The Ideology of Order

The Ideology of Order

A Comparative Analysis of
Jean Bodin and Thomas Hobbes

by

PRESTON KING

Professor of Government, University of Nairobi

BOOKS
10 East 53d St., New York 10022
(a division of Harper & Row Publishers, Inc.)

First published in 1974

Published in the USA 1974 by
HARPER & ROW PUBLISHERS, INC.
BARNES & NOBLE IMPORT DIVISION

ISBN 06 493710 0

Printed in Great Britain

*To my Fisk elders and age-mates
and particularly to nine among them:*

*Arna Bontemps, T. S. Currier, Robert Hayden, August Meier,
Bernard Spivack, David Lewis, Norman Hodges, Richard Thornell,
Eugene White*

*But most especially in memory
of my late brother
SLATER
whose charm, sympathy and intelligence
made him so tolerant a friend
and whose death proved so great a loss*

ACKNOWLEDGEMENTS

I am indebted to several friends and colleagues who kindly allowed me to address their senior seminars with a view to testing explicitly the main line of argument which is both assumed and stated in the text.

I am especially grateful to Maurice Cranston of the LSE, to Dr Parekh of Hull, to A. H. Birch, M. M. Goldsmith and Bob Dowse of Exeter, to Geraint Parry and Michael Evans of Manchester, to Jack Greenleaf, Jim McNamara and Graham Evans (a wonderfully acute and tenacious man whom I had not previously met), all of Swansea, to a measured D. D. Raphael and a vibrant Peter Campbell, both of Reading, and finally to Dr Berki and Professor Dodd, also of Hull.

In the text I have drawn attention to the notorious inconsistency of Bodin. This inconsistency is evident on any internal analysis of his *Six livres de la Republique* and can reasonably be assumed to obtain as between this work and the earlier *Methodus ad facilem historiarum cognitionem*. It is for this reason that my analysis of Bodin is basically restricted to the *Republique*. All the same, some scholars have made a point of arguing for a dramatic break between the *Methodus* and the *Republique* which I find it difficult to accept. The case is only rarely supported by tough, textual evidence, so that those who advance this argument are compelled to resort to historical evidence which is mostly circumstantial. A recent book of this type is J. H. Franklin's *Jean Bodin and the Rise of Absolutist Theory* (Cambridge, 1973). It provides the most careful of the conventional arguments so far marshalled in support of the *Methodus/Republique* hiatus theory (as discussed in Appendix 4 of this book). I think the argument of Appendix 4 stands, but the detail of that argument would naturally have been somewhat modified if the Franklin book had not been published too late to permit some formal account to be taken of his evidence. My basic view then remains that the more important hiatus obtains between Bodin and previous writers, not between an earlier and a later Bodin.

'The ground of the people to endure even the almost unendurable measure of sovereign power is . . . that its resistance to the supreme legislative power . . . must be thought of as destroying the whole legal constitution.'
Kant, *Foundations of the Metaphysics of Morals.*

'The notion that the state . . . would be no state if its will were tied by a higher norm, determining and limiting its range of action, poses a serious problem. To tell the whole truth, I do not think it has a solution. Despite the attempts which have been made, despite the prodigious subtlety which has been displayed, no satisfactory solution has been or ever will be provided. The most ingenious systems have merely concealed, but never resolved, the difficulty. For they have either ended up by affirming an all-powerful state or by entirely negating the state as such. They have oscillated between the absolutism of writers like Jean-Jacques Rousseau, Kant and Hegel, and the anarchism of writers like Stirner, Bakunin and Proudhon.'
Léon Duguit, *Jean-Jacques Rousseau, Kant et Hegel* (Paris, 1918), p. 4.

'Unlimited power, if it exists at all, must belong to a monarch, and least of all to a democracy, where the whole or a great part of the people wield authority collectively.'
Spinoza, *Tractatus Theologico-Politicus.*

'The defects of every government and constitution, both as to principle and form, must on a parity of reasoning, be as open to discussion as the defects of a law, and it is a duty which every man owes to society to point them out.'
Thomas Paine, *The Rights of Man.*

PREFACE

The history of politics appears very often to consist in a swing from demands for change to demands for order – and vice versa. In perhaps a more elevated style, political philosophy helps both to record and to provoke these swings, from 'liberty' to 'authority' and vice versa.

Every state, society or system, taken as an order, necessarily evinces a mixture of rights and wrongs. Every order in some degree establishes authority and protects liberties. Some liberty is restricted in every order; authority is absolute in none. To establish an authority or to protect a liberty may be just or unjust. Order *per se* is neither one nor the other. Every order will, in part, prove both just and unjust. Any order, therefore, will deserve in part both to be attacked and to be defended.

It is often held that order precedes justice. It is basically around such a formula as this that the ideology of order congeals. By the 'ideology of order' I have in mind a variety of arguments which are disposed to defend the consolidation of authority in an *a priori* way – whether that authority is fixed or expanding, stable or in process. The notion that order precedes justice most generally means that 'order' should be promoted or defended no matter what harm is done along the way. Such promotion or defence as this implies not that order is unjust, but that the supreme form of justice is order. This view is an ancient one, as old as Plato. But it should be established, and as plainly as possible, that justice no more equals order (or authority) than justice equals liberty (or anarchy).

If 'order precedes justice' means that order should take *precedence* over justice, the conclusion is to be rejected. Where we recognise an order, in some particular, to be unconditionally evil, we cannot intend that the evil should be preserved, since it cannot be right to preserve what is wrong. Of course no order is perfect; but imperfection still cannot claim any right to be preserved.

If 'order precedes justice' means that one grievance must queue up behind another for attention, then the test of the reasonableness of such patience is whether that other problem is genuinely more pressing; whether one cannot attend simultaneously both to the grievance in hand and to its rival; and whether in any event the one, as compared to the other, has or has not already been made to wait long enough. Certainly everything cannot be done, or reformed, at once; there are priorities; and while one priority takes its turn, some other must be required to wait. But one grievance can only be asked to wait upon the alleviation of another if it is clear that the other is of greater importance and that it is in fact being attended to: waiting one's turn cannot in fairness be made an endless occupation.

If 'order precedes justice' means – whether forever or only as far as we can see – that some particular evil is irremediable within a given system, then those who suffer the evil may understandably prefer to risk overturning the system. If indeed the evil is an evil, and is at the same time inextricably embedded within the system, then those who act against that system must surely be right to do so. I would argue that no evil is inextricably embedded in any system, and therefore that domino-type theories – which spring to the defence of particular evils on the grounds that they are necessary for the good of the political whole – are misguided. Revolutions are not inevitable. Nor are they illegitimate as such. Revolutions may or may not *tend* to arise, but it is perfectly legitimate that they *should*, in any situation where there is an accepted need for change which is systematically frustrated on the grounds that the effects of the change will be too sweeping, that all order will be undermined, and that the unintended consequences of these changes extend beyond our capacity to predict. No act, whether its character is evolutionary or revolutionary, can be usefully argued against on the grounds that it produces unintended consequences. For all acts are attended by consequences which no one can ever predict.

Every order instances control and lack of control, a degree of authority and liberty, both justice and injustice. No order is absolutely ordered. When we perceive the chinks, the discontinuities, in the armoury of order, we come closer to perceiving an important part of what it is – which is a perspective. A radical change of perspective may demolish *an* order but it would be extravagant to suppose that it can demolish *all* order. We cannot swim to shore if there is no sea; nor see the light if there is no dark; nor change a system and leave nothing the same. A change of perspective does not mean that all order is lost, and all order as such is certainly not bad. But ideologies of order are surely absurd: order cannot be praised, sanctioned or preserved *per se*. This is the slender point, in the analysis of Bodin and Hobbes, that we are ultimately concerned to set on its feet.

CONTENTS

PART ONE

INTRODUCTION

Chapter One

Introduction

ABSOLUTISM AND PLURALISM

Descriptions of group activity which posit such activity as involving, or tending towards, complete control from a discrete centre, as well as normatively espousing such a tendency, are often called absolutist. Descriptions of group activity which posit such activity as involving, or tending towards, the lack of control from a discrete centre, as well as normatively espousing this, are frequently labelled pluralist. In the case of absolutism we are concerned with a movement of thought which both describes and recommends the 'illimitable' concentration or integration of political power. In the case of pluralism we are concerned with the same process in reverse: description and recommendation of the 'illimitable' decentralisation, or indeed the dissolution, of power. Descriptively and normatively, the logical terminus of absolutism is *hier*-archy; that of pluralism is *an*-archy.

On one level, hierarchy may be described as a situation in which several groups are controlled by one (perhaps an imperial polity). On the same level, anarchy may be described as a situation in which each of several groups controls itself (perhaps a community of sovereign states). On another level, hierarchy can be defined as a situation in which one group is controlled by one of its members (perhaps a despotic state). On this same level, anarchy can be defined as a situation in which no member of a group is controlled by any other member (perhaps a Hobbesian 'state of nature'). Let us concentrate on this second level of hierarchy and anarchy. On this level, anarchy, for example, implies an absence of control by any member over others, but does not exclude the presence of control by each member over himself. Similarly, hierarchy implies a presence of control by one member over all others, but does not exclude an absence of control over the controlling member by another agent (perhaps a foreign power). Anarchy therefore defines not a total lack of control, but an absence of control from a specific centre. Hierarchy does not define a total presence of control, but the exercise of some degree of control from a specific centre. Anarchy, therefore, is compatible with the presence, and hierarchy with the absence, of control. They only define the absence or presence of control from a given locus, or from the perspective of a given agent, or as regards adherence to a specific rule (or rules).

To describe a society as anarchical must always imply, not that there are no rules, nor any authority, but that some particular rule or rules are inoperative, or that some particular agent is not authoritative. To describe a society as hierarchical must always imply, not that all activity is rule-bound, nor that some authority wields total power, but merely that a specific rule or rules, or a specific authority or authorities, wields or wield some determinate and ordering power. We may assume that any unit which we designate a society is to be understood to cohere by virtue of the sharing of some common rule or rules. In so far as such a unit gives evidence of some form of ordered character, it represents, to such a degree, a hierarchy. In so far as there is no formal limit upon the number of rules that such a unit may evolve, so far as it can always add more rules than it actually has, and so far as a society (accordingly) always exhibits fewer rules than it might, it follows (from all this) that every hierarchy – now observed from the perspective of rules which it does not observe – is also an anarchy.

Some aspects of political and social activity will be organised, others will be un-organised. No society or collectivity or state can be completely organised or completely un-organised. This is merely to say that in so far as a society exhibits *some* rule-bound behaviour it is organised; and that, in so far as *all* behaviour cannot be rule-bound, it is not nor can be completely organised. Any organisation, perceived from the perspective of one of its foci, may elaborate more rules, or fewer. An organisation may go on elaborating rules indefinitely, but it cannot go on subtracting rules indefinitely. When it has subtracted the last rule, if it leaves not a single one in force, then that organisation, as defined from a specific centre, ceases to exist. However, because one *focus* of control within an organisation ceases to exist, it does not mean that the organisation *per se* expires. Similarly, if that focus is itself identified as *the* organisation, it does not follow that, on expiry, those persons who were accounted the members of the organisation cease entirely to be related to one another in some rule-bound fashion. (An imperial polity, for example, might 'expire', in the sense that the central power is subsequently replaced by a series of independent states. The anarchy implied in the expiry of *imperial* control – a *particular* focus – is not equivalent to a disintegration of control *per se*.)

Hierarchy and anarchy may be regarded as interrelated phenomena: a given society always projects a hierarchy from one perspective, anarchy from another. The idea involved here is that within a society one may escape *some* organisation, but not *all* organisation. A further conjoint idea involved in all this is that, although one may promote *some* organisation, one cannot achieve *total* organisation. The ultimate sin of absolutism lies in the promotion of total organisation, that of pluralism in the promotion of no organisation. Absolutism and pluralism are inclined to fall overboard fore and aft in this way. Both, however, looking at the matter more charitably, merely define a direction of concern, where the direction seems to indicate an *a priori* disposition.

In so far as both absolutism and pluralism are descriptively concerned with the nature of social structure (however far they may tend to go in recommending divergent extremes of action), both reflect empirical interest in the nature and degree of organisation or non-organisation that obtains within groups. On the empirical level, absolutism and pluralism involve reflection on order, but from divergent standpoints: the one is largely concerned with those characteristics which make it possible to say that an organisation is an organisation, that it exists as a unit, as a whole; the other is largely concerned with the manner in which an organisation retains its identity as a unit while containing a variety of sub-units, and thus projects unity in diversity. Unity (the concentration of power or authority), whether it be considerable or minimal, still involves unity. Power or authority, whether diffuse or constricted, remains one or the other. An order, whether weak or strong, whether expressed through one rule or through many, remains an order. And absolutism and pluralism, in so far as they are concerned with unity or authority or power or order, may attach to this concern a measure of reverence for these things: which we may simply refer to as order, however absolute or plural a form it may assume. Pluralism, however, partly attempts to undermine the reverence for order which absolutism betrays. (For the moment it does not matter that the pluralist attempt is largely unsuccessful.) The result is that the ideology of order is a more distinctly absolutist than a pluralist concern. The present essay, accordingly, has essentially to do with absolutism rather than with pluralism.

When we think of political philosophies of absolutism, attention may be directed to writers like Niccolò Machiavelli, Jean Bodin and Thomas Hobbes. When we think of pluralism, however, no similarly immediate response is possible. In an earlier essay, *Fear of Power*, which is entirely continuous with the present book, I treated Alexis de Tocqueville, Pierre-Joseph Proudhon and Georges Sorel, in effect, as pluralists – as being more concerned, in an *a priori* fashion, with dismantling than with constructing power concentrations. There is no need to retrace here the steps of that earlier study. But it is in part because of it that I feel no need here to supply a portrait of pluralism, other than sketchily, comparatively, and as consisting in little more than a general current of ideas. More importantly, there are no individual 'pluralists' who will bear comparison with 'absolutists' like Hobbes (especially), Bodin, Spinoza, Rousseau, Kant, Hegel and, indeed, John Austin. Such men as these display analytical powers of the very first order. Men like Johannes Althusius and the Baron de Montesquieu are quite out of their depth in such company (although they might bear comparison with Bodin). John Locke would be an excellent recruit for the pluralist school, the only difficulty being that he points decisively in two contrary directions: the one towards some form of separation of powers, the other towards an unlimited concentration of power in the hands of *the people*.

There are at least two reasons why no individual 'pluralist' will stand comparison with the chief 'absolutists', why pluralism in itself tends to constitute a cluster of ideas lacking representatives as distinguished as Machiavelli, Bodin and Hobbes. In the first place, not one of the latter can actually be regarded as entirely anti-pluralist. Machiavelli had republican yearnings. Bodin was absorbed by a genuine search for justice. Hobbes remained to some degree an individualist. That is to say, none of these men would accept that a *complete* absence of independence or diversity was either possible or desirable (however far they might lean in that direction). Accordingly it would be difficult for any social or political theorist of note, following in their wake, to proclaim himself wholly uninfluenced by their arguments – at least in the sense that none is completely opposed to all they say. Secondly, pluralism has no entirely independent character since it consists largely in an attack upon absolutism: modifications to a plan do not mean much when examined out of the context of the plan they modify. Accordingly, those who might stand out by virtue of attempts to amend absolutist doctrines in a pluralist direction, find themselves, instead, enveloped in an historical shadow – the shadow of absolutist icons, the reach of which (for sound heuristic reasons) they never entirely escape.

In consequence, there are no truly notable theorists who can serve as worthy or appropriate respondents to absolutism. Hence it is best, as suggested, to portray pluralism as a current of ideas. Federalism, lying at the centre of this current, constitutes a species of float from and to which various pluralist notions spring and return. All about, a variety of nineteenth- and twentieth-century figures disport themselves: men like Tocqueville, Proudhon, Otto von Gierke, John Maitland, J. N. Figgis, William James, Ernest Barker, Harold Laski, G. D. H. Cole, Léon Duguit, and many others. It is this current of ideas, and such men as these who are drawn into it, that we should keep in mind as constituting or representing 'pluralism'.

Having briefly outlined what we mean by absolutism and pluralism, it will now be in order to state a broad assumption which I make in regard to them: this, in short, is that it is absurd to style oneself a proponent of either doctrine in any universal or even general sense. On the factual level, each describes a reality largely complementary to that described by the other: absolutists tend to be concerned with overall state structure ('sovereignty' is a central feature of this concern), pluralists with such subordinate corporate structures as figure in, or are embraced by, the state (like families, guilds, businesses, local government, and so on). On the recommendatory level, each proposes a course of action which may be appropriate in one situation but not in another: absolutists tend to favour increasing, pluralists decreasing, concentrations of power.

Absolutism and pluralism, therefore, do not consistently contradict each other, and neither is to be studied, promoted or praised to the entire exclusion of the other. Absolutism suggests firmness and single-mindedness of purpose; pluralism suggests a recognition of multiplicity as legitimate. A basic norm underlying absolutism is the appeal to strength; that underlying pluralism is an appeal to tolerance. There is no necessary contradiction in any given ruler or government proving both strong and tolerant. Further, a government may increase its strength by extending its tolerance; or it may be able to extend its tolerance by virtue of its strength. And where absolutism, in the descriptive sphere, merely seeks to portray the essential features of superstructures, it gives no necessary offence to pluralism, where the latter merely seeks to account for the general character of infrastructures.

Despite differential stress upon firmness and tolerance, as promoted respectively by absolutist and pluralist orientations, the central point of the present book grows out of the compatibility of these orientations. In so far as absolutism promotes greater concentrations, and pluralism smaller concentrations of power, both must still be regarded as promoting *concentrations* of power – even though differences in number, type and degree are important. Even where absolutism does not stop short of the assumption and recommendation that one centre possesses *total* power, nor pluralism short of the belief that all centres can and should possess *no* power, both are aligned on an identical continuum: that which has to do with *how much* power is wielded from a given locus. The amount of power that is and can be wielded is, of course, always more or less. Absolutism is always concerned with more, pluralism with less, but – as argued above – both are concerned with concentrations of power.

We may now touch on a point which, for our present purposes, is more important than, although directly connected with, what has just been said: any centre of power, however great, however small, can (and may be requested to) wield such authority as it enjoys with extreme resolution and vigour. The ideology of order, involving the acceptance, praise and promotion of the latter, can obtain in any form of order, whatever the degree of order. Any ordering or ruling element, whether it consists of one, few or many, may assume that its particular constitution and composition are ideal. In such circumstances, whatever the structure of the society or state, whether it be monistic or pluralistic, the crucial consideration is that the acceptance of its legitimacy may take the form of condoning whatever regulations are cast up by whoever or whatever organs are regarded as authoritative. In this respect, it does not matter whether a power concentration is highly restricted or very extensive: its legitimacy, and that of the rules or norms which proceed from it, may be regarded as virtually or entirely absolute. The consequence is as indicated: its utterances must be regarded as inviolate.

Absolutism is more dependent than pluralism upon the ideology of order. It attempts to validate norms almost exclusively by reference to *who* issued them. At first sight, pluralism appears to proceed in exactly the same manner: its arguments against absolutism lead into arguments for a different species of *who* (or persona), for a larger deciding body, or for a more diversified process of decision. The difference is that pluralist objections to absolutism may project at least some minimal disquiet regarding the notion that the rules thrown up by a deciding agent are necessarily legitimate (i.e. ought absolutely to be accepted) in so far as they proceed from some accepted source. Pluralism is continuous with absolutism but also less extreme. This continuity has to be demonstrated: as, most importantly, between federalism and absolutism; both can be said, obviously, to project significant forms of centralised power. But the ideology of order, though it may surface within any regime, whether labelled federalist or absolutist or other, is most conspicuously displayed by absolutism. The ideology of order, whether it surfaces in regimes that we call 'totalitarian', 'democratic' or other, is essentially a survival from absolutism, and is essentially to be attacked through a critique of absolutism.

In any study of absolutism or pluralism the general problem that we encounter is this: what can we learn about human organisation on both factual and normative levels? The severe answer, in the context of the present discussion, is – very little. The insights that we gain are more likely to be *logical* than either factual or normative, but since logic is fundamental to the marshalling both of facts and of norms this need not be regarded as an unworthy gain. In the present book we are less concerned with history than with philosophy, less with aptness of judgement than with the force of logic. It is this which explains my approach to Bodin and Hobbes, who are taken as the chief representatives of the absolutist tradition. Whereas *Fear of Power* dealt fairly fully with the detailed logical thrust of three pluralists, the general object of the present exercise is to consider in even greater detail the logical thrust of two major absolutists.

Our concern here is not just with what given historical figures thought, but with the nature and logic of social and political organisation in so far as it may be perceived through or contradicted in their thought. Absolutism is an excellent focus of attention because, more than most doctrines, it lies at the heart at least of all classical discussions of the nature of political power and social organisation. Here we are concerned with what power and organisation are, and with how we proceed when saying what they are. In this sense, therefore, we are also concerned with the methodology – the logic – of the social sciences.

The present focus on absolutism is somewhat vulgar and certainly preliminary, in so far as it involves an underlying concern with social science methodology. But absolutism represents one of the chief clusters of ideas about the nature of the political process, and thus contains notions that purport to be normative and factual, universal and (merely) general, simply 'true' and self-consciously 'ideological'. From an analysis of absolutist thinkers we may be able to begin to disengage some methodological principles for our own times.

THE METHODOLOGICAL RELEVANCE OF HISTORY

In social and political studies, the perennial debate, as also the most important, concerns (what we might broadly call) methodology. The latter is made up of a number of components, but most importantly the problem of distinguishing between values and facts; the possibility of achieving a 'value-free' description of social reality; the question whether all descriptions of social reality are 'ideological'; the question whether 'value-loaded' descriptions are necessarily 'unobjective', and so on. These problems shade into one another and interlock. Such clusters of problems will surface time and again during the course of the discussion which follows. They are set in an historical tradition of (what we might call) cumulative treatment. For not only have phenomena a history; so too, has the study of phenomena. In this connection, perhaps, the modern study of social science methodology most importantly commences in the sixteenth and seventeenth centuries. The writers of this period set out a basic range of problems which later students have come and continue to attack.

The doctrine of absolutism is basically the theory of sovereignty, and vice versa. These notions achieve their first and possibly their highest degree of theoretical significance as expounded by Bodin and Hobbes. Both men are concerned with achieving the profoundest possible understanding of what political reality is about. 'Sovereignty' is burdened with a variety of meanings which we need not explore. It does, however, cover at least one central concern which we shall take up: the notion of the actual character of state power, conceived in some universal sense. By many, Machiavelli is regarded as the initiator of this tradition. By others, Bodin is singled out for praise. For me, Bodin and Hobbes are the two chief figures; nonetheless, something will be said about Machiavelli. In any event, our concern is more with the reality of arguments and less with the precedence (or lack of it) of those who advanced them. Accordingly, we are concerned with the evolution and validity of key notions about the nature of political power – and with the way in which we discuss these notions. Pluralism is a more recent tradition of thought which contributes to this debate.

One of the first of our methodological interests relates to the designation of a writer's problem. Different writers, even living in the same period, see different problems, or perceive (what we might presume to be) the same problem in radically different ways. The question is not so much how problem-solvers come to perceive problems differently; it has to do, rather, with being reasonably clear about what is actually being perceived as a problem. It has to do, further, with recognising that what is perceived as a problem is at some point so perceived in a quite involuntary manner. We may say that we *choose* to deal with one problem rather than with another, and up to a point this is true; but the perception of the problem as such largely imposes itself upon one, communicating some sense of being obvious or self-evident (in its basic character if not in its solution).

In the case of a social or political writer, what is imposed, in some strange fashion, is a sense of what his own times are about. Because contemporaries will have different impressions about the salient features of their age, one must step back from any crude assumptions about the relationship between history and the variable impressions it makes. But impressions are made, and the receptive mind does not simply will that they be made. Thus it is useful to say, not simply that A's times imposed upon him a certain impression, but that his times were perceived by him in such a way as to generate a certain impression. In a loose sense, therefore, we can say that *history* imposes problems; but in the stricter sense we must say that the *perception* of history imposes problems. In order to understand a social or political writer it is useful, although not indispensable, to familiarise oneself, not (strictly speaking) with the history of his time, but with his actual or probable perception of the history of his time. In so far as the perception is ultimately involuntary, it is imposed: it is imposed as a largely uncontrollable interaction between the perceiver and his environment.

If we analyse the problems of absolutists and pluralists, we really ought to begin with some picture of the historical settings which they would regard as having imposed the problems with which they came to deal. In *Fear of Power* I discussed the historical problem-situation as perceived, for example, by Tocqueville. In general, his perception is not significantly different from that of pluralists as a whole. It usually consists in a view of state power as being highly concentrated, more than adequate to its purpose, and probably grossly inflated with respect to the latter. In the present book we shall reconstruct the historical problem-situations most probably perceived by Machiavelli, Bodin and Hobbes – featuring central awareness of and aversion to civil war, general disorder and gross insecurity.

The solution to a problem in political and social theory, in short, cannot be entirely divorced from the problem-solver's perception of the problem itself. This perception is necessarily an *historical* perception of the condition of the society or government for which the solution is designed. The definition of a problem is an act of judgement. Such acts, clearly, are far from entirely factual or rational. Given that this is so, given that the perception of the problem has a largely involuntary character, the problem should be understood to be at least partly submerged within its historical context, and to have partly emerged out of it. The history of a certain time comes to be seen in a common light by various sets of participant-observers. Because they *see* history in a certain light, they respond in what they regard as an appropriate manner – which is often, not surprisingly, a fairly common manner. Thus there is an important connection between perceiving history in a certain light, disengaging common problems from it when so perceived, and providing similar solutions to those problems. In all of this there is submerged some kind of fairly consistent connection between facts and values. Naturally, it does not follow that those who see history in a common light will necessarily disengage from it identical problems, nor that those who disengage identical problems will advance identical solutions. Men are too varied, and the process of reasoning too discontinuous, for this to be possible. Nonetheless the *tendency* holds: to move from common historical perceptions, to common definitions of problems, to broadly similar solutions to the latter.

In the case of the absolutists, in the case of Machiavelli, Bodin and Hobbes, the perception of their times as chronically unstable, as chaotic, tended to invite from them formulae or solutions designed to revise the state of affairs which they perceived (and assessed as evil). Accordingly, we devote brief historical chapters to each of the three writers in question and to their times. The object is not to provide a *history* of Italy or France or England, but an historical *perspective* on these states, one which would coincide roughly with Machiavelli's or Bodin's or Hobbes's own

25

perspective, and partially explain (albeit in a highly preliminary way) the work of each, conceived as a voluntary response to a more largely involuntary perception of the problem.

DISTINCTIVE FEATURES OF THE PRESENT ANALYSIS

Looking now beyond the contextual problem, we may see the absolutists and pluralists as argumentatively interlocked: Bodin swings away from a medieval pluralism, Hobbes more decisively into a seventeenth-century absolutism, and the pluralists back into a higher nineteenth- and twentieth-century theory of division of powers. In this scheme of things, the central figure is seen to be Hobbes: this central placement is justified by virtue of his uniqueness, as compared both to earlier absolutists and to successor pluralists.

With regard to Bodin, no contemporary treatment is available which compares in extent and analytical bent with the one provided here. Nor am I aware of the availability of any similarly extensive, comparative analysis of Bodin and Hobbes. Throughout the whole of the analysis of these writers, a persistent attempt is made to distinguish between factual and normative assertions. Underlying this attempt is a central methodological concern with the question as to how far such an attempt can go.

Although relatively little of substance has been written on Bodin, the same cannot be said of Hobbes who has been the subject of a vast literature. It has not been my intention to go back over this ground. Whereas Warrender, Mintz, Hood, Watkins and Goldsmith, for example, have been concerned to analyse Hobbes's theory of obligation, to set out the pattern of Hobbes's influence on later generations, to lay bare his theological presuppositions, to establish the connection between his metaphysical outlook and its practical applications, and to provide an overall account of his thought, the present approach is set apart by an attempt to see how far we may go in sorting out Hobbes's normative from his empirical ideas on political structure.

It is from this that the detailed discussion of Hobbes's ideas on command relationships springs – as between parent and child, master and servant, sovereign and subject. Whereas the present discussion of Bodin is novel by virtue of both (a) providing a detailed analysis and (b) being set against the backcloth of the value/fact distinction, no contemporary discussion of Hobbes (including that offered here) can lay claim to the same degree of novelty by virtue of either such approach. I believe, nonetheless, that my account of Hobbesian value assumptions is both novel and valuable. I feel no inclination to omit this self-serving conclusion since to state it clearly will at least have the effect of drawing the fire of critics in a disciplined and concentrated manner (see especially chapter 12 and appendix 5). To touch upon a different matter, I also believe that students of Hobbes have placed insufficient emphasis (or none at all) upon his failure to understand or explain the workings of corporate groups (better, the logic of collective control) – a failure which led Hobbes to support a form of absolutism which no *legislative* body can possibly sustain (see especially chapter 19).

INDIVIDUAL AND COLLECTIVE SOVEREIGNTY IN BODIN AND HOBBES

If we consider the essential character of human organisation, particularly from the political perspective, and more particularly still from the perspective of political sovereignty, we confront a central question in considering the difference in character between a single and a plural sovereign. This is a core concern of the present book, and is reflected in the analysis of Bodin and Hobbes. It is generally assumed that their conclusions are contradicted by federal experience and certainly by pluralist *theory*. The problem, however, is deeper than Bodin, Hobbes, federalism and pluralism, all of which – considered now as disembodied and depersonalised arguments – constitute accretions round the problem.

At an earlier time, it was thought important to consider, for example, whether monarchy or aristocracy or democracy were best. Today it is of course generally assumed that democracy is best. But, similarly, it was also considered important to establish what the nature of the difference was, if any, between these variant forms of organisation. This sort of question is seldom entertained today. One reason is that democratic (or 'plural') rule is almost everywhere assumed preferable to what we might call 'monarchic' rule. Accordingly, the factual question that tends to be asked is not so much how democratic and monarchic rule differ, but how to distinguish 'true' democracy from a *prétendu* representativeness which is really monarchic in essence.

As it tends to be assumed today that only democratic rule is legitimate, the important factual problem becomes that of determining what forms of political organisation can legitimately claim to be democratic. The trouble with the word 'democratic', however, is that it is too loose for our purposes. We can say that no government is completely democratic in the sense that none is based upon the direct participation of its entire membership. In so far as this is so, all government is aristocratic, in the sense that the ruling element, in so far as it is plural, does not encompass the entirety of the ruled. But the word 'aristocratic' will not serve either, because it is too likely to suggest a membership restricted by birth, as opposed to other, perhaps more functional, criteria such as skills of some kind. In any event, the problem, bypassing now the terminological question, becomes that of determining what forms of political organisation are plural, in the sense of being 'participative'. But the distinction between the 'aristocratic' and 'democratic', leading into the use of the expression 'participative', immediately raises another and now even more central problem: *how* 'participative'? Assuming that all governments effectively fall between the extremes of (*a*) complete control by a single individual and (*b*) total directive participation by the entire membership, then the only question of substance becomes that as to the degree to which the process of rule actively involves the ruled.

Virtually every government in the world today has what we might call a 'parliament'. Representatives of these parliaments or 'representative assemblies' regularly gather together in global conclaves to consider their common problems. This means that the United Kingdom, West Germany, Argentina, Ethiopia, Morocco, South Africa, South Vietnam, South Korea and numerous other states all assemble as 'parliamentary' regimes. They may have genuine, fraudulent or no elections. They may in varying degrees protect or stifle civil liberties. They may be effectively subject to a larger or smaller number of governors. But all meet as parliamentary regimes. So our original question may now be given a more contemporary twist: how representative is a government required to be to qualify as 'parliamentary'?

But at this stage we discover that we have returned to what is essentially a much older question. First, we may put it in this form: what is the difference between a parliamentary and a non-parliamentary regime? Secondly, we may put it in the older form: what is the difference between rule by one man and rule by many? And this is just another way of inquiring into the nature of the difference between rule by an individual and rule by a collective sovereign. Bodin and Hobbes lie at the source of this debate about structure. It has already been suggested, however, that it is difficult to conceive either of one man or of all men effectively governing a state. The very fact that a ruler has to be obeyed, and can therefore be disobeyed, implies in all circumstances some degree of participation by a plurality in the governing process. Thus the question has to be put in a far more hypothetical frame: if only *one man* ruled, in the sense that his word alone was regarded as legally final, what characteristics would accumulate around such a form of rule? Secondly, if *a group of men* ruled, in the sense that their collective word alone was regarded as legally final, what characteristics would accumulate around this form of rule? The beginnings of any answer about the characteristics of parliamentary rule or representative government must begin, and historically do begin, with these questions.

Bodin is largely inclined to believe that only one man, only a single individual, can be sovereign; and that all plural forms of sovereigns are in fact reducible to individual sovereigns. He broadly assumes that most organisations (most particularly the family and the state) can only enjoy a unity through the establishment and sharing of a single individual as head (a father or a sovereign). He is not absolutely consistent in this view, and that is why I resort to formulae of the kind 'he is *largely* inclined to believe'. In any event, given that the head of an organisation, for Bodin, is usually in all respects superior to all other members, there remains no way in which the members (within a system so constructed) can check his authority. Bodin's 'description' of unitary control does, of course, contain a recommendatory point: that every state ought to have an individual head as sovereign. But one can query the factual element by simply inquiring whether a given organisation, in order to have a unity, really must have *one* head. The answer is negative. What every organisation must have, however, is some rule or norm which stipulates a procedure by which its unity is established or maintained. The procedure must spell out some workable method of reaching decisions by the group as a whole. It may stipulate that a given *individual* should, in all areas of adjudication and administration, decide what is to be done; equally it may lay down that a *group* is to do this. Where a group is designated as sovereign, what must equally be stipulated is some non-contradictory means by which it makes its decisions – as by a majority or other vote. The procedure may, and in practice usually does, stipulate some separation of functions within the organisation. Where this is done it is important to ensure that the division of function is really clear, or if not that one of the elements within the organisation is designated as arbiter *vis-à-vis* the others.

The important point is that an organisation is only an organisation by virtue of the rules or norms, explicit or tacit, by which it is bound together. These rules may designate one or a variety of heads. It is only necessary, in the latter case, that procedures be elaborated which usually prevent these heads from clashing – by formally securing a self-consistent conclusion or decision. Unitary control is important. But one-man rule has to be seen as nothing more than one means to the attainment of this end. An undifferentiated group, like a representative assembly, may be made sovereign, but its ultimate coherence must be built upon some form of majority-rule norm. A differentiated group, like the officers and organs of a federal state, may be made sovereign, but the ultimate coherence of the federation must be built upon a fairly clear, internal differentiation of functions, together with the establishment of some final court of appeal to arbitrate in such conflicts as may arise between agents performing these functions. We may conclude that the descriptive element in Bodinian absolutism is correct in so far as it indicates that a group cannot exist without some form of common headship. But it is mistaken in so far as it separates common headship from common rules; it is mistaken in so far as headship is taken to mean anything other than a coherent system of decision-making; and it is mistaken in so far as it assumes that coherence must or can be absolute.

Moving now to Hobbes, we may concede that he is right in arguing that both an individual and a collectivity can wield sovereign power, i.e. can unite, in the sense of providing the leadership element in, a state. It would be wrong to suggest that Bodin did not grasp this point at all. He was aware of the existence of different forms of government, among which monarchy was only one. Moreover, he did speak of (what we might call) 'private corporate bodies' being governed by a conciliar or collective or non-despotic principle. Nonetheless, Bodin certainly supposed that any form of state organisation other than the monarchical was seriously defective. The state achieved true stability, or unity, through the sovereign, and the sovereign was not truly adequate for this purpose if not a specific individual. In this sense, Hobbes represents an advance upon Bodin in explicitly stating that a collectivity, as well as an individual, can be sovereign. Yet Hobbes raises a similar difficulty at a later stage. He does argue that there are individual as well as collective sovereigns. But after a time (see chapter 18, second section, and especially chapter 19) it becomes plain that he, too, impliedly means that the monarchical form of government is best – in the sense that only it provides true unity and stability.

The difficulty with Hobbes is that he does not unambiguously recognise that the 'absolutism' of a collectivity is, in immensely important respects, quite different from that of an individual. A collective sovereign might draw the same conclusions and take the same decisions as an individual sovereign, but its internal process of decision-making is not the same. The procedural differences are such that the two 'absolutisms' cannot meaningfully be equated. Procedurally, an individual sovereign is not required to consult others to issue a directive. A collectivity, by contrast, simply in order to know its own 'mind', has to accept the indispensability of some form of public communication otherwise known as debate (however irrational it may be).

The major difficulty with Hobbes's system, therefore, is less contradiction (which is Bodin's special preserve) than omission. He is right to point to an identity between an individual and a corporate sovereign, taking account of their *substantive* decisions; for they can clearly do the same things, whether for good or ill. Hobbes misleads, however, in so far as he fails to recognise or omits to note the significant difference in *procedure*. The critical analysis of Bodin makes it plain that no sovereign's power can be literally absolute (chapter 10 below). The critical point to be made against Hobbes is that a collective sovereign, with respect to the necessary and self-imposed limitations of its own internal procedure, is formally less absolute than an individual sovereign. To the extent therefore that a collective sovereign is deliberative or consultative, to that extent will it *tend* to act more slowly, to give less offence, and to draw greater support. It is for this reason that collective sovereigns (whether federal or other) are generally preferred to the individual variety. This is not because of the protection of civil liberties which sometimes characterises them, but because their more inclusive or consultative decision-making procedure increases, through the broader participation of the citizenry, the possibility of greater self-protection for those participants and their associates.

Having looked critically at the central assumptions of both Bodin and Hobbes on political structure, we can summarise and conclude the matter in the following terms. If an organisation necessarily receives its unity through the reduction of its members' wills to the will of a single individual, then it becomes absurd to assume that a group as such (i.e. one not commanded by a single individual) can exercise sovereign (or any other) power. Groups as such *can*, however, exercise sovereign (and other) power. A group which genuinely and consistently decides issues by reference, for example, to majority votes is not united by the acceptance of a single person's will. A group can continue in unity by referring decisions to a single individual (as under a monarchy) but of course it can also continue by referring such decisions to a collectivity (such as a parliament or cabinet or supreme court). If such a collective sovereign is not only a source of law but also subject to law, then it cannot possibly be absolutely sovereign – in the sense that Hobbes, in particular, requires.

The members of a sovereign group may indeed be placed above some laws (*vis-à-vis* non-members, as in the case of parliamentary or congressional immunity), but if an attempt is made to place them above the laws or procedures whence the group or assembly derives its character *qua* group or assembly, then the latter necessarily ceases to exist. Thus, where the rules of an organisation designate *a particular individual* as complete and final arbiter and initiator in all spheres, then he may reasonably be regarded as being formally above, in the sense of not being held to observe, any rules or directives which he himself promulgates under such authority. But where the rules of an organisation designate a body of individuals, like a legislature, as sovereign, then the sovereign cannot exist except where actually bound by rules of procedure, which means that it is limited by law (at least *some* law) which it itself promulgates. Even where it seeks to alter laws already made, it must of course adhere to some form of established procedure whereby this may be done. A sovereign assembly, therefore, is more limited than a sovereign individual. For it must be subject to (at least some of) its own laws, whereas a sovereign individual need be subject to none of those laws which he himself is empowered to issue.

As already noted, however, sovereign assemblies may be more or less inclusive. The fewer persons they include, the fewer guarantees are there that the 'interests' (however defined) of those who are excluded will be protected. It is at this stage that we touch upon a different type of problem – which is perhaps more nearly the province of political sociology – regarding the extent to which a given parliamentary regime is representative, and the manner in which it might be made more so. One quite conventional way of ensuring that a parliamentary regime is representative, or is made more so, is of course to extend the vote, with as few limitations as possible, to the citizenry as a whole. In such a case one could regard the citizenry as sovereign, i.e. as wielding an ultimate power of decision-making within the state system. If we can accept the notion of an assembly being sovereign, there is not necessarily any further difficulty in accepting the notion of the citizenry as a whole (more or less) being so. A group is basically such by virtue of the rules which impart to it its collective character. This must be equally true for a sovereign assembly. But what also characterises such an assembly is the fact that it actually assembles, comes together, within a defined spatial context. This spatial feature of an assembly, however, may be regarded as merely accidental, not essential. Spatial contiguity not being a necessary feature of group existence, there is no reason why the rules of inclusion and procedure defining the role of the citizenry should not be taken to constitute of the latter a sovereign unit. But once that is conceded we need only be reminded of what was earlier established: that such a sovereign, being a collectivity, has certain necessary, internal limits placed upon its manner of operating. The relevant descriptive implication contained in this is that a democracy cannot be as absolute in its operations as a monarchy. Further, in so far as the rules governing a democracy's procedures are more complicated than those governing those of an aristocracy, democratic rule must be regarded as necessarily less absolute than aristocratic rule as well.

It will be clear that, descriptively, absolutism is largely concerned with the character of *individual* decision-making. Pluralism, and federalism conceived as a pluralism, tend by contrast to be more concerned with the character of *collective* decision-making. It is a pity that, in reality, the distinction is not so clear-cut. It is equally unfortunate that the political theory of pluralism is not so incisive as that of absolutism. Pluralism requires, despite defects, to be discussed, and because of defects, to be criticised. Because it is less incisive, however, one cannot simply criticise absolutism from the pluralist perspective: the critique would not go far enough, it would not be good enough. The criticisms of Bodin and Hobbes provided here, therefore, are advanced in a manner virtually parallel to the exposition and without particular regard to pluralist critiques. In future, perhaps, the chief value of 'pluralist' studies will be to push much further the analysis of the character of collective decision-making. For the key point to be made against descriptive absolutism, as noted, is the fundamental logical difference in character between an individual and a collective sovereign, at least in respect to decision-making *procedure*, if not in respect to the *substantive* decisions actually reached. As for the substantive decisions themselves, there is the significant danger that, whatever their source, they may evoke an excess of zeal by virtue of their source.

FEDERALISM AND PLURALISM

Federalism evolved both as a political doctrine and as an historical experience. Historically it represents the most significant type of collective or plural sovereign the world has yet seen. It evolved legally from theories of collective sovereignty. If we label the history of federalism, institutionally conceived, as federation, it is clear that this tells us little *directly* about notions of collective sovereignty. Put another way, the history of federation, as it is frequently recorded, tells us much which is either false or misleading about the character of collective sovereignty. When we look more closely at the fundamental historical character of federations, what we see is that they generally represent attempts to achieve greater union, or as much in given circumstances as seems possible. Further, where federations survive, they usually, but not absolutely always, involve movement in the direction of increasingly integrated unity. Thus, in so far as doctrines of sovereignty and/or absolutism are regarded as describing or promoting greater concentrations of political power, they are in no way contradicted by the historical experience of federation.

The establishment of federations involves the elaboration of more complicated forms of unity than existed previously. 'Federation' affords greater unity than 'confederation', but less than that conventionally associated with the 'unitary' state. Federal government involves an elaborate parcelling out of powers. It requires the drawing up of a document assigning appropriate functions to central and local organs and/or governments respectively. This sharing out of functions always assumes the possibility, in most cases the probability, of jurisdictional clashes, and therefore assigns to some higher body the role of adjudicating in such disputes and therefore drawing the boundary between the different organs of government within the state. The experience of federation, therefore, does not contradict the doctrine of sovereignty or absolutism in so far as absolutism rejects as impossible or undesirable the parallel existence of 'autonomous' governments within a single government.

In short, federal government is not, in current phraseology, genuinely characterised by 'co-ordinate' spheres of control. In so far as any federation concedes the 'autonomy' of local units, it simultaneously ensures that the sphere of autonomy is interpreted or decided upon by an organ of the central government. If indeed any federal government were really built upon co-ordinate spheres of control, recognising in this the genuine autonomy of local organs, then the central government could not ultimately overrule the local, and the latter, if such were attempted, would enjoy and could exercise a right of secession. Since federal governments implicitly or explicitly exclude the right of secession, they must assume and assure, on all matters and at all levels, an internal – and indeed unitary – procedure of adjudication and reconciliation. Thus the federal experience does not in any way over-throw the traditional theory of sovereignty or of absolutism in the sense of demonstrating that there can be more than one power of final appeal within a single state.

Pluralism, as a throwback to medieval corporatism, but also building upon what were taken to be the implications contained in the evolution of federal government, often assumed that absolutism could be opposed by arguing that every state did or should contain a multiplicity of decision-making organs, no one of which was superior to all the rest. Where this was argued it would be pointed out that a multiplicity of governments or organs, operating with mutual independence, could not be described as *one* government. But when pluralists argued for the existence, factually and normatively, of unity in diversity, they were often accused of self-contradiction, of not being *true* pluralists. Many of them simply gave up the idea of protesting against the structural argu-ments of Bodinian and Hobbesian absolutism. Harold Laski despair-ingly suggested that the political theory of sovereignty, of absolutism (he explicitly regarded them as equivalent), had simply to be ignored because – interestingly – he considered the theory *logically* impregnable.

The pluralist camp, for all its virtues, was, perhaps inevitably, rife with confusion. Pluralists were even put into the absurd position of attacking unity *per se*. They stressed the divergence of organisations within the state. They stressed the notion of subordinate organs having distinct 'group personalities'. Gierke and Maitland went so far as to insist – nonsensically – upon groups being 'real persons'. Figgis argued that a group has 'a real personality, not a fictitious one'. In all of this they made an inadequate attempt to describe, as well as to recommend, the collective aspect of group unity and control. Figgis's desire to show that subordinate groups within the state really *are* autonomous (as well as that they should be) resembles Wheare's notion that federal systems enshrine co-ordinate spheres of control (between local and central organs). The difficulties created are the same. If a subordinate unit in the state really is autonomous then it can escape central control. If a subordinate unit within a federal system really wields a co-ordinate (which means some form of autonomous) power, then it can secede. (Otherwise it cannot ultimately defend its sphere of autonomy.) But in either case we are not speaking of one state, but of several. To point to any organisational experience and suggest that *subordinate* units are genuinely autonomous or *independent* is obvious nonsense. Such notions are no less nonsensical for being directed against some of the absurd dimensions of descriptive absolutism. What pluralists should have done, and what they (or others) still may usefully do, is to direct attention forcefully to the significant distinction between the internal character of individual and collective decision-making. Against the backcloth of that distinction, the point to be made (*contra* Laski and others) is that the doctrine of sovereignty or absolutism should not be ignored and that it is most assuredly *not* logically impregnable.

THE LEGACY OF ORDER

Absolutism, expressed in the simple form of a concern with individual sovereignty, survives virtually nowhere in the contemporary world. In this form it has been superseded by what we might call – somewhat misleadingly – the 'pluralism' of collective sovereignty. Despite the important difference in procedure between individual and collective sovereigns, it nonetheless remains that the substantive results they achieve, the specific decisions they reach, the types of regulations they produce, may all prove much the same. In this sense, a collective sovereign will not necessarily achieve results more *just* than those achieved by an individual sovereign. The subject or citizen, under (or within) a collective sovereign, may have a greater opportunity to participate in the governing process, but he will not necessarily be ruled less completely nor punished with more sympathy or less harshness. In any event, whatever the differences, the collective sovereign has displaced the individual sovereign – if not everywhere in *fact*, then virtually everywhere in *theory*; if not as an *actual* change of government, then as a *desired* change of government.

We spoke of absolutism as describing or espousing movement

towards complete or total integration. This means the concentration of all power at a fixed locus. Since the exercise of all control, of all power, necessarily involves a dual relationship, between subject and object, leader and follower, command and obedience, proposal and acceptance, the control or power factor cannot be completely concentrated at either one of these poles. The designated 'leader' must necessarily respond to the continuing initiatives of the 'led'; the 'led' are always initiating actions which generate 'official' response; the initiatives of a leadership necessarily involve some form of interaction with those of the led, most minimally by occasioning acquiescence or positive acceptance or complete rejection of initiatives by one or the other. Such interaction becomes the more complex as the size of a given social unit expands: any concentration of power simultaneously involves some diffusion of power.

The notion that political power can or should be completely integrated is roughly equivalent to the notion that perfect order can or should be established. But we have seen that power cannot be completely integrated. Similarly, no complete or perfect order can be established. Any existing order is necessarily elastic. In so far as it exists, it can always accommodate more rules, of some description, or fewer. The minimal number of rules that an order requires to exist is one; no theoretical limit can be placed on the maximum number that it may concoct. In the sense that an order (considered as a plenum of rules) could always expand to contain more rules, there is no logical terminus that the sheer quantum of rule-making can reach. One dimension of rule-fabrication is, of course, the generation of forms of punishment for the infraction of rules. The more rules there are, the more can be generated to govern their infringement. The more numerous the infringements, the more varied and severe can be made the rules governing infringements (i.e. the more intense can the entire process of punishment become) and so on *ad infinitum*. We must consider therefore that one aspect of absolutism is not only the virtually *a priori* concern with expanding in general the number of rules in society, but also, and necessarily, the concern with continually expanding the variety of punishments to be imposed for infractions of rules. We may take it as a matter of course that any society today which features high rates and severe forms of imprisonment is, in these particulars, absolutist and repressive.

Although absolutism, conceived as a concern with individual sovereignty, is dead, it remains fully alive when conceived simply as a concern with increasing the range, depth and harshness of control. This residual absolutism survives in some degree within all forms of collective government. Such residual absolutism involves the business of regarding the rules of any social plenum as absolutely binding – whatever these rules may be, whatever effects they may have. Thus a collective sovereign may elaborate as many or more rules than an individual sovereign, and it may prove equally or more extreme in applying them. What survives from absolutism, in most collective sovereigns, is the tendency to take rules too seriously, to interpret them too inelastically, and to punish infractions of them with excessive severity.

We frequently make a more contemporary distinction between 'totalitarianism' and 'democracy', as opposed, perhaps, to absolutism/ pluralism. Such a substitution, however, is inadequate, for all of the contemporary states which we describe as 'totalitarian' or 'democratic' either are, or affect a desire to become, collective sovereigns. They tend to have a corporate character and to promote some form of corporate interest. Although I take no particular care to avoid the use of the expression, 'totalitarianism' is clearly a misnomer. First, it cannot possibly label a reality since no central control can be total. Secondly, the term is mostly used to denote the dictatorship of a development-oriented oligarchy or individual, i.e. a variant form of *de facto* individual sovereignty or, more generally, a highly restricted form of collective sovereignty. In the case of 'democracy', which minimally means rule by the people, one is clearly dealing with a form of collective sovereignty. Further, all states which are or have been called democratic can easily be shown to operate in a basically oligarchic fashion, i.e. to exhibit the character of a restricted form of collective sovereignty. Thus both totalitarian and democratic states represent types of collective sovereign, which are in practice characterised by some form of restricted membership. A collective sovereign may establish greater or less central control, and where that control becomes greater it will not necessarily grow more unjust, just as government will not necessarily become more admirable where its range of control shrinks.

In view of all this, there has been a tendency to move away from the distinction between 'totalitarianism' and 'democracy'. The former expression, in any case, always had the character of a term of abuse. Every state which has ever been designated by outsiders 'totalitarian' has always labelled itself 'democratic'. A substitute distinction might be made between 'peoples' democracies' and 'liberal democracies'. But the first expression is so painfully redundant that I avoid using it too. The expression 'totalitarian', on the other hand, is so obviously exaggerated that one need not fear that any great danger, at the moment, derives from retaining it. So we come to speak of a contrast between totalitarianism and *liberal* democracy. These labels cannot, in themselves, be taken seriously. The differences between collective sovereigns have to be recognised in terms of differences of degree. These differences will essentially relate to the extent to which the governing element includes, and thereby represents, the governed; the variation in types of goals which are set for the collective membership (or citizenry); the degree to which the collective sovereign realises such goals; and the manner of their realisation. Totalitarian states may differ broadly from the liberal-democratic variety either in relation to degree of representativeness or goal achievement, but mostly in relation to the types of goal projected and (even more) the manner of their realisation. All that this means is that when people distinguish between 'totalitarian' and 'liberal-democratic' states, what they basically have in mind is an idea of the former being significantly more, and of the latter being significantly less, respectful of civil liberties. To the collective sovereign, in the one case, is attributed a basic concern with *what* is to be done (in a substantive, usually economic, sense); in the other case, the collective sovereign is attributed a basic concern with *how* things are done (in a procedural, legal, civil-libertarian sense).

Totalitarianism is largely regarded as a legacy of absolutism; in so far, however, as it embodies the principle and character of collective sovereignty, it is not to be seen in this light. Liberal democracy is often assumed to be entirely devoid of absolutism; in so far, however, as it puts forward unbounded claims for *order*, the assumption is unfounded. Given that both totalitarianism and liberal democracy feature collective sovereignty, they are in this fundamental particular alike. As collective sovereigns, each may perpetuate a feature of absolutism: the assumption that the stabler and more certain the political order, the better; that more political order always means a better political order. A demand for *more* political order often assumes that some absolute form of order can be reached; it often demands the promulgation of an illimitable string of laws to secure that order, together with bottomless harshness in applying the rules which define it. This aspect of absolutism may perpetuate itself through any form of collective sovereign, whether communist or capitalist. The twin assumptions that order *ought* not to be disturbed, and that it somehow *in fact* precedes justice, come together in the ideology of order. It is this ideology which, in all collective, even 'pluralist' regimes, is directly linked to the traditional theory of absolutism.

PART TWO

ABSOLUTIST PERSPECTIVES

'Everywhere it was feared that the entire social order, public welfare and culture would be undermined. Consequently . . . people began to seek salvation in a strong royal power.'
Zygmunt Izdebski, *Quelques observations sur les idées politiques de Jean Bodin* (Lodz, 1965), p. 35.

'The claims of Royalists and Parliament could be reconciled if it were realized that either Charles or Cromwell could be an absolute ruler by consent. The Royalists would have to give up . . . the theory of divine right; the Parliament men would have to waive their objections to absolutism.'
Richard Peters, *Hobbes* (Penguin, 1956), pp. 194–5.

'Plus qu'une autre sans doute la pensée politique paraît liée à la vie, aux événements de l'histoire et aux régimes au sein desquels ces événements ont surgi.'
Georges Davy, *Thomas Hobbes et J.-J. Rousseau* (Oxford, 1953).

Chapter Two

History: Italy and Machiavelli

In the fifth century, the Roman Empire collapsed. The Italian peninsula was overrun by loosely organised aliens. Centralised government in Italy disintegrated, and its former burdens were increasingly assumed by what had been a congeries of mere provincial towns. By the twelfth century these towns enjoyed considerable autonomy; in the meantime, Italy's early conquerors had been absorbed. For two centuries more the Italian city-states grew and flourished. But by the fifteenth century, when the Renaissance of Italian culture and art had reached an advanced stage of maturity and vitality, Italian political decline had become chronic and irreversible. From 1494, French, Swiss, Spanish and German armies invaded Italy. By 1530 Charles V had become her master, although this was not entirely and finally confirmed until the peace of Cateau-Cambrésis (1559). Italy was not to regain any real form of independence until reunited as a single state in the nineteenth century.[1]

During the Renaissance, the problem for Italy would be to determine how to avoid such subjugation to foreign rule. The independent city-states, confronted with the growing consolidation of monarchical power in countries like France and Spain, might try to survive on their own. They might, themselves, attempt to unite with one another under a monarchy. They might place themselves individually under the protection of different foreign champions. Underlying these options, however, was the question whether Italy was really any better off under Italian than under foreign rule. If the Italian states were genuinely republican, then their condition under external imperial rule would certainly be worse. But towards the close of the fifteenth century, there was little in the governance of the Italian states that could be regarded as genuinely republican.[2] Broadly speaking, Italian rule in the fifteenth century was

[1] For a summary view of these events, see J. C. L. Simonde de Sismondi, *A History of the Italian Republics* (Anchor Books, 1966), in one volume.

[2] See Simonde de Sismondi, *Histoire des rèpubliques italiennes* (Paris, 1807–18), vol. 12, pp. 17ff., where he discusses how severely limited were the numbers of 'citizens' (as distinct from inhabitants) in these states.

not of a kind to endear sovereigns to their subjects. Even in republican states (like Venice and Florence) where this was not entirely true, the endless attempts to subjugate smaller neighbouring states would not recommend to the latter the superior virtue of Italian rule. It may be useful to pass the situation under rapid review.[1]

The lords of Milan were, on the whole, a bloodthirsty lot. Many of them buried their adversaries alive, set packs of dogs upon them, were profligate in the dispensation of poisons, concocted elaborate and prolonged tortures and were both skilled and unrelenting in the prosecution of expansionist wars. The family of the Medici, apart from occasional expulsions, were dominant in Florence, where their rule was and had to be (given the city's republican character) far milder than that of their Milanese counterparts. But Cosimo de Medici, responsible for various persecutions, exiles and executions, was remembered for his reply to those who protested against these harsh measures, that states could not be governed with paternosters. Venice, rich and stable, unscrupulously promoted her interests at the expense of surrounding states like Padua, Verona and Vicenza, whose rulers she removed both by conquest and by assassination. Naples was in a chaotic state. No sooner had Ladislaus imposed a degree of order than he was presumed to have been killed by poisoning (1414). First, Alfonso of Aragon was invited to uproot the anarchical weed, then René of Lorraine, and thereupon these two traded blows to decide who was the better man. When Alfonso, the victor, died in 1458, his heir had to reconquer the kingdom, not only (like his father) by contesting the claims of René, but now also those of the pope. Rome itself was in a pitiable state. It had no commerce or industry and for the first part of the century its noblemen were essentially brigands, its territory full of thieves. Virtually all of the popes were guilty of cupidity and nepotism. According to Burckhardt,[2] Sixtus IV (1471–84) was 'the first pope who had Rome and the neighbourhood thoroughly under his control'. The pattern of rule was essentially tyrannical, and yet neither extensive nor sure. In 1492, during the mere eleven days which elapsed between the death of Innocent VIII and the accession of Alexander VI, 220 murders were committed. There is generally little evidence of any affection among the Romans for their rulers, which is readily understandable in circumstances where the pope sired numerous offspring, where one of these, Cesare Borgia, might freely murder courtiers, his brother-in-law and his brother, and where the pope might father a child (or generally be

[1] See Pasquale Villari, *Niccolò Machiavelli and His Times*, tr. L. Villari (London, 1878), vols 1 and 2.
[2] Jacob Burckhardt, *The Civilisation of the Renaissance in Italy* (London, 1937), p. 57.

reckoned to have done so) by his own daughter (Lucrezia Borgia).[1]

Under such circumstances as these, it is difficult to imagine so irrelevant a creature as the Italian 'patriot'. There could be no realistic object towards which to direct one's patriotism – unless of course one were looking backwards, to a point in time where such a political entity as 'Italy' actually existed; unless, in short, one cast a view back to so distant a point as that occupied by ancient Rome, and assumed that she represented a model worthy of imitation. But even in this case, one's primary concern (as in Dante and Marsiglio) would probably be with imperial, rather than with 'Italian', unity. One's primary concern, in short, would probably be with a non-nationalistic form of unity, over-leaping the bounds of Italian geography, grounded in the pursuit of a general peace, and possibly inclined to regard the most extensive unity as securing the greatest stability.

Niccolò Machiavelli, an official of the Florentine Chancery between 1498 and 1512, lived and worked during a period of truly extraordinary instability. He looked at Italy from a Roman political perspective. In so far as he had ideals, one might describe him as a republican. But Machiavelli was fundamentally interested in order and he sought some form of Italian unity as a means of promoting this. The harsh and anarchic circumstances (or at least such a perception of these circum-stances) which influenced Machiavelli's thought are reflected in his insistence upon the *arte della guerra*, on the horrors perpetrated by mercenary soldiers, on the importance of a citizen soldiery, on the need for princes to have knowledge of military affairs, on the indispensability of the military to the state, on the need for iron rule and unsentimental rulers, on the necessity for the prince to know everything about the elements of government, and generally on the legitimacy of losing one's soul to preserve the state. Machiavelli, unlike Sismondi,[2] could not regard republicanism as a solution to Italy's problems: the Italians were corrupt, and a corrupt people could not sustain free institutions. He did not envisage a confederacy: Italy would be united by a strong ruler utilising caustic methods or she would not be united at all. He was not a nationalist: he simply sought order and a state large enough to secure it, without being much bothered about the paths travelled to attain it.[3] Machiavelli, however, recognised the importance of popular support for strong and enduring rule. After the state had been founded and its

[1] See Villari, *Machiavelli*, vol. 1, p. 321.

[2] Simonde de Sismondi, *Histoire*, esp. vol. 12, argued that Renaissance Italy could only have been spared foreign conquest and subjugation by the revival of its republican tradition together with a confederation of such revived republics.

[3] Burckhardt, *Civilisation*, p. 15, *à propos* of size, remarks: 'it may be said in general of the despotisms of the fifteenth century that the greatest crimes are most frequent in the smallest states'.

security established, he believed it right and feasible to introduce a more democratic order, in the sense of admitting larger numbers of men to the direction of its affairs.[1]

Against a background of incessant turmoil, we see in Machiavelli something both of a monarchist and of a republican. It is a mistake to regard these items in his recommendatory repertoire as necessarily contradictory: they can be mutually supportive. The support of the people is the repository of a ruler's strength. And strength, through centralised leadership, is often the collective desire of a people. But in Machiavelli there is to be found no discussion of popular rights and limited sovereignty. Neither is there any discussion of the divine right of kings or of the unlimited sway of their authority. Accordingly, Machiavelli cannot easily be regarded as either an absolutist or a pluralist. In any event, a distinction must be made between absolutism and centralism. Machiavelli's centralism took the form of a concrete string of recommendations primarily intended to fit a concrete set of circumstances. Thus, while he was a centralist in one historical period (his own), he might have been a decentralist – taken as a proponent of limited sovereignty – in another. Although Machiavelli's political analysis was concrete and powerful, he raised, in the view of the present author, no genuinely important theoretical issues regarding the 'nature' or 'source' of political power. He took its nature and source for granted. His intelligence was not so much detached as engaged, so that he primarily raised questions – action questions – relating to his own historical-political circumstances. In his way, he was as much a classifier as Aristotle. But what he classified were not static entities, such as states, corporations and families, but dynamic entities, classes of acts, such as those that will win a state or lose it, subdue a people or rouse them to fury, and so on. To the extent that one persists in regarding Machiavelli as an absolutist, one must accept that he is highly pragmatic. Thus one can only argue with him by assessing his period, and the particular solutions which he proposes for the difficulties he thought were posed by that period. Machiavelli's writing was essentially policy-oriented. Although he thought about politics in a new way (in contrast to his medieval predecessors), he did not think about them in an abstractly logical way or even in what might be called a 'scientific' way (a perspective implying a divorce between the contemplation of politics and involvement in political activity). Machiavelli can only be called 'scientific' in the sense that he insisted upon ends always being matched by means appropriate to their achievement, whatever those means might be. But such a 'science' differs significantly from one which attempts to set out universal laws of human activity independent of human volition.

[1] *Discourses*, I, 9.

Machiavelli's concern with strong, centralised government, with eliminating ambiguous or uncertain centres of control and overlapping authorities, with creating peaceful and stable polities, whatever the cost, has an affinity with a like concern shared by Bodin and Hobbes. It is in this respect that his work is continuous with theirs. Although the political condition of the Italy in which he lived was not exactly replicated in either sixteenth-century France or seventeenth-century England, it was close enough to these to generate a similar stress, as reflected in Bodin and Hobbes, upon strong, well-articulated authority and an unambiguously defined centre of command.

It is far more misleading to refer to Machiavelli as an 'absolutist' than it is to apply such a label to Bodin and Hobbes. Machiavelli's 'absolutism', after all, is highly practical, not 'ideological'. His recommendations are so closely related to his historical circumstances, or (more strictly) to his perception of those circumstances, that it is difficult to imagine him as being at all concerned either to describe or to recommend 'illimitably' centralised power. Machiavelli's circumstances were such as were likely to produce an absolutist response, but his actual analysis betrays a greater concern with demonstrating how one may individually ascend a pinnacle of power than with demonstrating that sovereign power in itself is or should be unlimited, or that order, in some general sense, is or ought to be omnipresent.

There is a difference between concentrating power for some particular purpose and doing so in principle. There is a difference between seeking considerable power concentrations to achieve specific ends and seeking them on the assumption that they are good in themselves. Writers are often described as absolutists because they seek some concentration of power, or a considerable concentration of power, or an 'unlimited' concentration of power. But these are three very different degrees of concentrated power and it is undesirable that they be confused. Machiavelli is explicitly concerned with a considerable, but not necessarily with an unlimited, concentration of power. His period therefore may be regarded as relevant to absolutist theory, but his work cannot be held, in the fullest sense, to exemplify it.

Normative absolutism is most fully instanced in recommendations for unlimited concentrations of power. On one level it does not much matter whether power can or cannot in fact be unlimited. For even if we accept that it cannot be unlimited, we are not thereby accepting that the existing limits cannot be extended outwards, nor that there is some *a priori* way of stipulating an empirical point beyond which such outward extension ceases to be possible. Normative absolutism, defined as a recommendation for an unlimited concentration of power, can always be interpreted practically as a relentless *a priori* disposition to demand

45

an increasing concentration of power for its own sake. So conceived, absolutism is a psychological, philosophical and political possibility.

We shall find in Bodin and Hobbes far greater evidence of *a priori* absolutism than we shall be able to detect in the work of Machiavelli. This sort of absolutism involves an ideology of order: the unlimited concentration of power goes hand in hand with the total security of an order. In the same way that it does not necessarily matter that no power can literally be unlimited, so it does not necessarily matter that no order can be totally secure. Just as the actual limits of a given power can be extended, so the actual security in a society may be increased. There is no theoretical point that we can reach about which we are able to say: beyond this there can be no further centralisation, or beyond this there can be no greater security. Although the *a priori* disposition illimitably to concentrate power always contains the *a priori* disposition to make an order ever more secure, absolutism and the ideology of order are not the same. The ideology of order subordinates absolutism to the status of a means, elevates order to the rank of an end. The ideology of order has most significantly expressed itself through absolutism, but it is not historically exhausted by it, and it is not exclusively expressed through it.

If order is the end, and if pluralism instances one of its forms, then in this, too, we may discover a variant manifestation of the ideology of order. Order, as an end, may be served by pluralism, as a means. An order can, in varying degrees, be loose or tight. However an order is designated, in whatever way it is defined, the chief question that arises is: at what point may we say that it has disintegrated? We may say, for example, that the political order is threatened when the queen's name is taken in vain. Or we may say that an order only verges on collapse when the male citizenry refuse to be conscripted to wage foreign wars. In other words, an order may be designated in different ways and be held to collapse by virtue of a sustained challenge to any one or a number of a community's constituent norms. A plural order, however it may be defined, consists of a system of norms, however loose; some (or any) of these norms, when challenged, may generate within a dominant section of the community which applies them as outraged and intolerant a reaction, a reaction whose implications may be as extensive and as overwhelming, as any we might expect to be generated (perhaps more readily and for more trivial reasons) under an absolutist regime.

Chapter Three

History: France and Bodin

In the fifteenth century, France had probably become the most united country in Europe.[1] By the beginning of the sixteenth century the central authority of the king had been solidly established, as instanced by the reigns of Louis XI (1461–83), Louis XII (1498–1515) and François I (1515–47).[2] The survival of French unity during the mid-sixteenth century was partly attributable to the continuing conflict with Spain over the possession of Italy, a conflict which lasted up to 1559, and from which Spain (first under Charles V and later under Philip II) emerged the victor. But these wars, which had helped to consolidate French unity, also carried the seeds of its destruction.

The wars with Spain had flushed the French nobility from feudal isolation, brought them to the court and redirected their attention to the affairs of the realm as a whole in a highly competitive and potentially destructive manner. At the same time, the wars encumbered the king, Henri II (1547–59), with an enormous debt, such that he was compelled to default, as had the Spanish sovereign, Philip II, a few months earlier (1557).[3] The king's debt was mirrored in the even greater impoverishment of the people, upon whom these wars had brought ruin and in many of whom they had kindled the fires of rebellion. Among reformed Catholics (i.e. Protestants) political and military reverses were often attributed to religious impiety and corruption. As conditions grew worse, a seditious attitude towards the state was married to a growing irreverence towards the established church. The wars with Spain had compelled the French monarchy to exchange a modicum of toleration towards the Reform movement against a very substantial, even essential, quantum of financial and commercial assistance from those figuring in that movement. The Reform movement was inclined to assist the monarchy because the latter was locked in a deadly struggle with

[1] George H. Sabine, *A History of Political Theory* (3rd ed., London, 1951), p. 288.
[2] Roger Chauviré, *Jean Bodin, auteur de la 'République'* (Paris, 1914), pp. 209–10.
[3] J. E. Neale, *The Age of Catherine de Medici* (London, 1963), p. 31.

Charles V, emperor of Germany, Spain and the Netherlands, a ruler whose Catholicity was far more pronounced and dangerous than that of François I or Henri II. Thus the wars with Spain had the effect of delaying the conflict, as also the resolution of the conflict, between Protestantism and Catholicism within France; but they carried the danger of making that conflict more serious and more enduring when it did occur. Between 1557 and 1559 the ranks of the Protestants rapidly swelled. As the Spanish wars continued it became increasingly necessary for Henri II to decide whether to become Protestant, unite the country on that basis and so continue the wars against Spain, or to conclude an immediate and disadvantageous peace as an essential preliminary towards the suppression of Protestantism in France.

The question whether the French monarch could have become Protestant must inevitably, to some degree, remain open; but economic considerations of great importance weighed against it from the start. Financially speaking, France was the only country in Europe in the age of Luther which had already had its Reformation. This was due to the concordat of 1516, concluded between François I and the pope, which in effect allowed the French king to mulct ecclesiastical estates of vast sums. The German princes, by contrast, only came by their ecclesiastical levies on becoming Protestant; similarly, Henry VIII of England only profited from ecclesiastical wealth by establishing himself as the head of an independent, national church. But the French monarchy could anticipate no financial gain from conversion to Protestantism. If anything, conversion threatened to diminish the material benefits already accruing from the crown's spiritual allegiances, for such is the effect that the purifying zeal of the reformed church would almost certainly have produced. The Catholic church in France may have been corrupt, but its relations with the crown were still profitable to the latter. Thus, although the crown may not have turned away from Lutheranism for monetary reasons, neither could it accept it for these reasons. The absence of such a temptation must be regarded as having been a powerful argument against a reversal of loyalties. Genuine Protestant reform therefore threatened to deprive the crown of considerable sums of money; in addition to this, it simultaneously threatened to devolve increasing wealth and power upon a contentious nobility.[1]

Although persecution of the French Lutherans[2] began as early as

[1] Gabriel Hanotaux, *Études historiques sur le XVIe et le XVIIe siècle en France* (Paris, 1886), pp. 30–3.

[2] The French Protestants were called Lutherans, later Calvinists, and later still, Huguenots; but the reason for this last appellation is not at all clear. See J. W. Thompson, *The Wars of Religion in France, 1559–1576* (Chicago, 1909), p. 10 n. 1.

1520, François I did not push this policy to extremes. His son, however, gradually abandoned the more moderate practice of the father (who died in 1547). Henri II issued edicts against the Protestants in 1549, 1550, 1551, 1557 (when the death penalty was formally imposed on non-Catholics) and 1559 (when the death penalty was insisted upon for all heretical practitioners without exception for the well-born or wealthy).

Early in Henri II's reign, the 'Chambre ardente' was set up, a special court intended for the particular persecution of Protestants.[1] But it was towards the close of his reign especially that Henri II became genuinely obsessed by and fearful of the Protestant heresy. The majority of his soldiery were Protestant, as were so many of the merchants and bankers upon whom he depended for credit and supplies. Yet from Henri's perspective these people were unreliable, responsible for civil disturbances and given to religious innovation, thus offending against established practice. The conventional wisdom of the day argued that orderly government required – as even François I had insisted – one king, one law, one faith (*un roi, une loi, une foi*). Henri II and his advisers understood 'Reformation' and 'Protestantism', indeed, to be synonymous with rebellion and popular revolt.[2] And by 1559 he was being informed that from one-half to two-thirds of his subjects had fallen into heresy and that the number was increasing.[3] Henri decided that it was essential for him to crush 'cette infâme canaille Lutherienne'.[4]

The peace of Cateau-Cambrésis of 1559, concluding the wars with Spain over Italy, was a highly personal act. The fundamental motive underlying it was undoubtedly Henri's desire to uproot heresy in France. The treaty won nothing for France and surrendered much which it was unnecessary to yield. The effect was to bring external peace through submission to Spain, and internally to prepare the ground for civil war. Henri explained to the king of Spain, to the pope, to the Parlement de Paris and others, that his purpose in terminating these external wars was to be better placed to destroy 'l'hérésie de Calvin'. He instructed his judicial and administrative officials in the provinces to give all assistance in the elimination of heretical offenders – 'pour procéder à l'expulsion, punition et correction desdits hérétiques'. When a majority of the Parlement opposed the execution of his edicts against heresy, he marched into the chamber (June 10, 1559) and had six of them summarily arrested. Henri had not long to live, but he persisted in his determination to the end; even on his deathbed he swore to spare

[1] *Ibid.*, p. 11.
[2] Lucien Romier, *Les origines des guerres de religion* (Paris, 1913–14), vol. 1, p. 228.
[3] *Ibid.*, vol. 2, pp. 250–1. Romier argues that one-third is probably a more reliable figure.
[4] *Ibid.*, vol. 2, pp. 286–7.

no one who supported 'these new doctrines'. Calvin, safely ensconced in Geneva, interpreted Henri's death as a visitation of divine punishment, while Catholics deplored the French king's demise, fearing it would give courage to the Protestants.[1]

As Henri II was mortally wounded during that jousting match of June 30, 1559, which celebrated the marriage-to-be of his daughter (Elizabeth) to the king of Spain, he was succeeded (September 18, 1559) by his fifteen-and-a-half year old son, François II. The latter was far too young and inexperienced, far too weak and unwell, to perform the role for which he was now cast. Normally the care of the kingdom might have been informally entrusted to Antoine de Bourbon, king of Navarre.[2] But the Bourbons were adroitly eased to one side by the Duc and Cardinal de Guise, the uncles of François II through the latter's wife (Mary Stuart). The Guises arranged that the royal successor should assume formal control, but that they, rather than he, should actually direct affairs of state. The Guises intensified Henri's policy of religious intolerance and persecution. Predictably, the Protestant response became more violent. The Guises committed legal murder; the protestants replied with assassination. As Protestant opposition to Guise rule grew, so too did that of large numbers of the disaffected nobility, who were disinclined to favour the Guise seizure of power. The Constable (Connétable) Montmorancy and the Prince de Condé, for example, were deprived, respectively, of Languedoc and Picardy. Thus the Guises moved not only against the Huguenots but also against the princes of the blood and the lesser nobility. That is to say, they attacked political as well as religious opponents, and indeed the two types of opposition under the circumstances were disposed to converge.[3] The first attempt to unseat the Guises was the conspiracy of Amboise (1560). This event marks the beginning of serious bloodletting in the religious wars in France. The plot was betrayed and ruthlessly suppressed, costing the lives of 1,200 known or suspected rebels.[4]

This repression by the Guises (of the nobility in particular) was to have a significant and bitter effect. It marked the beginning of local risings, the smashing of images and the murder of priests. By 1562 civil war was an established fact. The thirty-six years which followed reflected an extreme confusion, the crown shifting its support from Catholic to Protestant to Catholic; the country being torn between the reformed and the established faiths; the nation lurching into war and

---

[1] Lucien Romier, Les origines des guerres de religion (Paris, 1913–14), vol. 2, pp. 295–390 for a fuller account of these developments.

[2] Neale, Catherine de Medici, p. 41. For a much more exact account see H. Hauser, La prépondérance espagnole (1559–1660) (Paris, 1933), pp. 42ff.

[3] Thompson, Wars, p. 16.   [4] Ibid., p. 39.

out of it; one war, truce, massacre, following hard upon another; each war becoming worse than the one before and every renewal of peace less certain. The wars which took place during this period are generally reckoned as eight: 1562–3, 1567–8, 1568–70, followed by the St Bartholomew's massacre in 1572, introducing the bloodier bouts which followed in 1572–3, 1574–6, 1577, 1579–80 and 1585–98. But the bare bones of such a chronology cannot capture the intensity of feeling, the animosity, which characterised these wars, nor the variety of stages upon which they were enacted, as between armies on battlefields and embittered neighbours in distant hamlets.[1] Thus we are confronted, not so much with a succession of distinct battles as with a continuing battle, not so much between distinct and disciplined armies as between compatriots and neighbours, consumed with religious and political hatred.

The St Bartholomew's massacre marked a turning point in the civil wars in France. Cathérine de Medici had persuaded her son, Charles IX, to try to resolve the conflict simply by eliminating one of the parties to it. The king's assent resulted in the virtual elimination of the higher nobility from the ranks of the Protestant leadership, a leadership which accounted for perhaps one-third of France's nobility as a whole. Henceforth the wars were limited to an almost exclusively religious, as distinct from a political, question: the survival of the Protestant faith. The Protestant leadership were subsequently of lower birth, and more fervent. The crown's position was now totally unambiguous: it had allied itself to a party. In consequence the wars could only grow more bitter and more difficult to conclude. It is estimated that those killed in Paris and the provinces during the St Bartholomew's massacre numbered between 10,000 and 20,000 people.[2] It is not merely that the response to the act was bitter: so was the act itself. The Spanish ambassador's description of the events of St Bartholomew is revealing: 'As I write, they are killing them [the Huguenots], ripping their clothes from them, dragging them through the streets, pillaging their homes, not even sparing a child. This morning, before noon, they had killed 3000 people . . . Praise be to God!'[3]

As the years went by, matters only worsened. Armstrong[4] provides a racy account of conditions in Paris during the Huguenot siege of 1590: 'Paris endured a famine to which that of 1870 was child's play. For some time rations of bread, with a piece of cat or dog, were served to the poor;

[1] For an excellent account of the entire period see John Viénot, *Histoire de la Réforme française de L'Édit de Nantes à sa révocation*, 2 vols (Paris, 1926–34). E. Armstrong, *The French Wars of Religion* (London, 1904) is convenient and brief but, like Neale, *Catherine de Medici*, not always reliable.

[2] Figures necessarily vary; these are taken from Armstrong, *Wars*, p. 33.

[3] In Hanotaux, *Études historiques*, p. 40.

[4] Armstrong, *Wars*, pp. 73–4.

but cats, dogs, rats, and mice rapidly disappeared . . . The Duchess of Montpensier advised the people to dig up bones from the cemeteries and grind them into flour [they did, and died as a result]. Noble ladies declared that they would eat their children rather than admit the heretic [with the consequence that the poorer people began to eat their children]. The German mercenaries chased the children down the streets, as the children had chased the dogs. Everything . . . was ruinous except sermons, of which the starving people could have their bellyful.'

France's experience of civil war in the sixteenth century was unique. There the Reformation did not triumph, but nor was it entirely defeated, whereas elsewhere clear success or failure was the general rule. The Reform movement touched Italy,[1] but there, as in Spain, it was wiped out by the Inquisition; in Germany, the north became Lutheran, the south remained Catholic; England and the Netherlands became Protestant. In none of these cases was the prospect or fact of religious reform accompanied by civil war. There was no serious religious strife in Italy or Spain or England in the sixteenth century. Even in Germany the struggles which ensued were essentially territorial, between north and south. In the Netherlands the Dutch wars against Spain (which resulted in the triumph of the Protestant cause) were largely seen as a national affair, being directed against Spain, a conveniently identifiable foreign oppressor. In France, by contrast, a civil war split the nation ideologically and territorially, lasted for almost four decades, forced the crown to lean first towards one side, then towards the other, and provided no credible foreign threat or enemy which might serve to unite the opposing parties. Against this backdrop the emergence in the sixteenth century of a French theory of royal absolutism is more easily understood. No such theory developed in England until the following century.[2]

Jean Bodin was the leading French political writer of the sixteenth century. Formally, his country was blessed with a legal and political hierarchy that ought to have been able to hold the country together, but which in fact was failing to do so. Early on in the civil wars, Bodin appears to have assumed that a show of strength and a bit of blood-letting would cure France of her civil troubles.[3] This expectation, unfortunately, was not met. Between the beginning of the wars and 1576 Bodin had much time in which to reflect upon the causes of the instability and insecurity of contemporary France, as well as time to revise his notions about the proper manner of curing those ills. We have already noted the ever-deepening tragedy of the French wars, especially

[1] Romier, *Origines*, vol. I, pp. 493–5.
[2] Sabine, *Political Theory*, p. 314.
[3] Chauviré, *Jean Bodin*, p. 272.

from 1562 to 1576, including the infamous massacre of Huguenots in 1572. By the time of the publication of the *Six livres de la République* in 1576 it was fairly clear that mere vigour and ruthlessness could not suppress Protestantism. This, in fact, was demonstrated soon after the St Bartholomew's massacre. For despite the crippling extent of the 1572 slaughter of Huguenots, Henri III (1574–89) did not take long to recognise the necessity of again granting concessions to Protestant practice. It was in fact these concessions which alarmed more extreme Catholics and justified their establishment of a 'League', as it was called, to proscribe further toleration of 'heresy'. More liberal Catholics, as represented by men like Étienne Pasquier, Michel de l'Hôpital, and, of course, Jean Bodin, opposed such extremism, considered it decidedly impolitic, and became generally recognisable as 'les Politiques', whose fundamental aim was some form of peaceful reconciliation with Protestantism.[1] Such figures canvassed not only for a strong state but also for one committed in a degree to the principle of religious toleration. For them, not only could a strong state afford religious toleration, but (as in French conditions) a state had to be tolerant in order to be strong.

If we compare Renaissance Italy with late sixteenth-century France we note an important similarity: both are characterised by an extraordinary amount of violence. But we also recognise an important difference: Italy continually suffered both foreign invasion and civil war, while France, which suffered no less for that, had only to endure civil war. In Italian circumstances virtually any form of order would probably prove acceptable. But in French circumstances, given the internal causes of the country's discontent, it is likely that no rule, however strong, could possibly succeed unless it held out some hope of truly reconciling the rival factions. In Machiavelli we see a diplomat who was passionately concerned with practical politics and essentially interested in imposing order by any efficient means. Bodin was interested in order, but unlike Machiavelli he could not be satisfied with just any form of order. In Bodin we discover a proponent of order but also of justice, not merely on the assumption that justice was as desirable as order, but on the additional assumption that (as in France) there could be no order without justice. Thus Machiavelli's concern was fairly elementary: roughly to establish any form of stable government. Bodin, operating in somewhat improved institutional circumstances, could take the existing governmental *framework* for granted: his concern was (*a*) to make that framework sturdier and at the same time (*b*) to render it sufficiently supple to tolerate such stress and divergent leanings of conscience as might destroy a structure more rigid and unbending. He

[1] See L. Couzinet, *'Le Prince' de Machiavel et la théorie de l'absolutisme* (Paris, 1910), pp. 84–6.

was concerned not only to increase power at the centre, but also to retain the independence of certain groups in certain matters at the periphery (like the family and the church), although on the assumption that the independence of the latter promoted the strength of the former. Bodin, in short, was not just an absolutist. He was also something of a pluralist. Despite the fact that he betrays little of Machiavelli's ruthlessness, he does reveal a far more deeply ingrained, indeed *a priori*, centralising tendency. Thomas Hobbes proved as ruthless as Machiavelli and far more centralist than Bodin.

As noted earlier, Machiavelli had stressed the importance of strong rule in an Italian context, arguing that, in periods like his own, a powerful prince was required to found and reform states. In the *Discourses* he has much to say that is favourable to republicanism, and in *The Prince* he elaborates in some detail upon the more extreme measures to which princely rulers might be obliged to resort. Neither work, however, reflected any generalised aversion either to princely or to republican rule and, as is generally recognised, the two texts are in no way incompatible. In both works Machiavelli stressed the necessity of princely rule in any state where order must be initiated or restored, while generally insisting that in corrupt and chronically unstable circumstances a prince must resolve to act alone.[1] Machiavelli did not advance these views within the context of a general analysis of the nature and structure of political power as such. His observations were recognisably important without rising, for all that, above the level of observations. Bodin, by contrast, went much further along the way to providing a general analysis of the nature and structure of political power. He attempted to analyse the general character of political order, integrally with an analysis of the conditions indispensable to its establishment and maintenance. His analysis of sovereignty lay at the heart of this concern. For this reason we shall pay very close attention to this concept. In it Bodin explored the general character of a hierarchy and the conditions for its maintenance. He was led on to advocate and explain the necessity for the concentration of greater power in the sovereign, without intending, at the same time, that the latter could or should do anything it wished. Nonetheless, his analysis of the conditions of a stable government, which also assumed the character of a recommended form of government, would have the effect of identifying its proponent (always with considerable justification) as an absolutist.

Bodin's analysis and recommendations were based on principles and were therefore deductive. But they were also related to existing circumstances and thus were existential and practical as well. His work provides us with an interesting and important contrast between style and sub-

[1] *Discourses*, I, 9, 55.

stance. The style is reflected in a tight and uncompromising deductivism, the substance in a practical concern with contemporary issues. The latter concern is encased in the former and for Bodin the two are inseparable. This inseparability has had a significant effect upon later generations of readers. If we invoke Machiavelli, we think it virtually impossible to explain him without introducing some consideration of the period in which he wrote. But if we invoke Bodin, such historical introductions generally appear less relevant. His application of a rigorous logic to political concepts goes far towards explaining this. And his logic has received far more attention by students of politics than has any other aspect of his work – such as his judgement, assessment of human psychology, or understanding of history. It is probably this purely logical understanding of Bodin – principally as reflected in his analysis of sovereignty – that so readily converts him into an absolutist. For the style so completely envelops the substance that it becomes difficult to conceive of Bodin altering his 'logic' or 'principles', no matter what historical period he might happen to find himself in. Thus he laid himself open to continuous attack over the centuries, in a way that Machiavelli, for example, did not. Machiavelli we excuse because his circumstances are so obviously unlike our own. Bodin it becomes more difficult to excuse, because the style in which he writes is such as to suggest that his analysis should hold for all politics at all times.

But, to paraphrase Couzinet: 'Absolute monarchy, based essentially upon the unlimited power of the prince, was born in circumstances where such a form of government was necessary and where its early defenders, like Bodin, were concerned to promote the well-being of the nation. He clearly saw absolutism as a means of improving conditions in France. But once the crisis was over, the absolutist principle degenerated into a dogma, converting the absolute power of the king from a mere means into an end in itself.'[1]

Absolutism, in short, was an understandable response to the political conditions we have described as obtaining in Italy and France. To put the case more neutrally, political theorists who accepted a reconstruction of Italian and French history during the Renaissance and Reformation similar to that advanced in this and the previous chapter, would be somewhat inclined to advance theoretical solutions similar to those put forward by Machiavelli and Bodin. To say this is not, of course, to advance a universal claim for these theories, but only a partial explanation of their historical relevance. Bodin was an absolutist in the sense that he can be taken, in considerable part, to have promoted in an *a priori* fashion the centralisation of government. The end which he sought through absolutism was 'order'.

[1] Couzinet, *'Le Prince'*, p. 286.

Chapter Four

History: England and Hobbes

Hobbes is all too often quoted to the effect that he and fear were born twins. Although Professor Goldsmith has rightly argued that this self-portrait is not altogether accurate,[1] one can also see that, in a deeper sense, it is not altogether inaccurate either. For it is true that Hobbes was not a timorous person, but it is equally true that his analysis reflects a fundamental fear of political disorder. The immediate aim of this chapter is to provide a description of those political circumstances within which Hobbes's political fears were embedded. The assumption underlying this description is not that political events automatically give rise to specifiable political thoughts, but, instead, that political events determine the limits within which political theory can relevantly operate. Civil wars involve problems which, when reflected upon, tend to give rise to explanations and remedies that differ significantly from those arising from, say, industrialisation, or rapid technological change, or the creation of empires, or racial conflict, or forced attempts at economic modernisation, or the rise of meritocracy. An age dominated by any one or a combination of these problems will produce corresponding variations in socio-political theory; it is only in this sense that conditions will determine ideas. The important point, albeit a conventional one, is to specify the problem; such specification admits a variety of responses or theories, but all of them gain their point and become simultaneously interrelated in consequence of being attempted solutions to the problem or problems specified. In the present context, the problem must be defined historically. Essentially it has to do with a perception of extreme disorder, civil insecurity or civil war. These are circumstances continuous with those instanced in the cases of Italy and France. In modified form, the problem presented itself to England at the time that Hobbes set about writing *De Cive* and *Leviathan*. An acquaintance with the general sequence of events to which these writings were related is not only essential to an understanding of the relevance of Hobbesian theory, or absolutism, but is also essential to an appreciation of that

[1] P. King and B. Parekh (eds), *Politics and Experience* (Cambridge, 1968), pp. 66–8.

theory which attempted to supersede it, i.e. the theory of limited or constitutional monarchy, of separation of powers, of federalism, and indeed of pluralism, under which heading all of these theories have from time to time been subsumed.

In the Italian circumstances of Machiavelli's time, the basic problem that presented itself was whether any form of settled rule at all could be attained. In the French circumstances of Bodin's time, the geographical definition of the state appeared fixed, as also the line of succession to be followed from one monarch to the next; thus the basic problem was less basic, and had essentially to do with the degree and range of power the government (generally assumed to be best when embodied in a monarch) legitimately and realistically required in order to produce a truly settled and orderly polity. In the English circumstances of Hobbes's time, geographical definition and line of succession appeared to be as clear as in France, so the problems of late sixteenth-century France and of seventeenth-century England were to some extent the same. But the distinctly English difficulty related, not to establishing just any form of orderly rule, nor to extending governmental authority in that degree necessary to ensure civil peace, but to effecting an harmonious blend between the discretionary power of a monarch (the king's prerogative) and the popular authority of a consultative assembly (parliament). It is because the king and parliament were parts of a governmental whole and because the immediate difficulty bore upon a relationship internal to that whole, that it is appropriate to interpret the English problem (particularly when compared with the circumstances in Italy and France) within a largely constitutional framework.[1]

In his sixteenth-century context, Bodin was concerned with supreme power in primarily personal terms. How much power should the king have? For how long? Was he completely above other powers? Was he somehow limited by them? Or was he only subject to God? Bodin's concern with these sorts of questions is easily understood against the backdrop of civil war in its endemically religious form in France. It was essential that supreme power be personal, and that the king, in whom it was centred, be above party and religious animosity and that he have sufficient power to contain these and other animosities. In a seventeenth-century English context, Hobbes is not formally concerned with supreme power in such exclusively personal terms. He did not conceive of monarchy as being *demonstrably* the best form of government (although

---

[1] Cf. I. Deane Jones, *The English Revolution, 1603–1714* (London, 1931): 'From 1603 to 1629 most of the religious and economic quarrels had a constitutional setting in the Courts or in Parliament; since the methods were legal and parliamentary, the whole issue can be called constitutional, in contrast to the period 1629–40, when the opposition could not appeal to parliament and ceased, save in Chambers's and Hampden's cases to appeal to law' (pp. 55–6).

57

he, personally, preferred it). For him the determination of the ideal form of government had to be left open. He argued, like Bodin, that one man or several could wield sovereign power. But he was less inclined to speak of the 'king' or 'prince' than of the 'sovereign', since the latter expression could cover either a ruling individual or group of individuals. Unlike Bodin, Hobbes was not formally concerned with promoting or extending *royal* power, but rather with urging that, within a constitutional framework, where there is ambiguity regarding the locus of supreme power, the structure of government will collapse and the state revert to anarchy. It is in this sense that Hobbes was not a simple royalist and for this reason that he was suspect among royalists. His theory of sovereignty as surely destroyed the theory of the divine right of kings as Locke demolished Filmer. By a contemporary, Hobbes could be read to mean that either a king or an assembly might be sovereign – i.e. have the final word – but that the two could not be so simultaneously. This would imply that it was wrong and mistaken to overturn King Charles but that, having overturned him, it would be equally wrong to challenge whoever subsequently and firmly held the reins of power (i.e. Cromwell). This would also imply that king and parliament could bring no true peace to the civil order except in so far as one was subordinate to the other. Hobbes, like Bodin, definitely *preferred* monarchical rule; but he was less ready to *argue* that it was best; he was content to demonstrate (or try to demonstrate) that no other form of government, if stable, was essentially different.

As already suggested, the English problem was largely constitutional; Hobbes's solution cannot be fully understood in abstraction from that context. The problem invited solution as it became increasingly clearly delineated during the course of the seventeenth century, and especially during the civil war of 1642–9. The civil war cannot of course be explained away by reference to one factor alone, apart from which it would in any event be out of place to attempt here a specific analysis of its causes. Speaking generally, however, I accept a multi-factor analysis of the revolutionary period, assigning prior importance to religious, constitutional and political conflicts and secondary importance to economic, class and technological factors.[1] Apart from such an admission it is only necessary to insist that the civil war be seen as a part of the

---

[1] Cf. Peter Laslett, *The World We Have Lost* (London, 1965), ch. 7. By contrast, Maurice Ashley insists that 'it was a real shifting of economic power that made civil war possible' (*England in the Seventeenth Century*, Penguin, 1961, p. 80). This sort of analysis is ultimately of course greatly influenced by Marx, but more immediately by the work of men like R. H. Tawney and H. Trevor-Roper. But even Christopher Hill, accorded popular recognition as a 'Marxist' historian, argues that 'we should not think *merely* in economic terms' and, further, that 'the civil war was fought about issues of principle' (*Puritanism and*

general historical movement of the seventeenth century. It is unnecessary to argue that it was an inevitable culmination of preceding developments, and impossible to argue that it was an indispensable source of subsequent English constitutionalism. All the same, the war was made the more possible by a political and constitutional ambiguity regarding the distribution of competences within the government; and it need not be deduced that, without the war, the constitutional position would not have been resolved in much the way it subsequently was.

The strong rule of the Tudors, especially of Henry VII, Henry VIII and Elizabeth I, brought an end to feudal anarchy. At her death in 1603, Elizabeth probably left England more unified than any European state had ever been. The Tudors created a firm governmental framework, an essential element in which was parliament, which was associated with and involved in all their great acts of state – such as the break with Rome under Henry VIII, the establishment of a common Anglican religion under Edward, the return to Rome under Mary, and the re-establishment of an Anglican religion under Elizabeth. The association of parliament with state activity served to make the state more, not less, powerful and explains much of the effectiveness of Tudor rule. This effectiveness, however, based upon parliamentary involvement, would tend to generate an ambiguity regarding the legitimate role and place of parliament in government. The problem was not immediately presented in the form, 'Who should rule?', but in the form, 'What are parliament's rights in the process of rule?' If parliament objected to an infringement of its rights, and if it were determined that they had truly been infringed, there then arose the question as to who would enforce those rights if the king himself declined to respect them. This was the nub of the difficulty. The king's response to it was wholly predictable: where there was any kind of conflict between king and parliament it was clearly the latter that must give way.[1]

Revolution, London 1962, pp. 30 and 23). We may agree that economic factors were important. But I agree even more with Gardiner's basic assumption (*History of the Great Civil War, 1642–49*, 4 vols, London, 1894) that religious and constitutional factors were of prior importance. Economic interests were reflected in the conflict between king and parliament, but they were not the only important interests reflected there. For it is not only the case that economic conflicts generate ideological conflicts, but also vice versa. Parliament was the great stage upon which was acted out all the significant forms of seventeenth-century conflict, whether legal, religious, political or economic. And that is why the evolving relationship between parliament and crown was, and was seen to be, so important.

[1] Margaret Atwood Judson, *The Crisis of the Constitution: an Essay in Constitutional and Political Thought in England, 1603–1645* (New Brunswick, N.J., 1949): see ch. 1.

James I (1603–25) argued forcibly for the divine right of kings, but still believed that kings were in some sense bound by the rules they created, that these rules entered into the general fabric of custom governing the land, and that the prince was bound to God (through his coronation oath) to observe these customs. The practical problem arose when James failed to do so. It might well be argued that James 'never did undertake any action for which there was not fairly good legal warrant',[1] but only in so far as one accepted James's own rather narrow reading of the law: which was that the king, virtually no matter what he did, could in effect do no wrong. When he imprisoned his parliamentary opponents, threatened to suppress the privileges of the Commons and tore the Protestation of the Commons from the Journals of the House (1621),[2] he no doubt had a 'fairly good legal warrant', but such a warrant as testified to his unfettered supremacy and which inevitably made a mockery of those customary rights and limitations upon arbitrary behaviour which he swore to uphold at his coronation. Thus to return to the core problem: the law posited parliamentary privilege; it also posited a royal prerogative; whether either of these was upheld might be affected by the persona of the decider. So far the decider was the king. But parliament, in order to protect its rights, might be forced to demote him. Such a procedure could only with difficulty be labelled constitutional. But it would be almost equally difficult to assert that it was unconstitutional. The constitutional arrangements of England did provide, after all, for some form of parliamentary privilege; what they did not provide for was its effective protection. Parliament, in insisting upon this, could only direct attention to a major constitutional incoherence; king and parliament, in going their separate ways, represented the dissolution of government, and therefore of constitutionalism itself.

James's first parliament met on March 19, 1604. During that year the right of the Commons to decide upon the legality of electoral returns was recognised by the king and the right of members of parliament to freedom from arrest was clearly set out on a statutory basis. But in 1606 James increased duties on imports without the consent of parliament. When the legality of these duties was tested in the courts the latter sided with the king, and parliament allowed the matter to subside. Parliament was prorogued in July 1607. Because of its persistent complaints and voicing of grievances it was not reconvened for more than two-and-a-half years. And when this parliament was finally dissolved in December 1610, no other was to be summoned until 1614.[3]

[1] F. D. Wormuth, *The Royal Prerogative, 1603–1649* (Ithaca, N.Y., 1938), p. 93.
[2] Cf. I. Deane Jones, *English Revolution*, p. 18.
[3] For a detailed summary of these events, T. F. T. Plucknett, *Taswell-Langmead's English Constitutional History* (11th ed., London, 1960) is useful.

When James's second parliament met in April 1614, it unanimously voted against the king's right to impose taxes without parliamentary consent, whereupon the king informed members that parliament would be dissolved unless they proceeded to vote the supplies required. But parliament insisted upon royal recognition of the prior right of parliamentary assent before such taxes could be deemed legal. The king would have none of this and did as he had threatened. This second parliament, which sat for two months without passing a single bill, was appropriately dubbed the 'Addled Parliament'. The obstinacy of this parliament was notable; it revealed remarkable agreement within the consultative branch of government as to the limits of the mere king's authority (not that of the government as such). Further, it revealed the extent to which an addled parliament meant an addled monarch, for the latter depended upon parliament to rule effectively and fully; but the effect of this dependence might be to make the monarch weaker, if making the government as a whole far stronger. The central dilemma therefore was that the king was weakened, *vis-à-vis* parliament, if he succeeded in governing through it; but he was also weakened, in respect of the country's total disposable power, if he did not.

Although the right of members of parliament to freedom from arrest was established on a statutory basis in 1604, four members of the Addled Parliament were arrested after parliament was dissolved. The king had naturally every right to arrest them on the assumption that he as king could do no wrong; but he could not be said to have such a right if it were assumed that the king, like everybody else, was obliged to observe certain relevant legal principles. But even here the matter was not so simple. James did not assume that he could do no wrong. Even Hobbes made no such assertion: Hobbes maintained that the sovereign might indeed act well or badly, but that he could commit no *injustice*. James's own position was not really very different. What it amounted to was the notion that even if the king behaved badly, such behaviour could never be taken to justify a mere subject's defiance of his commands; it meant that the king could be corrected by God, but not by other mortals, even where he was wrong. Thus the legal question was shunted from a concern with whether the king could act illegally to a concern with whether such illegality could possibly warrant disobedience. Thus the formula 'the king can do no wrong' really reduced to the proposition that the king could not be held humanly accountable for his wrongdoing.

This was the fundamental reduction that Hobbes's analysis achieved. Anyone who was adversely affected by the king's acts was likely to complain that the king was acting badly. According to Hobbes, the effect of any action upon us is assessed as good or bad depending upon whether it is pleasant or unpleasant. Thus the determination of whether royal acts were good or bad was endlessly subject to private interpretation. But if these conflicting interpretations of public acts came to be regarded as justifications for civil disobedience, then the maintenance of public peace must become an impossibility. It is out of this sort of ground that emerges the command theory of law. Law becomes regarded as a public fact having its source in a determinate human will, whether single or collective. Although one may disapprove of a law privately, to translate that disapproval into a publicly opposed stance presumably invites, according to Hobbesian logic, the disruption of the political order. The implication is that order always involves some inconvenience, but that the greatest inconvenience stems from disorder, and that the only sure way of avoiding this is to establish a determinate human superior to whom allegiance is given, entire and unqualified, such that what is lawful, and what is authoritatively commanded, are identical. This was essentially the position that James held, and which underlay his firm opposition to parliamentary demands. And James's second parliament, addled as it was, could be of no service to him essentially because it rejected that position.

After seven years without a parliament, James assembled a third (January 30, 1621). Parliament had not been called earlier because of its recalcitrance on previous occasions. It was summoned now because the king was sufficiently weak to feel the need. Once assembled, the Commons complained about the previous imprisonment of its members. The king wanted money. He was conciliatory, less high-handed, and promised to respect parliamentary freedom of speech. Parliament granted his request, voting him one supply and then another; and then sat for 'four months busily engaged in impeachments, inquiries into grievances and the preparation of bills of reform but without paying any attention to the King's request for a further supply . . .'[1] The exasperated James adjourned the parliamentary sitting to November. Yet when the Commons reconvened they still insisted on pressing their grievances, attacking popery, Spain and the proposed marriage of Prince Charles to the Infanta. James regarded their style as insolent, and when they protested he rounded upon them, threatening to restrict their privileges. They in turn protested their right to consider and debate a wide range of 'arduous and urgent affairs'. This was the protestation (December 18, 1621) that the king himself tore up, followed by the dissolution of parliament, the imprisonment of five parliamentary leaders and the banishment of others from England.

James did not have another parliament for more than two years; but need once more pushed him in a familiar direction. His fourth and last

[1] T. F. T. Plucknett, *Taswell-Langmead's English Constitutional History*, p. 356.

parliament met in February of 1624. As would be expected at the beginning of such an affair, king and parliament were mutually conciliatory. But matters went beyond initial expectations. For not only did the king allow parliament to advise effectively on matters of war and peace and to treat of the business of royal marriages, which he was previously unwilling to allow, but parliament too was prepared to make reciprocal allowances, and obligingly voted the royal treasury three subsidies. This final interplay of king and parliament represented a not unhappy end to James's reign. It was marked by a display of mutual concessions and the harmonious operation of the rather cumbersome machinery of English government. There was nothing inevitable about the breakdown of this machinery. But such a development was rendered more probable to the extent that one of its elements insisted upon a clear-cut supremacy which it did not in fact possess.

Charles I insisted upon this supremacy. His first parliament met on June 18, 1625. The new king, like the old, wanted money, in this case to fight a war with Spain. The new Commons, like the old, insisted upon redress of grievances. It was not that they wished to be involved in the process of government: they already were. But they wished their involvement to be accepted with all its implications on a basis of right. There was in fact nothing unusual in this demand. The demand did not in itself imply a principle of parliamentary supremacy. But it did imply certain limitations upon the royal prerogative, which limitations in fact formed a part of the common or customary law of the land. Parliament naturally employed such *de facto* leverage as it had to achieve its ends. It voted only meagre subsidies and proposed to grant customs duties (tonnage and poundage) only for a year (rather than for life, as was customary). This denial of tonnage and poundage was unusual, as also the insistence upon the dismissal of the king's favourite minister, Buckingham. Charles's response was to send parliament packing, although he was forced to recall it only six months later.

Charles's first parliament lasted for only two months. His second, which assembled on February 6, 1626, lasted for less than five. During the years 1626–8 the rumour began to circulate that Charles would dispense with parliament altogether. Given popular agreement that parliament was essential to government, opposition to Charles quickly increased.[1] He proceeded to collect revenues to prosecute the war with Spain, but without parliamentary consent. Recusants were induced to pay for relief from religious persecution. From the rich, extra payments were demanded. Fort towns were ordered to provide the king with war vessels and from all subjects a general loan was exacted. But under pressure of foreign involvement none of these measures was adequate to

[1] Judson, *Crisis*, p. 69.

Charles's financial needs and he was driven, for the third time, to summon parliament.

When parliament met (March 17, 1628), Charles invited it to make the appropriate financial concessions, without which, he stated, he would be obliged to achieve his end by other means. His warning was ignored and the Commons proceeded anew to raise such questions as the legality of forced loans, arbitrary imprisonment and quartering of soldiers on civilians, culminating in a composite Petition of Right (June 7, 1628) which declared illegal all these procedures, together with summary executions and arbitrary appropriations of property. In these circumstances it was clear that parliament was not merely protecting its own rights, understood as freedom of debate, protection from arbitrary arrest in consequence thereof, and a right of regular assembly, etc., but was also claiming as its right the protection of what were regarded as generally accepted customary arrangements, such as property rights. The king parried their thrust by ordering a recess. This recess lasted for almost seven months, and during this time Charles continued to raise customs duties as before. Several merchants who refused to pay were imprisoned and their goods appropriated. In November the king also declared the legal incompetence of the Commons to treat religious questions. The issues of religion and taxation were especially sensitive and when the Commons reassembled (January 1629) they passed resolutions which declared their competence to deal with religious matters, as well as the criminal liability of any who advocated or exacted or even paid 'unlawful' taxes. In all of this they revealed a 'disobedient and seditious carriage', to quote the king; so parliament was dissolved and not summoned again for eleven years.

This period has subsequently become known as the 'eleven years' tyranny', a formula accurately recording the parliamentary perspective and the degree to which parliament and king had moved apart. It is pointless to speculate whether Charles could have survived had a train of fortuitous circumstances not conspired against him. He was certainly stubborn and inflexible to a degree which cautions one against the view that his fate was settled by mere chance. He set himself firmly and resolutely against the express interests of the Commons in determining to free himself from financial dependence upon the latter (which would effectively confer upon him a power to rule without them); and the same effect was achieved in insisting upon the imposition of a uniform religion throughout his kingdom,[1] when his beloved wife was a Catholic, as well as conspicuously meddlesome, making it difficult for Protestant subjects to take His Royal Majesty's Protestant orthodoxy on trust. Charles's Calvinist, Covenanting subjects in Scotland were the first to oppose

[1] C. V. Wedgwood, *The King's Peace, 1637–1641* (Fontana, 1966), p. 160.

him. Of course they might be written off as mere rebels; but the question inevitably arose as to how they were to be written off militarily. Charles naturally fell back upon his presumably loyal English subjects for support which, unfortunately for him, could only be obtained effectively through parliamentary channels. And thus, whether fortuitously or inevitably, Charles found himself confronted with a parliament whose support he badly needed, but which he would require to milk with all the care that one bestows upon a gaboon viper in parting it from its venom. Charles himself was so quick to recoil from the task that this parliament has subsequently become known to history as the Short Parliament. Nothing was achieved by dissolving it, and so, soon after, another was called: the last of Charles's reign and perhaps the most fateful in English history.

The Long Parliament met on November 3, 1640, and its leader, John Pym, argued that parliamentary grievances must first be resolved before further business could be conducted. The ancient privileges of parliament, he insisted, must be upheld: parliament must be fully consulted and its members must not be made liable to arrest for speaking their minds; further, Protestants must not be persecuted for their religious beliefs; finally, Pym opposed all taxes not approved by parliament, together with the 'revival of obsolete laws' and monopolistic trading practices.[1] The king had blundered in all these respects and it was natural that parliament should wish to prosecute officials responsible for such alleged breaches of law. Either the king could do no wrong and was in principle irremovable, or the king was *de facto* irremovable and therefore could do no wrong. But his chief officers, in principle and practice, were not incapable of wrongdoing, nor were they irremovable. They were the natural objects of parliamentary attack. But where parliament could successfully remove these officers the king was or became less powerful than he appeared: the effective flow of his rule would make a forced descent into the even calm of a reign. For to attack a king's ministers was, of course, to attack the king's own substantive powers. Despite this, the king's principal advisers were brought down, one after the other: the Earl of Strafford, Archbishop Laud and Lord Keeper Finch. Despite this, the king agreed that parliament, which had effected this work of destruction, should be reconvened at least once every three years, and that the Long Parliament in particular should never be dissolved except by its own consent. Charles could only agree to these things because the alternatives seemed even worse. He needed the support of his English parliament to be able to contain the rebellion of the Scots. But to do this he needed to be able to contain the demands of the Commons, which he found increasingly difficult to do.

[1] *Ibid.*, p. 335.

65

It was a gamble as to how far he could go in appeasing the Commons to contain the Scots, and within a few months of the opening of the Long Parliament he had gone very far indeed.

The revolt of Charles's Catholic subjects in Ireland in October 1641 forced the king's relationship with parliament into its most critical phase. Given Puritan successes in parliament, the Catholic Irish anticipated that further measures would be taken against their religion and that more of their land would be appropriated for and by British settlers. Accordingly they attacked the settlers and drove them out, claiming to restore the king's rights with his support. An army had to be raised to suppress the rebellion. The danger was that if the king controlled this army, he might well use it against parliament rather than against the Irish. The danger to him was that if he did not control it, he would have no means whatever of asserting a power either equal or superior to parliament's. Parliament, more naturally than the king, wished to act against the Irish. But in this connection they asked, in effect, that they be conceded the right to approve all chief appointments to the army, including its head. To drive home their point, the Commons drew up a Grand Remonstrance (November 23, 1641) against Charles's rule, with a view to proving categorically that 'the king was unfit to choose his own counsellors or to control his own army'.[1]

The king responded to the Grand Remonstrance by indicting the leaders of the parliamentary opposition for treason (January 2, 1642). But neither of the houses of parliament would surrender these men. Accordingly, the king himself, supported by troops, came to the Commons to seize the accused men (January 4, 1642). They fled shortly before his arrival. The king's act constituted a clear breach of parliamentary privilege. On January 10, 1642, regarding his position as far too vulnerable, Charles retreated from the capital. There was little room left for debate. The king organised his forces, parliament organised theirs. The war was a continuation of debate by other means.

The advent of civil war represented the breakdown of the constitution. The latter provided no clear answer to the question as to which side in the dispute was legally right. The Tudors had left unresolved the constitutional question as to who was the final legal authority in the realm: king, Lords or Commons.[2] On the one hand, not only the parliamentary but also the royalist side held that the king was subject to law. On the other hand, not only the royalist but also the parliamentary party held that the king could not be disobeyed. These two principles, obviously, might come into conflict where the king, in some serious matter, had violated the law. Two contrary courses of action might be

---

[1] C. V. Wedgwood, *The King's War, 1641–1647* (Fontana, 1966), p. 20.
[2] Judson, *Crisis*, p. 7.

deduced: either that the king be punished, or that his lawlessness be suffered in silence.

The logic of the anti-royalist argument was roughly as follows. Disobedience to the king is sinful but the king's violation of the law is not to be endured. As the king can do no wrong, it is not he, but his ministers, who violate the law. To punish them is not to punish him and involves no disobedience to his will. In so far as the king himself did wrong, the wrong was not consistent with his real intentions but was attributable to evil counsel. Counsellors advised evilly to the extent, essentially, that their advised courses of action were not coincident with those advised by parliament. But where it became clear that the illegal course of action taken was taken essentially by the king alone (as when Charles entered the Commons to arrest the five members) then the blame for it (and therefore the punishment) must be visited upon the actual offender, but without prejudice to the office he held.[1] Thus arises a distinction between the king as a person and the crown as an office. In so far as they were detachable, the subject's prior obedience was to the crown (the office) rather than to the king (the incumbent), and to the king only in so far as his actions did not violate the legal restrictions which inhered in the exercise of his authority through the crown. The law defining the operations of the crown was to be regarded as the *common* law; its interpreters were the judges who presided over the ordinary courts of justice; their decisions, in limiting the crown, also limited the operations of a lawful king. Where the king himself acted in a clearly unlawful manner, parliament must appeal from what he did to what he ought to have done, from his arbitrary to his rational will, from the king above law to the king under law, from his arbitrary commands to his courts' reasoned rulings, from the king out of parliament to the king in parliament. All of this, naturally, implied a co-ordination of authority, not the supremacy of one type over another. But where the king attempted to impose his will upon parliament by force, then parliament must oppose him to support and uphold the law of the land. From this last position would finally issue the doctrine of the sovereignty or supremacy of parliament.[2]

Charles, having lost the war, was put on trial and executed by the parliamentary forces in January 1649. It is significant that he was not killed secretly, nor tried as a *usurper* of royal authority. He was tried and executed as 'King of England'. The principle thus advanced, that the king himself could be guilty of treason, was novel; for it was generally assumed that one could be guilty of treason towards a king, but not that a king could be meaningfully guilty of treason towards the state. The

[1] Cf. Wormuth, *Royal Prerogative*, pp. 110–11.
[2] Cf. Jack Hexter, *The Reign of King Pym* (Harvard, 1941), p. 190.

parliamentary conclusion followed, however, from the principle that the king was under the law, not above it, and, being under it, must serve rather than subvert it. The parliamentary indictment read to the effect that Charles had attempted 'to overthrow the rights and liberties of the people',[1] principally by making war upon parliament, which was taken to embody and express those rights and liberties. Thus Charles was adjudged guilty of treason. The chief problem for this line of argument, naturally, was to establish *towards whom* the king's actions had been treasonous.

The logic of the distinctly royalist argument starts from this point. Charles argued, quite simply, that he was the highest court of appeal in the land, and therefore not subject to any other. The legal implication of Charles's defence was not that he was in principle above the law, that he could make it or break it at will (he conceded that the Commons exercised certain privileges and that he respected those privileges), but that there was no other corporate body or agent to which he was legally subject nor by which he could legally be tried. Thus if he had done wrong there was no one who could call him to account for it: 'a king', he said, 'cannot be tried by any superior jurisdiction on earth'.[2] If the king had been elected by the people or by parliament there might of course be a case for arguing that he could be removed by them. But Charles took the position, which could not be gainsaid, that England was not an elective 'but a hereditary kingdom for near these thousand years'.[3] The people had no authority to give him office and they had none to take it away. By implication, any attempt to punish the king was really an act of treason *towards him*.

Whereas the parliamentarian began from the premise that the king was subject to law, without directly repudiating the notion that he must be obeyed, the royalist began from the premise that the king must be obeyed, while admitting nonetheless that he was in some sense subject to the law. In a crisis, both of these principles could not be upheld. Thus, while the parliamentary position led to the conclusion that the king, in certain circumstances, could legitimately be punished or overthrown (i.e. that even the king could be guilty of treason to the state), the royalist position led to the contrary conclusion that the king could not be legitimately punished or overthrown, no matter what laws he had violated. It was natural that each party should attempt to advance its position as the correct one, from a legal or constitutional point of view. But it is essentially because no legally or constitutionally *correct* position could be clearly maintained that the argument quickly leapt from the level of law to that of political philosophy.

[1] C. V. Wedgwood, *The Trial of Charles I* (Fontana, 1967), p. 146.
[2] *Ibid.*, p. 156.   [3] *Ibid.*, p. 150.

Miss Wedgwood is right: 'It was possible for an honest partisan of either side to argue a convincing case although the political theory in which most Englishmen had been reared gave little help. Since King and Parliament made up the body politic it was a clean impossibility for the two to be at war. Each man solved the problem by deciding to the best of his judgment which of the two had temporarily forfeited his function.'[1] Thus for some, the king had surrendered to evil counsellors, while for others, parliament was the instrument of a seditious faction. English constitutional practice provided a place for both king and parliament, but there was no clear provision for the one to overthrow or destroy the other. Yet they were at war, on the assumption that neither would respect the privileges of the other. The only legal means of deciding between them lay in falling back upon that rule indicating, in case of conflict between the two branches of government, which was superior. But no such clearly established rule was to be found. The political theories which emerged during the course of this crisis were most relevantly concerned, therefore, not with advancing an estab-lished point of law, but with recommending more forcefully some final locus of decision-making in the state. And it was this issue which many thought the civil war should settle.

Let us look for a last time, in the most skeletal form, at the manner in which this conclusion falls out. Constitutional practice established a king, but also that this king must be bound by certain laws. To be *effectively* bound, some sanction must be held out against him should he violate those laws. He is not *effectively* bound where no such sanctions are or can be imposed. If it is genuinely intended that the king should respect, for example, the property rights of subjects, where the latter have no real means of securing that their rights *are* respected, then in effect they have no such rights. Either the king can be punished for violating established rights, in which case they have force, or he cannot be, in which case they do not. Either the king can be punished for overthrowing the law, in which case he is under it, or he cannot be, in which case he is effectively above it. Where parliament exercises established (for how long is immaterial) constitutional rights, it may seek redress from or against the king where he violates those rights: this is to follow out the constitutional logic of its position. Where the king exercises a prerogative constitutionally provided for, but which con-flicts with parliamentary rights, he may attempt to override those rights: this is to follow out the constitutional logic of his own position. But here we are presented with a conflict potentially implied in the constitution itself in so far as it does not clearly stipulate that in case of conflict between royal prerogative and parliamentary rights either one or the

[1] Wedgwood, *The King's War*, p. 122.

69

other must take precedence. An important point to be advanced in some of the political theory of the time, then, was that the position of precedence or superiority must be clearly established on the part of some agent within the state if a minimal condition for stability was to be met.

Now the position that there must be one clearly established superior within the state apparatus could not be described as exclusively royalist. Philip Hunton's *A Treatise of Monarchy* (1643), for example, while declaring that the existing English constitution provided no *legal* means of resolving the conflict between the king and parliament, argued that the collective judgement of a parliament was better than the individual judgement of a king (and ought therefore to be preferred). Dudley Digges, by contrast, in *The Unlawfulnesse of Subjects taking up Armes against their Sovereigne in what case soever* (1644) also argued that there could not be 'two supreme authorities' within a state 'to proclaime and manage' its laws, but was led from this to the contrary conclusion that the king actually was sovereign and that parliament could not legally act against him. Thomas Hobbes, writing more forcefully than either of these men (*De Cive*, 1642), and also more neutrally, held with them that the 'peace and self-defence' of citizens required that they all be subject to one will within the state, but that this will could be of 'either man or council'. Hobbes did not so much propose to demonstrate that the king rather than parliament was or should be sovereign, but only that, for peace and stability, one or the other must be clearly dominant.

Historical conditions provide a setting for social ideas. In conditions where control mechanisms (not just governments) are regarded as omnipresent, clumsy and oppressive, it will not be surprising if a general reaction sets in against such mechanisms. In conditions, by contrast, where control mechanisms (but most particularly government) are regarded as inadequate, where violence is regarded as too commonplace, or where social institutions within one society are regarded as too conflict-prone, it will be equally unsurprising if the demand for greater unity or order or harmony should be repeatedly advanced. All the same, it is difficult to predict when either liberty or authority will be judged to have gone too far. We are accordingly bound to stress that the historical conditions, which impose relevance or irrelevance upon socio-political ideas, are never just external circumstances, but a *perception* of external circumstances. Thus historical explanation is always partly circular. The particular facts which we record may be said to explain the relevance of certain theories that emerge. But those very facts have been selected largely because they cohere with these theories. Thus to know the 'facts' may not merely help to explain a theory but the 'facts' will to a degree concretely embody it.

PART THREE

TWILIGHT OF THE PLURALIST STATE: JEAN BODIN

'We must not forget that the end of the state is not liberty, but a well-ordered life.'
Jean Bodin, *La méthode de l'histoire.*

'There is nothing in the world pleasanter to behold, or which more deliciously revives the mind, or which serves us more commodiously, than order . . . By contrast, we may discover nothing more unpleasant, or more difficult to understand, than that which is confused and disorderly . . .'
Jean Bodin, *Le théatre de la nature universelle.*

'Taken in perspective and as a whole, Bodin was a thinker with a liberal disposition; his logical mind and the desire to impose greater order, which was current in his time, led him to the doctrine of absolutism.'
E. Fournol, *Bodin, prédécesseur de Montesquieu* (Paris, 1896), p. 112.

Chapter Five

Bodinian Overview

Jean Bodin was born in 1529 or 1530 and died in 1596. His principal work, which appeared in 1576, was a hefty tome of over seven hundred pages, entitled *Les six livres de la Republique*. There were ten French editions of the *Republique* during Bodin's lifetime, together with three Latin editions, the first of the latter being published in 1586. The present analysis is almost exclusively centred on the *Republique*.[1]

Jean Bodin made a significant contribution to the history of ideas, but the fact that this study begins with a detailed analysis of Bodin's ideas, rather than with those of any other writer, is partly a matter of convenience. The doctrine of sovereignty does not entirely originate with him, as he insisted. If so, it would be difficult to know what to make of Ulpian, writing in the third century, to the effect that the ruler is above the law and, indeed, its source (*princeps legibus solutus est* and *quod principi placuit legis habet vigorem*). On the face of it, the suggestion that Ulpian was the originator of the theory of sovereignty seems absurd. But what is really absurd is the notion that the theory of sovereignty has an objectively specifiable, as opposed to an arbitrarily specifiable, origin at all. In the end, 'sovereignty' is only a word indicating the supremacy of some person or group over others, which logically and by extension may imply that no similar supremacy is held by still others over this person or group (thus leading into the notion of 'independence' – especially that of a state). We cannot even credit Bodin with inventing the word, which in itself, of course, is of little importance. What Bodin did was to offer important assistance in elaborating upon

[1] In English there are only two translations of this work. The first (1606) by Richard Knolles is surprisingly good. The second (1955) by M. J. Tooley belongs to an entirely different category. It has been abridged to perhaps a quarter of the original length, generally fails to provide any indication as to what has been excised and where, and is clearly intended for cursory perusal and not for serious study. An excellent amended version of Knolles's *The Six Bookes of a Commonweale* has been produced by McRae (Cambridge, Mass., 1962), but where the Knolles translation is quoted in my text this is always expressly indicated and the edition intended is always that of 1606. Details of Bodin's other works are provided in the bibliography.

some of the implications contained in the concept. But it is impossible that the basic concept, that of making some agent or agents in the community superior to all others, with a view to concentrating further the power of the government, should be exclusively peculiar to the Renaissance or even to Europe. Any community whatever will at times be forced to think in terms of centralisation, most especially when warring with itself and with other communities. To restrict ourselves to the West, we may see that various writers before Bodin, especially from the thirteenth century onwards, were very much concerned with such concentration. The more important names are perhaps those of Dante and Ockham and certainly Marsilius. Thus must Bodin be seen as part of a procession, which has no clearly ascertainable beginning. If not, we might do well to begin with Hobbes and ignore Bodin; or begin with Austin in the nineteenth century and ignore Hobbes in the seventeenth. Because *this* analysis begins with Bodin, for which there is good reason, it is not to be assumed that *the* analysis does.

Our concern with Bodin is largely a concern with sovereignty, which itself derives from our concern with absolutism; and the relevance of absolutism is grounded in the view of it as a path to order. Although we cannot say that the theory of sovereignty began with Bodin, we can say, with Merriam, that he provided us with 'the first systematic discussion of the nature' of the concept.[1] Emphasis here must be placed upon the adjective 'systematic' (although 'systematic' remains, all the same, a highly permissive adjective). The theory of sovereignty attempts to provide us with some understanding of what politics is and ought to be. But it is more expressly concerned with the *is* than with the *ought*. The theory of sovereignty in effect assumes that an order cannot exist without an orderer, and that if an orderer is to create order he requires a power that is absolute. From this flows the association between sovereignty and absolute power or between sovereignty and (quite simply) absolutism.

In saying that Bodin was one of the first writers to pay systematic attention to the theory of sovereignty, we are trying to make at least two points. The first is that he paid particular attention to the logic of the notion of wielding a supreme power in the state. The second is that he was particularly concerned to demonstrate – and this consciously – what it is to have an order, what the chief characteristics of a state (of *any* state) actually *are*, rather than (certainly far *more* than) with what sort of order a state *ought* to have, with what features *ought* to be incorporated into its structure. The theory of sovereignty, therefore, in attempting to be positivistic, immediately raises the question of the relationship

[1] C. E. Merriam, *History of the Theory of Sovereignty Since Rousseau* (Columbia, 1900), p. 13.

between *describing* a social reality and (covertly) *recommending* or *approving* it. All the same, it is a distinction which Bodin sought to make, and he must be accorded his due – at least from the perspective of novelty – for having attempted it.

There is a significant difference between merely assuming the state is universally structured in a certain way, and actually arguing, however inadequately, that it *is* so structured. Plato erected an ideal state. Aristotle, too, was largely concerned with such a state. Cicero sought to inculcate a sense of duty towards the Roman Republic. Augustine was primarily concerned with problems like justice (without which kingdoms were but great robberies) and obedience. For Aquinas the state was natural, while monarchy was demonstrated to be the best of its forms, but Aquinas made no attempt to discuss or advance a general or universal model. Machiavelli, certainly, was primarily concerned with the means by which power *is* acquired or preserved, but in too fragmented a manner to be of much use to us. Bodin, by contrast, was convinced that he had done something new and different. To a certain extent he was right; for although there was some discussion of political structure in Greek, Roman and medieval times, it was mostly incidental, being expressly subordinated to other concerns of a more distinctly moral character.

Bodin, and certain writers who follow him, such as Hobbes, Spinoza, Austin and Kelsen, may be described as writers on 'political structure' to the extent that they are primarily interested in determining *what it is*, *how it works*. Many other writers, by contrast, such as the Monarchomachs (i.e. George Buchanan, Junius Brutus, J. Boucher, Mariana *et al.*), Locke and Rousseau, were less directly concerned with the empirical nature of politics in that their primary interest was to determine who *should* exercise sovereignty, that is to say, a final power of decision in the state. It is partly, as Merriam says of the Monarchomachs, that their 'effort was not . . . the determination of *what* sovereignty is, but rather *where* it is; or better, the defence of the original and inalienable sovereignty of the people'.[1] When one says in any universal way what one takes politics to be about, one may in fact be disguising – or simultaneously expressing – what one thinks is politically valuable and, therefore, what one thinks *ought* to be done. One inevitably raises the question, therefore, as to how genuine a distinction can be made between saying what sovereignty is and indicating the manner in which power ought to be exercised. Our purpose here will be to set out deliberately on the road to positivism, to political 'science', and see just how far – in the case of two of the earliest positivist writers on politics – it will take us. There is the likelihood that the search for political *truth* always leads us back to considerations of what is morally *right*, even if

[1] *Ibid.*, p. 18.

we can follow no path whatever that will lead us to a determination of what is *universally* right.

In our own century, sociological and anthropological studies have vastly expanded our knowledge of political and social structure, mostly by means of empirical analyses of different societies, as also by detailed studies of specific aspects of organisation along class and administrative lines in highly technological societies. Assertions that originally were really definitional or deductive in character have increasingly been approached from an empirical point of view. The assertions that (*a*) every sovereign must be absolute or (*b*) every state must have a sovereign, could be advanced by Bodin and Hobbes in what was basically a deductive or definitional guise. But it was always possible to test these assertions against particular empirical contexts to see how they would hold up in fact, and against fact. It was important to ask how the Dinka or the Nuer or the Kwakiutl were actually organised, and to what extent, and to achieve what aims, and in what sense they had recognisable governments at all. Hence the importance of the studies by men like Malinowski, Pitt-Rivers, Evans-Pritchard, Firth, Boas, Fortes and Robert Lowie, *inter alia*, and on a more theoretical plane, the work of men like Max Weber, Mosca, Pareto, Michels, Durkheim, Simmel, Sorokin, Parsons and others.

The difficulty is, however, that very few attempts have been made to integrate the findings of twentieth-century research into the valuable models of political structure provided by earlier classical writers, and here I make particular reference to Bodin and Hobbes. The effort expended on compiling information often appears to be inversely proportional to the effort devoted to imposing upon it some degree of coherence. In fact, it is astonishing how wide a gap there is between the substantial theoretical analyses of political structure in the sixteenth and seventeenth centuries, and the thin and restricted renewal of this sort of analysis by Austin in the nineteenth, more vigorously matched by Kelsen in the twentieth. Carl Friedrich sees this gulf as one aspect of a more general fall in political literature. 'Only since the 19th century', he writes, 'have we begun to pursue systematically the topics which the generations from Machiavelli to Hobbes envisaged.'[1] Friedrich tends to attribute this subsidence of political inquiry to the waning of Italy and central Germany in the seventeenth century and the settling down of the rest of Europe 'under more or less absolute monarchs, fully occupied with organizing their national communities'. These correlations between ideas and events are never sufficiently precise, but much can be said in support of Friedrich's suggestion.

[1] Johannes Althusius, *Politica methodice digesta* (reprint of 3rd ed., 1614), Introduction by C. J. Friedrich (Harvard, 1932), p. ix.

There is certainly a striking correlation between the conscious need for greater political integration towards the close of the Middle Ages and the articulation of highly theoretical models of political structure presented under the title of 'sovereignty' during the period immediately following. There is no doubt that students of law and politics, like Bodin, were overwhelmed by the variety of overlapping and conflicting authorities, by the confusing autonomy of corporate groups, such as guilds and ecclesiastical bodies, by the persistence of archaic customary law, all of which were so characteristic of the time. Civil war, naturally, breeds upon conflicting authorities, and it is scarcely necessary to do more than note the total abhorrence of internecine conflict felt by Bodin and Hobbes.[1] These men recognised the need to eliminate the tendency towards civil war which inhered in a system so chaotically structured. They were plainly aware of the need for a more unified and coherent political system. And it may well be that where a need is real and generally recognised as such, truly outstanding minds will address themselves to the business of meeting that need, or to the business of analysing the means by which it can be met. This certainly happened as regards the analysis of sovereignty (conceived as the promotion of absolutism), and the need reflected in that analysis.

It is clear that Bodin was concerned to extend the range and to confirm the finality of the king's power. But this concern also involved an analysis of the nature of governmental power. Bodin spoke of sovereign power as being absolute, when he also meant to argue that it ought to be so. The use of the term 'absolute', however, involved him in the exaggeration of his case. He made much of it, but the word did not adequately express what he in practice appears to have intended. 'Absolute' may be understood in several senses. It is unnecessary to take it in more than one at this stage of the proceedings: that is, in respect of the demand that the king should wield a complete and unabridged power of command. This was not a demand which Bodin made consistently, although clearly his favourable use of the word 'absolute' would suggest that he favoured this demand. Bodin was practically concerned to extend and confirm the king's power; he also spoke more exaggeratedly in terms of making this power 'absolute'. Commentators are aware of the oddities of Bodin's use of the word 'absolute', and also that he was not entirely committed in practice to what it meant in the abstract. His position, accordingly, has been judged inconsistent.

Max Shepard argued against the conventional case for inconsistency

[1] Cf. Abel LeFranc, *La place de Jean Bodin dans la Renaissance et dans la science politique* (Paris, 1929), p. 408: 'Mais la grandeur de l'attitude de Bodin se révèle pleinement dans l'opposition irréductible qu'il fit à la guerre civile.'

several decades ago.[1] Shepard states that 'Bodin never meant that law is merely and always the command of the sovereign . . .'[2] The *leges imperii*, which might be called the basic or constitutional law, for example, were not the command of the sovereign. Further, even where a law is promulgated by the prince, which the *leges imperii* are not, if that law corresponds to natural law or divine justice (such as laws against theft), then Bodin's assumption, which is medieval on this point, is that 'in such a case the "legislative" authority does not really make law but merely "establishes" it'. Shepard concludes: 'Bodin's position is perhaps theoretically consistent enough; natural law simply lies outside the scope of the sovereign's competence to affect in any way.' Thus the sovereign cannot make any law he wishes, nor is he above being bound by any law he enforces. Thus the possibility of 'absolving the sovereign from all law cannot be carried to its logical conclusion in Bodin's theory'.[3] Shepard works out the legal consequences of this position in the following way: 'If the sovereign clearly violates a well-known rule of natural law, this releases the magistrate from all obligation to carry out the sovereign command or law, and the subject from all duty to obey it. Bodin explicitly enunciates this right of passive resistance, although he emphatically denies any right of active rebellion or tyrannicide, except against a "tyrant without title".'[4] In my own view, indeed, the problem with Bodin's analysis centres somewhat less in inconsistency than in exaggeration. Nonetheless, the assertion that the sovereign (in Bodin's theory) cannot be absolved from all law does fundamentally contradict Bodin's argument about sovereign power being absolute and perpetual.

Let us elaborate for a moment upon Shepard's position. It is suggested that Bodin sees the law as a species of command to which the sovereign is subject and which he, somehow simultaneously, is above. This means that the law has other sources than the sovereign, who only serves as one such source. When the sovereign acts within his proper sphere, his word is law. But when he steps outside that sphere, his word ceases to be law. It is in this sense that the sovereign is both a source of law and subject to it, is both above and beneath it. Thus not all laws are the consequence of a sovereign command nor can a sovereign command anything he wants.

The position outlined above is a reasonable one. It is, however, a *reconstruction*, one indeed which plays down the absolutist exaggeration

---

[1] Max Adams Shepard, 'Sovereignty at the crossroads: a study of Bodin' *Political Science Quarterly*, vol. 45, no. 4 (1930).

[2] *Ibid.*, p. 597.

[3] *Ibid.*, p. 601.

[4] *Ibid.*, p. 599.

built into Bodin's own formulae. Bodin was particularly concerned to extend the authority of the crown so that the incumbent should be able to confirm or break customary law, and there is nothing necessarily absolutist about this position (unless we regard any demand for centralised power as an expression of absolutism). But Bodin also spoke in terms of sovereignty being absolute, perpetual (*la puissance absolue & perpetuelle*), total (*toute puissance*), and unlimited (*la souveraineté n'est limitee*, etc.). Statements such as these, to put it mildly, may be accounted as exaggerations. All the same, they were set down on paper, form part of the record, and their logic was elaborated upon. Even as exaggerations, it is plain that such claims as these are not entirely consistent with that view of the sovereign which holds him to be limited by and in law.

All the same, Shepard's piece is useful. It suggests that many of the elementary inconsistencies for which Bodin has been held accountable reflect an inadequate appreciation of the basic character of his work. There remains, nonetheless, a more fundamental inconsistency from which in any circumstances it becomes difficult for Bodin to escape. Thus, even where we say that the sovereign is only so in his sphere and can be denied obedience where he steps outside it, the question of *who* defines that sphere and of *how* that obedience is to be effectively denied becomes crucial. If it is suggested that the recognition of the point where the sovereign oversteps himself is or can be spontaneous, this must argue for what is already an extremely cohesive society. If it is suggested that the recognition of this boundary has to be urged upon the citizenry, and that they must be persuaded that it has been overstepped at some given point rather than another, then this implies a less cohesive society and the *organisation* of opposition to the sovereign. If Bodin rules out any form of organised opposition to a lawful sovereign, this substantially eliminates – in Bodin's historical circumstances – any *effective* opposition to the sovereign. Thus, given that Bodin denies that there should be any form of organised resistance to the sovereign, and given, too, that he characterises the latter as absolute, it becomes clear that there is no great difficulty in describing Bodin as an absolutist. It is indeed because of Bodin's fundamental inconsistency that some commentators will argue that he *essentially* promotes some species of limited power and others that he essentially promotes the reverse. Both elements, indeed, are present.

The sort of defence which Shepard provides for Bodin does at least demonstrate the insufficiency of a variety of commonplace criticisms of Bodin's inconsistencies. But, at the same time, this sort of defence can sin in the opposite direction. It is easy to swing from the argument that Bodin does not believe the sovereign to have an arbitrary right to create law (and that this belief reveals no real inconsistency in his position) to the argument that Bodin sees the power of the state essentially as a means of concretely establishing intangible norms, which are expressions of natural law and justice. This was the position taken by a Spanish commentator, F. J. Conde, five years after Shepard's article appeared.

Conde argues that: 'La virtud, no la utilidad, es el fin último del Estado, define su sentido y encierra su justificación.'[1] The stress on virtue is exaggerated, because Bodin stresses also the importance of utility. Conde then proceeds (correctly) to locate the source of virtue in God: 'La idea de un Dios rector del universo y el principio de la virtud como fin último del Estado, implican la existencia de un núcleo intangible de normas, contra las que el Estado no puede atentar sin perder su razón de ser.'[2] From this location of virtue in God, one then deduces that he is ultimately the source of *all* law (which is not Bodin's position), and that the laws of the prince are merely a reflection of the will of the divinity. 'Como la ley es obra del Principe y el Principe es imagen de Dios, las leyes del Principe deben ser fiel reflejo de las leyes de Dios.'[3] This account fails to recognise that Bodin does confer upon the prince a degree of *arbitrary* power which is not a reflection of divine or natural law, the rightness of which is only calculable in terms of utility, and thus relative to an arbitrary end. This failure is shared by Shepard's account. But Conde goes much further and suggests that the power which Bodin assigns to the prince on the basis of utility is not really assigned to him on that basis at all. Even his arbitrary power is a reflection of what is in itself right (*droit*), of natural law. 'Bodino', writes Conde, 'va a definir la "Puissance", es decir, el poder del Estado, "en termes de droit". El poder del Estado puede haber nacido de la fuera, ser mero poder de hecho, "car en matière d'estat qui est maistre de la force est maistre de l'estat", pero nuestra publicista se dispone a constrúirlo "en termes de droit", es decir, a fundamentar juridicamente el poder del Estado.'[4] In this manner, the apparently arbitrary power of command conferred by Bodin upon the prince is misleadingly reduced to the relatively innocuous business of interpreting an already existing law, whether called natural or divine, such that interpretation merely 'establishes' rather than 'creates' law. Such an account is not faithful to Bodin's intention.

Bodin *was* interested in royal absolutism. He insisted upon the need for one most powerful and unified directive agency in society, to declare or enforce or interpret law. Bodin was as much interested in *droit* as in

[1] Francisco J. Conde, *El pensamiento político de Bodino* (Madrid, 1935), p. 45.
[2] *Ibid.*, p. 47.
[3] *Ibid.*, p. 59.
[4] *Ibid.*, p. 65.

loi, but also vice versa. He was interested in a *de facto* state of order, but also in a just order. That is why he found both obedience and passive resistance to the prince appropriate, given appropriate circumstances. For Bodin not only believed that the absence of an absolute prince causes anarchy, but that the presence of one who is unjust (in refusing to observe the dictates of divine and natural justice) does so too. Bodin, of course, conceived of the prince as inferior to God. This may mean either (*a*) that he is not absolute and sovereign in the strictest sense, or (*b*) that he is simply a divine intermediary. Neither alternative can be jettisoned entirely. The prince 'establishes' and interprets law which is natural and divine; and because such laws do not really proceed from him, but through him, he is bound by them. But not all law is natural and divine, and even though it is not, it is equally necessary as that which is. And it is in regard to such law as this that the prince is properly supreme. Bodin nowhere pretends that he who is just necessarily has power. Nor does he suppose that he who has power is necessarily just. *Droit* and *loi* he does not suppose to be mutually entailed. Both *droit* and *loi* constitute principles which are incorporated into *de facto* legal codes. Bodin recommends complete obedience of subjects to princes in regard to the second (these are stipulations which do not reflect divine or natural law); he recommends complete obedience of subjects *and* princes in regard to the first (which do reflect principles of divine or natural law). Thus, in so far as the prince is absolute, Bodin conceives of him as such within a certain sphere. And in so far as he is supposed to require a complete and unfettered right of command, it is in regard to principles of regulation, or to laws, which are neither just nor unjust, neither right nor wrong. But, as we have noted, Bodin does not make these points without ambiguity and even contradiction.[1]

Bodin's system is rather less inclined to confer total and unlimited power upon the sovereign than to endow him with the greatest, the ultimate power of decision, in certain matters. The concept of ultimacy places Bodin's sovereign at the apex of an hierarchical pyramid of authority. His system, in effect, depicts the state's hierarchy. This hierarchy, which one can disengage from illustrations and examples littering the hundreds of pages of his work, provides his nuclear conception of the character of political and social structure. This conception is nowhere clearly stated as such; it must be reconstructed from the odds and ends of his analysis. As Bodin concludes his *Republique*[2] he provides a primitive diagram of his conception of this structure. It is at once revealing and inadequate to his purpose (as shown by the analysis provided in the body of his work); but we shall nevertheless

---

[1] See further appendix 2 below.
[2] *Les six livres de la Republique* (1579 ed.), p. 736.

begin with his diagram. It consists simply of two intersecting lines, one horizontal, the other vertical. At the top of the vertical line (1) sits the sovereign. Distributed along the horizontal line are three estates, (2) the clergy, (3) the military and (4) commoners (scholars, merchants, artisans and unskilled labourers), in that order (from left to right). Thus, the only point which Bodin's diagram really depicts is the supremacy of the sovereign, within the state hierarchy, over all other orders. The *numbering* does not represent a chain of command but a quite different order, which is that of public honour or esteem: number (1) is more honourable than (2), (2) than (3), etc.

As Bodin's diagram only indicates the legal superiority of the sovereign to the estates, the lower-level relations of inferiors to superiors must be sorted out. Now the first point of importance is that Bodin does not see governance of the state in terms of class rule, or in terms of the formal or substantive superiority of one estate over another. Estates might be and were organised as coherent legal groups, but in so far as this was the case, they were essentially autonomous *vis-à-vis* one another, and were only commonly subject to the sovereign, or to the public officers of the sovereign. Bodin saw the clergy as attending to the spiritual needs of the people; but they were corporately organised, and so the chains of command were internal to their organisation, as supervised ultimately by the sovereign and mediately by his corporation of magistrates. The military might, of course, be required to subdue internal rebellion, but their primary purpose, whether offensive or defensive, was directed externally; so that they also were corporately organised, with an internal chain of command overseen by the sovereign and his officials. Lastly, the fourth estate (perhaps they might be called civilians) was not viewed as a mass of individuals, but as a corporately organised unit with its various subdivisions, of guilds and fraternities and towns; and these corporations were mainly private, and were supervised by the public officials (who also constituted a corporation) of the king. The king's officials settled disputes where necessary between the various sub-units of the estates; while the sovereign, ideally, settled disputes between the estates or the highest autonomous corporate units, and directed the activities of the state from the highest level and in regard to matters appropriate to his authority.

Bodin's overall position on the structure of the state implies the supremacy of the sovereign, public corporations following at the next level, and private corporations last. Thus, the ultimate or last legal unit within the state, for Bodin, was not the individual but the group, such as the guild, or – most importantly – the family. The corporate community of the family Bodin assumed to be more important to the state structure than any other apart from the office of the sovereign. He therefore recommended that the sovereign treat it as inviolate. In fact, Bodin regarded the inviolability of the family more as an item of natural law (of *droit*) than a conventional principle (*loi*), so that he did not view the rights of the family as falling within the *discretionary* preserve of the prince. Other private corporations, however, Bodin did not regard as inviolate. They were considered entirely subject to the prince's command, which was assumed to be directed to the general good, which in turn was partly determined on utilitarian grounds – which means conventionally and arbitrarily. The borderline between private and public corporations in Bodin is shadowy; but it is sufficiently precise for one to say that public corporations are those which are conceived in the main as instruments of the sovereign will. They basically constitute, in short, the administrative machinery of the state. They are not represented in Bodin's diagram, but would have to be located there either as an extension of the sovereign authority or as a connecting (and overlapping) link between the sovereign and the estates. Private corporations would be located within the estates in descending order, with the exception – as noted – of the family, since this communal unit fed individuals into other corporations and into the state more generally conceived, without at the same time being hierarchically subordinate (in *droit*) to them *qua* families.

Thus we see a communal whole, consisting of a variety of enclosed communities, most having an appropriate sphere, which (for each corporation) was not conceived as opposed, but as complementary, to the overall state structure. This is a typically medieval view; but it is medievalism in decline. This partially pluralist conception of the state primarily depends not only on the assumption of natural law (as one or a few absolute, but abstract, ethico-legal principles), but also upon the assumption that certain positive laws are naturally or divinely ordained. Where such positive laws can be regarded as natural (as, for example, regarding the prerogatives of the family or the church or private property), the attitude of the state towards the affected institutions (like the family or church) and practices (like usury and heresy) will tend to remain static. But once reduce the sphere of natural law, thus expanding that of conventional law, and society tends to move automatically away from fixed or pre-ordained spheres of corporate authority, away from fairly distinct spheres of control, and towards the prospect of greater centralization.

Bodin moves decisively towards a centralising, law-creating sovereign, following his recognition that not all public decisions can be either right or wrong from a natural law point of view. Conflicts between decisions or courses of action or rules which are neither right nor wrong must be settled arbitrarily – which is to say by an arbiter; it does not matter whether the arbiter is a person or a rule, so long as one is led to a conclusion. As no natural justice attaches to such decisions they cannot be settled on a strictly rational basis. Bodin does not omit *all* references to external standards in the matter of deciding between conflicting conventional laws; for he evokes the spectre of utility, which the prince is enjoined to hold before him in the form of a decision-calculus. Thus, when confronted with conflicting conventions the prince may resort to Bodin's embryonic calculus of pain and pleasure. But if, in the political sphere, the calculus means little more than that in indifferent matters one should be governed by the wishes of the people (their 'pleasure'), then it is clear that these wishes, these utilities, are never uniform and often conflict. Thus we return to the inevitability of arbitrary decision-making. Where this is arbitrary it cannot search for abstract or divine reason behind the conventional. Hence Bodin's concern with a uniform source of law – within the conventional sphere – rather than with the abstract 'rightness' of the law. He assumes that 'natural justice' within a world of convention is essentially to be obtained through order, harmony and uniformity; and he further assumes that a single, individual source of law is more likely to produce this than a multitude (or group) of individuals attempting to act as one. What concretely springs from this is a demand for greater centralization. What tends abstractly to emerge – in his own case – is a doctrine of 'absolutism' (where centralisation is universally recommended as an ideal good-in-itself). Although Bodin envisaged theoretical limits upon the sovereign's power, he almost nowhere envisaged any concrete means of making such limits operational. His contradictoriness largely derives from combining notions about the evils of unlimited power with notions about the necessity of eliminating virtually all effective human restraints upon princely rule.

Chapter Six

The Family

Bodin was concerned with several distinct matters in *Les six livres de la Republique*.[1] The core concern was an interest in centralising national authority, in placing it in the hands of the monarch, and in determining which of its uses were just, as well as what customs and rules the king should feel obliged to obey. These interests, given the manner in which they were promoted, revealed an absolutist orientation on Bodin's part. We shall be concerned with analysing this orientation largely against the backdrop of Bodin's assumption that he was stating political facts rather than projecting political ideals.

For Bodin, political organisation implied a chain of command consisting of superiors, intermediaries and inferiors. The actual links of this chain comprised, naturally, those corporate elements with which the author was familiar. The most conspicuous of such elements, as a prevalent and viable organisational unit, was the family, or household. Bodin's *Republique* consisted in sovereign power 'justly' governing many households (*mesnages*) in those matters of interest common to them all.[2] The household itself was regarded as a discrete sub-unit of the state, which embraced several persons, under obedience to one head, who was guided by the common interest, although the organisation was subject to his exclusive will.[3] For Bodin, the family was the most fundamental unit of political organisation. Within it, the father was compared to God: 'le pere est la vraye image du grand Dieu souverain' (*SLR*, p. 20). To this godlike being a wife and children were entirely subject. Bodin even considered it necessary to grant the father authority of life and death over his wife, his children[4] and even over adopted children (*SLR*, pp. 30, 32). If, for example, a wife were found adulterous or a

[1] All subsequent references are to the French edition of 1579, henceforth abbreviated as *SLR*.

[2] 'Republique est un droit gouvernement de plusieurs mesnages, & de ce qui leur est commun, avec puissance souveraine': *SLR*, p. 1.

[3] 'Mesnage est un droit gouvernement de plusieurs subiects, sous l'obeïssance d'un chef de famille, & *de ce qui luy est propre*' (my italics).

[4] 'Il est besoing en la Republique bien ordonnee, rendre aux peres la puissance de la vie & de la mort': *SLR*, p. 22.

daughter in sin or a son incestuous, their lives were his to take or spare. The chains relating subject to object, command to obedience, were firmly attached. To this scheme of authority paternal power supplied the key.

Beyond the immediate family, paternal power increasingly conflicted with the various degrees of liberty enjoyed by other men. Servants owed 'service, honour, and obedience so long as they remain in the master's house'; but should they fail in obedience, respect and allied virtues, the family head could do no more than 'chastise and correct them with moderation and discretion' (*SLR*, p. 34).

As for slavery, Bodin, unlike Aristotle, did not consider the institution 'natural'. In his experience it was as rare as in Aristotle's it was common. Slavery was only natural in the sense that it existed, not in the sense that it conformed to human nature. He advocated its gradual abolition. Slaves were only reliable if they loved their masters, which on the whole they did not. They were inefficient, vengeful and dangerous. In support of this view, Bodin cited 'l'ancien proverbe, qui dit, autant d'ennemis que d'esclaves' which, to Bodin, 'montre assez quelle amitié, foy & loyauté on peut attendre des esclaves' (*SLR*, p. 45). Bodin's anti-slavery argument had a normative aspect, but it was most importantly empirical. In effect, he deplored the slave–master relationship because it bred more in seething discontent than it produced in the way of order, and thus, structurally, stood condemned.

For Bodin, a household – in the Platonic sense of the ideal – consisted of at least four or five persons: a father and mother, together with children or free men or freedmen ('ou affranchis, ou gens libres') or slaves (*SLR*, p. 8). This position was consistent with that of Aristotle. However, the family was not viewed in a purely economic light. Indeed, Bodin complained (*SLR*, p. 7) that Xenophon and Aristotle had divorced family economics from a concern with disciplinary power. By contrast, Bodin's purpose was to bring them together, to underline the role of the family within the political hierarchy, which was to serve as a school of discipline for citizens and as a reproductive source of life to the state.

As for discipline, Bodin was of the opinion that the power of life and death over children should be *restored* to parents, since the absence of such power made his conception of the disciplinary function of the family difficult to attain. He believed that disobedience, irreverence and contempt towards parents constituted a danger to the state (of which danger, nevertheless, magistrates could not take cognisance). His assumption was that children who were not awed by parents were not fearful of God, and nor, therefore, of magistrates. Paternal authority, in particular, contained a disciplinary idea, the implementation of which was essential to the prosperity and good order of the state.

As for procreation, Bodin ascribed to the family 'la source & origine de toute Republique' (*SLR*, p. 7). A state was understood to consist of a people which did not merely exist for a moment but endured through time: which, according to Bodin, never died – 'ne meurt iamais' (*SLR*, p. 9). A people never died because it was continually reproduced. Because the family was the procreative fount of society, the *fons et origo* of every state, Bodin concluded that it was indispensable, and – in this sense – the state's indestructible ground.

In Bodin's logic, the importance of the family argued for its inviolability, since upon its life depended that of the state. However, he did not elaborate upon any means by which the family would remain inviolate in cases of conflict with the state. For many commentators, G. H. Sabine[1] among them, family inviolability is necessarily inconsistent with state supremacy. This is of course true, on the assumption that the powers of the state and of the family conflict. In Bodin's recommendation that paternal power be restored, however, his intention was that the state order be completed, not interrupted; thus he requested an act by, and not against, the government. In respect of protecting the family and its property from violation, Bodin regarded such protection as a matter of right, not of fact; as a right to be protected by, and not directed against, government; as a recommendation to power, and not as an attack upon it. None of this entails that Bodin understood rights to be created by the state, only that *one* of the functions of the state was to defend them.

Bodin's analysis of the household delineated a precise hierarchy of command. The household composed a realm, set upon a flat, ordered from a peak, together entire, somehow, and self-contained. Such a view reflects a commonplace of sixteenth-century life. The pattern of order here involved features a head, wielding supreme authority over members of, and adjuncts to, the family. Bodin advanced a fourfold typology of command relations. A husband commanded his wife; a father, children; a lord, slaves; a master, servants.[2] The very fullness of this enumeration, however, is evidence of Bodin's general uninventiveness: the actual

---

[1] 'But to combine an *inalienable* right [to private property] in the family with an absolute power in the state made an insuperable logical difficulty' (my italics): *A History of Political Theory* (3rd ed., London, 1951), p. 344. The contradiction referred to is partly based on a misunderstanding. First, Bodin's rights are not thought to oppose, but to complete, the state structure. Secondly, Bodin's absolute power is only regarded as absolute within a restricted sphere – i.e. where a decision to be taken is in itself neither right nor wrong. All the same, the logic of Bodin's position is unenviable.

[2] 'Le comandement des mesnages se prend en quatre sortes, du mari envers la femme, du pere envers les enfans, du seigneur envers les esclaves, du maistre envers les serviteurs': *SLR*, p. 13.

phrasing of the typology is almost Aristotle's (*Politics*, bk. I, 1253b), and for that fact alone somewhat out of date.[1] Indeed, the lord–slave relationship of antiquity had virtually ceased to exist by the close of the High Middle Ages within Western Europe, and was certainly over in France when Bodin wrote.[2] Slavery is, of course, a condition in which a man finds himself when he bears no rights and is regarded as a thing. Nevertheless, rights and 'thingness' are measured in degrees: they are not absolutes. Thus there was a transition – albeit tediously slow – from the Roman slave (*servus*) to the medieval serf (*servus*), marking a movement from one subordinate position to another less subordinate. It is worth noting that Bodin's analysis failed to take sufficient account of this change, but only because the failure underscores his sometimes uncritical dependence upon past writers. One may nonetheless set aside this minimal inadequacy to grasp the central point: that for Bodin, even in the relations between husband and wife, children and servants (and this means from the very start) there was, and must always be, a clearly established chain of command.

It will now be appropriate, given Bodin's dependence upon Aristotle, to take note of the differences (there are only two) between the types of household control which they advanced. (*a*) Aristotle did not distinguish between masters and *servants*, but only between masters and *slaves*: for he knew all 'household servants' as 'household slaves' (*douloi*). There seems to have been no servant function distinct from a slave function. Fustel de Coulanges, for example, did not even bother to discuss the matter, but merely stated that 'a family', in antiquity, 'was composed of a father, a mother, children, and slaves'.[3] (*b*) Aristotle assumed the control of husband over wife, but he did not distinguish between the control of husband and wife over children; he referred only to the control of *parents* over children.[4] Now these two differences, though small, provide a clue to Bodin's purpose. First, Bodin revealed

[1] Bodin, however, was at least abreast of his time in the sense that the three estates of the realm which he designated excluded a distinct class of slaves. But his classification of estates was unoriginal, nevertheless, because it took no account of a rising merchant class (see p. 97 n. 3 below).

[2] See the second part of a two-part article by Marc Bloch, 'Comment et pourquoi finit l'esclavage antique', *Annales*, vol. 2 (1947), pp. 30–44, 161–70. This is also published in M. I. Finley (ed.), *Slavery in Classical Antiquity* (London, 1960), pp. 204–28.

[3] *La cité antique* (Paris, 1864), translated by Willard Small, *The Ancient City* (London, 1873): Doubleday Anchor Paperback (1965), p. 86.

[4] Following the Barker translation, Aristotle's phrasing is as follows: 'The primary and simplest elements of the household are the connection of master and slave, that of the husband and wife, and that of the parents and children' (*Politics*, bk. I, 1253b). One can, of course, *infer* from this typology *paternal* control over children; and such is the order stressed by Coulanges. Aristotle,

an increased interest in detail of control (not merely over slaves but, equally, over servants). Secondly, he showed a concern for the elimination of *conflicting* controls (to invoke not merely parental command over children, but *paternal* command over children).

The logical character of Bodin's conception of paternal authority was dual: he meant, first, that the father ought to have ultimate and absolute authority; and secondly, that fathers – at least in some degree – actually possessed such authority. For example, in respect of the second point he argued that the domination of women by men was characteristic of all societies. In his own words: 'la puissance des maris sur les femmes, a esté generale à tous les peuples' (*SLR*, p. 16). With regard to the first point, he argued that the justification for the universal recurrence of this situation lay in the need to eliminate rival authorities and so the conflict bred by such rivalry; for rival authorities would issue contradictory commands and the family would find itself, as he put it, 'en trouble perpetuel' (*SLR*, p. 15). This formula was intended to contain both an explanation and a justification.

There are two points of relevant interest arising from Bodin's discussion of the chain of command within the household. The first has to do with the factual assertion that the condition of dependence which he described was universally characteristic of women. The second concerns his empirical explanation *cum* normative justification of this dependent condition, which he thought to be scientifically and ethically inescapable because of the need to ensure against competing chains of command. The first attempted to say what the structural hierarchy of the family was. The second was designed to explain why the family was and had to be so structured. It is interesting and inescapable that his conception of family structure should largely reflect his knowledge of the households of his day. It is equally interesting to note in what respect he erred in his attempt to explain the universality of this situation.

Bodin's first error took the form of a *non sequitur*. It does not follow from the assertion 'every household must have an ultimate arbiter' that any particular person (e.g. a man as opposed to a woman) should be that arbiter. Thus, Bodin's designation of the male will as exclusive

in fact, assumed paternal finality, but here only stresses, perhaps significantly, the third control category (over children) as *parental*, thus impliedly reducing the importance of the father's separate authority (over children) by placing it on the same level as the mother's. For purposes of comparison, the Bodin variation on Aristotle, quoted above p. 87 n. 3, may be translated as follows: 'Household authority is divided into four types, that of a husband over his wife, of a father over his children, of a lord over slaves, and of a master over servants' (*SLR*, p. 13). Here there is no evasion: the husband commanded his wife, the *father* his children.

does not follow from his stipulation that a single and exclusive will must prevail.

But Bodin could have argued far more seriously than he does that 'men are more intelligent than women', which (though false) would imply that, since someone must govern the family, and since men are supposedly better endowed than women, the former inherit a sounder title to the offices of direction than the latter. Such an argument was, of course, a commonplace among Greek and Roman theorists. Plato, Aristotle and Cicero, for example, all contended that the justification of male dominance derived from superior intellect. This idea was closely associated with the notions that rule requires skill (which it does) and that legitimate rule is solely derived from supreme intelligence (which it is not). Plato assumed, Aristotle stated and Cicero repeated that the justification of slavery lay in the stupidity of the slaves, a failing made good, however, by the leading light of a lord. There was, of course, a connection between being a wife and being a slave. In fact, rule in general, for these writers, was legitimated by intelligence (in spite of disputes regarding which intelligences – of one, few or many – were superior).

Bodin's position was rather different. There is no question of *formal* disagreement: his own, often unspoken, emphasis simply led him elsewhere. As shown, he opposed slavery. By contrast, he supported male domination (superfluously so, in regard to the internal logic of his own system). Principally with Eve in mind, he briefly alluded to a contrast between male reason and female concupiscence. He also called attention to a putative lack of foresight and prudence in women. Together with these beliefs he advocated a monarchical regime of hereditary succession in the male line (*SLR*, bk. VI, ch. 5). He believed, in fact, that a 'state, properly speaking, loses its name when a woman possesses sovereignty'. But it is of interest to note that appended to this conclusion was the protest: 'pour sage qu'elle soit'! In other words, no state should suffer a woman's rule *no matter how wise* she might be! (*SLR*, p. 699). This addendum is significant because it directly contradicts the classical justification of male domination. According to Aristotle, 'the element which is able, by virtue of its *intelligence*, to exercise forethought is naturally a ruling and master element' (*Politics*, bk. I, 1252a). According to Bodin, women ought not to be permitted to rule, irrespective of their skill or intelligence.[1] Commentators invariably fail to see this contradiction.[2] Bodin does suggest that women are intellectually inferior to men, but his position on this issue is highly inconsistent.

[1] See further appendix 1 below.
[2] E.g. J. W. Allen, *A History of Political Thought in the 16th Century* (London, 1960), p. 408: 'Bodin asserts that it is not woman's physical weakness but her

Bodin's overall position suggested less that woman's 'inferiority' resulted from unintelligence, than that it was established by decree, sometimes natural, sometimes divine, but nevertheless *commanded*. Female inferiority was more a matter of 'right' than of fact, more a 'jural' than a natural condition. Thus, to come to the heart of the matter, 'gynecocracy is directly contrary to the laws of nature', and this seemed to mean that 'God's law has expressly ordained that woman is subject to man, not only in the governing of kingdoms and empires, but also within each particular family'. As for proof, Bodin adduced such as this: that 'the most terrible curse laid upon an enemy was that he be ruled by women' (*SLR*, p. 698). There is no doubt that Bodin abhorred female rule with something of the horror of a plague. Yet there is no doubt either that this simple abhorrence was never accompanied by any serious or consistent attempt to justify it. Even where Bodin accepted that women were intellectually superior to men he would not concede that they should serve as a ruling element.

Bodin employed incongruous borrowings from the Old Testament and from Aristotle, but he nowhere advanced an even superficially convincing argument to explain or justify the subordination of women. This fact, combined with his insistence upon such subordination, again betrays a want of imagination. So long as man could consistently foster the myth of female inferiority, so long could one appear to justify, or, indeed, merely to explain, the fact of the *paterfamilias*, of male domination. But once call into question the Eve myth, once doubt the feasibility of the Graeco-Roman intellectualist argument, and little is respectably left in support of sixteenth-century anti-feminism. Bodin, unhappily, retained the conclusions of his predecessors, but virtually jettisoned the arguments that produced them.

It emerges as significant that intelligence in general essentially *did not matter* to Bodin, either as an explanation or as a justification of rule, and it was because of this that he had to make do with explanatory

moral and intellectual inferiority that makes her the natural subject of man. It is a primary law of nature, he declares, that reason should rule appetite. Man in relation to woman represents reason.' This interpretation is based on the mistaken assumption that Bodin was simply and seriously following Aristotle. This assumption is explicit in Sabine, *Political Theory*, p. 344: 'He merely followed Aristotle in arguing that men are the embodiment of reason, as against the more passionate nature of women.' That this interpretation is somewhat mistaken is suggested by the following typical quotation: 'The laws of nature have endowed men with strength, foresight, weaponry and authority, while women have been deprived of them' (*SLR*, p. 698). Here there is no clear suggestion that women have been deprived of intelligence. Women might be evil, sinister, fickle, oversexed – but in the *SLR* Bodin does not insist that they are stupid. In opposing monarchical succession in the female line he stressed its *inconvenience*.

small-shot, such as universal practice, natural law, divine sanction, male strength, etc. Such trifles were intended to show why women do not (because they do not) and should not (since Nature wills that they should not) command. Still, the fustian that covers the pit may be displaced. Peering in, one observes the Bodinian shaft that takes us deeply towards Hobbes. There is no Platonic vision of human intelligence binding men to justice, nor a Thomistic vision of divine intelligence ordering the world, nor the surface confusion and cynicism of Machiavelli's *Prince*.

Instead we see the undermining of a belief in the rationality of human affairs. The Bodinian principle of human order was more hierarchical than rational. Its axes were more command and obedience than question and answer. None of this in itself need be taken to mean that he was an unsavoury fellow or dogmatic. But there had appeared a philosophical-legal chink in Bodin's divine defences. He still believed in Good and Evil. But in Bodin a gulf was insinuated between them: there was right, and wrong, and actions, properly speaking, which were neither. Right and wrong were somehow manifest, as decreed by God or as embodied in Nature. Duties so declared were beyond dispute, or, if not, were amenable to settlement by reference to their source, conceived as God, Nature or Reason. For the rest, there was no alternative to human authority, whether a father, bishop or king. And so we return to the significance of Bodin's *non sequitur*.

Bodin's prior concern was that there must be order, security – not simply because of the presence of disorder and insecurity, but (philosophically) because there existed a broad spectrum of choices which were not rational, and so dependent upon the exercise of will (not reason). However, he made the mistake of assuming that this ordering will must be of a particular sort, i.e. paternal, whereas, given choice indifferent to reason, the question of the sexual locus of the will had already lost its antique importance. But this Bodin did not grasp.

With this failure, however, one may contrast his success in grasping the demise of slavery. The intellectual prop supporting it had been removed; the Aristotelian view that the slave (at least the European slave) was an 'animate object' was dead; so, too, was the complementary view that the master's intellect was necessary to infuse such objects with purpose. Bodin, an admirer of order, was not susceptible to the charms of *all* orders, of prostituted orders, of the slave regime. Christian (theoretical) ethics had played its part and smoothed his way, but had in no way ceased to defend the superior interests of man over woman. Bodin leaned heavily towards his fellow men, but this unfortunate tendency – in the absence of the now untenable Aristotle prop – meant swift descent into error. For it did not follow from the assumed necessity for order that males alone should provide it, especially if the keeping of that order did not require any significant virtue in which, it might be argued, women failed to share.

Bodin, however, committed a second error – at once less revealing and far more serious than the first. It lay in the assertion that 'a household may tolerate only one head, one master, one lord'.[1] This idea is transferred to his later discussion of sovereignty. Bodin's general meaning – interpreted empirically, not definitionally – seems clear. Given a household unit, its continued orderly existence must depend upon the unambiguous recognition and acceptance of some *one*, single and final arbiter, having sufficient power for overall direction and settlement of disputes. However, what is not clear is whether he meant that *every* household must have one head or only that *some* households require one head.

Thus, Bodin may have meant the assertion 'a household may tolerate only one head' to apply either universally or only generally. Before proceeding, however, it is as well to remark (first) that, either way, Bodin's purpose was not to argue that all or most families *actually were organised* in this way, but rather that all or most families *must be* so organised to escape disintegration; thus (secondly) that his purpose was not merely to relate an observation but also to advance an explanation bearing a predictive value, in the form: given F (family), if O (ordered), then H (head); and (lastly) that this explanation proceeded from the *assumption* that either all or most families – he does not make clear which – were, in fact, ruled by a solitary will. Now to return to Bodin's assertion.

If the proposition were intended generally, it would reveal little, since it would then have to be hedged about with conditions, with a view to explaining why only *some* families demand a single head while *others* do not; just as one is told little about gravity when informed that most projectiles (e.g. tennis balls) come down while some (e.g. rockets) do not.

If Bodin's proposition were intended universally, a single counter-example would show that it was false. There is in fact no difficulty in producing examples of families in which authority is shared among several persons (and not merely exercised by one) without the harmony of the family unit, for that reason, being vitiated. Possibly no such examples were available to Bodin. But even here the fact that all families were organised in a particular way would not entail that they could not be otherwise arranged; no more than the fact that all industrial countries lie in temperate zones entails that states otherwise situated

[1] 'Le mesnage ne souffre qu'un chef, qu'un maistre, qu'un seigneur': *SLR*, p. 15; also, for example: 'La famille, qui est la vraie image d'une Republique, ne peut avoir qu'un chef', etc. (p. 674).

93

cannot become industrial. But even if sixteenth-century examples were available to Bodin, it is most probable that he would neither have looked for nor recognised them – just as he ignored the significance of Elizabeth I's reign in respect of female rule. For, to Bodin, the indispensability of a single, exclusive arbiter over the family was more a tenet of faith than a working hypothesis: just as he believed, despite the evidence, that female rule (*as such*), whether domestic or other, was bad.

This brings us to the purely definitional (*a priori*) aspect of Bodin's assertion. This may be worth considering for the simple fact that one may reasonably argue that a family, conceived as *one* unit, subsumed under *one* order and as expressed in a single hierarchy, certainly cannot have *two* or more heads. Thus, assuming the structure of this unit, order or hierarchy to be triangular, it could have but one summit, one base. And, to conclude the argument, if one chose from any triangle a given side, enclosed by two vertices, and called the enclosure the base, the remaining point would automatically become the summit, top or head.

Now the trouble with the foregoing approach – which is purely definitional – is that it assumes what has to be proved. It incorporates into the subject, family, a predicate regarding its structure, while this relation is immunised against doubt by the following understanding: that whatever hasn't this structure *cannot* be a family. Definitions, of course, are useful, but this particular use of a definition is not; for there is little point in trying to prove a 'fact' simply by juggling words. Thus, Bodin's assertion could only be usefully accepted as an hypothesis. So understood, it would raise a two-part question: (*a*) *Is* every family governed by a single head? and (*b*) *Must* every family be so ordered? The second question need only be entertained if the answer to the first is positive; and the answer to the first is negative. Families, as we know them, are both loosely and tightly organised, while many are scarcely organised at all. They often betray a considerable diffusion of authority. If one attempts to argue that a family, as such, necessarily has a single head, one merely begs the question.

Bodin's analysis of family structure, then, threw up two basic errors. His analysis could be shorn of these by removing the expression 'only one' in referring to the need for a family head, together with the expressions 'paternal' and 'male' as referring to some supposedly exclusive sexual locus of control. Given these emendations, however, the position advanced would not, of course, be Bodin's – not as we know it. We would emerge with a more minimal statement of more or less the following kind.

The family is an elementary unit of human society; within it, the activities of persons, at least partially, are made to dovetail with one another, and this through the instrument of conscious controls; if a family is to remain a unit, i.e. to retain its organised character, it must also retain the conscious controls which (partly) make its existence possible; and as there must be conscious controls, some persons, not necessarily always the same, and not necessarily one person alone, nor one sex alone, must exercise them. In short, if we cut out many of the convolutions of Bodin's argument, we are left with a hard, nuclear statement regarding family and, therefore, political, organisation.

Chapter Seven

Private Corporate Bodies

Bodin wished to describe the general nature of corporate functions and structure. With regard to corporate bodies, he wrote: 'it is necessary to speak of their power in general, which is not determined by the various articles of incorporation, statutes and particular privileges' (*SLR*, p. 334).

Bodin's general position in regard to such bodies is clear. Though he thought they originally evolved prior to the establishment of the state, he believed that, once the state was in being, corporations had to be sanctioned by it. Corporate bodies were essentially artificial and extra-familial. They responded to specific needs and interests. Some were legally inferior, some equal, others superior to one another. Within them, family heads were divested of all 'natural' authority and corporate associates met on an equal footing. The fact that individual members met as equals entailed that the decision-making process peculiar to corporations was deliberative. Decisions had, therefore, to be established either through unanimous agreement or by the will of the majority.

What gave a corporate body substance and justified its existence – indeed, made its existence possible – was the delineation of the purposes underlying it. In so far as the state sanctioned a corporate body, it sanctioned *pari passu* the pursuit of that common interest which constituted such a body's underlying aim, end or purpose. It was only in respect of realising this purpose that a corporation could, on the one hand, take decisions, and on the other, impose penalties to ensure its members' observance of such decisions. Neither a corporation's decisions nor its punishment of members could conflict with either its specified purposes or the more general purposes of the state.

The state, nevertheless, was not a completely separate and self-contained institution. Members of the judicial profession, for example, were part of government, but not the whole; they exercised rule, but were also subject to it. The body of judges was itself a corporation and was thus governed by purposes distinct from those of other corporations. The purpose of this body was to mediate in disputes affecting the general welfare of the entire state, whether between individuals or between corporate bodies; to see that state law was not infringed and that corporate authority was not exceeded. But these functions were performed subject to, and as an expression of, sovereign power. It is in this sense that the judicial power was only a part of the state. The judicial power, at the same time, was only another – albeit distinct – sort of corporation. And what this implied was that it was not only a part of the state, but equally a part of, and continuous with, society at large. Thus Bodin's conception of 'political' structure is really *social*, and entails an upward spiral of organisation, authority or government, from the smallest to the greatest locus of social power. The significant point is that this view of government cannot accommodate any assumption of an essential and generalised opposition between the *individual* and the state.

Corporate bodies were in general fitted onto two levels which were not completely separate but simply distinct and continuous. One was private (non-state), the other public (state). The family, as shown, was regarded in an evolutionary sense as a nuclear pre-state community, possessing peculiarly basic rights, offering a microcosmic preview of the state's structure.[1] Other private corporations were held to be less privileged and rightly subject to more complete and arbitrary state control.

Private corporations were pyramided in an interlocking series of controls. The most elementary grouping was the college (*colleges*, *collegiorum*); a union of these formed a corporation (*corps*, *corporum*); and a union of these formed an estate (*estat*) or university (*universitas*). Otto von Gierke's formulation, which is not exactly the same as Bodin's, was as follows: 'A *collegium* is the legal union of two or more persons of like status: a *corpus* is the union of several colleges: a *universitas* is a local community . . .'[2] The three estates (the *universitas* or *estat*)[3] therefore

---

[1] Bodin regarded the family as such a unique structure that he tended not to see it as a corporation at all. He formally distinguished, for example, between *familles*, *colleges* and *corps* (or between *familiarum*, *collegiorum* and *corporum*). But when he asserted that 'a corporation is understood to consist of divers families, or colleges, or of many families and colleges together' (this from Knolles, *The Six Bookes of a Commonweale*, p. 361), Bodin may have meant both that the family is some form of college, and that it goes directly into the making of larger corporate bodies.

[2] Otto von Gierke, *Natural Law and the Theory of Society*, tr. Barker (Cambridge, 1934), vol. I, p. 64.

[3] The three estates which Bodin designated were the church, the military and the common people (cf. *SLR*, p. 736). The omission of specific reference to a merchant class reveals the extraordinary tenacity of the medieval outlook. King Alfred the Great (849–99) is quoted to the effect that a king's instruments of rule are 'men of prayer, men of war, and men of work'. Bodin, over six hundred years later, still failed to differentiate between workers and burghers. As early as the fourteenth century, however, an English manuscript, while asserting

allowed the highest possible articulation of particular interests. Above the estates was erected the machinery of state control – judges and magistrates – which was merely another, although higher, form of corporate organisation. This machinery, then, was made up of public corporations (or, as we shall often have occasion to say, of public corporate bodies).

The *exact* relationship which Bodin intended to suggest between public corporations and the sovereign will directing them is difficult to grasp. The question was: *how much* independence (from the sovereign) did public corporations wield, or how little? In general, the position which appears most sound is that these agencies, though in many respects necessarily independent, were conceived as the institutional reification of sovereign power, and were thus an extension of the sovereign. So one finds in Bodin, on the one hand, those institutions and agents exercising 'public' control, including that of sovereign authority (all elaborately architected into an ascendant whole); and on the other hand, a broad proliferation of inferior associations, revealing their own hierarchies and systems of control, catering for interests less public and general, more private and particular. The point is that Bodin's transition from 'private' to 'public' is not abrupt but continuous. It is in respect of the twofold division between private and public, however, that Bodin began a process of analysis which Hobbes may be said to have completed. Hobbes's basic structural distinction was between sovereign and subject, whereas Bodin's was between sovereign authority and a diminuendo of many other corporate authorities.

Bodin defined a corporate body as a 'lawful community under sovereign power'. He added that 'the word lawful signifies the authority of the sovereign, without whose permission no corporate body exists' (*SLR*, p. 333). Thus, for Bodin the existence of a corporate body required the *express sanction* of the sovereign. Such a statement might appear to contradict Bodin's view of the manner in which states were formed. In respect of their formation he had written: 'men progressed through alliances and communities of estates, corporations and colleges to create in the end the states with which we are familiar' (*SLR*, p. 345); and this implied that corporate bodies were *established without the sanction* of the sovereign – since they were supposed to exist before he did.

However, there is no contradiction. It is perfectly possible to say

that 'God made the clergy, knights, and labourers', went so far as to admit that 'the burghers and usurers' did in fact exist (as a class) – even though they were created by the Devil. Cf. H. St. L. B. Moss, *The Birth of the Middle Ages*, *395–814* (Oxford, 1963), p. 271.

that fraternities, corporations, guilds and the rest grew originally of their own accord; and also to say that, with the advent of the state, such bodies subsequently had to be either established or sanctioned by it. For assuming that state organisation was meant to entail a uniform legal system, Bodin believed that corporations, which are sub-systems, must either blend or conflict with the former. If a corporation did or was thought to blend, it would be established, or its establishment would be sanctioned or agreed to. If it did not, it would be, and would have to be, suppressed. In short, the existence of corporations did not necessarily imply the existence of a state; but the existence of a state required that it sanction the continued existence of corporations.[1]

For Bodin, one of the basic implied characteristics of the corporation was its voluntary character. (The family, conceived as a 'natural' institution, he believed had no such character.) This implication is derived from the contractual nature of corporations, and from the idea that the head of the household, in his relations with other heads, was an equal. The voluntary character of corporations and the equality of members entailed further implications regarding the decision-making processes peculiar to these organisations.

Within a corporation, which Bodin conceived of as catering for a particular interest shared by several men, decisions taken regarding the direction of overall affairs could not be made by a single person in his own name. The decisions taken had to express the consent of members in general. Bodin thought there were two ways in which this could be done. In the case of certain decisions, it would be necessary for the consent of each and every member to be given; in others, only the consent of a majority of members was necessary (not exclusively represented by the formula of one-half plus one). The principle which Bodin invoked to distinguish between the two methods of deciding was as follows. First, some decisions affected every member of a corporation individually without affecting the general structure and purposes of the corporation itself. Secondly, other decisions, while affecting every individual, were also essential to achieving the purpose of the corpora-

[1] Gierke misread Bodin on this point. 'Local communities and *corporate bodies*', Gierke wrote, 'as distinct from the family, *were regarded as only arising after the constitution of a system of political order*, and within the limits of that system' (my italics). The italicised part of the above (intended to apply mainly to Bodin) is false. Cf. Otto von Gierke, *Das deutsche Genossenschaftsrecht*, vol. 4 (1913), Barker translation, p. 62 (ch. 1, sect. 5, para. 15); *Natural Law and the Theory of Society*, vols 1 and 2. Later, however, Gierke (cf. Barker translation, p. 65) stated (correctly) the reverse: 'Associations arose, in Bodin's view, at a time long before the foundations of the state . . .' Gierke's tergiversation – indeed, his self-contradictory exposition – probably sprang from his failure to see clearly that the prior evolution of corporations is compatible with their being subsequently controlled by the state.

tion.[1] Bodin did not illustrate this distinction, but it is not difficult to do so: a savings association which sought to have members wear black suits would be an example of the first; an example of the second would obtain if a savings association sought to raise or lower its interest rates. On the Bodinian model, the first decision would have to be assented to by every member for it to take effect; the second would require only the assent of a majority (variably defined).

So long as a corporation restricted itself to those actions which were true to its nature, it could (in catering for the distinct interests which gave it birth) demand compliance from all its members.[2] When it went beyond this, Bodin implied that its only means of binding members lay in their own free decision to bind themselves. Here we may note, however, that individuals can scarcely be said to 'bind' themselves if they merely decide to take a certain course of action, since in deciding otherwise they could at any time unbind themselves. Where a corporation can only bind members if they bind themselves, the corporation cannot, in such a case, properly 'bind' members at all. This is not to say that a corporate body cannot in general or in principle bind itself. It is only to say that it makes little sense to speak of a group being 'bound' in cases where the decisions that are regarded as 'binding' it have to be unanimous. A group may be regarded as binding itself where it takes a *unanimous* decision in the sense that all who later decide to withdraw their support from that decision are nonetheless compelled to comply (despite their change of view). A group may also be regarded as binding itself where it takes a *unanimous* decision even though those who later withdraw their assent are in no way compelled to comply (despite their earlier commitment). These two cases are significantly different: as a result I would speak of the first case, but not of the second,

---

[1] 'Car en toutes communautés, quand il est question de ce qui est commun à tous en particulier & divisement, le consentement expres d'un chacun y est requis: mais s'il est question de ce qui est commun à tous par indivis, & conioinctemēt, il suffi que la pluspart soit d'une opinion, pour obliger le surplus: pouveu qu'il ne soit rien ordonné contre les statuts du college, establis par le souverain . . .': *SLR*, p. 357.

[2] It will be clear to the reader that the application of such a principle of distinction would, in practice, raise certain difficulties. In the first place, the purposes of an association are rarely or never defined so strictly that there remains no latitude for the widening of its actual range of activities. Now, it is only by comparison with the *purposes* of an organisation, that one can tell whether its activities remain 'relevant' to its existence. So, in the degree that these purposes cannot be entirely and unquestionably defined, in such degree does it become impossible always to say when a decision does or does not affect the essential character of the organisation; and thus to that degree equally impossible to say whether or not a majority or a unanimous decision is logically required to settle a particular question.

as an example of a group binding itself, since in the second case, whatever the group decides is necessarily vitiated should any particular member change his view. The second case illustrates a coincidence of decisions, not a corporately binding decision. This case of a corporation only binding members if they bind themselves is then in reality only a case of a corporation not binding members at all. This can only suggest that where a corporation ventures beyond its agreed aims its decisions cannot be enforced upon the membership, but can only function as a coincidence of views among the membership. The difficulty at this point, of course, arises in respect to the exact nature and implications of the 'agreed' aims of a group. Given the flexibility of such aims, there will presumably always arise boundary problems regarding the right of an organisation to bind its membership to one course of action rather than another. Where, however, such aims are assumed to be clearly defined, the implication contained in Bodin was that a corporate body's decisions can only bind its membership if the questions being decided remain relevant to the essential purpose of the organisation. Bodin believed the essential purpose of a corporate organisation, in effect, to consist in nothing more than the specific, common interest which brings its members together.[1]

The definition of a common interest, for Bodin, drew a ring around that area in which the majority of a corporate body might exact obedience from the rest. Within that area, such a body could punish its members if they ran foul of its regulations. 'I am not of the same opinion', wrote Bodin, 'as those who hold that colleges can establish rules without invoking some form of penalty, since law is useless and silly if those who disobey it cannot be punished' (*SLR*, p. 340). However, Bodin thought that such a body could punish its members solely in relation to their membership; so that the ultimate sanction would be expulsion (not death or imprisonment). Thus, though a corporate body might discipline members, it could do so neither excessively nor arbitrarily. In this connection, Bodin remarked that 'although Frederick II granted broad jurisdictional scope to University Rectors, and though college principals have always disciplined their students, such authority relates only to matters of little import'.[2]

The definition of common interest also drew a ring round that area

[1] 'Le mot communauté signifie qu'il n'y a point de college, s'il n'y a rien commun: aussi n'est-il pas necessaire que tout soit commun: il suffit que l'assem blee soit commune à tous les collegues . . .': *SLR*, p. 333.

[2] 'Et combien que l'Empereur Frideric [*sic*] II donna aux Recteurs des Universités iurisdiction, & que les principaux des colleges ayent tousiours eu la correction sur leurs disciples, cela toutefois ne s'entend que des choses legeres': *SLR*, p. 336. Also: 'celuy qui fait l'ordonnance, n'ayt la puissance de la faire entretenir par peines arbitraires': *SLR*, p. 340.

in which a corporate body was empowered to act at all – both *vis-à-vis* the functions of similar bodies and *vis-à-vis* those of the state structure itself. If a private body exceeded its mandate or acted beyond the sphere of its interests or ran afoul of state law, then it could itself be punished, just as it could punish its members (*SLR*, p. 340). Thus the state could restrain or limit such punishment as was meted out by inferior corporations. But as the state was not an entirely discrete unit of control, as it was continuous with social control generally, and as it was itself hierarchical, the activities of inferior judges and officials were subject to checks and restraints imposed by superior officials until there existed no higher power to place similar limits on the highest; and the latter, Bodin argued, could not (sovereignly) place such limits upon itself.

For Bodin, towns or provinces were as much corporate communities as were guilds or universities. And he explicitly recognised that the punishment of a corporate body could not be quite the same as the punishment of an individual. If the corporate body legitimately took the offending step, which is to say, through proper procedure and with the support of the members, Bodin felt that the entire corporate community could be punished: by disbandment, fines, by removal of privileges and civil rights, and otherwise. But corporal punishment or execution would only be fitting for those who actually committed or directly supported the unlawful act. Bodin viewed individuals in terms of their corporate interrelations, but nowhere assumed that any individual member of an organisation could be held fully responsible for whatever was done by the latter.

Bodin regarded every corporate body as a community catering to a particular interest. Both family and state were communities as well, but distinct in kind. Private corporate bodies were generally not thought to be *hierarchically* superior to families, but merely extensions of them. Moreover, Bodin suggested that they embraced more spheres of interest than those embraced by the family, and with greater particularity. Thus the private corporate body might be regarded as greater in *extent* in that it gathered together a number of families in respect of the prosecution of a particular interest. But the family, unlike the corporate body, was 'natural', not artificial, and this meant that it was both indispensable and prior to any other form of human organisation, and sometimes, therefore, more *fundamental*. There is thus a tension in Bodin's analysis: in one sense, private corporate bodies are superior to the family; in another, they are inferior. The overall conclusion to be drawn is that Bodin insists upon an essential, qualitative difference between the family and other corporate bodies, but that the basic hierarchical relationship between the two is one of equality.

Bodin thought family structure was inevitably based upon paternal despotism. By contrast, he pictured corporate structure as based upon the voluntary adherence and assent of members. Given this distinction, together with Bodin's general approach, he would most probably have assumed that any family not based upon paternal despotism was not 'truly' a family at all; for he did, in fact, believe that a private corporate body not based on voluntary adherence somehow, for that reason, became something other. When confronted, for example, with the fact of a private corporate body (i.e. the church) based upon an authoritarianism parallel to that which he thought characteristic of the family, he could only recognise the similarity in order to show that such bodies were more nearly families than 'true' corporations. Thus, if he had ever been confronted with a family run on joint and participative – let us say 'democratic' – lines, he probably would not have yielded to the evidence. He would probably have concluded that such a family was not 'really' a family.

It seems fair to say that Bodin had a virtually intuitive understanding of the distinction between family and other private corporate organisations and that he did, and would, remain impervious to the disintegrative appeal of contrary evidence tending to subvert that distinction. His inclination was to manipulate definitions in order to preserve distinctions, rather than to dismantle the latter in view of newly arisen, contradicting facts. If he had been brought consciously to recognise the insufficiency of his distinction, he could readily and openly have admitted the fundamental similarity between family (noting, for example, the marital contract) and private corporate structure, rather than stress a putatively essential difference between them. This would have permitted him to say of his own time that corporations were usually, though perhaps not always, run democratically; and that families were usually, though not always, run despotically. He would have been able to say of the future that neither the family nor the corporation would necessarily or even probably maintain their then respective and characteristic modes of administration.

Bodin, however, did not revise his conception of the essential difference between family and other corporate structures, and this created a minor difficulty. As family and corporate structure were somehow supposed to be inherently distinct, there arose the problem of determining which was superior to the other. As shown, Bodin supposed one to be superior in extent, the other more fundamental, i.e. superior in quality. This arrangement is not quite satisfactory, and so we come to the conclusion advanced above: that the basic hierarchical relationship in Bodin between the family and private corporate bodies is one of equality.

As against this conclusion, one might argue – falsely, to my mind – that a wider extent of authority conveys, as such, a 'higher' authority.

One could note, for example, that a trade union, in expelling or fining one of its members, reduces or eliminates the wages available to the family of that member and thus significantly affects family life itself. But the relevant reply to such a position as this is that there is an important distinction between affecting a community and controlling it, between influence and formal domination. A wider extent of authority implies a 'greater', but not necessarily a 'higher', authority. This distinction, one must add, Bodin did not make. But to accept it would not prove incompatible with the position he took. He appears to have assumed that guilds and such similar private corporations only acted towards a man in his capacity as a member of such bodies. Thus they did not or could not or should not attempt to discipline his wife and children and servants nor to dictate to the family as such. They therefore could not be said to control the family nor to be hierarchically superior to it. This would be true even though a given guild might influence a particular family far more profoundly than the decisions of the latter could generally influence the guild.

It may be appropriate to remark that any centre of control or administration is subject to a thousand and one influences. What a churchman says may readily affect what families do, as families; but as long as he merely exhorts and recommends, he does not, logically, coerce or control. (If he can coerce, in respect of the family, then he represents an order legally superior to the family.) Instances of such influence are everywhere. It is the influence of the non-legal upon a legal hierarchy that Dicey attempted to account for through his (otherwise inadequate) distinction between a political and a legal sovereign.[1] The former influences the machinery of control, but does not in itself constitute a sufficient condition of control. There is a difference between organisations influencing one another and the same controlling one another. Those which do not control (though they may influence) one another are legally equal. This does not mean that they are the same or do the same things or act in the same way or wield the same power. It merely means that, within the legal structure of the state, they stand, vis-à-vis one another, at par.

The implication in Bodin is that the family is autonomous vis-à-vis other corporations except for those which directly represent the power of the state. All non-state corporations, however, are not equal to one another, for they can be pyramided and they thus control one another. Bodin stated the position at reasonable length: 'A college can represent a particular skill or science or jurisdiction or marketable good. Also, several colleges may be united into a body – as of craftsmen, or merchants or professors or judges. Further, separate colleges may lawfully

[1] A. V. Dicey, *Law of the Constitution* (9th ed., London, 1945), p. 429ff.

constitute a general community – indeed, a university. Not only may all colleges and corporations constitute lawful communities, but these, together with the entire population of a town, district, or province, may assemble as estates' (*SLR*, pp. 332–3).

Bodin's exposition, however, of the hierarchical relation between corporate bodies was not entirely clear. One of the basic reasons for this lay in his failure properly to differentiate between several distinct orders of relation between communities: particularly between (*a*) their order of historical evolution (*mesnage, corps, estat*); (*b*) their relative strength of influence; (*c*) their comparative range of control (e.g. New York city government *v.* Albany city government); and (*d*) the order of control or the hierarchy obtaining between them (e.g. city–county–state–nation; or pope–archbishop–bishop, etc.). Since these different relations were not properly differentiated some confusion was inevitable.

Chapter Eight

The Family and Private Corporate Bodies

Bodin regarded the family as a self-contained community. Corporate bodies were assumed chronologically to evolve from it. Thus the family could exist separately; but the precondition of corporate existence was the existence of the family.

Corporate bodies embraced every aspect of communal life, the latter being governed by guilds, corporations, fraternities and colleges. These covered trades, recreation, education and religion. Bodin wrote that men originally established such associations for purposes of common defence ('pour defendre leurs maisons', *SLR*, p. 330) and in hopes of re-establishing and maintaining friendship among kinsmen, who were thought to be more and more divided with the increased proliferation of communities (*SLR*, p. 331). Friendship, he felt, was the real and 'sole foundation of every society and is required far more between men than justice' (*SLR*, p. 332). Artisans and merchants, priests and pontifs, indeed even philosophers, and all other sorts of men, had their own particular fraternities and colleges.[1]

In his discussion of corporate bodies, Bodin was concerned with at least three distinct matters. One had to do with the manner in which these bodies were founded, another with the function they performed and a third with the nature of their political structure.

(1) Bodin's conception of the manner in which corporate bodies arose (a confused mixture of violence and contract theory) is not directly relevant to our study.

(2) Bodin's treatment of the functions served by corporations is more complete than his treatment of the functions of the family. He explicitly assigned two major *functions* to the family. One was to teach children obedience.[2] Another was to handle family disputes, through

---

[1] 'Les artisans, marchands, prestres, pontifes, & toutes sortes d'hommes avoyent leurs confrairies & colleges, aussi avoyent les Philosophes entre eux': *SLR*, p. 332.

[2] Bodin believed that order in the family was the condition of order in the state; children who were not taught obedience by fathers would prove incorrigible to judges (*SLR*, p. 24).

the agency of paternal power – disputes which magistrates would have no time to deal with. Such functions, for Bodin, were important but not stressed, since they were incidental to, and not the effective reason for, the existence of the family. By contrast, purposes and objectives were necessarily antecedent to (and indeed the occasion for) the existence of corporate bodies.

Bodin divided the functions of corporate bodies into two. The first was to promote fellowship (*la religion*), the second to secure administration (*la police*). Although he distinguished between the two functions, he did not distinguish clearly between the guilds, etc., serving them. He remarked, for example, that guildhalls held frequent banquets and festivals, while the smallest villages set up communal halls. This suggests that Bodin believed any one corporate association could perform both roles. In any case, examples of the administrative functions of guilds consisted in dispensing justice, parcelling out responsibilities and regulating the conditions of trade. Corporate bodies could be formed in as many spheres as required the institutionalisation of fellowship and the administration of affairs. The enumeration of such spheres is not directly relevant to our concern.[1]

(3) Bodin's delineation of the character of corporate organisation partly involved an attempt to distinguish between it and family organisation. He made three broad attempts to distinguish generally between the two structures.

(*a*) Within the family, Bodin thought, the father must be god, guide and guardian. But in those relations extending beyond the family, he was reduced to an equal *inter pares*. A family head, on quitting the home which he commanded, was immediately divested of his title of 'master'. He must thenceforth treat and negotiate with other family heads. He was no longer lord and master, but rather 'a companion, peer and associate of all the rest'.[2] So when men stepped outside the family circle, thus ceasing to be masters, they became colleagues with one another. Bodin implied that in corporate bodies, a *principle* of control was substituted for the complete individual authority of one person.[3] Being colleagues necessarily entailed the principle of consultation, of deliberation, by which means majority or unanimous agreement could be reached; this was distinct from Bodin's concept of family organisation which depended upon the *plena potestas* of a single will.

---

[1] Cf. *SLR*, pp. 332–3.

[2] 'Or quand le chef de famille vient à sortir de sa maison où il cõmande, pour traitter & negocier avec les autres chefs de familles, de ce q leur touche à tous en general, il despouille le tiltre de maistre, de chef, de seigneur, pour estre compagnon, pair & associé avec les autres . . . il s'appelle citoyen': *SLR*, p. 47.

[3] 'Quand ie dy collegues, i'entens qu'ils soyent egaux en puissance, pour le regard de la communauté, ayans chacun voix deliberative . . .': *SLR*, p. 333.

Bodin remarked, however, that certain corporate bodies were organised on the principle of personal control rather than on that of
deliberate agreement. Bishops and abbots, for example, had the power
to punish canons and monks. But in these cases, such authority was
bestowed either by the prince or by colleagues. Bodin did not say so,
but it is assumed, in respect of authority bestowed by colleagues, that it
could always be resumed by them, thus implying that the relationship
of equals had not been infringed. As for the authority bestowed by the
prince, the hierarchy created within the corporation (which was no
longer subject to the control of its members) implied that the organisation was no longer, in effect, a 'corporate' one. As Bodin argued:
'if a leader has such power over all members of a corporate body . . .
it is no longer properly speaking an association, but a sort of family
instead'.[1] Thus, when Bodin discovers a corporation which does not
behave as he says a corporation must, he calls it something else.

Bodin's attempt to characterise the difference between family and
private corporate organisation in terms of a difference between collegial
and individual leadership is inadequate. That it is so can be plainly
demonstrated from his own text. He argues, for example, that the
exclusive authority of the father characterises family organisation. But
immediately he indicates that heads of non-familial corporations may
wield a similarly exclusive authority (abbots over monks, etc.). To say
that the family is distinguished from private corporate bodies by a
particular species of leadership, and then to instance precisely the same
form of leadership in various non-familial bodies, can only subvert the
original distinction advanced. This objection to Bodin's first distinction
between familial and non-familial corporate organisation only becomes
important, of course, with reference to Bodin's purpose: whether it was
simply to say that this familial/corporate difference generally obtained
in his own time or that it obtained *de facto* everywhere or that it necessarily *must* obtain everywhere or that it *ought* to obtain either generally or universally. We cannot in fact tell what Bodin's precise purpose
was, assuming that he had one. But given that he intended to say more
than that (in his own time) fathers generally exercised autocratic control,
it will be useful to note (i) that any private corporate body can in principle
be controlled in the same manner as an autocratically governed family,
and (ii) that any family (assuming that its membership contains two
adults or at least more than one non-infant) can in principle be governed
collegially.

(*b*) Quite separately, Bodin attempted an alternative distinction
between the family and the corporation, but without overruling the

[1] 'Mais si le chef a cette puissance sur tous en corps, & en nom collectif, ce
n'est pas droitement college, mais plustost une forme de famille': *SLR*, p. 333.

first. In effect, he said, accept that not all corporate bodies (e.g. the church) are governed through a deliberative process; there nonetheless remains within such bodies a distinction between the *person* of the leader and his *office*. Leaving aside, he wrote, the argument whether a body governed by a single will is a family or an association, 'it seems that he who is elected by the association or the prince to command any or all of his colleagues has a double character, one in respect of individual relations, the other regarding his relation to the association as a whole'.[1] (This distinction was familiar to medieval theorists; Gierke cited several examples with regard to it.)[2] Bodin implied that no similar distinction could be established within the family; for the father did not merely hold an office since he was not, apart from his office, an equal or colleague of his wife and children and servants. His person and function were fused, as opposed to those of a corporate head; for the latter had a dual character, to whose personal aspect no reverence was attached.

Unfortunately, this distinction also seems to be defective, since we may cite Bodin's own example to illustrate corporate organisation structured in a manner contrary to that which he conceives essential to its nature. Thus, if a bishop's authority extends into every dimension of the lives of his subordinates, the difference between his authority and the father's could not be described in terms of the former having a dual, and the latter a single, capacity. Obviously, there would be no definable respect or sphere in which the subordinate ceased, *vis-à-vis* his bishop, to be anything other than what he was, i.e. a subordinate and not an equal. There would be no respect in which he would not owe obeisance as well as obedience to his superior. If the differences between the bishop's authority and the father's consisted in, for example, the absence of the former's command of life and death over his charges, this difference would still involve no more than a variation in the extent of control exercised by each of them. If the difference between the bishop's authority and the father's consisted in the alienability of the first (since a bishop can be removed by a higher authority), this would offer no support to Bodin, since he himself asserted that a father's authority was also, under some circumstances (suppose he were mad), alienable.[3] Modern law, certainly, assumes that paternal authority is alienable

---

[1] 'Mais, laissant la dispute à part, il semble que celuy qui est esleu de college ou du Prince, pour commander à tous les collegues en particulier, a double qualité: l'une pour le regard de chacŭ, l'autre pour le regard du college . . .': *SLR*, p. 333.

[2] Baldus, John of Salisbury, Marsilius of Padua, and Nicholas of Padua, *inter alia*. Cf. Gierke, *Die publicistischen Lehren des Mittelalters*, tr. Maitland, a section from the third volume of *Das deutsche Genossenschaftsrecht* (1881), rendered as *Political Theories of the Middle Ages* (Cambridge, 1900).

[3] *SLR*, pp. 20–32 (bk. 1, ch. 4).

since it provides that parents can be relieved of the custody of their children should the latter be neglected or abused. In sum, this second distinction between the principles of family and corporate organisation is inadequate, because corporate administration does not always imply in practice the personal equality of associates and because paternal authority does not exclude either in theory or practice the separation of the father's personal from his 'official' capacities.

(c) What might appear to be the soundest formulation advanced by Bodin regarding the distinction between paternal and associative authority runs as follows: the difference between the family and its corporate extensions is that the former is natural while the latter are artificial.[1] The sense of this was that a family community was based upon birth and a corporation upon interest.

Nevertheless, even where one takes the narrowest formulation of this idea – to the effect that babies (at least) are born into families, but not into corporations – it does not work. For it is easy to see that there is a difference between merely being born, in itself, and being attached to the community or communities to which birth ordinarily gives access. The family, as Bodin saw, is a 'community' (*communauté*) in some sense like any other. What he did not note, however, is that the attachment of offspring to parents is not 'natural' in the sense that birth is. Although parents may form one community, offspring can either be transferred to another or indeed abandoned: for offspring may be treated like stray animals, or like fallen apples which no one disturbs. Parents, moreover, sometimes do not themselves form a community, since the relationship between them is not necessarily a marital one. In the same way that a child may be born, and yet not be attached to any community at all (i.e. be abandoned), so may a child be born and attached to a community other than the family (e.g. a church or an orphanage), or, in short, to a non-familial corporate body. If children *can* be 'born into' families, then so too can they be born into churches, orphanages, nurseries and businesses (e.g. in this last case through rights of inheritance). This is to say that children can readily be attached to corporate communities other than the family; it is also to say that they can be just as much, or as little, born into one community (the family) as into another (other corporate bodies). But the real point of this is that children, strictly speaking, cannot be 'born into' any community. So much for Bodin's three distinctions between the family and private corporate bodies.

We have already seen that Bodin believed the power of the father was and had to be virtually absolute. It was a belief grounded in sentiment and mistaken reasoning. But we have seen, too, that this belief was

---

[1] 'La famille est une communauté naturelle: le college est une communauté civile . . .': *SLR*, p. 330.

supported by the underlying idea, the unformulated assumption, that conscious controls had to be exercised if an orderly household were to be kept. This same assumption underlay Bodin's view of corporate bodies. It is important to note here this general assumption, since Bodin's views on family and corporate organisation are otherwise distinct.

The *paterfamilias* figure does not recur as the soul of conscious control in Bodin's treatment of the workings of corporate associations. Bodin saw the family as governed by an absolute ruler; he saw the operation of controls within the corporation or guild as being otherwise. Both types of order required control, conceived as a regulatory function, along with some means of hierarchical transmission of control. But they did not require the same type or procedure of control. Bodin saw the *paterfamilias* as a *ne plus ultra*, while the head of a guild or college was represented as a *primus inter pares*. He saw no distinction between the person and office of the father, while the corporate head was thought to play two roles – the first being that of an official and formal superior, the second that of a private individual who, as such, was merely the equal of his associates. Bodin regarded the family as a natural community while extra-familial associations were artificial. But in his attempt to formulate a general distinction between their procedures of control he failed. It may be that any such formulation is in any case impossible. That contingency apart, the immediate reason for his failure arose from the fact that he did not grasp the full implications of the idea that the family, like the corporation, is also a community or association and thus as natural, or as artificial, as the latter. Given this similarity, there is no necessary reason why family organisation should be less deliberative than other associations nor the organisation of these any less authoritarian than that of the family.

In any case, Bodin believed that the principle of political organisation within corporate bodies was consultative. He argued the reverse in the case of the family because he had not fully grasped the implications of the assertion that it, too, was a community. Hence variant theories were aired, and not a uniform one, regarding the nature of political organisation and actual procedures of political control. What remained common was an assumption regarding the need for conscious political control. Although Bodin wrote that 'Every state, corporation, college and family is governed through command and obedience',[1] it becomes clear from his analysis of corporate bodies that he believed the procedural relationship between 'command and obedience' was not always identical in type.

[1] 'Toute Republique, tout corps & tout college, & tout mesnage se gouverne par commandement, & obeïsance . . .': *SLR*, p. 13.

One is particularly concerned with how Bodin saw the *hierarchical* relationship (within the state) between the family and corporate bodies. The fact that he never adequately distinguished between them (despite his efforts to do so), and never shed the idea that they were essentially distinct types, might lead one to think that no clarification of the question of their precedence can be achieved. In any case, Bodin had three choices open to him. He could have looked upon the family as either (*a*) hierarchically inferior or (*b*) hierarchically superior. Alternatively, he could have regarded it as (*c*) merely another corporate body, equal in status to all the rest. We may consider only the second of these possibilities as unquestionably excluded. Bodin could not entertain the idea of the hierarchical superiority of the family, since he thought the latter was included within a hierarchy of which it constituted the fundamental, associative unit; it would thus be impossible for the family to subsume other associative units under itself. The real question then, is whether Bodin considered the family to be subsumed under, or equal to, other corporate bodies. The means of testing this question lies in determining whether or not he believed that other corporate bodies directly mediated between the family and the organs of the state.

The evidence in Bodin's work leads in two directions. First, when he argued that 'every state, corporation and household is governed by command and obedience' (*SLR*, p. 13) the very order in which he mentioned these units might be taken to imply a hierarchical relation between them, with the family at the bottom. When he discussed 'the differences between the family and the corporate body, and between the latter and the state' in terms of a relationship between 'the whole and its parts',[1] he seems to have implied an order ranging from the family at the bottom, through the corporation, to the state at the top. In short, there is some suggestion in Bodin that he conceived of the family as a distinct, nuclear community, hierarchically inferior to corporations.

In the case, however, of the second direction, Bodin's definition of the state does not even mention corporate bodies, quite apart from any implication that they are hierarchically superior to the family. He asserted that the state merely consisted in the (just) governance of several households through sovereign power.[2] This implies no mediation by private corporations between the state and the family. The implication was later made explicit. The state, he wrote, 'can be restricted to the point that it possesses neither corporations nor colleges, but a few

[1] 'La différence de la famille aux corps & colleges, & de ceux-cy à la Republique, est telle que du tout à ses parties': *SLR*, p. 330.
[2] Cf. *SLR*, p. 1.

families only'.[1] This would imply that there was no necessary mediation between family and state, and thus that the former was essentially equal to other corporate bodies since it was no more subsumed under them than they under it.

Thus Bodin's view of the hierarchical relation between family and corporations is less explicit than his (defective) formulations of structural distinctions between them. Nevertheless, it is easier to clarify the first than to justify the second. It is no doubt easier to accept that Bodin understood the family to be in general hierarchically equal to other corporate bodies than that he thought it inferior or that he was guilty of contradiction (for this is at no point perfectly clear). In short, I suggest that the overall weight of Bodin's work implies the basic equality of the family with (other) private corporate bodies.

My first reason is that although Bodin wanted to distinguish between the nature of the family and corporate structure, this does not necessarily imply that he wished to place them on distinct *hierarchical* levels. For example, if he had tried to distinguish between the structure and purpose of a masons' guild and the order of Jesuits, it is clear that the distinction would not have entailed the implication that he believed one to be hierarchically superior to the other. The same argument can apply to the family.

My second reason is that the statement that society is a *whole*, constituted of family, corporation and state, need not necessarily be interpreted hierarchically, since it can equally, and more reliably, be interpreted historically. For Bodin did assert that the family existed first, and that corporations grew from it. His formulation was as follows: 'et l'origine des corps et colleges est venue de la famille, comme du tige principal'.[2] This suggests that he was plotting a putative course of historical evolution and not offering an administrative ranking. My general conclusion, therefore, is as previously stated.

Despite muddled efforts to distinguish between the internal *structure* of the family and the corporation, the overall weight of Bodin's analysis does imply his acceptance of their *hierarchical* equality. Although he argued that they were distinct types of organisation, this does not imply that he thought them distinct in the sense of being superior or inferior to one another. What he clearly did was to conceive of the family as a fixed type of community which was *indispensable* to human life and political organisation, which he believed other corporations were not. Thus he concluded that the family community, *as he conceived it*, should not be tampered with since it was somehow inherently good;

---

[1] 'La Republique . . . peut estre si estroite, qu'elle n'aura ny corps ny Colleges, ains seulement plusieurs familles': *SLR*, p. 330.

[2] *SLR*, p. 330. Cf. pp. 345 and 350.

other corporate bodies could not justify equal immunity from state control.

We have noticed a gap in Bodin regarding his ideas about the nature of family organisation and his ideas about the organisational principle underlying private corporate bodies. This gap is unsatisfactory and the question is whether, and at what cost, it can be eliminated. If it is to be eliminated, the family must certainly not be regarded as 'natural' and the corporate body as 'artificial'. The phenomenon of birth is not of sufficient significance, or at least has not a relevant significance, to justify this sort of distinction. Families can in part be regarded as voluntary organisations (people do join them, both through marriage and adoption), just as corporate bodies can in part be regarded as involuntary organisations (people are often attached to them by birth, as in many religions, or through inheritance of positions of control in business and politics, or through automatic inclusion in age-grades in many small-scale societies, etc.).

Our question here is whether it would be easier logically for Bodin to modify his views on the family in the direction of those he advanced relating to the private corporate body, or the reverse. Indeed he could do both. For it is clear that a family, considered as a corporate group, can, just like other corporate groups, be governed both despotically and democratically. There is no reason why a family, as distinct from an association or corporation, requires to be ruled exclusively by one head. There is no less reason why a corporation than a family should require or will involve some degree of arbitrary control. In so far as there are necessary and significant organisational differences between familial and other associations, Bodin fails to marshal them convincingly.

Nonetheless, Bodin could maintain that the family has prior rights in a strictly historical sense. This sense would exclude the notion of the family having *imprescriptible* rights. Being original, the family could not have started with a constitution. Over time, of course, it might evolve one; or, at a given point in time, it might be given one. If the family confers upon itself its own constitution, then it must be sovereign, i.e. a state. If it operates according to a constitution that is imposed upon it, then it must be a sub-unit within a state. If the family's constitution is imposed, then whoever imposes it may be assumed to have the capacity to alter it. The interesting case for us, as for Bodin, however, is that which more nearly corresponds to the reality: where the family actually exists as a sub-unit within the state, but is neither given nor evolves any purpose or aim so express and plain that it might be called a constitution. But it is in precisely such a case that the uniqueness and importance of the family can best be expressed in terms of its historical priority.

The difference between the family and private corporate bodies can then be seen in terms of a difference between initial and derived existences. An associated difference is that the character of the initial organisation is always modified by the simple emergence of those derived from it, and defined in contradistinction to it. An entire procession of 'derived' organisations would necessarily affect, or alter, the purpose or – more simply – the activities of the mother organisation (the family). That is to say, the activities of the family necessarily shrink in relation to the absorption of specialist functions by the derived organisations. In so far as the derived organisations exercise control over their members, who are also members of families, their existence places limits upon the range of control originally exercised by the family over its membership. The problem is to remove the suggestion that such limitations imply 'infringement' of the family's prior or 'imprescriptible' rights. If now we assume that only the derived corporate bodies have legally defined purposes, which we might call charters, for example, then only they are in a position to be revoked, that is, to have their charters annulled. The rights and duties of the family, not being formally defined, have to be regarded as characterised by an extreme elasticity. If they are defined, if families are in effect simply given charters, then of course they simply become like all other private corporate bodies. (In the present world that is, of course, basically what they are.)

But we may suppose, as seems reasonable, that Bodin does not regard families as having such charters. Accordingly, he regards the purpose and functions and rights of the family as primordial; and yet, since these rights, etc., have never been formally stipulated, he simultaneously puts himself in a position to maintain – should he have wished to – that they could never be 'infringed' or 'proscribed', no matter how circumscribed they became.

If the family is assumed to represent the first and (at the time) only form of social organisation, its original powers must be regarded, *formally*, as having been complete or unlimited, in the sense, that is, that there existed no rival organisations to lay claim to a share in the direction of the affairs of its members. In so far as there existed no rival competences against which the family would have been required to set out its own, there would have been no original necessity to specify, and therefore to set limits to, the powers of the family. But the failure to set limits to the family's authority equally represents a failure to reserve specific family powers against encroachment. If the original character of the family is regarded as entailing the quality of being inviolate, then we are placed in a strange position: just as the family can be regarded as original whether it wields almost all power or nearly none, so then could it be regarded as inviolate whether it alienated considerable power or no power at all. The family may be considered as original, but it is consistent with this that it is and constantly has been surrendering one power or another and one power after another. Where a part of its originality is held to consist in its inviolability, then of course the family can be regarded as remaining 'inviolate' however much authority it may, over time, surrender.

'To violate' may involve the notion of 'taking away'. If the family is inviolable in the sense that nothing can be taken away from it, and remains inviolate even when much *is* taken away from it, we are obviously trapped in a contradictory position. From this there is no genuinely satisfactory escape. But one last desperate recourse is held out to us. We might say that in so far as a family in any degree remains a family, it retains some inviolable – i.e. some unviolated – character or 'essence'. Constitutionally, we can translate this notion of an essence into the notion of 'residual' powers. We can then distinguish the latter from either 'delegated' or 'appropriated' powers. In response to gradual but increasing complications (such as population growth, economic specialisation, war, etc.) the family can be regarded as delegating – or as being forced to surrender – certain successive areas of control and responsibility to parallel, intermediate or sovereign authorities. Such a process necessarily involves the constant depletion of the power and responsibility vested in the family; it involves a gradual narrowing of the breadth of the family's functions. But in the sense that the family always retains what is left, in the sense that this is a sum of residual powers, in the sense that the latter are regarded as retaining the essential element, and in so far as this is regarded as the inviolable element, the notion of the family's inviolability may be awkwardly reconciled with the fact of a continuing alienation of its powers.

It seems clear that Bodin wanted to perpetuate some of the power and independence reserved to families. But it seems equally plain that this desire was founded on the assumption of an absence of conflict between family heads and their sovereigns. One could always argue that the prince should regard the family as inviolate, without meaning that the prince should yield to the family head in cases of conflict. 'Inviolability' becomes a legally empty phrase where there is no stipulation of the particulars with respect to which the family is not to be interfered with, or if it is left to the prince to interpret those stipulations where made. If the family has no defined character, then powers can continually be subtracted without formal violation. If it has a defined character, either conferred or merely recognised by the state, it must be left to the latter to say what that character is. Such is the form of reconciliation which Bodin might have sought to achieve between apparently disparate elements in his argument.

Chapter Nine

Public Corporations: *Iuges et Magistrats*

Bodin argued that the singular difference between (*a*) the colleges of judges and magistrates and (*b*) all other corporate bodies was that the latter were only established to deal with specific and limited common interests in the community. The former, on the other hand, were established to deal with relations between all subjects generally, even to regulate the conduct of corporations and to mete out discipline to them should they offend against the law.[1] This notion implied a loose assembly of associations, each appropriate to a particular sphere of activity and activated by a specific interest (common to its membership), all spiralling upwards to be embraced by an ultimate authority, an apex of sovereign and pyramidal power, by which the divergent elements of social structure were clasped in harmony. Thus Bodin's manner of conceiving the hierarchical order of relations between distinct associations within the state was largely medieval in inspiration.

One would say today that Bodin conceived judges, magistrates and officers to be component parts of the state structure. But because we habitually contrast rulers and ruled, government and citizenry, we tend to assume that judges, magistrates and officers are in some sense opposed to the generality of individuals in the society (the 'masses', the people, the public). This opposition Bodin did not assume. There was a difference between public and private corporations, but it was merely a matter of degree and not absolute. The state, for Bodin, did not consist merely of individuals or of indiscriminate masses, but of associated individuals; it primarily contained groups, corporate bodies, associations, fraternities, guilds, estates, cities, and so on, and not mere individuals. The colleges of judges and magistrates, then, were also corporate bodies; they were pyramidal and superior, but not absolute and arbitrary. They formed a part of the state structure, not as opposed

[1] 'La difference de ceux-cy aux autres colleges, est notable, en ce que les autres sont establis chacun pour le gouvernement de ce qui leur est commun: & les colleges des Iuges & Magistrats sont principalement erigés pour les autres subiects: & mesme pour reigler les autres colleges, & les corriger s'ils mesprennent contre les lois & statuts . . .': *SLR*, p. 335.

to an inchoate mass of individuals, but as the topmost element (under sovereign authority) in a pyramid of corporate institutions, which touched and regulated every aspect of social life.[1] The magistracy was superior to all other individuals and groups, save the sovereign, because with it lay the most general authority – to apply the laws of the sovereign and to adjudicate general disputes under his authority and so secure the peace of the realm.

Bodin applied the term 'magistrate' indifferently to the highest, most commanding and independent offices in the state. The hoary distinction between legislative, executive and judicial powers is traditionally (even if misleadingly) attributed to Montesquieu. It would be injudicious to attribute it to Bodin, who reveals remarkably little concern with such categories. Bodin's significant distinction was between an ultimate and absolute authority, on the one hand, and an inferior and subordinate authority, on the other. He did not sort out, in the strict terminology of a later age, the particular divisions within this authority. Such divisions as he was concerned with were primarily vertical (or hierarchical), not horizontal. For him, magistrates in their generality were not merely the 'judges' of our present day; they were also the executive officers of the realm. Thus the *chancelier*, the *connétable* (constable), *chambellan* (chamberlain) and *marechaux*, amongst others (as well as *iuges*), were all magistrates.

It is not the case that Bodin simply and confusedly misunderstood the distinct functions of executive and judicial officers. The fact of his day was that such functions were not performed in the highly compartmentalised way characteristic of contemporary practice.[2] All officers of the realm held their authority from the king, and the functions they were expected to perform were many-sided. There existed in France no genuinely distinct law-making body, and the monarch was himself usually regarded more as a supreme arbiter of conflicts than as a supreme director of constructive social efforts – except in certain spheres, such as diplomacy, defence, etc. Bodin's primary effort consisted not in redrawing competences within the state, but rather in the extension of the

---

[1] 'Les premiers corps, & colleges, & qui plus ont de puissance en la Republique, sont les colleges des Iuges & des Magistrats: car non seulement ils ont puissance sur la moindre partie du college en nom collectif, & sur chacun de tous les collegues en particulier: ains aussi sur les autres subiects a leur iurisdiction, hors leurs college . . .': *SLR*, p. 334.

[2] For the 'confusions' of competence relating to the constitutional structure of sixteenth-century France, see R. Doucet, *Les institutions de la France au XVIe siécle* (Paris, 1948), vols 1 and 2, with particular reference to the following chapters: vol. 1, pt 2, 'Les conseils' (ch. 7), 'Les cours souveraines' (ch. 6), 'Le parlement de Paris' (ch. 7), 'Les offices' (ch. 18); vol. 2, pt 4, 'La justice', 'La hiérarchie judiciaire' (ch. 1).

sovereign's authority throughout the entire range of competences available to state control. His primary emphasis was *not* upon the legislative authority of the sovereign as the *pierre* upon which secular power must be built (which is the current opinion).[1] Bodin emphasised instead that the sovereign must be supreme in every sphere, *including* the legislative (apart, of course, from the limits imposed by divine or natural law). Public corporations, subject to sovereign control, must operate as extensively as the community's general interests (however defined) demanded. The point about these corporations, and their chief agents, was not that they performed executively, judicially or otherwise, but that they did so subject to an integrated and sovereign authority (the monarch) and with a view to promoting and preserving the general interests of the community or commonwealth or state.[2]

Bodin thought that public (corporate bodies or) corporations, like private (corporate bodies or) corporations, could, within the legal confines of their charters or commissions or orders, both create and enforce laws. For example, he understood adjudication to be partly a legislative function, both in practice and in principle. He established a hard and fast distinction between the judicial determination of fact and the assessment of causes in equity. The former category of decisions was entirely bound by law; the latter created law. 'In one case', he wrote, 'their position [that of the judges] is servile, in the other honourable, because in the first they are bound by law while in the other they

---

[1] See further appendix 3 below.

[2] *SLR*, bk. III, ch. 2, pp. 259ff. Bodin distinguishes between two sorts of officers: 'les uns qui ont la puissance de commander, qui sont appellés magistrats: les autres de congoistre ou d'executer les mandeměts: & tous sont personnes publiques'. In short, superior magistrates have the power to issue orders; subordinate officials merely carry them out. Bodin did not bother to distinguish between 'magistrates' (*a*) as judges, and 'magistrates' (*b*) as executive officials. He only stressed the difference between *public* officers who command and others who obey – irrespective of judicial, executive or other competences. In fact, he tends to think of the magistrate as a living law who both declares and enforces what is to be done.

Bodin did distinguish *types* from *degrees* of state competence. But *sovereignty* was basically distinguishable by degree, not by type, of competence. What was distinctive about sovereignty was the general 'supremacy' and 'finality' of the sovereign – which is to say, his ultimate right to interpret, as well as (in some cases) to create law. It is true that the state fell under the *command* of the sovereign, but Bodin by no means understood the sovereign command to be coextensive with the power to create law. For not all law was created; in fact, only very little of it was. So command covered the interpretation of (already existent) law as well as, occasionally, and in certain spheres, the creation of new law. Commentators conventionally assume (as, for example, do Sabine, Merriam, Gierke and C. J. Friedrich) that Bodin understood sovereignty essentially to involve a supreme legislative capacity, rather than a judicial one – that it implied a type, rather than a degree, of power. Although Bodin does say that the first

are not.'[1] The clear implication here was that judges sometimes made law – though it lay with the sovereign to say (in the end) whether such law was sustained. Thus, for Bodin, judges could take decisions independently of established law, although not contrary to it; and because judges were inferior to the highest source both of law and judgement, their independent decisions were subject to appeal, while the decisions of the sovereign, and the sustained application of his law, were final.

One may bring further evidence to show that Bodin conceived public (like other) corporations and their agents to be capable, within their stipulated spheres, both of creating and of enforcing laws, thus performing a generally undifferentiated function. Marshals, for example, whom we today consider to perform in an executive capacity (or as an extension of such a capacity), Bodin explicitly conceived to perform in a total capacity – within the confines of their commissions. They made war and directed its course, without restriction to particular procedures; and they judged their men in accordance with how they complied or otherwise with orders given. For Bodin, all was left to 'their judgement and discretion'. And they could not be regarded as 'simple executors of the law' since there was 'no law governing their modes of action.'[2] Their commands (implicitly authorised by the sovereign) were law; in short, they not only interpreted law but also created it.

Public officials (*personnes publiques*) were assumed to be the agents of public corporations and were of two sorts. Some, whom Bodin called 'officiers', occupied a position natural to the state, and thus an enduring one, even though a given holder of the position might be relieved of it. Others, whom Bodin called 'commissaires', occupied a position specially created to serve a specific and limited purpose.[3] Bodin made no attempt to establish this distinction in terms of the type of job done, but, it would appear, merely in terms of its duration. Thus, persons

mark of sovereignty is to command law, the general tenor of his work suggests that these commentators have mistakenly read the legislative emphasis of Hobbes backwards into Bodin. Bodin mostly meant by sovereignty an *ultimate* control or a *highest* human authority, whether in the interpretation or promulgation of laws.

[1] 'Or l'un est servil, l'autre est noble: l'un est obligé à la loy, l'autre ne l'est point: l'un git en faict, l'autre en droit; l'un est propre au Magistrat, l'autre est reservé à la loy: l'un est escrit es loix, l'autre est hors la loy' etc.: *SLR*, p. 306.

[2] 'Si donc les Magistrats militaires, & Capitaines en chef, ont en toute Republique puissance du glaive, sans aucune limitation, ny restriction de la forme de proceder, ny des peines, pour la varieté de crimes & forfaits, le tout à leur discretion & iugement, on ne peut dire qu'ils soyent simples executeurs de la loy, attendu qu'ils n'ont point de loy à laquelle pour ce regard ils soyent subiects', etc.: *SLR*, p. 305.

[3] 'L'officier est la personne publique qui a charge ordinaire limitee par edict. Commissaire, est la personne publique qui a charge extraordinare, limitee par simple cõmission': *SLR*, p. 259.

who held jobs which always had to be done, whose execution was
uninterruptedly necessary to the functioning of the state, were called
officers. Those who held special commissions, limited to a specific (not
necessarily designated) period of time, were called commissioners.

Public officials were, then, both officers and commissioners. (Church
officials were also 'public', according to Bodin, but not in the same sense
as the others, since the former were administratively subordinate to
those public officials who, let us say, represented the sovereign.) But
not only were public officials distinguished from one another on the
basis of the length of their appointments. They were also distinguished
in terms of their mutual relationships of command and obedience.
Those who were free to give orders, issue commands and, in short, act
creatively within the sphere subject to their control, were called 'magistrats'. Those who had no such authority, who only carried out orders
and did strictly what they were told, were minor officials.[1] (Bodin had
no specific term for these.)

From all of this, it is clear that Bodin applied the term magistrate to
the highest officers of state, i.e. to *personnes publiques*. Their offices
could be permanent or temporary, ordinary or extraordinary. Further,
Bodin explicitly argued against the notion, among other similar ones,
that the magistrate was merely a counterpart of the present-day judge
(in his words, 'une personne publique qui preside en justice', *SLR*,
p. 260). The term magistrate he understood to cover a wide number of
functions, legislative, executive and judicial in character, all of which
could be combined. For Bodin, in short, the magistrate was simply an
omnicompetent public official who had the power to command obedience.[2]

This formulation might suggest that the highest power in the
state, after all, *was* conceived as legislative. But not so. For Bodin, *all*
relations (except, generally, those within private corporate bodies)
entailed command and obedience. All authority was based on command
(*SLR*, p. 13). This would apply as much to a judge as to a soldier. It
emerges, from a close reading of Bodin's text, that the only separations
of power which he conceived of were incidental and *ad hoc*. In book III,
where he dealt with what might today be called the machinery of government, the first chapter deals with advisory bodies (*le senat, le conseil*),
the second with administrative personnel (*officiers et commissaires*), and
the remaining five (apart from the last) with the highest branch (*les*

[1] 'Il y a deux sortes d'officiers & de commissaires: les uns qui ont puissance de
commander, qui sont appellés Magistrats: les autres de congoistre ou d'executer
les mandemēts: & tous sont personnes publiques . . .': *SLR*, p. 259.
[2] 'Magistrat est l'officier qui a puissance en la Republique de commander':
SLR, p. 273.

magistrats) of such personnel. No chapter deals with legislative or judicial branches as such. For the author, such 'branches' did not exist. The judge was a magistrate just like any other. He issued orders, and he could enforce them. Where judges 'merely' applied the law, Bodin only thought of them as persons holding commissions from magistrates, with a view to doing a job with which the magistrate for some reason could not cope. The lord of a manor was a magistrate, and so was a military commander; the idea of a judge 'pure' had not quite arrived.[1]

Bodin designated a hierarchy of public officials, and supreme among these were magistrates. They were of three orders which ranked one above the other.[2] 'The first constraint', wrote Bodin, 'wielded by those who have power to command, is the seizure of persons as well as goods' (*SLR*, p. 300). Every magistrate exercised such power as this, paired with the right to convict or acquit. Some magistrates, however, only dealt with property relations; others with both the latter and disputes governing honour (*l'honneur*); and a last category with property and honour as well as with the dispensation of corporal punishment, up to and including the sentence of death (*SLR*, p. 300). The relevant point about these distinctions lies in the fact that they were based not so much upon the question of *what* was done, but rather on that of *how much* was done. Different magistrates did not simply have different sorts of tasks to perform; rather, they were distinguished from one another on the basis of their having a wider or narrower realm of authority within which to operate. In respect of one another, some were sovereign (*souverains*), others intermediate (*moyens*) and the most inferior just that (*les derniers*). The chain of command ran from the top, to the middle ranks, and to the last (*SLR*, p. 284).

The most elementary act of authority, as mentioned above, consisted in the power to seize both persons and goods. This function would today be regarded as purely executive. It is clear that Bodin realised that the arresting officers would generally not be the same as the presiding officers in a court; but he made no distinction of principle between

[1] *SLR*, p. 299. Bodin states that the magistrate is the living law, 'who commands, prohibits, permits, and punishes'. The magistrate was as much an executor as adjudicator of law: 'la loy qui dit, que la force des loix gist à commander, defendre, permettre, & punir, est plus propre aux Magistrats qu'à la loy, qui est muette: & le Magistrat est la vive loy qui fait tout cela . . .' This suggests that adjudication is an integral and perhaps indistinguishable element in the promulgation of law. But it does not follow from the idea that the magistrate is a living law that he is the exclusive creator thereof. Cf., for example, 'Olivier brings Hamlet to life'. This statement implies interpretation, the overlay of an actor's creativity upon a documentary sub-stratum provided by Shakespeare.

[2] 'Aussi pouvons nous diviser les Magistrats en trois sortes, pour le regard de leur puissance . . .' etc.: *SLR*, p. 254.

the two. Such officers were under the command of magistrates, constituting the concrete and visible extension of the magistrate's verbal authority. The function of a magistrate was not merely to judge but also to command. Today, the term magistrate implies solely a judge; for Bodin, it implied the highest public officials in the state. There is obviously a close connection between the act of judging and possessing high authority in the state. But the implications of the term, for Bodin, were wide-ranging, whereas now the term's meaning is more restricted.

It should, therefore, be clear that Bodin was not particularly concerned to distinguish between separate competences (between who legislates, executes, adjudicates). These competences he generally conceived to be merged, and, if separated, to be separated by chance devolution and not on principle. His interest lay in the designation of the order of superior and inferior command assumed to inhere in the state structure. For the rest, judges could legislate; soldiers could adjudicate. What mattered was the inferiority of both, in every hierarchical respect, to the sovereign. The sovereign had the *ultimate* right of command in every sphere and over all public corporations and their agents; while these exercised a like authority over all private corporations and their private members.

Bodin's intention, however, was not to say that the magistracy (a composite term for public corporations) had unbridled authority over private bodies and persons who were subject to it. His purpose, on the contrary, was to establish a distinction between the *ultimate* sphere of public authority and the immediate spheres of private right. Although Bodin's conception of the difference between public authority and private right is imprecise, he nevertheless assumed a *differentiation of functions* between them. Those corporate bodies which we would call public performed a role hierarchically superior to those we would call private, since the public corporations catered for the community's most general interests. Public corporations could not do, and were not intended to do, any and everything. Their basic purpose was to ensure that private corporations and individuals did not infringe state law, and so the most general interests of the community (which this law was intended to uphold). Private corporate bodies operated within defined spheres, and the magistracy did likewise.

Bodin's distinction between private and public corporations, however, was inadequate. Any proper distinction between them would really have to turn upon drawing a firm line between their separate spheres of concern. But if this were ultimately done by the sovereign, the line could be so drawn that the interests of private groups were readily subsumed under the general interest of all – which is to say, of public groups, compositely termed 'the state'. The problem of what is of public interest, and what private, does not appear susceptible to any universal solution. But Bodin nonetheless assumed that a formal distinction between them could be couched in universal terms.

Now the point of immediate relevance is that Bodin understood the machinery of state to be subject to the control of the sovereign. The sovereign bore ultimate responsibility for the appointment of all public officials. These created or applied such laws as the sovereign deemed adequate to serve the general interests of the community. The distinction between public and private must turn, however, upon what was meant by the general interest. And as the ultimate determination of this lay with the sovereign, further discussion of the matter (in the general interest of an orderly unfolding) must await the discussion of sovereignty proper. But it is as well to remark that the concept of the general interest is tautological in form and highly variable in content. The (laudable) uses to which the American constitution's 'general welfare' clause has been put provides evidence of the enormous elasticity of such formulae.

Bodin believed that the ultimate function of the sovereign was to maintain a just order within the state; this meant eliminating conflict. One realises, however, that all social conflict cannot be eliminated. (It is even questionable as to whether all of it is bad.) This poses the problem as to what spheres of conflict the state should attempt to control. On the basis of some such distinction as this, one could differentiate between the type of control which public corporations, as opposed to private ones, exercise. Bodin lived at a time when this question was more crucial than it is at present. There existed a multiplicity of rival authorities and rival laws. These structural squabbles were the remnants of baronial authority and of ecclesiastical ascendency. In this context, the important question for Bodin was not whether the state could perform functions never before exercised, but whether it could appropriate functions exercised hitherto by others.

For example, one of the most important rights exercised by private, and particularly ecclesiastical, corporations was the meting out of punishment to associates who violated public law. Bodin argued, however, that both civil and criminal procedures fell under royal authority, irrespective of the offender's corporate affiliation (*SLR*, p. 336). Here was implied a logical integration of control, not – from a general social perspective – an absolute extension of control. Bodin cited the case of Gregory XI, who claimed that any student (*echolier*) in the University of Paris charged with a criminal offence must be judged by the bishop. Bodin claimed, to the contrary, that neither the king nor any public officer was in any way obligated by such declarations. He also insisted that it was absurd to permit the church to grant refuge to criminal offenders. Sanctuary, he argued, should only be granted to the young, and then for 'fautes ligeres' (*sic*). His reasons for supporting such integration of control never quite become explicit. But there is a suggestion that, where it is possible for offenders to receive judgement at the hands of their colleagues, general unrest is created by the possibility of their receiving partial judgement and perhaps escaping punishment altogether. Here, too, we have further evidence of Bodin's general concern to concentrate within the hands of the sovereign all competences, and not just to attribute to him the legislative or executive power.

Bodin does not consistently attribute to the sovereign *all* legislative power. He attributes to him a power of command in those matters where divine and natural law are silent, and where the public power, guided by the public interest, must ultimately command what is (and what is not) to be done. Bodin does not consistently attribute to the sovereign a legislative power alone or exclusively, but instead an unfettered right to interpret, create and execute in so far as his judgement, legislation and execution (his commands) do not conflict with law divine or natural.

Public corporations preserve the unity and harmony of the state, by virtue of interpreting and creating and executing its laws. Laws, in part, are arbitrary and 'artificial'; in part they are divine and 'natural'. The laws regulating the affairs of state come from man, and from God. Public corporations, which utilise both the laws of man and of God, to attain justice, peace and prosperity for the commonwealth, do not exclusively execute either the will of God or the will of man. Public corporations are not therefore exclusively subject either to the sovereign's will or to that of God. Bodin, therefore, to whatever extent he may have wished to integrate social control, did not consistently envisage the complete subjection of private to public bodies nor of public corporations to the prince.

Bodin conceived of the public corporate body as based upon command and obedience, and of the private corporate body as based upon a conciliar principle of control. The gap between the control principles governing the family and the private corporate body is therefore reproduced in regard to the latter and the public corporation. But, as in the first case, there is no good reason why we should regard the control principles operating in the cases of public and private corporations as being fundamentally different. The public corporation need not necessarily be governed in a fashion either less conciliar or more despotic than the private corporation. It becomes plain that Bodin's general inclination is to assume and argue that human organisation is based on an absolutist principle – of command and obedience; but it is equally clear that this is not a position to which he is rigorously faithful.

Chapter Ten

The Sovereign: Exposition

For Bodin, sovereignty was not equivalent to the power of the state. Nor was it equivalent to the power of public corporations. It was the term covering the logic of power wielded by the highest or supreme agent in the state. The sovereign was not necessarily a monarch. It might be an *élite* or a *populus* – an aristocracy or a democracy. For this reason Bodin's analysis implied that the sovereign was not merely a person but an office, though he did not clearly or explicitly formulate the distinction. His major problem became that of determining the essential characteristics of this power, both *irrespective* of who wielded it and also in order to determine who wielded it. In short, the assumed question from which his analysis proceeded was: what is the nature of that control exercised by the highest power in the state? Thus he was concerned with an important aspect of the general character of political power.

Bodin's argument assumed that the best type of sovereign was a 'royal' monarchy – as distinct from the rule of tyrants and despots. Not only did his argument assume as much, but he later went on to put forward other arguments offering explicit support in the matter. However, as distinct from this concern, whether concealed or explicit, with what type of sovereign is best (i.e. with who should rule), Bodin's analysis revealed a formal logic distinct from both ethical and factual judgements. His *basic* arguments relating to the nature of sovereignty do not plead directly *for* a particular type of sovereign nor do they stipulate that *practice reveals* that sovereigns always operate in a certain way. His basic arguments, in form, are less normative and/or empirical than *conditional*, not in the sense of being tentative but in the sense of drawing out conclusions from initial premises.

Bodin wanted to say (as distinct both from what a good type of sovereign is and as distinct from how sovereigns actually operate) something about what seems logically to be implied in the term 'sovereign' itself. This was a matter of definition, deduction and classification. In short, Bodin (in part) wanted to construct a model of the state and of the power-relations comprising it, but most importantly to delineate within this model the implications involved in the idea of supreme power, or sovereignty.

The topmost power in the state, called sovereign, entailed, for Bodin, certain attributes. If these attributes properly belonged to the highest authority, then they could not be considered the province of inferior authorities. Thus the proper power of the sovereign was quite distinct from that of his or its subordinates. And this power, whatever it was, could in no way be shared with subjects.[1] Bodin did not stress this argument, but its implication was that the attributes of sovereignty were in some sense indivisible. The sovereign was the topmost agent in, or servant of, the state. This was taken to mean that its authority was superior to that of any other agent. And, in so far as it was superior, it could be neither equal nor inferior to any other person or group. In short, the idea of a hierarchy implied a point, not a plateau, at the crest. As applied to political society, the existence of a sovereign implied the subordination of all other persons and groups in the state. Such subordination affected principally the nobility and the church. Thus, no agent – whether called duke, count, governor, magistrate, regent, dictator or king – was sovereign if his power was derived from or obligated to the superior power of another. The sovereign was above all subjects ('celuy qui est par dessus tous les subiects', *SLR*, p. 149).

Bodin's argument regarding the indivisibility of sovereignty was not intended to suggest that the power of the state could not be divided. On the contrary, it was based on the assumption that it *was* divided. It was not power, as such, but *sovereign* power which could not be held in common with subjects. In the state, such power as was shared was not sovereign; and most power exercised was shared. Bodin briefly enumerated certain of those areas in which power was shared: in 'the administration of justice',[2] in the appointment and dismissal of officials (covering judges, administrators, accountants, soldiers, commanders and so on), in dispensing rewards and punishment, and in debating affairs of state (as would a privy council or a senate). In all these areas, subjects and sovereign shared power; hence the power exercised was not sovereign. But Bodin did not stop there. He went on to argue that even the making of law, understood as such, did not constitute sovereign power. Neither the people of Rome, for example, nor the magistrates in any state, could be called sovereign merely by virtue of the fact that

[1] 'Or à fin qu'on puisse congnoistre celuy qui est . . . Prince souverain, il faut sçavoir ses marques, qui ne soyent point commune aux autres subiects: car si elles estoyent communes, il n'y auroit point de Prince souverain . . .': *SLR*, p. 147.

[2] *SLR*, p. 150. This phrase is somewhat awkward. Knolles (p. 155) uses it. Tooley, however, rather enigmatically speaks of 'rights of jurisdiction' (p. 42). Bodin's own wording was 'faire justice'.

they made laws.[1] Any argument against Bodin to the effect that power was in fact divided in many states would, therefore, be irrelevant. Bodin's model suggests that power is divided in every state, and indeed in every sphere – which would mean for us legislatively, executively and judicially.

From Bodin's analysis, it is clear that sovereign power was not merely a power to command, for fathers, bishops and magistrates also commanded. Nor was it simply a capacity to command within a restricted sphere of government, for example in the legislative. Sovereignty, being the highest power in the state, consisted in the *ultimate* and most general power of command over all subordinate branches of government, however conceived, and without exception.

Bodin's terminology was not put to consistent use, but he drew a sharp distinction between commands (*a*) which were either inferior in sweep or subject to appeal, or both, and others (*b*) which were neither – i.e. which were final. The second type of command was peculiar to the sovereign, and the first to his subordinates, in whatever sphere. Although some commands originated with the sovereign, others did not. By implication, what was required of a law was not that it be commanded by the sovereign, but (if it originated with an inferior) that it *at least* should not conflict with the sovereign's express will; or (if it originated with the sovereign) that it should not conflict with other law, i.e. that which was natural or divine.

Commands were laws and laws commands. Both were the preserve of the sovereign, although, as stated, not all indiscriminately. Bodin distinguished between 'laws' and 'edicts' (*loix* and *edicts*) (*SLR*, p. 151) as a means of formalising the distinction between sovereign and in-

---

[1] 'To understand the attributes of sovereignty it isn't enough . . . to have the power of making laws and appointing Magistrates . . .': *SLR*, p. 150. Knolles translated this passage as follows: 'That the people ought to content themselves to have the power to make laws and magistrates; that is not sufficient to declare a soveraigntie of power in them, as I have before declared concerning the magistrates. Yea the power to make laws is not the proper marke of soveraigntie, except we understand thereby the soveraigne princes laws . . .' (p. 156). Knolles's translation suggests less that the first mark of sovereignty is to command law than that the highest and final form of law is that which the sovereign commands.
Bodin's own formulation (*SLR*, p. 150) runs as follows: '. . . que le peuple se devoit contenter d'avoir la puissance de faire les loix, & les Magistrats: ce n'est pas assez dit, pour faire entendre qui sont les marques de souveraineté . . . le Magistrat peut donner [la loy] à ceux qui sont au ressort de sa iurisdiction, pourveu qu'il ne face rien contre les edicts & ordonnances de son Prince souverain'. Here Bodin does not make an *exception* of 'the soveraigne princes laws', but merely enjoins the magistrate not to make laws which conflict with these.
The point about law-making not being, in itself, an attribute of sovereignty seems to escape Tooley entirely; at least it is omitted, for his translation simply reads: 'appointing to office is not an attribute of sovereignty' (pp. 42–3).

ferior commands. 'Law' was intended to apply to the most ultimate
category of command, 'edict' to commands inferior to 'law'. But Bodin
does not keep strictly to this distinction.[1] Thus, 'law' generally means
any public regulation governing corporate bodies, public corporations
and individuals; law is a command, at whatever level it may be issued,
whether by God, by Nature, by the sovereign, by magistrates or by
heads of families. But 'law' nevertheless contains two levels or types of
command: the *supreme* and the *subordinate*.

Laws supreme, as distinct from laws subordinate (which are sometimes called edicts), fall within the province of the sovereign. In respect
of law understood as a supreme command, Bodin wrote that it 'means
the just government of whoever has complete power [*toute puissance*]
over others without the exception of anyone: whether such governance
affects all subjects in general or in particular, apart from them (whether
one or many) that give the law . . .' Law, he added (intending this to be
understood as law supreme) 'is the command of the sovereign as it
affects all subjects in general or matters of a general nature'.[2] It should
not be overlooked that Bodin stressed continually – though, as usual,
not consistently – the idea of *generality*, as being peculiar to the sorts
of law commanded by the sovereign. For him, 'only sovereign princes
can give law to all subjects, without exception, whether in general or
in particular' (*SLR*, p. 151). This mention of the 'particular' was to
reaffirm, not the illimitable power of the sovereign, but the illimitable
range of applicability of that power peculiar to the sovereign.

The essential characteristic of sovereignty, therefore, was not the
power to command (any) law, but the human power to issue commands
of the highest and most general kind. Thus, although the sovereign's
command (within certain limits) was law, not all law was the sovereign's
command. (For Hobbes, on the other hand, the sovereign's command was
law, and law was the sovereign's command.) Sovereignty, for Bodin,
merely consisted in the highest and most general, the ultimate and final
power of command. Bodin continually stressed the idea of absolutism
conceived as hierarchical superiority, as distinct from absolutism

[1] *SLR*, p. 154. At this point, for example, only three pages past his initial
elaboration of the distinction between laws and edicts, Bodin writes that it is
'only the sovereign Prince who can append to his edicts the death penalty'. The
word to underline is *edict*. Just the page before he writes that 'the Magistrate
can give law [N.B.] to those under his jurisdiction, provided he does nothing
contrary to the edicts and ordinances of his sovereign Prince' – 'pourveu qu'il
ne face rien contre les edicts & ordonnances de son Prince souverain'. It is clear
that Bodin is not terminologically consistent. In this case, the sovereign is made
to issue 'edicts' while magistrates promulgate 'laws', whereas previously (e.g.
p. 151) the situation was the reverse.
[2] 'Loy est le commandement du souverain touchant tous les subiects en
general, ou de choses generales . . .': *SLR*, p. 150.

conceived as the simple exercise of arbitrary control. The power of a sovereign, in order to be such, must entail an authority to command which was unlimited by any other agent greater, less or equal to himself (*SLR*, p. 154). As sovereign, presiding over a hierarchy of control, such commands as he issued did not require the consent of inferiors, since their power could not be equal to the sovereign's, given that they were subsumed under a power pyramid which he controlled.

Bodin's assertion did not constitute a fact, but a model of analysis. It *could* be taken to mean that a sovereign's power was absolute or that it should be so. But it could also be used to show that *no* sovereign's power either was absolute or could be so. When he argued that the power peculiar to the sovereign was not shared with subjects, he immediately went on to show that there was no sphere in which governmental power was not shared. This move merely implied that sovereign power was of a specific and restricted nature, that the sovereign was not and probably could not be strictly absolute or sovereign – in a *total* sense. In short, within the model the very idea of sovereignty would be inconsistent with such notions as 'absolute' or 'total'. This implication would tend to force upon Bodin's concept of royal absolutism more of an identity with the idea of *finality* or *ultimacy*, as opposed to *totality* and *arbitrariness*.

Sovereign power, for Bodin, was in effect the supreme power of command. But this implied command equally over every department of government. The sovereign's command was law; but not all laws were sovereign, i.e. they did not, or could not, all follow from his command. The sovereign's command directed the general affairs of state. Such commands not only established laws in the contemporary sense; they directed diplomatic negotiations, the appointment of senior officials, the denial or acceptance of appeals against the decisions of inferior magistrates. Whatever the sovereign spoke or commanded (*qua* sovereign) was law. Because all laws were not manifestations of sovereign power, there was implied and required and established a distinction between at least two distinct types of law, of command. With this, we return to the first sentence of this paragraph: sovereign power involved *supreme* command. It was not total. It involved the highest authority, but not all authority. Thus, the idea of sovereign power tended to lead Bodin to the notion of *final* power. As for facts, it is plain that Bodin did not believe actual rulers could do whatever they liked. As for norms, Bodin did not advocate that actual rulers ought to do, or be permitted to do, whatever they liked.

The idea of the sovereign, conceived as a final and highest arbiter of disputes within a polity, is, of course, as old as organised society itself. Bodin, probably for that reason, deliberately underplayed this strictly judicial aspect of the question. The sovereign, conceived as interpreter of law, is generally characteristic of static societies. The sovereign, conceived as maker of law, is generally characteristic of dynamic societies. Bodin was interested in extending the conception of the sovereign's range of power to fit a traditional society increasingly subject to expansion and change. Sovereign power implied a final authority in the settlement of disputes. Bodin intended it subsequently to embrace also final authority in either the initiation or the sanctioning of law. In any case, judicial pronouncements were commands, although not necessarily laws. They were pronouncements deduced from or implied in other pronouncements, usually more general in character.

Bodin usually understood by sovereign power not only final authority to settle disputes within the context of traditional society, but final authority, too, in the rearrangement of that society. If the purpose of the sovereign were to attend to the common good, however defined, this task not only could but, as Bodin saw, did lead into the need for administrative initiative as well as for judicial conservation; it required the rearrangement of social relations as well as their preservation. This attitude is expressed in Bodin's discussion of the difference between law and custom. Law was made by the sovereign, custom by subjects.[1] But there was no doubt that custom could carry as much force as law.[2] The basic implied difference between them did not lie in the degree of strength of either type of regulation; nor really in the source, or point of origin of either. Bodin did not say, but seemed to imply, that the *essential* difference between law and custom lay in the realm of finality. For law had the power to displace, break and amend custom, as well as to sanction it, while custom had no similar authority over law. Magistrates could interpret custom as they saw fit, but law must be strictly applied (*SLR*, p. 155). In other words, the sovereign's command was final, while the pronouncements of tradition, habit, and magistrates – conceived independently of the sovereign's command – were all subject to appeal. It was the sovereign's ultimate prerogative to decide upon the meaning of law, and although this prerogative embraced the (limited) need for its creation as well, decision about the meaning of law was regarded basically as a matter of interpretation.

Law could be decreed both by sovereigns and by magistrates, but if derived from the latter, they were necessarily subject to the sanction of the sovereign. In other words, there were supreme laws, on the one hand, and mere edicts (and customs) on the other. Both carried force.

---

[1] 'Le Prince souverain est maistre de la loy, les particuliers sont maistres des coustumes': *SLR*, p. 154.

[2] 'Il est certain que la coustume n'a pas moins de puissance que la loy': *SLR*, p. 154.

The fundamental difference implied was that one sort were final and the other were not. Bodin also argued, however, that the sovereign could not be bound by his own laws. This meant not only that the sovereign was above the laws but, by virtue of being so, could change them at will. And since even sovereign laws could be changed at will, there would appear to be no obvious reason for supposing that these laws were, in themselves, any more final, in the sense of *enduring*, than customary laws. Thus it is important to note that the finality in Bodin's conception of sovereign law cannot be taken to imply its duration. So one is brought back to the idea of hierarchical supremacy as the proper meaning of the sovereign's legal finality.

But Bodin offered no developed legal theory. He seemed to waiver in his general conception of the nature of law. On the one hand, law was 'the command of the sovereign touching all subjects in general, or matters of a general nature'; on the other, it was still the command of the sovereign, while affecting 'all subjects in general or in particular' (*SLR*, p. 150). Were all laws *general* in nature, or were they *particular* or were they both ? The answer is not clear. But it is perfectly possible to reduce the ambiguity and latent conflict here by saying that Bodin understood or assumed the purpose of law to consist – most generally – in promoting the common interest. Thus, laws were usually general in nature, but sometimes particular as when applying only to one or a few persons. In such cases the law, though particular or severely limited in general application, was either in the public interest or at least not contrary to it. The difficulty with this possibility, however, is that Bodin distinguished between justice and legality, or between *droit* and *loy*. The two were not identical although they might coincide. In so far as they conflicted, *loix* could not be called state regulations promoting (or preserving) the general interest. For Bodin seemed to assume that the general interest of the community could not be served contrary to what was right. Law might be either right or wrong, or neither; but where wrong its observance was bad for the state. The idea that laws can be bad might appear to weaken any justification of the perpetual and absolute power which Bodin attributed to the sovereign. But we have previously seen how fast and loose Bodin played with terminology. The sovereign could do wrong, but only when he acted outside his sphere of control. He was absolute, and so was above the law and could change the law and create none that was bad. But he was only absolute *within his sphere*, which was simply the highest and most general level of jurisdiction, subsuming *at this level* all aspects (legislative, judicial and executive) of governmental activity. He was above the law and could change it, but only *that law which he was empowered to enact*: civil law. And such law as he had authority to enact was necessarily devoid of wrong – because it was not natural law, because it was utilitarian in character, because its very nature was arbitrary and eternally subject to dispute, because, in short, it projected the need for will, not reason, if order were to be more securely established or maintained.

For Bodin, the prince was bound by covenants between himself and his subjects. These covenants the prince had no more right to break than his subjects. Laws were different from covenants, in the sense that the prince could be bound by the latter while it was impossible for him to be bound by a law of his own making. The prince was, of course, bound by *some* laws – by those that did not proceed from him, that did not receive their rightness and justice from him. Such laws were natural laws, as opposed to those that were civil or positive. As Bodin put the point, speaking of the oaths taken on the assumption of royal power: 'there is no royal obligation to keep the law, unless the failure to do so constitutes a denial of right [*droit*] or justice'.[1]

From an absolute point of view, Bodin neither stated nor implied that the sovereign could do no wrong. He could do no wrong only for as long as he operated within his sphere. What that sphere was, we have already discussed. It will now suffice to say that there is no necessary contradiction between the idea of the sovereign being absolute (in his sphere) and the idea that his power is (otherwise) limited. Contradiction is only absent, however, on the assumption that a clear line of demarcation can be established between those spheres where the sovereign's prerogative may and may not operate. Even geographical boundaries are subject to dispute. This is all the more true for boundaries that are purely legal and normative in character. In order to demarcate sovereign from non-sovereign authority, some referee is required to say when the boundary demarcated is or is not being violated. If the referee is the sovereign himself, there can be no guarantee that he will not stretch the law to suit his own needs, and in this case the distinction between sovereign and non-sovereign power becomes untenable. If the referee is some agent other than the sovereign, then such an agent necessarily has the power either to increase or restrict the range of royal power; and in so far as an external agent can do this, the sovereign cannot even be 'absolute' within its (his) own sphere since the supervisory agent is effectively empowered to say what that sphere is.

The limitations upon sovereign power which Bodin put forward were essentially logical and deductive in character. Bodin made a distinction between basic and non-basic law; between law that was and was not essential to the continuation of a political order; between law that was and was not fundamental; between law that was and was not

[1] 'Il n'y a aucune obligation de garder les loix, sinon que le droit & iustice le souffrira': *SLR*, p. 95.

constitutional. The sovereign, of course, did not materialise out of nothing. The polity which he governed evolved through time. Sovereign power, therefore, was as much created by, as it created, the state. Because the sovereign was only part (although the highest and most important part) of the state, he was in some degree a creature of its making, as was it of his. This did not imply equality, but merely mutual participation in a unique, a single, a unitary process of human association. For this reason, the sovereign could not merely act as he pleased, but his acts must be conditioned (and this means limited) by the total historical process in which he was only one, though the most important, participant. He issued laws governing the state, but behind the laws decreed were overs governing the very activity of declaring law. 'The Prince cannot infringe those laws, such as the Salic law, which concern the condition and very nature of the realm, in the degree that these laws are attached to and joined with the crown . . .'[1] The Salic laws, of course, governed the conditions of succession to the French throne. And Bodin argued that any laws passed by a ruler which prejudiced this succession could be thrown out by his successor.[2]

Bodin thought it necessary to extend the power of French kings to make new laws and break established customs. If the king, however, were strictly bound by existing law and custom, his authority would be severely curtailed. The king, on accession to the throne, did, of course, swear an oath before the ecclesiastical authority. But even where kings swore to support ancient laws and customs, 'the Prince can act contrary to the laws, or break and annul them, should they cease to be just'.[3] In the case of the kings of France, the oath sworn, according to Bodin, carried 'no obligation to keep either the laws and customs of the country, or of previous kings'.[4] Bodin cited in full the oath sworn by Philip I in 1058 along with other oaths of a similar kind. What he sought to draw attention to was the fact that, although such commitments were perfectly valid, they all carried formulae (equivalent to that of the American constitution's public welfare clause) which left the keeping of the law to the discretion of the prince in cases where it (the law) had become obsolete or created injustice. For what the prince

[1] 'Quant aux loix qui concernent l'estat du Royaume, & de l'establissement d'iceluy, d'autant qu'elles sont annexees & unies avec la couronne, le Prince n'y peut deroger, comme est la loy Salique . . .': SLR, p. 95.

[2] 'Tousiours le successeur peut casser ce qui aura esté faict au preiudice des loix Royales, & sur lesquelles est appuyé & fondé la maiesté souveraine': SLR, p. 95.

[3] 'Ie dy que nonobstant tous ces sermēts, le Prince souverain peut deroger aux loix, ou icelles casser & annuller, cessant la iustice d'icelles': SLR, p. 94.

[4] 'Aussi le serment de nos Rois . . . ne porte rien de garder les loix & coustumes du païs, ny des predecesseurs': SLR, p. 94.

promised to do essentially was to 'govern well and justly the subjects committed to my care' ('de gouverner bien et deuement li subiects commis en me garde', *SLR*, p. 95).

For Bodin, then, there was a real distinction between the fundamental law of the realm and that which was not fundamental. But he seemed to imply that much law, although thought to be fundamental, really was not; he certainly believed that much law that was not fundamental, despite long establishment, certainly was not just. The king's oath of allegiance to support the laws and customs of the realm rested on the assumption that these laws were just and equitable. Where, in fact, they were not, Bodin implied it to be the duty of the king not only *not* to enforce them, but to quash them. Thus, the prince was both above and below the law; in the first case, when it was civil and unjust, in the second when it was fundamental, natural and divine. The prince was obligated primarily to observe *jus*, not *lex*; *droit*, not *loy*; and because he was subordinate to the former, he was above the latter. And all this simply meant that he was only above that law which did not conflict with justice.

Bodin's argument ran more or less as follows: the prince must be just; therefore he is not strictly obligated to observe the civil (or positive or established) law. If he swears to uphold positive law, then either he is no sovereign or he will break his word. A magistrate or an officer cannot break the law laid down by the sovereign. And the sovereign cannot suffer the continued application of law which is unjust. The sovereign prince must break, change or correct positive laws according to the demands of the particular time and circumstance.[1] Bodin even went on to argue that should one attempt to prevent the prince from altering positive law, he would be encouraged not only to violate 'civil law, but also the laws of God and of nature, thus cumulatively [domino-like] ignoring the difference between them'.

It was inevitable for Bodin that a sovereign, in being above the law, should change the law out of the need to meet changing conditions and the dictates of justice. This was his duty; and if he were always and everywhere bound to observe the law, civil law, and preserve it as it stood, he would violate rather than fulfil his duty. In short, the prince was sworn not only to keep the law, but to promote justice, and where conflict occurred the concern with justice took precedence over the letter of the law.

---

[1] 'Mais il faut de deux choses l'une, c'est à sçavoir que le Prince qui iure de garder les loix civiles, ne soit pas souverain: ou bien qu'il est pariure s'il contrevient à son serment, comme il est necessaire que le Prince souverain y contrevienne, pour casser, ou changer, ou corriger, les loix selon l'exigence des cas, des temps, & des personnes . . .': *SLR*, p. 101.

In order clearly to state the limits within which the prince could and could not act, Bodin entered into a detailed discussion of law. Thus he would be able to say what law the prince could and could not command, and from that, what law the prince was or was not above. In effect, Bodin distinguished between laws which were (*a*) just, (*b*) neither just nor unjust, and (*c*) unjust. As usual, he stated the case far more elaborately. But that this was, in brief, his meaning is supported by the fact that Knolles's translation interpolated, as an integral part of the text, a clarifying sentence to this effect: 'for there be some things honest, some things dishonest, and some in a meane betwixt both' (*SLR*, p. 105). Bodin himself explained what he meant by 'honest' or 'honour': 'when I say honour, I mean what is honest by natural right'.[1] Those laws which were agreeing 'unto the equitie of nature' or in conformity with 'what is natural and right' were not inferior to the prince, but he to them. The limit of the sovereign's power was that it should not infringe *jus* or *droit*.[2] For natural justice was the command of God, and not the preserve of the sovereign.

Thus, according to Bodin the sovereign was absolute, but only within a given sphere; in respect of laws that were divine and natural he was himself subject. To 'divine and natural laws', he wrote, 'all the Princes of the earth are subject. It is not in their power to contravene them if they would avoid high treason, and war, against God. Beneath his grandeur all monarchs of the world must bear the yoke and bow their heads in fear and reverence.'[3] For Bodin, then, 'the absolute power of Princes and sovereign lords by no means extends to the laws of God and nature'.[4] Thus the sovereign could revoke ordinary or civil law (*droit ordinarire*) but not 'divine and natural law.'

Law, then, was either right or wrong or neither. If it was *right* – in itself or 'naturally' – it did not proceed from the prince but from God. As a command emanating from a source superior to the prince, the latter was bound by it. If a law was *wrong*, it not only did not proceed

---

[1] *SLR*, p. 105. Bodin's phrasing is as follows: 'quand ie dy l'honneur, i'entens ce qui est honneste de droit naturel . . .' My translation is quite literal, particularly in the case of *droit* as right. Knolles's version runs: 'And that I call honest, which is agreeing unto the equitie of nature' (p. 105); Tooley's: 'When I say honour, I mean that which conforms with what is natural and right' (p. 33).

[2] 'Cette puissance est absolue, & souveraine: car elle n'a autre condition que la loy de Dieu & de nature ne commande . . .': *SLR*, p. 89.

[3] 'Mais quant aux loix divines & naturelles, tous les Princes de la terre y sont subiects, & n'est pas en leur puissance d'y contrevenir, s'ils ne veulent estre coupables de leze maiesté divine, faisant guerre à Dieu, sous la grandeur duquel tous les Monarques du monde doyvent faire ioug, & baisser la teste en toute crainte & reverence': *SLR*, p. 92.

[4] 'Et par ainsi la puissance absolue des Princes & seigneuries souveraines, ne s'estend aucunement aux loix de Dieu & de nature . . .': *SLR*, p. 92.

from God, but opposed his will; and in such a case, the prince was, himself, bound to oppose it, and not to incorporate it into civil law. Finally, a law might be neither *right* nor *wrong*, in which case, it neither proceeded from nor opposed the will of God, and so either existed or was created at the discretion of the prince. In such cases, the prince was above the law, which was created or merely retained at his will. The prince equally created law in situations where all the choices before him were right, but conformed with varying degrees of usefulness.

Even, however, where the prince was above the law, his authority was not arbitrary for he was to be guided by (if one likes) the principle of utility. In any conflict between what was profitable and what was proper, the merely profitable must perish. But in situations where the choice was not between right and wrong but between the right conjoined with different degrees of utility, the prince should choose that law which was not only right but most useful. And in cases where the choices before the prince were all equally indifferent (morally) he should settle upon the option which conferred the greatest utility or benefit. It ought to be kept in mind that Bodin recognised a distinction between what the prince was bound to do and what he (merely) ought to do. He was *bound* to act in no way contrary to the will of God, i.e. contrary to natural right or divine justice. In other respects (that is, where natural right was not impugned) he either did or *should* act according to the dictates of utility. In the former case, subjects were bound by the will of God, in the latter by that of the prince. Bodin pointed out that subjects sometimes disobeyed their sovereign's laws on the grounds of a prior obligation to obey the laws of God. Such moves were generally dishonest or wrong. It was to be remembered, in any case, that it was 'a divine and natural law to obey the edicts and ordinances of him whom God has given power over us' (*SLR*, p. 106, l. 15). Still, the condition of such obedience was that these 'edicts not be directly contrary to the law of God, who is above all Princes' (*SLR*, p. 106, l. 16). Thus, the subject's right to disobey the prince clearly turned upon whether what the prince ordered was contrary to the law of God. Here arose a problem which Bodin was incapable of settling. For God commanded obedience to his laws, and one of these stipulated obedience to the prince; but the prince, nevertheless, could *de facto* issue commands contrary to other laws of God. In searching out one ultimate authority, Bodin threw up two; the subject, therefore, had no option, in cases of conflict, but to choose between them. It is not difficult to see that Bodin leaned, in principle, more towards one (obedience) than towards the other (conscience). All the same, his attempt to pinpoint *clearly* an ultimate locus of control, i.e. of obedience, failed. It is difficult to believe that any other result was possible. In the attempt to designate a particular will as the state's locus of control, he (understandably) found it impossible to say either that the sovereign should always be obeyed or that the sovereign should never be obeyed. Bodin suggested, in fact, that the sovereign should *almost always* be obeyed, but sometimes not. He further suggested that though the sovereign might occasionally be disobeyed, no subject could ever (justifiably) attempt to kill him. Let us now summarise the position.

For Bodin, the sovereign was the ultimate source of law; thus, he was not bound by it. Not to be bound by it meant that it did not apply to him and that he could change it at will. Nevertheless, Bodin distinguished between different types of law. Logically, there was the distinction between laws that were good, bad and indifferent. The sovereign's authority was absolute only in respect of laws indifferent. This distinction was matched by another between natural law and civil law. Only in respect of civil law was the sovereign absolute (*SLR*, p. 107, ll. 7ff.).

Natural law, in effect, embraced natural justice or divine law, and it emanated from God himself. Civil law, in effect, embraced Roman, canon and customary law, and either emanated from, or must be sanctioned by, the prince. The absolute power of the sovereign, involving the superiority of the latter over the law, was understood to be strictly confined to a specific sphere: 'absolute power', Bodin wrote, 'entails nothing more than superiority over civil law'.[1] It involved no control over the laws of God. Good laws were commanded by God, and bad laws were prohibited by him: these commands, either to act or forbear, were expressions of divine justice or natural law. Commands of neither sort fell properly under the control of the sovereign. They, strictly speaking, constituted the realm of civil law, in respect of which no clear decision about rightness or wrongness was available, and it was in such circumstances that the will of the sovereign must be accepted as the final, arbitral and directive principle of the state.[2]

Bodin's analysis, however, created an extraordinary tension in political theory. There was natural law, to which the sovereign was subject, and civil law, which he was above. He could break customary law; and he could subvert those elements in natural law that were not really 'natural'. If there were customs which the sovereign supposed to be unjust, he could break them – whether his inferiors thought them to be expressions of divine and natural law or not. This means that what was conventionally received as natural law might be demoted (at will) by the sovereign to the status of the non-natural, and thus quashed. This tension, therefore, which centres in the question 'How much authority is

[1] 'La puissance absolue n'est autre chose que la derogation aux loix civiles . . .': *SLR*, p. 108.
[2] See further appendix 2 below.

to be vested in the sovereign?' arises from the fact that there is no obvious line of demarcation between the civil law and the natural law;
no obvious distinction between what is conventionally right and what is
naturally right; between the will of God and that of the prince. Where
these distinctions weaken or fail, the result is that far more power is
conferred upon the sovereign than Bodin may have intended, or desired.

It is clear that Bodin appealed for a greater concentration of state
power. It may be misleading to suggest that he really wanted such
power to be 'absolute'; yet he himself so describes it. Certainly his
absolutism involves a demand for power concentrations greatly in
excess of what was in his time acceptable by ordinary men. His 'description' of sovereign power simultaneously involves an appeal for it.
There is nothing necessarily mistaken about an appeal to concentrate
more power at a given locus. The difficulty contained in Bodin's position primarily relates to its relative lack of limits, its tendency to appeal
unceasingly for further (if not strictly or consistently for *unlimited*) concentrations of power. It is true, as I have been at pains to show, that
Bodin wanted sovereign power to be regarded as subjected to divine
and natural law, as being guided by principles of public utility when not
subjected to such law, and as requiring passive disobedience by magistrates when conflicting with the laws of Divine Reason. But given the
difficulty of divining Divine Reason, and given that collective judicial
disobedience is virtually impossible to achieve anyway (and not necessarily effective when achieved), we must accept that Bodin in fact envisages no meaningful institutional limits being placed upon the operations of state power and in this sense qualifies as, and can appropriately
be labelled, an 'absolutist'. What we should note in this absolutist
tendency is the marked assumption that 'order' is some form of fixed
state which the conferment of ever-increasing power can somehow
achieve. In this sense, Bodin's 'description' of sovereignty partly constitutes what we might call an ideology of order.[1]

[1] See further appendix 4 below.

Chapter Eleven

The Sovereign: Analysis

ABSOLUTE POWER

Bodin insisted upon two vague but fundamental characteristics of sovereign power, understood in the most general way: that it was absolute and perpetual. He called sovereignty 'the absolute and perpetual power of a state'.[1] In the present analysis I shall treat perpetual power as a function of absolute power. In so far as any sovereign possesses an absolute power, this is probably most easily and meaningfully identifiable as the state's highest or 'greatest power of command'.[2] The state, for Bodin, consisted (minimally) in the good government of several distinct families from within, and in the regulation of matters of common concern between them by the sovereign. This could imply, therefore, that the sovereign had not the entire power of the state, but only that of one of its parts (the highest). All the same, the notion of an absolute power can imply far more than a highest and/or greatest power of command. It will be of interest to note the different possibilities involved.

The term 'absolute' can embrace such ideas as 'highest', 'greatest', 'total' and 'unlimited'. (One dimension of unlimited power is the time factor: thus 'perpetual' power.) These are distinct notions and their implications differ. Highest suggests the apex of an *order*, or of a hierarchy, of control. Greatest overlaps that meaning, but may also suggest a *limited*, if major, *quantity* of control. Total overlaps this idea in turn, as it contains the notion of a major quantity of control but adds to it the idea of a *complete quantity* of control. Unlimited control differs significantly from complete control: the latter implies that the potential objects of control (like the possible openings in a game of chess) are finite, while the former implies that the potential objects of control are infinite. Thus unlimited power may subsume the notion of complete control over an exhaustible series of acts, but it additionally implies further control over every possible, every conceivable, over a literally unending, series of acts.

---

[1] 'La souveraineté est la puissance absolue & perpetuelle d'une Republique': *SLR*, p. 85.
[2] 'La plus grande puissance de commander': *SLR*, p. 85.

All of these notions are not necessarily compatible with one another. One may exercise what is formally the highest power without exercising what is *de facto* the greatest power, and vice versa; and if one exercises either or both, it is not necessarily implied that one's power is more than partial – i.e. such power is not necessarily total or unlimited. One may exercise, at least formally, a total power, in the sense that one exercises a final authority over the entire range of governmental competences, but this is plainly not coincident with an unqualifiedly unlimited power. Finally, the possibility of exercising any form of unlimited power is more conspicuously doubtful than the possibility of exercising a highest, greatest or total power.

We may now explore these concepts in reverse order: we shall proceed from the general concern with (*a*) absolute power, to (*b*) temporally unlimited (perpetual) power, to (*c*) unlimited power generally, to (*d*) total power, to – finally – (*e*) a highest/greatest power. The assumption underlying this progression is that 'absolute power' is merely a framework concept whose content should accordingly be analysed from the perspective of an increasing empirical possibility of achievement. That is to say, it is less likely that an unlimited power can exist than a total, and less likely that a total power can exist than a highest or greatest power.

PERPETUAL POWER

There remained in Bodin a basic contradictory pull between the ideas of a highest and/or greatest power (*la plus grande puissance*), on the one hand, and the ideas of a total and/or unlimited power, on the other. The possession of a highest or greatest power implied limits, while the possession of total or unlimited power implied remarkably few or none. Bodin was inclined to suggest that sovereign power was the highest or greatest in the state, and thus limited. He was also inclined to suggest that sovereign power, within its sphere, within its limits, was total. But, finally, he was equally inclined to omit to say how any agent, other than the sovereign himself, could authoritatively say what those limits were.

We have already remarked that 'unlimited' does not quite equate with 'total'. For here we confront the difference between *infinite* and *all*. The latter suggests the possible exhaustion of a category, the former that the content of a category cannot be exhausted. If one understood Bodin to mean that the sovereign had total power, such an understanding would lead one to ask: in what respects, over what matters, governing which spheres? But if one understood that Bodin assigned to the sovereign unlimited power, there would be no occasion for queries: such a sovereign's authority must apply in whatever respects or spheres one thought or might think of. It would make no sense to make sure that *unlimited* control could operate in any sphere if it did not extend to all. A sheriff's authority, for example, can scarcely be described as boundless, however great it may prove, if he is not empowered to pursue felons across the boundaries of neighbouring counties.

Power may be regarded as unlimited in a number of respects. We noted that one of these, to which Bodin attached particular attention, was the temporal. At times Bodin appeared to suggest that the sovereign's power was unlimited in sphere and degree, in jurisdiction and extent – but also in time; in his words: 'sovereignty is unlimited in power, competence and time'.[1] This third characteristic has to do with perpetual power.

In discussing the character of perpetual power, Bodin had in mind two distinct concerns. One was to justify the right of a monarch to rule in perpetuity. The other was to show that the very idea of sovereign power, irrespective of its possessor, contained the implication that it existed in perpetuity. On the whole, he used the second argument to prove the first, providing a classic example of (what C. L. Stevenson has called) a persuasive definition. What Bodin meant, in arguing that sovereignty involved a perpetual power, could itself, however, be debated in perpetuity. For this reason we might do best to quote his own formulation and then inspect it more closely.

'I have said that this power is perpetual. For it may be conferred upon one or several persons for a certain period, at the end of which they are still subjects. Thus, even when in power, such persons cannot be called sovereign princes. For it is seen that they are no more than depositories and custodians of this power, since it can be revoked by the sovereign (whether Prince or people) whenever he wishes. A sovereign retains his power always. He who lends his goods to others remains the owner of them. And so it is with those who confer power and the authority to judge or command. Whether they confer their power for a specific period and in limited degree, or in unlimited degree and for so long as they wish, they retain their right to the power and jurisdiction which others are lent or permitted to exercise.'[2]

It seems that Bodin's main intention, in the above, was to argue that

[1] 'Or la souveraineté n'est limitee, ny en puissance, ny en charge, ny à certain temps': *SLR*, p. 86.

[2] 'I'ay dit que ceste puissance est perpetuelle: parce qu'il se peut qu'on donne puissance absolue à un ou plusieurs à certain temps, lequel expiré, ils ne sont plus rien que subiects: & tant qu'ils sont en puissance, ils ne se peuvent appeller Princes souverains, veu qu'ils ne sont que depositaires, & gardes de ceste puissance, iusques à ce qu'il plaise au peuple ou au Prince la revoquer: qui en demeure tousiours saisi: car tout ainsi que ceux qui accōmodent autruy de leurs biens, en demeurēt tousiours seigneurs, & possesseurs: ainsi est-il de ceux là qui donnent puissance, & autorité de iuger, ou commander: soit à certain temps &

no time limit could be placed upon the duration of a sovereign's rule, and that, if it were possible to do so, he who was restricted by this limit was no sovereign. In short, a sovereign ruler could not be restricted to a specific term of office; and if a ruler were so restricted, he was subordinate to the restricter, who was sovereign. This position could be put somewhat differently, but to the same effect: no sovereign's rule can be revoked by another agent in the state; if a ruler's authority can be revoked he is not sovereign, but subordinate to the revoker, who is sovereign. Bodin's argument that sovereign power could not be restricted in *duration* (as distinct, for example, from *quantity*) appears in practice to have meant little more than that the executive ought to be appointed for life and that his office should be hereditary: in the circumstances of his time there are concrete arguments, not wholly ridiculous, which one could have advanced to support such a position. Bodin so inflates the position, however, that he sins by excess. Hence the argument that sovereignty involves a 'perpetual power'.

What Bodin *basically* meant by perpetual power seems clear. How he meant to argue his case in detail seems less clear. We are compelled to resort to conjecture: what he may well have intended was to *deduce* the characteristic of perpetual power from that of unlimited power. If we assumed that it was possible for an agent to wield an absolutely unlimited power, then it would naturally follow that such power would also encompass the idea of its infinite duration, which is but one dimension (the temporal) of illimitability. Assuming that one agent can possess a power which is – in every sense – unlimited, it can clearly be deduced from this that such an agent possesses a power perpetual. Bodin does not explicitly advance this entailment, but it is not unreasonable to think that he may have intended it.

One obvious and general difficulty, however, relating to the attribution of any form of *unlimited* power to a *limited* agent (whether single or collective) is the apparent inconsistency of attributing infinite power to a finite being. This difficulty would attach of course to the notion of a finite power being capable of unlimited duration.

Another difficulty in the notion of sovereign power being perpetual – where 'perpetual' describes a power or authority which continues unending through time – is that such perpetuity could only be regarded as an essential characteristic of sovereignty at the expense of demonstrating that sovereignty never did, does not, and never could, exist. It is clear, from an empirical point of view, that no sovereign need ever have continued unending through time, or (historically) ever did. Where one

limité, soit tant & si long temps qu'il leur plaira, ils demeurent neantmoins saisis de la puissance & iurisdiction, que les autres exercent par forme de prest ou de precaire': *SLR*, p. 85.

incorporates into the meaning of sovereignty the idea that it exists in perpetuity, the term becomes empty since it is robbed of any sphere of application. States are destroyed by other states; they disintegrate; they integrate; rulers are replaced by other rulers; distinct types of sovereign are replaced by other types of sovereign. To insist that sovereign power exists forever is merely to insist that the term 'sovereign' never be used to refer to any actual state at all.

Bodin, however, was aware of at least some of the difficulties peculiar to the argument that only the holder of *perpetual* power is sovereign. Since kings die, and lines of kings cease, it would seem somewhat absurd, even to Bodin, to argue that to be sovereign a king must never die. 'One must therefore understand by this word perpetual, the life of him who has power.'[1] This qualification makes Bodin's abstract insistence upon perpetuity more intelligible. It merely means, as already suggested, that Bodin believed that rulers should receive or be granted office for life; he also believed that they should be able to appoint their successors, as a rule following an hereditary principle. All the same, Bodin says too much about perpetuity in general and loose terms to be permitted to escape censure so easily. It must doubtless have impressed him as being more admirable to construct an argument which favoured 'perpetual' power than to restrict himself to the more concrete and less impenetrable argument that sovereigns should have power for life, conjoined with the right to dispose of the succession. Because scholars have taken his stipulations about perpetuity seriously, considerable time and effort have been lavished upon refuting him. We need only reply as we have already done: no power, whether of an individual or of a group, has existed in perpetuity. Further, since perpetuity includes the past, it becomes logically impossible, equally, that any future sovereign could ever *become* perpetual. This impossibility is, of course, distinct from the *improbability* that any state which now exists, or any future state which comes into being, will so continue without end. For it is scarcely necessary to remark that kings die, that lines of kings end, that monarchies, aristocracies and democracies supersede one another, and in no unvarying order, and are sometimes superseded by nothing at all. Thus one cannot say that sovereign power exists, and assert at the same time that it necessarily exists in perpetuity.

Formally speaking, Bodin very probably meant to argue that from the fact that X (understood as a monarchy, aristocracy or democracy: i.e. as a type of sovereign, not a person) *ceases to be* a 'sovereign', it follows that X *never was* a sovereign. If so, such a move constitutes a *non sequitur par excellence*. To see more clearly that this is so, the posi-

[1] 'Il faut donc entendre ce mot perpetuel, pour la vie de celuy qui a la puissance': *SLR*, p. 88.

tion attributed to Bodin may be distinguished from one which we may correctly attribute to Hobbes. The latter argued that the sovereign, to be a sovereign, must wield virtually unrestricted power, failing which he *ceases to be* sovereign. Bodin's argument, in respect of unlimited duration, was that a sovereign, to be a sovereign, must exercise perpetual power, failing which he *never was* a sovereign. Such a concept of sovereignty, it will again be seen, robs the notion of any possible sphere of application. Suffice it to say that the more meaningful notion of a greatest or highest power in the state does not, of course, entail that such power must have no limit in time.

Bodin's formal argument (that the highest and greatest power in the state is perpetual) and the different empirical and logical props it might be made to rest upon are shaky in the extreme. The illogic of the position is indeed so transparent that we might suggest a psychological reason for it being advanced in the first place – this stemming perhaps from a (sometimes blinding) desire to defend monarchical right.

UNLIMITED POWER

Bodin's position as to whether sovereign power was or was not unlimited always remained confused. His general formulations in respect of absolute and perpetual power prejudiced the extensive qualifications he later placed upon them. He was so immensely inconsistent, at least *formally*, that his position makes little sense until one takes his qualifications as constituting a more carefully tailored statement of what he really intends. Then one can interpret the general formulae as broad attempts to encapsulate more specific truths. This, however, is to treat Bodin rather gently, more so certainly than have most of his critics, more so perhaps than is even proper; for it involves paying rather less critical attention to certain of the sillier and more exaggerated assertions that he made.

Bodin said that the sovereign was (in some sense) absolute and yet (in another sense) not so. Students of political thought are aware that Bodin was concerned with the character of absolute power. They are less often aware that he remarked that he considered its exercise impossible. Although Bodin argued for some sort of absolute power, he nonetheless advanced the opposing case, with approval, in the following terms: 'For if we say that he has absolute power who is not subject to the law, no such Prince can anywhere be found, given that all Princes in the world are subject to the laws of God and of nature and to many human laws which are common to all peoples.'[1] Absolute power, in this context, relates to some generally unlimited form of power. Again, in

[1] 'Car si nous disons que celuy a puissance absolue, qui n'est point subiect aux loix, il ne se trouvera Prince au monde souverain, veu que tous les Princes de la

this context, it is plain that Bodin is disavowing the possibility that such a generally unlimited power might exist. Here, however, we run up against the question as to whether Bodin saw himself as describing an empirical/logical impossibility, or effectively recommending some form of moral self-restraint upon authority. It is certain that he was doing the latter; it is less certain to what extent he was doing the former. It is certain that he thought of a sovereign agent as one wielding at least a highest and greatest power in the state, and that no such agent should regard himself as free to behave in a manner morally unrestrained or unlimited. It is less certain to what extent he conceived of a sovereign agent, if truly sovereign, as being in fact limited in respect of the powers which he actually wielded. On the whole, Bodin was far more inclined merely to advise the sovereign not to go too far than to attempt to devise institutional means by which sovereign abuse of power could be checked.

Bodin's difficulty regarding unlimited power was peculiar neither to himself nor to his cause. The simple but fundamental difficulty involved was exaggeration. Bodin advocated the extension of royal power; but he formulated and became identified with the idea of an unlimited state power. Acton desired caution in the surrender of power to government; but he became identified with the notion that power is evil and, through this, with the cause of strictly limited government. Absolutists and pluralists are equally concerned with the question how much centralisation there ought to be. Bodin and Hobbes ask for more; Tocqueville and Acton ask for less. These demands cannot be assessed in the abstract. But there is a tendency to do so where they are abstractly formulated (and often even where they are not). The absolutist usually argues that sovereign power is or should be *unlimited*, the pluralist that it is or should be *limited*. Their universal arguments against specific evils or abuses are rarely helpful or relevant.

It is illogical to argue for unlimited power, since such a thing is impossible. It is superfluous to argue for limited power, since all power is limited. There might be good reason, under certain circumstances, to increase control, and, under others, to decrease control – sometimes in depth, sometimes in breadth. Where one argues in specific cases for an increase or decrease of control at a given centre, one enjoys the advantage that such formulae are difficult to universalise, that their applicability is necessarily restricted in time and space.

However, specific recommendations (and the arguments which support them) can never serve as complete substitutes for the theoretical frameworks within which they must be located. A basic theory or model of state structure, of what a state is, must serve as a form of limiting

terre sont subiects aux loix de Dieu, & de nature, & à plusieurs loix humaines communes à tous peuples': *SLR*, p. 91.

condition upon all recommendations regarding what such an entity should become. If, for example, we conclude that the highest power wielded in a community (by the government) *is* necessarily limited, then we can no longer meaningfully *recommend* that state power be either unlimited or limited. If we are confronted with abuses, we can see – from the fact that abuse may be occasioned as much by the distribution as by the concentration of power – that any universal recommendation urging either is worse than useless. The case must be more carefully investigated and the proposed solution more precisely formulated.

TOTAL POWER

Bodin conceived of absolute power (sovereignty) as involving some species of total power, of *toute puissance*. This concept was certainly related in some way to his ideas about unlimited power. We noted that he spoke of sovereignty not being limited in power or competence or time: 'la souveraineté n'est limitee, ny en puissance, ny en charge, ny à certain temps'. We have already discussed the unlimited time – or perpetual power – factor. We have also had something to say about the notion of unlimited power generally. In Bodin there is no express separation of total power from unlimited power and where we make the distinction we must ourselves assume the responsibility for doing so. There are various reasons which we need not review for dismissing the notion of unlimited power. But Bodin's argument for sovereignty being unlimited in power (*puissance*) or competence (*charge*) can be reinterpreted as an argument for at least two distinct types of *total* power: one in sphere, the other in degree. If we keep in mind the notion of 'total' as implying finiteness and 'unlimited' as implying infinity, then we can conclude that *perpetual* power has more to do with an unlimited than with a total power. We shall now interpret spheres and degrees of power as involving 'total' spheres and degrees of power and see what conclusions we come to.

Bodin appeared to suggest that sovereign power involved some species of total control both in *sphere* and *degree*. The distinction here, if one likes, is between horizontal range (competence or *charge*) and vertical depth (power or *puissance*). As between (*a*) sphere and (*b*) degree of control, Bodin did not establish and maintain a truly clear distinction; but a distinction between the two is important. For although a ruler may exercise ultimate control in every jurisdictional sphere (and in this sense wield a total range of power), no ruler can exercise an unlimited degree of control within every sphere (since this would imply – among other things – that his power was equal to that of an entire hierarchy, which a ruler's power can never be).

(1) There is no need to discuss at length the idea of sovereign power implying a total range of control. A sovereign's power can be total in the sense that he – as a single or collective agent – *exercises control over every governmental sphere*. There is no need to quibble about the word unlimited, but it must be said – as regards spheres of control – that no agent's power, strictly speaking, can be unlimited, in so far as the number of jurisdictional spheres in government is accepted as limited. Given that the number of such spheres is limited, then control over them can be made total. Thus a ruling agent can be said to have total power in the sense that any type of problem arising at any point or time within a defined organisational unit can be referred to that agent for final decision.

(2) A ruler, however, cannot exercise a total depth or *degree* of control over any community. A community must contain at least two or more individuals. A control function consists in the issuance of instructions or rules and obedience being rendered to those instructions or rules. Given that the issuance of rules, etc., is not identical with their acceptance, there can be no way of guaranteeing that all that is ordered will be obeyed. Given a further physical and spatial distinction between the person or persons issuing a rule and the other or others complying with it, most of what is actually done by subjects cannot be read as any form of response to orders issued by rulers. A total degree or depth of control is impossible, minimally because total supervision is impossible.

(3) If we now take sphere (or range) of control together with degree (or depth) or control, we may conclude that although a range of control (assuming it to be limited) may be total, the degree or depth of control exercised cannot be. A sovereign may wield a *total* range of control combined with an *intensive* degree of control, of course – but only within a very small community. To rule alone and effectively in a small community is possible. To rule without the assistance of others in a large community, however, means that virtually nothing is done. Thus it often happens that the more concentrated (in sphere and degree) a ruling agent's power becomes, the less effective it becomes; and vice versa, that power often becomes more effective as it becomes more diffused or shared.

Although a ruling agent's power, on one level (range), may become total in a small community, on no level and in no community can it be regarded as unlimited. The actual spheres of control are limited. *Complete* control over them, therefore, is also limited. Further, since items of control are unlimited in potential degree or depth or intensity of control, no limited agent – which every ruling element is – can totally or illimitably control them in degree, depth or intensity. No one rules forever. No sovereign can do everything that might be done. Even were the availability of time unlimited (infinite), what can be accomplished by one agent is not. Where a sovereign governs through officials his power is limited. Where he governs without officials his power is limited. Although a ruler may not require subordinates to implement his orders, he will always require subjects to obey them. And obedience cannot be guaranteed. It is never absolute, or given unconditionally, illimitably, or irrespective of the ruler's behaviour, or irrespective of the subjects' needs or desires. And, in any event, the power of a limited being (as we have noted) cannot be unlimited and the power of a part of a hierarchy – even the highest – cannot be identical with that of the whole.

If an agent exerts a particular (a maximum) quantum of power through a hierarchy, which power is distributed along horizontal as well as vertical axes of control, then any extension in range of control is paralleled by a decrease in depth of control, and any intension in depth of control is matched by a decrease in range of control. At the same time, narrow range does not *entail* intense depth of control, and shallow depth does not *entail* a broad range of control. In short, assuming a ruler to be operating at maximum capacity, any extension of his authority implies less intension, while greater intension implies less extension.

Every head of state and every parliamentary body probably recognises that there is a maximal effort of which he or they are capable. If an individual's labour never ended, that individual's life very soon would. Even if one – whether an individual or a group – worked always as hard as possible, all extension of control could only be won at the expense of its depth within particular spheres, and vice versa. Concern with one matter distracts from another. The sole eyes and ears of the king would rarely suffice to keep him king. Where he *needs* officials, the need of itself implies limitations upon his ability to control them. As his control is selective, not total, limited, not unlimited, partial, not whole, his power is not that of the state but merely that of a part of the state. It is in this sense that sovereign depth of control is necessarily limited, most especially and obviously where we are dealing with an individual rather than with a collective sovereign.

At this stage we have now formulated fairly precisely the idea that sovereign rule in breadth (range) can be complete, but that sovereign rule in depth (degree or intensity) cannot. If the actual spheres of power are limited, the potential degree of control that can be exercised within each such sphere is not. Thus a complete range of control means simultaneously fairly shallow depth of control. Since potential items of control (in depth) within a single sphere are unlimited, then complete or unlimited vertical control in any given sphere is unattainable. Total horizontal control over all (i.e. a limited set of) spheres of power is formally possible, but we may now remark that it is also in practice, or *de facto*, selective. Total vertical control over any given sphere of power is impossible and therefore *formally* or *necessarily* selective. Since in practice rule always combines breadth with depth, since both are on different levels selective, both are in fact limited, and no power or authority in general can be held to be total.

Most of the remarks made about the character of rule where exercised by a single individual will equally apply to any form of collective or collegial government. Any ruling element that can be differentiated from the ruled may wield a total power in the sense that the entire range of competences, every distinct sphere of control, is concentrated in that element. Total power in this sense, referring as it does to a range of competences, is necessarily limited since the range of competences involved is limited. It is only in this sense that an 'absolute' monarch or a 'sovereign' legislature may wield total power.

The *degree* of control which any sovereign exercises, however, cannot be total. A sovereign may exercise total control over all distinct spheres of government only because there is a limited number of such spheres and only because the control exercised over each is merely ultimate or final (rather than total). But a sovereign cannot exercise total control in depth (a total degree of control) over every or any sphere of governmental activity. A sovereign, whether individual or plural, cannot exercise total control in depth because the sovereign is not coincident with the subject(s). Since every agent, whether individual or plural, sovereign or subject, represents a distinct but continuing centre of activity, there is a necessary time-lag – equivalent to a control-gap – between the initiation of a proposal and its communication (and acceptance). Further, the member or members of every ruling element must also attend to their own affairs, which reduces the time available to direct the affairs of others. Also, every agent, whether sovereign or subject, is a source of initiatives, and also a respondent thereto, which means that the formal sovereign is constantly and necessarily modifying his own initiatives in response to those of citizens or subjects (again implying that the ruling element never exercises a total depth or degree of control). Finally, of course, the initiatives of any sovereign or ruling element can always, quite simply, be rejected: where potential rejection remains, no total (degree of) control obtains.

It is one thing to describe a controlling element as all-powerful; it is another to recommend that it become so. An ideology of order, where it recommends that a ruling element become all-powerful, must assume not only that such a development is desirable but that it is possible. Power can be concentrated in one or a few hands, in the sense that final authority in all spheres of government may be delegated to one or a small group of persons. But total power cannot be concentrated in one or a few hands, in the sense that a sovereign can exercise complete control over all the activities of all persons who may qualify as subjects or citizens. Where the power of a governing agent can be increased in scope and/or depth, it is logically possible, with entire consistency, to recommend such increases. The actual spheres of power, however, are limited in number, while the potential degrees of power are not. Where an ideology of order calls for a concentration of all jurisdictions or spheres in one centre, the thing is possible. Where it calls for a concentration of all *degrees* of power in one centre, the possibility disappears. Given that the actual exercise of power combines both spheres and degrees, total power, in the broadest sense, cannot be achieved. Consequently, it cannot be described, nor can it, with consistency, be recommended. It is not unnatural, however, for the impossible not to be recognised as such, and in these circumstances to be recommended. The recommendation for total power can always be read, in any historical context, as a minimal recommendation for the attribution of *greater* power to some specific centre or agent. It can also be read as recommending as great a concentration of power *as possible* at some specific point.

THE HIGHEST AND GREATEST POWER

In the discussion of absolute power, Bodin definitely meant that he who possessed it was (*a*) superior in status to all other persons and agents in the state, and (*b*) superior in quantitative power to any other person or agent in the state. Thus we come to Bodin's conception of sovereignty as the highest and greatest power in the state. Bodin, however, did not distinguish between these two ideas, although the distinction is indispensable. In fact, he covered both of these notions with the term 'la plus grande puissance', which literally means the greatest power but may also suggest the highest. Although the two ideas were not identical, there is no doubt that Bodin believed, in respect of sovereign power, that they were inseparable. Their conflation may be seen as the source of certain of his analytical difficulties.

Bodin was particularly interested in the relation between superiors and inferiors. Looking at the matter afresh, we can see that if we failed, like Bodin, to keep in mind the difference between, let us say, *status* and *influence*, the general conclusions which he drew, regarding the logic of relations between superiors and inferiors, would prove valid. The difficulty is that one may easily have the *highest* status within a community without necessarily enjoying the *greatest* influence.

To begin, it may be well to recall Bodin's formulation of the nature of absolute power, suggestive as it is of Hobbes's contractualism. 'For the people or lords of a state can bestow sovereign and perpetual power upon someone purely and simply that he may freely dispose of goods, persons and of the entire state, and also leave it to whomever he chooses. It is in this way that an owner can quite simply give away his property, and from no other reason than generosity. For such is the nature of a true gift that, once bestowed, it bears no conditions, since things given upon condition are not really given. So it is with sovereignty, that if given to a Prince conditionally, it is not given at all, except for those conditions which attach to the very creation of the Prince, whether derived from the laws of God or of nature.'[1]

The suggestions contained in this declaration are manifold. My immediate concern lies with its hierarchical implications. To begin, the sovereign was to be regarded as sovereign of right. (In a later discussion of tyranny, however, Bodin also suggested that a sovereign could be such against right.) He who was sovereign was so absolutely. This meant nothing more than that no one else could dictate to him or otherwise tell him what he must do. From this point, Bodin's position becomes unclear. Obviously, if anarchy is not desirable, it is a bad thing should anyone at all be able to tell a ruler what to do or to check his initiatives at will. On the other hand, if official licence is not desirable, it would be a bad thing for a ruler to be able to take whatever initiatives he wished. It is between these reefs that Bodin had to steer; given the dilemma, he was more aware of the first danger than of the second. Thus, Bodin stressed the point that the sovereign wielded power as of right (and by right) and that right (consent) and might (force) made him superior to all other persons or agents in the state.

From this rough-hewn view of sovereign superiority Bodin drew certain conclusions. He did not state them formally, but one can grasp the logic of his position from the following argument: 'If absolute power, as conferred upon the Prince's lieutenant, were called sovereignty, it could be used against the Prince, which he would no longer be except in name. The subject would command his lord, the servant his master. This thing would be absurd, given that the sovereign's person is, in law

---

[1] 'Car le peuple ou les seigneurs d'une République peuvent donner purement & simplement la puissance souveraine & perpetuelle à quelqu'un, pour disposer de biens, des personnes, & de tout l'estat à son plaisir, & puis le laisser à q il voudra, & tout ainsi que le proprietaire peut donner son bien purement & simplement, sans autre cause que de sa liberalité, qui est la vraye donation: & qui ne reçoit plus de condition, estant une fois parfaicte & accomplie: attendu que les autres donations qui porte charges & conditions, ne sont pas vrayes donations: aussi la souveraineté donnee à un Prince sous charges & conditions n'est pas proprement souveraineté, ny puissance absolue: si ce n'est que les conditions apposees en la creation du Prince, soyent de la loy de Dieu ou de nature': *SLR*, p. 89.

[*droit*], beyond the reach of that power and authority he gives to others. For however much power he gives, he always holds more. And of command and supervision he is never deprived, whether he exercises it by veto or by concurrence, or by issuing summons, or by whatever means he pleases, as regards the responsibilities he has laid upon his officials, both high and low . . .'[1]

In the above is to be found the partly distilled logic of sovereign power, as processed by Bodin. The basic idea was that the greatest power in the state was superior to that of every other person or agent. The analysis which supports this notion did not, properly speaking, constitute either a recommendation or a statement of fact; rather, it was a model of analysis. It offered a skeletal outline, or classificatory model, of actual political relations. Bodin, of course, also used this model persuasively, to suggest that a *monarch* should be sovereign.

To Bodin, it was *absurd* to think (*a*) that an inferior could *wield more power* than a superior, (*b*) that an inferior could *act against* his prince, (*c*) that an inferior could actually *check the initiatives* of his lord, (*d*) that an inferior could *overthrow* his lord, and (*e*) that a subject could *replace* his sovereign. These conclusions are purely logical in character, but one can readily appreciate their persuasive force. Persuasion apart, and assuming a conflation of status with influence, all of these assertions carry logical force. It is only if one recognises that superiority may connote status or influence or both together (and not necessarily this last alone) that one can see that an inferior (in status) might (in fact) wield more power than a superior, or act against him, or check his initiatives, or, indeed overthrow and replace him. In short, as superior influence does not necessarily accompany superior status, and vice versa, it cannot be said that an agent who is superior in certain respects is necessarily superior in others; thus in this matter Bodin's conclusions are not logically watertight.

CONCLUSION

Bodin's general case was awkward. He described the basic character of government in terms both of a conciliar and a despotic principle. It is in this sense that he partakes of both pluralism and absolutism. His

[1] 'Si la puissance absolue, ottoyee au Lieutenant du Prince, s'appelloit souveraineté, il en pourroit user envers son Prince, q ne seroit plus qu'un chiffre, & le subiect cômanderoit au seigneur, le serviteur au maistre: chose qui seroit absurde, attendu que la personne du souverain est tousiours exceptee en termes de droit, quelque puissance & auctorité qu'il donne à autruy: & n'en donne iamais tant, qu'il n'en retienne tousiours davantage: & n'est iamais exclus de commander, ou de congnoistre par prevention, ou concurrence, ou evocation, ou ainsi qu'il luy plaira des causes dont il a chargé son subiect, soit commissaire,

pluralism is architected as a medieval hierarchy of groups, but almost all of which Bodin regards as requiring to fall more fully under state control. He regarded the family head and state sovereign as largely despotic, by contrast with the private corporate body which was essentially conciliar. His normative aim, perhaps, was primarily to make intermediate (or 'private corporate') bodies more susceptible to sovereign control, on the assumption that the family, in the form it then assumed, presented no particular obstacle to sovereign control and stable government. The more fundamental question here, however, is whether, on the descriptive level, Bodin's insight into the general nature of control operating in human organisation is coherent. We can see in the case, for example, of the contrast between sovereign control and private corporate control that it is not.

Bodin's work is not impressively consistent. He attempts nonetheless to achieve a basic, factual characterisation of the nature of rule, particularly sovereign rule. He attributes to sovereignty at one time or another, with greater or less coherence, a variety of features. The most fundamental of these is the notion of its being 'absolute'. We have seen that the notion of absolute power contains a number of possible implications, such that it is a perpetual, unlimited, total, highest and/or greatest power. We have analysed these concepts in ascending order of tenability. That is to say, we have assumed it to be more likely that one could wield a highest and/or greatest power than a total power; that the latter is more likely than an unlimited power; that an unlimited power either seems less obviously absurd than a perpetual power, or merely that the latter can be regarded as the temporal dimension of unlimited power. Our general conclusion is that a ruling element cannot be regarded as wielding an absolute power where this means that such power is perpetual, unlimited or total. But a ruling element can be regarded as wielding an absolute power where this means that it is the highest or the greatest power in a society, organisation, state, or whatever. In this last case, however, the distinction between a highest and greatest power, considered as a distinction between formal status and actual influence, is crucial.

I suggest that a hidden argumentative, normative assumption contained in Bodin's view of *la plus grande puissance* in the state is that that authority which is formally highest should be conceded an actual influence equal to its formal status. Bodin was obviously inclined to regard formal authority as holding a state or society together, and to believe that where such authority could not fall back upon a substantive

ou officier: auxquels il peut oster la puissance qui leur est attribuee, en vertu de leur commission, ou institution: ou la tenir en souffrance tant, & si longuement qu'il luy plaira': *SLR*, p. 85.

influence, there was a grave threat to the preservation of order – the order in question being that projected, of course, by the existing formal hierarchy. In this we discover a very early form of the domino theory: take away one item, and everything else collapses.

This form of domino theory in politics only works, of course, on the assumption that any socio-political system is or can be supported by only one of its elements. Where this is true, however, it is reasonable to suggest that such a system, *qua* system, scarcely exists at all. For this to be intelligible, we must be clear as to what we mean by a system. A system can be defined as constituting some form of norm-governed relationship between its members. A system exists where the sharing of a rule or rules creates a community among two or more persons. Minimally, we might say that a society, system or organisation exists where at least one rule can be taken as shared among certain individuals. But one rule always implies more. Thus an 'order' always refers to a complex of behaviour within which individuals are related to one another in some patterned fashion. The 'order' requires one rule, the one will imply another – or others – and it is impossible to establish a limit upon the number of rules an order will contain.

What we normally think of as an 'order' or system or society does not, of course, have only one rule, but often hundreds and even hundreds of thousands of rules. A sporting association (including the rules of the game), a business, a university or a government as a whole will display a surprisingly large number of rules. To change any one rule in any such system may indeed require adjustments in many of the other rules governing it, but it is difficult to imagine that the removal or adjustment of any one rule could equate with, or empirically produce, the collapse of the system as a whole. It is difficult to suppose that a system so complex and involuted as a society or state might ever collapse. However much we may speak of coups, revolutions and decay, *collapse* is always an inappropriate synonym. What we are more concerned with in any social plenum is the juggling of elements, sometimes the exclusion of elements, but not with the destruction of the plenum itself. Since the number of rules that are actually changed in a given society are almost always and necessarily a small percentage of those that actually obtain, it will prove useful to pay closer attention to *which* rules have been, are being, or are desired to be changed, and rather less attention to the question whether the alteration of those particular rules will equate with the *destruction* of the society as such.

A writer like Bodin seeks to concentrate as much power as possible in as few hands as possible. But the domino theory of systems maintenance which underlies this approach is misleading and inappropriate. An order simply consists in the sharing of a larger or smaller number of rules. Since no systems are in fact bound together by only one rule, since it would seem logically impossible exhaustively to tabulate the number of rules underlying any system, and since few challenges to governmental systems either do or effectively can challenge all or even a majority of those rules which have been explicitly projected, then virtually no prospective change of a rule, or non-observance of a rule, can be equated with an undermining of the system *per se*. Order exists where certain rules are complied with. The rules which such an order can contain are innumerable. It is only where *all* rules are overturned (not observed) that one can speak of disorder *per se*. Since that never happens in reality, any reference to disorder must be more precisely formulated as non-compliance with some particular norm or norms contained in the existing order.

Since the impingement of human individuals upon one another virtually always constitutes some kind of order, it is less appropriate to fear disorder *per se* than to inquire into the nature and desirability of the actual order that exists. Order cannot, of course, simply be read as involving the exclusion of violence. Every existing governmental order at some point sanctions the use of violence. If an order *per se* is not necessarily upset by governmentally sanctioned violence, then we need not suppose that it is necessarily upset by non-governmentally sanctioned violence. There is disorder where rules of some description are not complied with. But in every order innumerable rules are not complied with. In any event, since many rules may be evil, much disorder may be good. Any form of order is not necessarily good and all forms of disorder are not necessarily bad.

The ideology of order, as in Bodin, might simply be equated with the notion of concentrating as much power in as few hands as possible. This view is not an unreasonable one. The difficulty is that it appears to clash with a pluralist position which demands as great a diffusion of power as possible. However much diffusion of power there is within a given system, the difficulty arises when one stipulates that some particular rule or set of arrangements is to be defended at all costs. In general, this is what the demand for 'order first' reduces to. It does not mean that the system as a whole is being defended for the system in part is always undergoing change. It only means that some particular part of the system should not be allowed to change. And many proponents of this view will often be prepared to concentrate quite as much power as they can to secure that such change is not carried out.

Disorder is always specific and it means that specific norms are not being complied with. The 'order first' principle intends that as much power should be concentrated and as much force should be used as is necessary to achieve compliance with that specific norm (or norms) which is (or are) not being observed. One is normally disposed to think of the absolutist position as being maximalist and of the pluralist position as being minimalist in regard to the concentration of power or force. But the priority-of-order position, which we may initially assign to absolutism, can and often does surface – however inconsistently – under pluralism. For where the pluralist adopts a priority-of-order position, and in this identifies the maintenance of the entire system with one of its parts, and consequently prepares to defend this conception of the system by whatever means and with whatever force necessary, then the recommendatory position reached is this: go as far as you need in the use of force, up to and including execution, to punish infractions of some of the existing rules, on the assumption that this will preserve the existing order as a whole. This is another way of suggesting the propriety of concentrating as much power as one requires, and sometimes deploying it as ruthlessly as one desires, to defend some particular concept of 'order'.

PART FOUR

DAWN OF THE ABSOLUTIST STATE: THOMAS HOBBES

'I finished a book in my native idiom . . . From the press in London it sped to neighbour regions. Its name was *Leviathan*. That book now fights for all Kings and for all those who exercise the rights of Kings.'
Hobbes, *Autobiography*.

'For every man is desirous of what is good for him, and shuns what is evil, but chiefly the chiefest of natural evils, which is death; and this he doth by a certain impulsion of nature, no less than that whereby a stone moves downward.'
Hobbes, *De Cive*.

'If a man . . . must sometimes do by the commonwealth's order what he knows to be repugnant to reason, that harm is far compensated by the good, which he derives from the existence of a civil state. For it is reason's own law to choose the less of two evils; and accordingly we may conclude, that no one is acting against the dictate of his own reason, so far as he does what by the law of the commonwealth is to be done.'
Spinoza, *Tractatus Politicus*.

Chapter Twelve

Hobbesian Overview: Facts and Norms

Both Bodin and Hobbes were concerned with, and frightened by, the prospect of civil war. If an harmonious society was the ideal, then the least desirable society was one hung upon civil dissent and internal conflict. The problem was to determine how to avoid such conflict, how to ensure against it. But the answer to this must lead into a discussion of the causes of conflict; and the delineation of these causes must in turn be tied to an understanding of what an ordered society or state really is, how it operates, of what it is constituted.

Hobbes wished to show that good government is strong government, that any established government is best, that competing authorities are bad, that subjects should obey their sovereigns, and so on. He invokes and elaborates upon various arguments to prove these points. My purpose is to attempt to set aside moral considerations and scrutinise exclusively the manner in which Hobbes understands the factual nature of social and political structure, to see *how far* these factual considerations can be divorced from the ethical, to detect weaknesses, and to dismiss (where necessary) merely apparent, but unreal, weaknesses.

In *Behemoth*[1] Hobbes was directly concerned with the causes of 'the civil wars of England ... that were carried on from the year 1640 to the year 1660'. He puts forward seven reasons for these wars, which may summarily be stated – in reverse order – as (7) the ignorance and gullibility of the people; (6) the scheming of ambitious men who had either lost or desired a fortune and sought this through war; (5) the unpatriotic inclinations of merchants who believed the end of monarchy would bring an increase in trade and wealth; (4) the election to the Commons of eloquent men, intoxicated by the Graeco-Roman example of popular government, which they wanted to see established in England; (3) the

[1] Thomas Hobbes of Malmesbury (1588–1679) published his first book – a translation of Thucydides – in 1629. He wrote five major works of political analysis. *The Elements of Law* was completed by 1640 but never published. *De Give* appeared in 1642, *De Corpore Politico* (derived from *The Elements of Law*) in 1650, *Leviathan* in 1651, and *Behemoth* in 1679. His English works (11 vols, 1839–45) and his Latin works (5 vols, 1839–45) were edited by William Molesworth.

religious dissension of sects such as the Independents, Quakers and Anabaptists, who claimed for themselves 'private interpretation of the Scripture'; (2) the claims which Papists laid upon secular power; and (1) the similar claims laid by Presbyterians upon this power.[1]

Reason 7 (since it is constant in all societies) was not so crucial: 'The common people have been, and always will be, ignorant of their duty to the public.'[2] Nor was reason 6 crucial, since ambition (like ignorance) is also constant (ambition for power): 'it is the desire of most men to bear rule'.[3] Similarly, the greed of merchantmen is timeless: 'London, you know, has a great belly';[4] but businessmen (he implies) must be taught to see that the exactions of a republic are no less onerous than those of a monarchy.

It is only reasons 1 to 4 that are really important to Hobbes. And these ultimately reduce to two. The first is the desire by several bodies to share sovereign power (causes 1 and 2). The second is the desire by individuals and sects for free expression of religious and political opinions (causes 3 and 4). The free and irresponsible expression of opinion and competition for office constituted, in Hobbes's view, the chief impediments to civil peace. Ignorance, ambitious scheming and greed were important. But what was most important was the unchecked promulgation of seditious notions together with the attempt to limit or subtract from the plenitude of sovereign power. Thus the cause of civil disturbances in general was the absence of a truly sovereign power, and the essential function of a sovereign power (essential to the keeping of peace) was to state what opinions were or were not seditious, what rules were or were not lawful, and to possess a monopoly of force sufficient to ensure that inadmissible opinions were not disseminated and that rules declared to be law were not ignored.

Such is the indicative content of Hobbes's analysis. It consists in the assertion that every ordered (or 'well'-ordered) state features a central figure or body wielding a complete monopoly of force, and that it is free to use, and must use, this force to thwart the expression of opinions whose circulation might lead to unrest. In the *De Cive* and in *Leviathan* Hobbes tried to show that in every ordered state there is no more than one source of legal power; that that source is only sovereign to the extent that it is granted obedience by the people; that it is able to fall back upon force where that obedience is withdrawn or turns into hostility; that it is only sovereign to the extent that it is regarded as the sole arbiter of

---

[1] Sir William Molesworth (ed.), *The English Works of Thomas Hobbes* (London, 1839–45), vol. 6, pp. 167–9 (or *Behemoth*, pt 1).

[2] *Ibid.*, p. 212.

[3] *Ibid.*, p. 404.

[4] *Ibid.*, p. 292.

doctrinal and religious truth; and that no subordinate individual or group can be permitted to speak against the sovereign's pronouncements (without danger of civil war). We need only remark now upon the difficulty of testing these propositions until it is shown, minimally, whether they are to be taken factually or normatively – or, indeed, as purely logical statements derived from more basic axioms or principles.

Now, from even the most cursory appraisal it becomes plain that Hobbes's argument contains factual, normative and logical elements. The problem is to determine the relationship between these elements. Hobbes is of considerable interest because he is one of the first important political philosophers to begin his analysis, not with a statement regarding the nature of man's duty, but with a statement regarding the character of man's nature. He begins, in short, or appears to begin, with an *is* rather than with an *ought*. His argument is so devised as to suggest that the 'ought' somehow flows from the 'is': given that men *are* of such and such a character, they *ought* to act in such and such a way. This implies that what ought to be done is ultimately dictated less by God or the sovereign than by Nature. Our nature encapsulates a primal fact, and we must act in such a way as to harmonise with that fact. The primary 'fact' to which Hobbes draws our attention is this: men have a fundamental urge, he says, to preserve themselves, to avoid violent death, to live in peace and security. And it is upon this 'fact' that he somehow builds the conclusion that men ought or must obey a single and exclusive sovereign, general obedience to whom can usually be expected to yield (to those obeying) security and protection.

This statement of the position raises the question whether one can meaningfully deduce an ought from an is, a norm from a fact; and, also, whether and to what extent Hobbes made such a deduction. I accept as elementary logic that one cannot legitimately deduce a norm from a fact. They may be, and some facts and norms always are, *related*; but they are never related in the strict sense that one entails and can be deduced from the other. From the fact that I wish to preserve myself it does not follow that I should; from the fact that I seek peace (or revenge) it does not follow that I ought to; from the fact that a boy is determined to steal it does not 'follow' morally that he 'must'. This negative position is matched by a positive one, namely, that only from one fact can another be deduced; and, equally, that only a norm can entail another norm. It is only where my inclination to preserve myself or turn the other cheek or seek revenge or thieve is judged apt or good or *right* that I may possibly deduce the notion of my being *obligated* to adopt some means of doing these things.

If, therefore, Hobbes was *deducing* a norm from a fact, in the above sense, he would have to be judged seriously mistaken. Further, if he were so mistaken, and could not otherwise be defended, the logical infrastructure of his state would actually collapse (of its own illogical weight). Macpherson has made an elaborate attempt to rescue Hobbes's system from this tragic *dénouement*. One agrees that such an outcome is by all means to be avoided. But Macpherson's lifeline has to be rejected because it requires that we now regard Moore's 'naturalistic fallacy' as being itself fallacious. What Macpherson demands, in short, is that we accept that Hobbes *did* deduce norm from fact, and, further, that *Hobbes's* deduction be regarded as valid. And yet one must hold to the illogicality of such a deduction, no matter whose it is.[1] Macpherson attempts to strengthen his defence with the argument that Hobbes's society was of such a kind (extremely competitive, contentious and materialistic) that his conclusions as regards the recognition of an all-powerful sovereign were particularly appropriate: society being what it was (or being conceived as Hobbes conceived it), it should be governed as Hobbes stated. But this does not help us much, since it only takes us back to the statement that, 'from "f" fact, Hobbes derives "n" norm'. It really does not matter whether the fact (the picture of human nature), although false in some universal sense, is possibly true in some more local sense (for seventeenth-century English society). What is still asserted, and what must still be rejected, is the propriety of deriving a norm from a fact.

It is as well to remark that Hobbes, like every writer, made various unstated assumptions which affect the intelligibility of what he said. The exploration of such assumptions can be invaluable, although there are certain limits upon how far it can usefully proceed; it is in its nature to lead into logically swampy territory of an infinitely regressive kind: for since every statement is based on assumptions, then every statement of assumptions will imply still further assumptions. It must also be recognised that too great an obsession with assumed but unstated social conditions can easily lead us to believe that the writer under review, whoever he chanced to be, was more concerned with those limited and unstated social conditions than with what he himself (often consciously) regarded as a universal problem and even as a universal solution to the

---

[1] See C. B. Macpherson, *The Political Theory of Possessive Individualism: Hobbes to Locke* (Oxford, 1962). Macpherson concedes 'that on the model of formal calculi, moral utterances cannot be entailed in factual statements' (p. 82), although this slightly mis-states the point, which is that moral statements cannot be logically deduced from factual statements (whatever the model). That 'oughts' are often stated as 'facts' in ordinary language, and are often *disguised* as such on a higher, philosophical level, does not really damage this conclusion. Thus, when Macpherson argues that Hobbes's '*deduction* [my italics] of obligation from fact may be allowed to be valid' (p. 87), what he says is mistaken and misleading, as well as unnecessary.

problem. Hobbes was largely provoked to write as he did by the civil war: the universality of the style was built around this particularly of content; his desperate view of human nature, conceived as grasping, aggressive and self-interested, was no doubt influenced by those circumstances, as also by the growth of new economic relations of a capitalistic kind. But despite all this, we must remember that Hobbes was concerned to make a fundamental political point which he regarded as being of universal application: that man's nature is essentially such as to require in every society a superlatively powerful sovereign to keep him at peace with his fellows. We can recognise at once the exaggeration, which is a source of error, and which was largely inspired by a perception of local difficulties; but we must also leave room for exaggeration and error occasioned by the very attempt to lift perception beyond those local difficulties and to understand the functioning of human society from some higher, even universal, perspective, in the hope that the understanding obtained in one context can be activated in another (which is almost always likely to be mistaken in some particular). Indeed, if Hobbes had not projected a more universal concern it is very unlikely that contemporary writers would show such extraordinary interest in his work. On this point we must accept the common-sense of Oakeshott's judgement: 'the masterpiece, at least, is always the revelation of the universal predicament in the local and transitory mischief'.[1] In Hobbes we are concerned with a writer who made a passionate attempt to thrust beyond the particular to the general, from the transitory to the universal.

It is now necessary for us to retrace our steps. Hobbes's argument is so constructed as (often) to give the impression that the relationship he establishes between 'is' and 'ought' is deductive – involving a movement from what human nature is like to how human beings ought to be governed. I have suggested that, if this relationship *is* deductive – as there is certainly some evidence for thinking he saw it to be, and as Macpherson has argued that in some sense it is – Hobbes's conclusions must simply collapse. I have argued that this will follow, no matter what we say about the accuracy of Hobbes's facts or the extent of their applicability. I have also argued that although an awareness of a writer's unstated historical, social and economic assumptions can be enlightening, they should not always be emphasised to the extent of suggesting that these particular assumptions eliminate the universality of his concern either to explain or resolve some aspect of the human condition; that a writer's times, and his understanding of them, will always limit his outlook, although it does not follow that one ought necessarily to attempt to limit the validity of his point to his own times.

[1] Michael Oakeshott, Introduction to *Leviathan* (Oxford, 1955), p. xi.

What I have not discussed, however, is whether Hobbes can really be said to have been guilty of committing the naturalistic fallacy, to have deduced 'ought' from 'is'.

On one level, Hobbes would deserve to be charged with the fallacy: for he clearly suggests that one can deduce from man's nature his duty to the state. The question, however, is whether there is an alternative interpretation of Hobbes's argument, as plausible as that interpretation which accuses him of the fallacy, but which leaves his logic basically unimpaired. Following this line, one might argue, as I do now, that whether or not Hobbes *deduced* his norm from his facts, the latter already disguised a norm, from which a second norm was, in effect, derived. Hobbes certainly *attempted* to deduce a norm from a set of facts (in which he was mistaken), but he simultaneously derived a norm from a norm (which, in principle, is a legitimate procedure). Hobbes's basic mistake, therefore, arose from disguising, both from himself and his readers, the underlying norm – the rightness of self-preservation – which shaped the selection of his facts (about human nature).

To say that Hobbes derived a norm from a norm does not necessarily say anything about the nature of the first norm from which the second is drawn. It does not say that the higher norm is represented by, for example, God or a contract. Hobbes does suggest, of course, that one has a duty to perform an act if one has, in some way, consented to do it; that one is obliged to act in such and such a way, if God has, somehow, willed it. But the real question is, in the former case, why should one in the first place consent to perform a particular act ? and in the latter case, how does one reliably elicit the will of God ? Hobbes's suggestion is clearly that one should consent to do that which preserves oneself. His further suggestion is that what is universally so is willed by God; and thus that man's universal motivation towards self-preservation is willed by God. After a point it becomes futile to continue asking whence the first norm – positing the good of self-preservation – was derived. The essential point is that it is there. Man should *consent* to act in such a way as to preserve himself. He should also do what God wills. Since what God wills is expressed in Hobbes's interpretation of what is true about human nature, then man is additionally commanded *by God* to preserve himself. But this is only another way of saying that God as well as man approves of self-preservation; or possibly that God approves of self-preservation *because* man does; whence we may conclude that Hobbes, as one of these men, regarded self-preservation not only as a *desired*, but as a *desirable*, good.

It is not enough to say that Hobbes believed men to be guided essentially by the motive of self-preservation. One must see that he regarded it as *proper* that they should be. It was perfectly plain to Hobbes that many people do not seek to preserve themselves – else why should there be suicides ? A man who kills himself can scarcely be said to *preserve* himself. Thus, to a person on the verge of leaping from the Empire State Building, it makes far more sense, logically, to argue that he *ought* not to do it, than that, in the act of leaping, his intention cannot really be to destroy himself. Of course, for a person to be told that he does not, cannot want to destroy himself, that his soul goes marching on even when the body is still, that the purpose of life is living and so forth – such a marshalling of facts or putative facts may have an overpowering psychological effect. But these 'facts' cannot expunge an even more basic fact: that all such statements are essentially intended to persuade him not to leap, on the obvious assumption that he *ought* not to do so. Similarly, Hobbes is not merely saying that men do seek to preserve themselves (he could see as easily as we that some do not); he is also assuming that they ought to, that they are right to do so (for virtually everyone is in a position to decide whether he shall live or die). It would be unnecessary for Hobbes to render this assumption explicit, for the simple reason that most of his readers, then and now, would agree with it, and not require to be persuaded on the point. And it is only from the assumption that men *ought* to preserve themselves (the first norm) that one can deduce that they must take the necessary steps thereto (the second norm).

Of course, Hobbes might object, as he does, that anyone who kills himself is mad: bringing to mind the coroner's customary 'explanation' in cases of suicide that the act was committed while 'the balance' of the agent's mind was 'disturbed'; the clear assumption being that anyone who commits suicide is necessarily deranged. The proof of derangement, however, is built into the definition of the act; the derangement is not a matter to be investigated. For Hobbes, a suicide was mad by definition, since the only *sane* (i.e. right and proper) thing was to preserve oneself. If, no matter what one does, the observer always contends that one's act stems from self-preserving motives (Hobbes) – it might be from economic motives (Marx) or from sexual motives (Freud) – his contention can only be regarded as trivial, since there is no way in which he will allow the matter to be tested. But there is another consideration. And this is that such a closed understanding is as likely to express a *moral* commitment as an hypothesis about the facts. I am suggesting that the closed circularity attaching to Hobbes's basic understanding of human nature (as inspired by self-preserving motives) was more definitional than hypothetical; and that his commitment to it flowed as much from supposing that the motive was acceptable as from supposing it to be universally present – or true.

In objection to the above, it might be argued that Hobbes, in regarding his view as correct, need never have regarded the situation he described as *desirable*. This is certainly true. Hobbes regarded the human motive towards self-preservation as a universal fact (barring mental aberrations) and took it to be undesirable in certain of its manifestations. To accept this, however, implies no contradiction in the analysis so far: Hobbes thought the drive towards human self-preservation desirable, and also undesirable – in neither case universally, but in respect of different aspects of its manifestations. The drive towards human self-preservation was undesirable in so far as it led towards war, instability, collapse of order. It was desirable in so far as it was rationally directed to avoid such chaos. The objectionable and immoral man, for Hobbes, was not one who sought to preserve himself, but one who, through vainglory, narrow greed, selfishness and gross miscalculation, aborted his own end and that of every other. We need not carry this further; only one point requires to be driven home: human self-preservation, *when rationally pursued*, was regarded by Hobbes as desirable. Because it could not be achieved if irrationally pursued, it can be assumed that only *effective* human self-preservation, for Hobbes, was desirable. It is because this was *desirable* (proper, right, fitting, etc.) that Hobbes could conclude that his solution *ought* to be adopted: there was, he believed, no other means of actually achieving the desired end.

It is not from the 'fact' that men attempt to preserve themselves that Hobbes deduces they should; rather, it is from the assumption that they ought to do so effectively that he concludes they should take up his solution. Thus, from the very start we are dealing with Hobbesian assumptions about what men ought to do, and not merely with assertions about what they are like. It is largely because the norm ('preserve thyself') lay from the start in the Hobbesian description of human nature that it is so difficult to trace the *source* of political obligation in his work. The source of the norm is another norm – except that the source-norm is not explicit and therefore remains unargued. Accordingly, speculation has continued over a number of years regarding the manner in which Hobbes derives a duty to obey the sovereign. Is the duty to obey derived from force, consent, self-interest, divine command, natural reason or some combination of these? Numerous writers have commented on the matter, the more interesting among them being Taylor, Warrender, Strauss, Oakeshott, Brown, Krook, Macpherson, Goldsmith and Watkins. It is impossible here to do justice to the views they have expressed. To do so would defeat the object of my purpose, which is to discuss Hobbes's views regarding what the state is, not what it *ought* to be, except in so far as the second question significantly impinges upon the first. Thus, although something more must be said here about Hobbes on obligation, it would be irrelevant to say much more.[1]

Among all of these interpretations, that advanced by Watkins seems to me to be most nearly correct (as regards our immediate concern). Following Kant, Watkins distinguishes between categorical imperatives and hypothetical imperatives. The first are acts that are good in themselves, the second are acts that are necessary to achieve a given end, whether actual or merely possible, whether good or bad. An act that is prescribed as the practically necessary means to achieve an actual end is called an 'assertoric hypothetical imperative', and Watkins suggests that Hobbes's normative argument may be so labelled. This means that Hobbes, in Watkins's view, assumed that the basic aim shared by all humans is that of self-preservation; that this aim is not merely one that they might, but one that they do, share; that recognition of, and obedience to, the sovereign is the practically necessary means of achieving it; and therefore that this means *ought* to be (not necessarily *will* be) followed.[2] I accept this interpretation. Its only defect, in respect of the previous discussion, derives from an ambiguity: does Hobbes regard the end (self-preservation) as desirable, good; or merely as actual, a fact? The interpretation just advanced provides no answer to this question. But the answer, as previously suggested, is not difficult to find. To the extent that Hobbes believed that all men aim at self-preservation, he, being a man, must be included in their number; therefore Hobbes impliedly aimed at self-preservation. This conclusion is, of course, reinforced by Hobbes's commitment to the notion of generalising from one's own motives to those of other men. But what does it mean to cite as a 'fact' the 'fact' that Hobbes (as implied in his own argument) aimed at self-preservation? It can only mean that he thought it *right* or *fitting* or *proper* that he should be so motivated. For Hobbes to *describe* his motivation is merely to present, in a disguised and non-argumentative form, a key element in his *morality*. Once more we can see that Hobbes's means-norm (regarding obedience to the sovereign) is derived from a logically higher norm (his personal commitment to self-preservation as a justifiable end of human activity). Now it will be possible to state the logic of Hobbes's position far more clearly than before: 'I (Hobbes) am motivated by the desire to preserve myself; this is fitting and justifiable; and certainly no different from the motives of other men; as all men share this aim and fundamentally think it right, they must be logically compelled to recognise and adopt such means as will achieve it, which we can only do by rendering virtually entire obedience to a mutually recognised sovereign.'

[1] For further comment on the source of political obligation in Hobbes see appendix 5 below.
[2] J. W. N. Watkins, *Hobbes's System of Ideas* (London, 1965), pp. 82–3.

It may be useful to draw the reader's attention to one moral flowing from this discussion. Political theories always involve assumptions, explicit or otherwise, regarding human nature. Sometimes these assumptions are stated explicitly and in universal terms – as in the case of Hobbes's notion of the self-preserving motivation of human activity. Where such statements are made, however, it has to be recognised that, since they are universal in character, they subsume (by implication) the motives or character of the person making them; and to *describe* one's own personal motives is simultaneously to take an *ethical* stance. The moral, consequently, is this: where any writer states what he takes to be the universal facts of human nature, always understand him to be talking about his own commitments and acceptances as well as about the supposed ends of others. Further, where he attributes such ends to all men, he will often be disguising or concealing, deliberately or subconsciously, his own personal inclinations and motives. From this it does not necessarily follow that it is 'wrong', either morally or intellectually, to make universal statements about human nature; it is simply necessary to recognise that such statements are likely to conceal an ethic, especially that of the propounder. A moral for the writer is this: try also not to expand such statements (about human nature) to the point where they are simply identified in an uncritical fashion with those shared by 'everyone else'. If Hobbes had done the first of these things, he might have avoided the second, and he would certainly have made it far easier to understand the recommendatory or normative logic of his argument (the derivation of norm from norm).

One final item ought to be taken up before continuing with this general review of Hobbes's position. I argue that Hobbes does not deduce an 'ought' from an 'is' (or a norm from a fact). The question that now arises, however, is whether and in what sense it is even possible to deduce an 'ought' from an 'ought' (or a norm from a norm). The position taken here is that the deduction of one norm from another is sometimes as illegitimate as deducing a norm from a fact. Let us take two quite different types of norm (or imperative) to illustrate the deductive illegitimacy referred to.

We might say, for example: one should never steal. We might also say something like: *X* should reach the British Museum as quickly as possible. In the first case one may cite the rule (Never steal), provide a concrete instance of an act that would contravene the rule (making off with the child in the pram) and deduce that the latter act ought not to be executed (Do not make off with the child in the pram). Such a deductive procedure is quite straightforward, providing a clear example of one norm (or imperative) being strictly entailed by or deduced from another. But let us examine the second case. To begin with, the rule appears to have too limited a range of application to be called a 'rule'; we might better speak of it as an 'injunction' or 'imperative' instead ('rules' may be regarded as 'imperatives' of a more general kind). In this case, we may cite the injunction (X to reach the British Museum as quickly as possible), instance a programme of action that will subserve the injunction (run? take a taxi? commandeer a car? ignore traffic lights? proceed along route A? or B? or C?, etc.) and 'deduce' that that programme of action should be carried out. I write 'deduce' because the form of deduction that obtains in the second case is certainly not the same as that in the first.

I am not here concerned to make any sort of exhaustive statement about the different types of normative 'deduction' that it is possible to make. The elementary point to be established is merely that there are different types. For our purposes it is convenient to distinguish between *universal norms* (e.g. the prohibition on theft), which subsume a variety of concrete cases, and *end-norms* (e.g. the injunction to proceed most expeditiously to B) which require the application of some means if the end projected is to be served. In the case of universal norms, the deduction of what we ought (or ought not) to do is relatively simple – because the concrete cases to which universal norms refer are almost always easily recognised. In the case of end-norms, the 'deduction' of what we ought (or ought not) to do is both practically and theoretically far more complex – because the middle term, the concrete case, appears virtually nowhere to be a sole and exclusive means of achieving the projected end-norm. When we accept that we ought not to steal, we are not required to choose between different acts of theft: all are excluded as illegitimate, and one may deduce that indulging in any such act (certified to be an act of theft) is wrong. But when we accept, for example, that we ought to move from A to B (as quickly as possible or otherwise), we are virtually always confronted with a number of obviously distinct and *mutually exclusive* choices, any one of which might satisfy the end, but no one of which could be regarded as being entailed by the end. In almost all cases we know what it is to steal, so that if we are enjoined not to steal we almost always know concretely what it is we are enjoined not to do. But if we are enjoined to achieve a specific end in the most expeditious manner possible, it is always empirically difficult – perhaps theoretically impossible – to assume that any given procedure will necessarily satisfy the end projected better than any other possible means that we might devise or later find ourselves presented with.

From an end-norm, to which is attributed an overriding importance, one can only deduce *that* it ought to be realised, one cannot deduce specifically *how* it ought to be realised. One could of course deduce how an end ought to be realised if one could prove that there was *only one way* of realising it. But to *prove* that there was only one means of achieving an end would involve demonstrating not only the inadequacy of those possibilities that had occurred to one, but equally the inadequacy of (presumably unnumbered) possibilities which had not. This would certainly seem to be impossible.

In this discussion of end-norms, we are in no way concerned with the problem of competing ends. This raises a very different sort of problem. One might, for example, project two ends – one the early capture of a town, another the protection of the lives of the citizens inhabiting the town. But the early capture of the town might involve the sacrifice of many lives, while the protection of these lives might delay the town's capitulation. This is a very commonplace type of moral conflict, where the decision regarding concretely appropriate action is complicated by virtue of the potentially and actually contradictory character of the ends which we wish or are compelled to serve.

If we direct our attention to some specific and uncontradicted end-norm (not to the more complex phenomenon of parallel and possibly inconsistent end-norms), what we usually note, immediately, is that there appear to be different ways of achieving the end projected. If the requirements incorporated into the end are rendered more precise (not merely to go to the Museum, but *as quickly as possible*), there may still be *different* means (different routes, procedures, forms of transport) which will nonetheless satisfy the same end. To deduce a specific means from a given end we must demonstrate that the means in question is the only means possible. (I have already said that it would seem to be logically impossible for us to satisfy such a demand.)

The point of this discussion is to suggest that we cannot 'deduce' a means from an end. It is one thing to say that a particular means can in fact achieve a given end. It is another matter to say that it is the sole means available to achieve that end. As long as one cannot say that a particular means is exclusively necessary to achieve a given end, one cannot deduce the former from the latter. As long as there is a variety of means available to achieve a given end, as long as these means are genuinely and materially different from one another, then the distinct character which each exhibits, the distinct consequences which each sets in train, cannot be indiscriminately attributed to the initial end to which each such means may be related. If the means as a whole, in its character and in its consequences, cannot be shown to be exclusively and distinctly *necessary* for the achievement of the end, then the one is in no way *deduced* from the other. For to accept the end is *not* to accept the means, but only that there be a means.

An essential point about any means is that it is only a possibility. It is impossible ever to prove that a particular possibility is the only possibility capable of achieving a given end. It is impossible to show that *no* other possibility could have done the same: for one most certainly cannot prove a negative. It happens, of course, that one runs out of ideas. In such circumstances one may understandably plead that, in pitching upon a particular possibility, a particular means, this was the only possibility or means *which occurred to one*, or that it seemed to be the best among a variety *which occurred to one*. But we may reasonably assume that the means which occur to one are not coextensive with all the means, even the best means, that might possibly be devised.

Means-norms are various. No exclusivity of possibility ever attaches to them. They are culled from imagination; they are simultaneously hammered out of fact. And it is because they are so ephemeral in quality, a material so difficult to work, that we often concede that 'the end justifies the means'. This formula, which appears so logical, is, however, only a lazy man's conclusion. He who wills the end assumes *some* means. He who justifies the end assumes *some* means. But because the means must always be assumed to be multiple and mutually inconsistent, it can never be said that the acceptance of an end *entails* some specific, related means. The formula which stipulates that 'the end *justifies* the means' is logically mistaken in so far as 'justifies' implies 'entails'. Ends do not *entail* specified means: to suppose that they do merely betrays a want of imagination. We can never prove that a particular means is the only possible means; we cannot *deduce* a specific means from a general end; we can only conclude that the projection of an end entails nothing more than the general requirement that there be a means. In so far as it is clear that no specific means can be deduced from any particular end, we may say that means are *related* to ends rather than *deduced* from them. It will suffice to say that 'relating' has a looser sense than 'deducing'. *Deduction* implies an exclusive entailment, *relation* suggests variable connections with something other. A means is not logically contained in, and deducible from, the end; it has merely an empirical relationship to it.

To some, Hobbes appeared to have deduced a norm from a fact. From the proposition that men *in fact* seek to preserve themselves, conjoined with the proposition that the establishment of an all-powerful sovereign was the sole means of doing this, he concluded that men *ought* to establish such a sovereign. Such a procedure, in so far as it actually involves the deduction of a norm from a fact, is certainly indefensible. It in no way follows that, because men *do* seek to preserve themselves, they *ought* to – whatever the means one might project to achieve such an end. If Hobbes is read as having deduced a norm from a fact, and this deduction is taken to be central to his argument, then – on such a reading – his argument must collapse. I have suggested, however, that what we discover, on investigating the matter more closely, is that Hobbes can be read – both more generously and more plausibly – as having merely concealed a norm within a fact, and therefore as having deduced a norm from a norm. Hobbes most probably assumed, on the factual level, that men *usually do* seek to preserve themselves. By contrast, he clearly appears to have assumed, on the normative level, that men *always ought* to seek to preserve themselves. It is only on this assumption, of course, i.e. that men *ought* to seek to preserve themselves, that one can deduce that they *ought* to fashion some means by which this might be done. Whatever *means* Hobbes might produce to achieve this end could only be regarded, for our purposes, as being related to, rather than deduced from, the end (or end-norm) initially posited (or assumed).

In Hobbes, however, there emerges some suggestion that he actually saw himself to be *deducing* a means from an end, or the means from the end. This is because he places considerable stress on the notion that the means which he improvises (virtually total obedience to a sovereign) enjoys an exclusive claim to securing the projected end (individual self-preservation). Although it is perfectly legitimate for Hobbes to deduce from the desirability of self-preservation the consequential desirability of *some* means of achieving such preservation, he certainly cannot *deduce* any means in particular of achieving it. In so far as he assumes that his end 'justifies' his means, in so far as he assumes that his singular means is 'entailed' by his end, he is simply mistaken.

So much can be said on a purely theoretical level, with no need whatever to look at the 'evidence': for, as we have stated, one cannot demonstrate a negative; one cannot ever prove that there exist no other possibilities (or means) besides that one or those few which one has oneself thought up or merely recognised. But we need not leave the matter there, since, as it happens, more can also be said on a purely practical level, without ignoring the 'evidence'. For, as we shall have occasion to argue in the final chapter, although a state may secure considerable peace (and security) where subjects are completely obedient, a state may also secure considerable peace where citizens are consulted and rulers are more fully and continuously responsive to their wants and needs. In short, complete obedience may be one means of attaining security; but it is plain that representative and responsible government is equally a means of attaining security. And in so far as these are distinct and even incompatible means of achieving the goal of self-preservation, neither of them can ever be regarded as being exclusively 'entailed' or 'justified' by the end in question. The demand for security, in short, does not necessarily lead us into a commitment to absolutism.

It is of course conceivable that all men might wish to preserve them-

HOBBESIAN OVERVIEW: FACTS AND NORMS

selves. But it is obvious from the fact of suicide, war, inordinate risk-taking and the like, that men are at least as much committed to living in a certain way or ways as they are committed to living *per se*. It is similarly conceivable that all men ought to wish to preserve themselves. But it is obvious that there are very often strong arguments for surrendering one's life when set against the surrender of honour or integrity or justice or even a satisfactory sense of purpose in living. In any event, assuming that I want and *ought* to preserve myself, it can only be deduced that I ought to seek some means of doing this; it cannot be deduced that I ought specifically to seek peace (if I am always a pacifist I may be unable to preserve myself) or that I ought specifically to obey my sovereign (he may wish to destroy me – as Hobbes admits) and so on. Hobbes argues from the good of self-preservation to the good of peace to the good of an all-powerful sovereign to preserve the peace (implying the good of virtually total obedience to the sovereign, without which he could not be all-powerful). It is not necessary to rehearse considerations of the invalidity of this argument; it is only necessary to point out that it is not constructed around a train of deductions, however much Hobbes would like to persuade the reader that it is 'logically' watertight; for, as suggested earlier, we cannot deduce an exclusive or specific means from an end; we cannot *prove* the non-existence or impossibility of all alternative means. Thus, when we are confronted with the argument that Hobbes is *necessarily* right if his premises are once conceded, we must recognise this to be simply an empty argument. Hobbes can only demonstrate that absolutism is (sometimes) *a* means to self-preservation (which he cannot demonstrate purely deductively); he cannot prove that it is *the only* means thereto. It was the only means *that occurred to him*.

The primary concern of this analysis is with the indicative content of Hobbes's understanding of politics; with what he thought it is about, not what it ought to be about; with the objective character of political order, not with ideal projections of that order; with the universal facts (if there be any) of political life, less with the norms by which it might be guided. Hobbes is especially amenable to this sort of indicative analysis because he made such a clean break with obviously moral formulae: he sought expressly either to exclude such formulae or somehow to objectify them, put them on a level with the sciences; his prior commitment, especially in *Leviathan*, appeared to be to determine what man's nature simply is, not what it should be. And yet we are already in a position to see how impossible this divorce really is. Hobbes appears to be simply concerned with facts, and yet his facts are shaped by norms. He appears to deduce norms from facts, while really deriving duty from an already existing concept of *right* conduct. Indeed, when we push our consideration of the matter far enough, we may even conclude, aptly and logically, that Hobbes's major concern, that which frames and renders coherent his factual analysis, is the question: how should the state be constructed? how should politics be conducted? When we pare Hobbes's logic down to the core, it becomes apparent that he is a moral universalist, who attempts to persuade men to a course of action in the most ruthlessly intellectual manner open to him. The primary question that he tries to answer for all of us, against the backdrop of civil war, past and present, is whether we *ought* to obey the state. His answer to this question is unequivocably affirmative. His analysis attempts to demonstrate why that obedience should be virtually unlimited, why it is that one agent's will should be accepted as unquestionably binding upon the wills of others, why a strict hierarchy of command and obedience is necessary and should be accepted. The concern with whether and why we ought to obey the state is peculiar to both Bodin and Hobbes. In Hobbes it constitutes merely one aspect of a more general moral problem: what criterion will permit us, universally, to distinguish between right and wrong. Hobbes believes that it is more or less universally right to obey the sovereign, the state. Thus he considers it important not only to show men what state structure is, but to convince them by reference to the 'facts' of self-preservation that they ought to accept the state and obey its agents. This is the reflection, within the sphere of politics, of Hobbes's general concern with a universal criterion of proper conduct. For he believed 'that which is clearly wanting [in books on ethics and politics] is a true and certain rule of our actions, by which we might know whether that we undertake be just or unjust'.[1] And what he wanted to do was to supply such a criterion in respect of political obedience.

It was inevitable that something be said about the connection between facts and norms in Hobbes. It is not my principal intention, despite this, to embark upon another analysis of Hobbes's theory of political obligation; nor to lay bare his theological presuppositions, nor to give an overall account of his thought, nor to explain the continuity between the metaphysical and practical aspects of his thought, nor really to set that thought against the background of political developments in Hobbes's own and later times (although something has been said about this in chapter 4). All of these things have in some degree been done before.[2] It is not surprising, perhaps, that no one has at-

---

[1] Molesworth, vol. I, pp. 9–10 (*The Elements of Philosophy* or *De Corpore Politico*, I, I, 7).

[1] See, in the following order: H. Warrender, *The Political Philosophy of Hobbes: His Theory of Obligation* (Oxford, 1957); F. C. Hood, *The Divine Politics of Thomas Hobbes: An Interpretation of Leviathan* (Oxford, 1964);

tempted to disengage in any degree of detail Hobbes's views on the general and/or universal facts about politics given the considerable dependence, on reflection, of the latter upon his values. Nonetheless, that is what we are about to pursue here, since it may prove instructive in determining how much of a disengagement we can achieve.

M. M. Goldsmith, *Hobbes's Science of Politics* (Columbia, 1966); Watkins, *Hobbes's System of Ideas*; S. I. Mintz, *The Hunting of Leviathan* (Cambridge, 1962).

Chapter Thirteen

Hobbesian Overview: Family and State

The first thing we shall do, although briefly, is direct our attention to Hobbes's conception of the origin and evolution of the state. This is not a crucial question, but it is fairly germane simply because Hobbes is a contractualist, and builds upon this his general theory of state structure. (There is hardly any excuse for examining this question in Bodin because he is not a contractualist.) The most elementary *social* unit for Hobbes is the family. He establishes no essential distinction between the family and the state: where the family is independent it is a state; where dependent, it is merely a part of, and subject to, the state. Thus the family is the first social unit with which we are familiar, and its evolution merely means expansion (by procreation, voluntary adhesion and conquest) into a larger unit – i.e. the state – based upon an identical internal principle of organisation and control.

The fullest statement of Hobbes's conception of the origin of the family (and one therefore worth quoting) is to be found in the *Dialogue between a Philosopher and a Student of the Common Laws of England*: 'And first, it is evident that dominion, government, and laws, are far more ancient than history or any other writing, and that the beginning of all dominion among men was in families. In which, first, the father of the family by the law of nature was absolute lord of his wife and children: secondly, made such laws amongst them as he pleased: thirdly, was judge of all their controversies: fourthly, was not obliged by any law of man to follow any counsel but his own: fifthly, what land soever the lord sat down upon and made use of for his own and his family's benefit, was his propriety by the law of first possession, in case it was void of inhabitants before, or by the law of war, in case they conquered it. In this conquest, what enemies they took and saved, were their servants. Also such men as wanting possession of lands, but furnished with arts necessary for man's life, came to dwell in the family for protection, became their subjects, and submitted themselves to the laws of the family. And all this is consonant, not only to the law of nature, but also to the practice of mankind set forth in history, sacred and profane.'[1]

[1] Molesworth, vol. 6, p. 147.

178

Hobbes then proceeds to state his view regarding the manner in which states evolved from families.

'Great monarchies have proceeded from small families. First, by war, wherein the victor not only enlarged his territory, but also the numbers and riches of his subjects. As for the other forms of commonwealths, they have been enlarged other ways. First, by a voluntary conjunction of many lords of families into one great aristocracy. Secondly, from rebellion proceeded first anarchy, and from anarchy proceeded any form that the calamities of them that lived therein did prompt them to; whether it were, that they chose an hereditary king, or an elected king for life; or that they agreed upon a council of certain persons, which is *aristocracy*; or a council of the whole people to have the sovereign power, which is *democracy*.'[1]

Clearly, for Hobbes, the family is the most elementary and (historically) the earliest social unit. As the state merely evolves from the family, or, to be more precise, since the state is merely a larger form of the family (and this a smaller form of the state), it is necessary to understand the structure of Hobbes's family if we are to understand the constitutive elements of his state. Hobbes understands structure in terms of hierarchy, in terms of command relations between superiors and inferiors. The important question for him is not, Is rule, law or command just? but rather, What is the *source* of the command? *who* issued it? There is no room, therefore, for natural law in Bodin's sense. What is right or wrong (we shall return to this question) is completely absorbed by a different question: Who is the source of the distinction between right and wrong? Within the family, this source is the head, i.e. the father. The patterns of control exercised by the father over the family constitute its structure and its unity.

Hobbes actually calls the family 'a *father* with his *sons* and *servants*, grown into a civil person by virtue of his paternal jurisdiction'; but he does not intend this definition to be entirely exhaustive.[2] It does and does not exclude slaves. It should obviously include mothers (wives) and daughters. What Hobbes seems to be doing is stressing the essential importance of a chain of command within the family. The father is a pure source of command. A son is subject (to the father) but is a potentially independent source of command, and (where the father is absent) an actually independent source. The servant, of course, is an object of command; mothers, wives and daughters are equally objects of command: unlike sons, they are not even potentially independent orderers, and thus there is no essential difference between them and

[1] *Ibid.*, pp. 150–1.
[2] *De Cive*, II, 9, 10, p. 110. Unless otherwise indicated *page* citations refer to Sterling Lamprecht edition (New York, 1949).

servants, or even 'slaves'. Hobbes, naturally, juggles his terminology with dexterity. Those (like T. S. Eliot) who think him a fraud, from the point of view of substantive analysis, are sometimes right. For he defines 'slave' in such a way that the word becomes synonymous with 'prisoner'. For Hobbes, the distinctive characteristic of the slave is that he is held in his position purely by force. A slave is, in some sense, a man outside society, literally an *hors la loi*, since he cannot be bound by any tie of obligation. He cannot be obligated because he is not free to accept or relinquish his servitude. But, by contrast, a man who serves another, and is not in fetters, must obviously (in some sense) serve *willingly* (since he can flee or attempt to flee), and thus must not be called a 'slave' but a 'servant'. The effect of this is that persons whom we would normally call slaves become, in Hobbes's terminology, servants, and are assimilated to the rule of the father in essentially the same way as are all other members of the family. Hence the family features 'a *father* with his *sons* and *servants*, grown into a civil person by virtue of his paternal jurisdiction. Hence it develops that Hobbes is not interested in the family as a unique social unit, but merely as a repository of command relations of different types, all of which ultimately reduce to an identical type.

This description of the family applies only to a Western or – putting the position more generally – patrilocal type of family. Hobbes speaks of it as *the* family. The question arises: did Hobbes simply make a mistake in assuming that his definition of the family was universally valid? Or does he perhaps mean that the family type with which he was familiar ought to be universally followed? There is doubtless something of both positions involved. What is certain is that Hobbes's definition approved an established practice.

The family, as a concrete, corporate unit, impliedly entails every conceivable method of creating order among individuals. For there is no essential difference between the autonomous family and the state, since 'a great family is a kingdom, and a little kingdom is a family'. The family may involve relations grown out of procreative activity (offspring), out of contract between husband and wife (marriage), and out of conquest (of spouses, slaves and servants). The family may be built upon relationships between parent and child, husband and wife, master and servant, and – if the family is autonomous – between sovereign (understood as its head) and subject (understood as any other member). All of these relations (except the last) were essential to the classical conception of family structure. But because Hobbes sees them as distinct, and yet continuous with the principle underlying all social organisation (even including the political tie of sovereignty), he can find no justification for analysing the family separately. He does not deal with it as a unique social structure, as does Bodin, but reduces it to the specific relationships of obligation which it may contain.

As *all* social structure, for Hobbes, is essentially a matter of command and obedience, the problem of analysing it is greatly simplified. It is not Hobbes's position that subordinate groups within the state are unimportant. But it is essential for him that they recognise and accept their dependence upon the sovereign. More importantly, Hobbes assumes that to understand any instance of corporate structure is virtually to understand all instances of such structure. Thus, although inferior corporate groups are important, the separate and detailed analysis of them is not. For Bodin, there is a difference in structure between the family and other corporate bodies. When the family head leaves his home, he relinquishes his superiority, to meet with peers in guilds and church as an equal: hence the importance of debate, and (in part) of natural law, which debate may help to reveal. But no such idea is to be found in Hobbes. For him, there is no essential difference between the organisation of family, corporation and state. If the state is the final unit of command, then it wields an absolute right of control; so with the corporation and the family. Thus in all social structures and inquiries, the only important question must be: who rules?

Hobbes's concern with specific relationships of command and obedience makes it unnecessary for him to deal independently with family and corporate structure in any substantial degree. What is important for him is not the control of one group over another, but the control (through command) of one individual over another. Order within a small group like the family reduces to such control. Order within a larger group like the state involves merely the broadened and deepened range of this control. Debate over political and social issues is irrelevant and dangerous, except where it involves nothing more than counsel directed towards the promotion of an express end, which a single person or *body* (here lies the difficulty) must define. Without this, debate can only reflect partial interests and divergent ambitions, and so serve as a prelude to the collapse of the harmony it seeks to build. The idea of order and control built on command and obedience really goes to the heart of the matter. The relationships involved are basically between individuals, not groups. Thus it would suffice, for Hobbes's purposes, to demonstrate the way in which he believes individuals come to be related in – or as – groups.

Hobbes argues that individuals should be viewed 'as if but even now sprung out of the earth, and suddenly (like mushrooms) come to full maturity . . .'[1] This does not mean that he believed men were sprung up out of the earth. It suggests rather that a coherent explana-

[1] *De Cive*, II, 8, 1, p. 100.

tion of social structure can be reached by regarding individuals (rather than any corporate unit whatever) as fundamental. This does not mean that individuals are more important than groups, but merely that groups are always constituted of individuals. And the conclusion to be drawn is that one can only properly understand the character of social organisations if one understands the character (i.e. the human nature) of the individuals who compose them.

Hobbes believes that it is inappropriate to view the state or commonwealth as a mere multiplicity of individuals. Any assembly of persons does consist of biologically autonomous agents, but Hobbes believes that a state is *more* than a mere mass of such agents. He regards it as a whole, although not as a 'natural' or biological whole. It is not a whole which is based upon actual physical union; but it is based upon a principle of identity. When Hobbes wishes to stress that Leviathan is not a 'natural person', he says that 'he is a *feigned* or *artificial* person'.[1] When he wants to stress that Leviathan represents an identity, he says that this unity 'is more than consent, or concord'; that 'it is a real unity' of citizens in the person of the ruler, 'in one and the same person'.[2]

In so far as Hobbes is concerned with a general explanation of social structure, his analysis must be seen as an attempt to account for the manner in which men 'transcend' their individuality in order to establish an effective union or identity among themselves. He supposes that they are separate, but not isolated, that they can be united through organisation, but not obliterated by it. Thus his problem is not that of determining how putatively isolated individuals can be absorbed within a state, but how mutually insecure individuals remain or become united in peace with one another.

As indicated, Hobbes's perspective on unity led him to believe that it was not so much achieved by virtue of individuals co-operating with one another, as by virtue of their acquiring control over one another. He outlined three ways in which such control could be acquired. One is when 'there is a right acquired over the person of a man by generation' (parenthood); another is when 'a man taken prisoner in the wars . . . promises the conqueror or the stronger party his service' (conquest); a last is when 'for peace and self-defence's sake' individuals agree among themselves to confer power and authority upon one man or a body of men (contract).[3]

To effect unity among or between individuals is for one or some to acquire control over others. To say that 'there are but three ways only,

[1] *Leviathan*, I, 16, p. 105. Page citations, unless otherwise indicated, refer to the Oakeshott edition (Oxford, 1955).
[2] *Ibid.*, II, 17, p. 112.
[3] *De Cive*, II, 8, I, pp. 100–1.

whereby one can have a dominion over the person of another' does not mean that the nature or principle of control varies, but only that the means by which the control is acquired varies. Thus, the parent–child relationship is originally based upon birth or 'generation'. The master–servant relationship is originally based upon defeat in war. The sovereign–subject relationship is based upon a 'mutual contract' which individuals have 'made between themselves'.[1] Hobbes also argues, however, that the sovereign–subject relationship can be established 'by force' (which takes us back in effect to the arrangement between master and servant).[2]

All these methods of creating an ordered society, or of establishing 'the right to dominion . . . over the persons of men',[3] reduce to the same basic principle. The different relationships are, in themselves, the same, differing only in the way in which they were established. They do not imply distinct principles of rule, but are distinct examples of the same principle at work. The citizens contract to institute the sovereign, who either has or acquires both the right and the might to control the state. When this is done freely, they choose their sovereign from fear of one another; when they are forced, they 'subject themselves to him they are afraid of'.[4] The soldier spares the life of an opponent, who in consenting to render faithful service is tied by obligation to the victor. The child is at the mercy of its mother, as it is borne and cared for by her, and its implied acceptance of this situation enjoins its obedience to her. All of these cases involve a conjunction of either tacit or explicit consent with sovereign power, which expresses, in Hobbes's view, the essential character of rule or social organisation.

There are, then, significant differences between the Hobbesian and Bodinian views on political and social structure. We shall briefly compare their views on men, women and children – the constituent units of family and state – and then remark upon their views relating to the family and the state in general. For Bodin, the father's right is natural, whereas for Hobbes it is derived from that of the mother, which alone is 'natural' (in the sense that it is based upon her 'original' power over the child). Bodin believed that men, rather than women, should bear rule, without suggesting that men were more intelligent than women. Hobbes also believed that 'males carry the pre-eminence',[5] while giving as his reason the supposition that 'they are fitter for the administration of greater matters, but specially for wars' and that (subsequently) their

[1] *Ibid.*
[2] *Leviathan*, II, 20, pp. 129–30.
[3] *De Cive*, pp. 100–1.
[4] *Leviathan*, II, 20, p. 130.
[5] *De Cive*, II, 9, 16, p. 112.

supremacy simply became a matter of custom.[1] In *De Cive*, Hobbes does not suggest that men are more intelligent nor that they are vastly stronger than women. But in *De Corpore Politico* (which appeared in manuscript form in 1640, two years before the publication of *De Cive*), he had declared 'that generally men are . . . endued with greater parts of wisdom and courage . . . than women are . . . Not but that women may govern, and have in divers ages and places governed wisely, but are not so apt thereto in general, as men.'[2] It is probable that the central place which the theory of equality held in Hobbes's analysis, together with his belief in the superior importance of will over reason in the art of rule, led him to omit (although not to repudiate) these conventional remarks on female character. Both Bodin and Hobbes accepted primogeniture, with the difference that Hobbes provides (as usual) a reason for doing so: 'usually it is so [that the eldest] is the wisest'. This position, unlike the earlier position on women, could easily be made compatible with an egalitarian philosophy: since it is equal natural ability, *plus* equal experience (of which age has more than youth), that makes for truly equal men. Even at this point, however, Hobbes continued to fuss over his proof. To those who might discount it, he appealed on a different ground: even if one assumes that 'brothers must be equally valued', primogeniture must be understood to constitute 'a natural lot [by which] the eldest is already preferred . . .'[3]

For Bodin, the family was the irreducible unit of social organisation; for Hobbes, it was merely the smallest (and even then with no absolutely fixed character). For Bodin, individuals were born into families; for Hobbes, they were merely born, being related to other individuals on the basis of force and consent. For Bodin, the family was necessary and natural, whereas for Hobbes it was useful and artificial. For Bodin, the authority of the state was derived from families, as represented by the father; for Hobbes, it was derived from individuals, as represented by themselves. For Bodin, there was between families a common area of interest, in which the absolutism of the sovereign must be unlimited (but also *to* which it must be limited) in the interest of a common good; for Hobbes, a common interest could be established between individuals, but it required the complete absolutism of the sovereign to be made secure.

Hobbes takes for granted, where Bodin repeatedly states, that order is built upon a clearly established chain of command and obedience. The difficulty in Bodin is not so much the conflict between the 'immunity' he claims for the family and the 'absoluteness' he claims for the state.

[1] *De Cive*, II, 9, 16, p. 112.
[2] *De Corpore Politico*, II, 4, 14.
[3] *De Cive*, II, 9, 17, p. 113.

Bodin's basic difficulty derives instead from the conflict between his general claim that *all* power (with the exception of private corporate bodies) is based upon command and obedience (which suggests unlimited and arbitrary power) and his belief that only *some* acts require to be commanded – there being others which are naturally right or wrong, thus implying no need for an unlimited and arbitrary human power (to proclaim and enforce law). It is such a muddle as this that Hobbes *formally* cleared up, but could not really and effectively resolve. Because Hobbes jettisoned the view that any acts were 'naturally' right or wrong (in Bodin's sense of being above command), and accepted that all were only conventionally so (as the expression of a particular interest or of a point of view), it was necessary for him to see any fixed social order as based upon an (ultimately) arbitrary or artificial arrangement of rights and wrongs. There could be no 'natural' limitations upon nor 'immunities' from the power required to install such an order, given that its sole feasible aim was to keep the peace. Where Bodin wanted to show that the arbitrariness of the social order was partial, Hobbes wanted to show that it was virtually complete. Where Bodin thought it necessary to bestow 'absolute' power only in certain spheres, Hobbes thought that it could be excluded from virtually none.

Hobbes's analysis, in effect, jettisons traditional concepts of natural law, despite his adopting the terminology. Bodin insists upon the importance of command and obedience, but his analysis suggests that this principle of control is really restricted to the sphere of conventional law. God, of course, is the source of divine law; he commands it; but this, impliedly, is not quite the same as natural law. For, following Bodin, there are some things that even God cannot command. He cannot, for example, make natural law other than what it is. There are some things that are right and wrong irrespective of who commands. Bodin accepted, naturally, that God could do no wrong. But this would not mean that he could act arbitrarily (with his arbitrariness automatically constituting the ideal good), but simply that his nature was such that he could not so act.

In Hobbes, little trace of this idea remains. God is the source of law. His commands are final. His power to enforce is sufficient to his power to command. What he commands is, of itself, natural law; the dictates of natural law, which are of God, bind man to a code of moral conduct, even when he is not governed by an earthly sovereign. The most important of these commands is that men seek peace by all available means. But the limit of this peace-seeking consists in whatever evasive action is required for self-preservation. This not only implies that what God commands is necessarily in the interest of those commanded, but also that, from *de facto* self-interestedness, particularly as manifested in the drive for self-preservation, one can infer the will of God (this self-preserving drive being assumed present in everyone). A man's self-interest consists, maximally, in the attainment of felicity and, minimally, in the avoidance of pain and violent death (or acts which unhappily lead thereto). Thus, what is right and what wrong is a function of man's interest and from this can be derived God's command. Indeed, since men can only know *themselves* directly – not God – it is to be assumed that the surest means of divining his will consists in knowing one's own nature, which God made and presumably wanted to be as he made it. If it is in man's interest – the condition of his preservation, peace and felicity – that he be governed by an absolute sovereign, that interest must be read as God's command. In any event, in whatever way men may presume to know God's will (Hobbes mentions reason – the eliciting of what is, including one's own nature – revelation and prophecy), it is not God but man who is bound by the expressions of that will (his commands); for God, being their source, may change them as he thinks fit. The order of the world does not so much reflect an ultimate Reason as an ultimate Will. Seen from this perspective, no law is 'natural' for Hobbes, and they are all conventional. God's will, the sovereign's will, the pontiff's will, the father's command: these are the declaratory chains which bind one agent to another, and constitute the essence of political structure and social order.

Thus, for Hobbes but not for Bodin, command is the exclusive means of creating order. Command is the essence of all political organisation: whether in the family, the state or intermediate groups. Hobbes also suggests that command is the essence of order in the universe as a whole. Not only do men command, but so too does God. Men only command one another, while God commands the whole of nature, including man.

Hobbes's insistence, however, upon command as the only source of order in the state tends to minimise the important consideration that people, ultimately, require to be convinced that it is *right* to obey the commands issued them. Thus, although commands are essential to order, what is equally essential, after a point, is the belief (on the part of those obeying) that those commands are not unjust. Although every state requires direction, the acceptance of that direction requires that those accepting it feel they are right to do so. Hobbes's principal objective is to convince subjects that they ought not to have too many qualms about obeying their rulers no matter (virtually) what these command them to do.

Chapter Fourteen

The Individual

Hobbes's analysis does not begin as a study of men leading an ordered life in society, nor does it begin as a study of men leading a disordered life outside society; it begins as a study of the individual (who actually lives in a society, but who is conceived in abstraction from present ties and obligations) with a view to determining how his *de facto* ties and obligations are grounded in or derived from his 'basic' nature. For Hobbes, it would be impossible to understand how and why society exists without, first, understanding the nature of its most elementary constituent parts, which are human individuals. From this flows the concern with man, his nature, psychology, basic character and 'natural' state – all of which terms I use to cover a single concern with the individual, conceived in analytical abstraction from any specific social context.

Because the Hobbesian notion of man seems to invite such immediate and withering fire from some who view it as abstract and artificial, it may be appropriate to attempt a brief defence – or explanation – of Hobbes's approach. Those who object to Hobbes's abstraction of the individual from social ties, and insist that man cannot even hypothetically be placed in a state of nature, may consider the following point. Their case rests on the assumption that the individual must always exist within a social context, or perish – by which it is meant (to fall back upon alternative phrasing) that no man is an island entire unto himself. Against this assumption it is easy to reply that it is partly true and partly false. On the side of truth, the dependence – the complete dependence – of the individual during infancy and early childhood is beyond reasonable dispute. It is nevertheless the case – here the assumption becomes false – that individuals do transcend infancy; they develop sufficient strength and skill (in an underpopulated world) to acquire for themselves food, clothing and shelter, and these skills will often enable them to survive unassisted by others. Such an existence might be precarious; Hobbes suggests that it would be filled with terror; but it would nevertheless be possible. It is around the *possibility*, not the fact, of individual isolation that Hobbes's initial analysis is built. Given the possibility, thus the question: why do men remain together, when they might well drift apart and live alone?

For Hobbes, men do not live together primarily because they are political animals, falling back on one another in quest of an aesthetic ideal of perfection, nor because of an economic appetite which dictates the necessity of self-interested, productive co-operation with others. They remain together, paradoxically, because of their mutual fear of one another: 'not in the mutual good will . . . but in the mutual fear'.[1] They are not *forced* together; so their remaining so must be freely willed – hence consent, or *contract* as an explanatory model. Contract does not explain the literal origins of society but its perpetuation, its continuance in being. The individual's allegiance to his fellows is not grounded in fear of mere solitude, but in fear of isolation in the face of external encroachment, of attack, of loss of property, and most importantly of loss of life.

The reason why men do not drift apart, or attempt to live in isolation, is that, although some might succeed, most could not. The reason why men do not generally attempt to live in isolation is that the attempt would usually end in failure. Thus, those who object to Hobbes's state of nature, and believe it nonsense to think that man could be, or ever was, placed in it, find themselves in general agreement with Hobbes without realising it. A man here or there might live in isolation; but isolation is impossible for men in general. The state of nature, in fact, as Hobbes describes it, is not one where men have no contact with one another, but one where contact is unregulated, unpeaceful, warring – which thus compels them to lead lives that are 'nasty, brutish, and short'.

Isolation, *in the face of attack*, does not literally mean that one is alone, but that one is being subjected to a certain sort of treatment, both from and in the presence of others. The state of nature is, for Hobbes, not one where individuals are insulated against one another, but one – which is quite a different thing – where they have reached the nadir of mutual impingement, i.e. a state of war. Thus Hobbes's theory assumes that an individual *may* retreat into isolation, but this would only imply that he thought such retreat *possible* – not easy or probable. What it primarily suggests is that individuals are almost always exposed to one another, and that to this usually constant mutual exposure there attach two major poles of conduct: peace (in civil society) and war (in the state of nature).

Thus, for Hobbes, there should be two questions: (*a*) Assuming that an individual might live alone, why would he live with others? (*b*) Assuming that an individual can usually only choose between war and peace, why does he choose peace? Actually, Hobbes has no explicit

[1] *De Cive*, I, I, 2, p. 24.

answer to the first question. But his general position implies that men can never ensure that they are *truly* alone. The second question answers itself: war brings pain and sudden death (which men do and should avoid); peace is a condition necessary for felicity. For Hobbes, then, the *primary* question has not to do with why we live among (rather than in complete isolation from) other individuals. Instead, it is about how we come to be united with (rather than warring against) fellow individuals. Here we can see that Hobbes is not really concerned with the individual in an actual situation where completely deprived of all social intercourse, but rather with explaining how individuals avoid being overwhelmed by the evil of war, with how they make the transition from war to peace, with how and on what basis they establish orderly – if not amicable – settlements among themselves.

The state of nature, then, is not intended as a point in time but as a condition or state of being. In that state, the condition depicted is one of mutual antagonism and conflict between individuals. It is not intended as an historical age which existed prior to the establishment of government; rather, it is a condition and disposition which exists where government is suspended or destroyed. Hobbes was fairly explicit on this point. He believed that families, for example (which were miniature states) had always existed – which means that almost all men at all times had lived with one another. He even went so far as to claim that 'a son [daughters were obviously unimportant] cannot be understood to be at any time in the state of nature, as being under the power and command of them to whom he owes his protection as soon as ever he is born, namely, . . . his father's or his mother's, or his that nourished him . . .'[1] Complete individual isolation was at all times unlikely and improbable. Hobbes's state-of-nature model, therefore, was not intended to depict what would happen once men were *alone*, but what would happen once government was removed – whether represented by the head of a family or by the head of a state ('to be a king, is nothing else but to have dominion over many persons; and thus a great family is a kingdom, and a little kingdom a family').[2]

As for those who maintained that 'there was never such a time, nor condition of war' as that Hobbes described, Hobbes agreed with them: 'I believe it was never generally so . . .'[3] Like Bodin, he believed that families had always existed, but that larger aggregations – which might be called commonwealths or states – had not. To put it differently, he believed that states had always existed, but that at an earlier time and on

[1] *Ibid.*, I, I, 10 (note), p. 28.
[2] *Ibid.*, II, 8, 1, p. 100.
[3] *Leviathan*, I, 13, p. 83.

a smaller scale they were called families, and that later and when they became larger, they were called states. In short, political and social structure are omnipresent, although it is possible that an adult individual may (and that such an individual occasionally does) escape all traffic with his fellows. When Hobbes says, for example, that 'the savage people [as he calls the Indians] of America . . . have no government at all' (the problem being 'at all'), his qualification of the assertion is immediate: 'except the government of small families . . .'[1]

It should therefore be clear (a) that Hobbes does not suppose that individuals ever generally exist or existed in complete physical isolation from one another; (b) that he believed individuals were almost always contained within some formal organisation, whether large (like the ttate) or small (like the family); (c) that social organisations, whether or not they have contained all individuals at all times, have existed as long as men have existed; (d) that the 'state of nature' does not refer to the absence but to the presence of a relationship between human individuals – but in an unfortunate condition where they (whether as individuals, families or states), although 'contiguous', share no common arbiter or will in exercise of a unified power over them; and (e) that this state of nature is characterised by mutual fear, misunderstanding and conflict (or the disposition thereto).

To be able to avoid conflict among and between individuals, it becomes necessary to know what they are like as such. The pre-eminent characteristic of the individual is not physical isolation but psychological self-containment. This belief, together with the doctrine of equality, constitute the central ground upon which Hobbes stands in his view of the individual. Hobbes therefore does not toy with the notion of empirical investigation, with 'psychology' in the modern sense. For since men are equal, an individual's knowledge of himself will suffice for his understanding of the basic impulses and motives of others. Hobbes retreats within himself to discover his own nature, to compare his experiences of different men, and to distil a residual understanding which might serve as a model of human nature in general. To understand the nature of the individual is to understand the basic character of all social structure, since families, corporations and states are only composed of individuals fixed in determinate, mutual relationships.

It is individuals who are always found in juxtaposition to one another. Their contiguity sometimes waxes into war, at other times it congeals into a fixed state of peace. The question is not what individuals are like in isolation, but what they are like within themselves, apart from varying circumstances. The first point is that they are much the same. The second is that they are psychologically self-contained. A third is that this

[1] *Leviathan*, I, 13, p. 83.

imposes severe limits on mutual understanding. And a last is that misunderstanding is compounded (or made simply inevitable) for men
understand what is good as a function of 'whatsoever . . . is pleasant',[1]
and what is bad as a function of what is unpleasant. Hobbes veers
between the notion that the individual is an animate solipsis (for which
he cannot be blamed) and the view that he is merely selfish and egoistic
(for which he must be blamed). For either of these reasons, and perhaps
for both, Hobbes believes that the individual, although born in need of
society, is born unfit for it. Solipsism is natural, but the solitude it
imposes 'is an enemy'.[2] Man is not alone, but he carries an island within
himself. The establishment of links between himself and other selves is
a function of education, of learning, and of experience. And the result is
that though men are almost everywhere and always found together,
conflict is more natural than harmony, war than peace. The whole art of
education, in effect, is to teach men peace – both its basis and the means
to its attainment: 'man is made fit for society not by nature, but by
education.'[3] And it is this education which equips men, not to *live*
together, but to live together *in peace*. The avoidance of war, therefore,
although it is what men naturally desire, is not an end they obtain
easily; a state of peace is not natural but artificial: it is an art or skill to
be acquired.

Politics (as opposed to war) is not natural to men, but merely an
accomplishment; man is not born a political animal: force of circumstance compels him to become one. Not even birth affiliates him to the
society 'into' which he is born; for birth does not automatically provide
the protection of a family; blood itself does not tie one to those among
whom one initially or subsequently appears. To be a member of a
family, ultimately, is to be accepted by its head. And the alternatives to
acceptance are abandonment, exposure and abortion. However natural
birth may be, the family is not. It is a political arrangement, a contrived
state of peace which presupposes a knowledge of duty. Acceptance into
a family, like acceptance into the state, is not natural but 'artificial'; not
inescapable, but the consequence of a decision; a decision not merely on
the part of those who provide succour, but also impliedly on the part of
the being who accepts it (at whatever stage it may be most appropriate
to speak of his 'acceptance').

Social peace does not exist naturally or automatically. It exists as a
result of contrivance and decision. It exists, writes Hobbes, 'not so
much for love of our fellows, as for the love of ourselves'.[4] 'Civil'

[1] *De Cive*, I, I, 2, p. 24.
[2] *Ibid.*, I, I, 2(note), p. 21.
[3] *Ibid.*, p. 22.
[4] *Ibid.*, I, I, 2, p. 24.

society does not exist for its own sake; it exists as an expression of the interests of its individual members. What they seek, in the perpetuation of peaceful arrangements, is their own good. The important question was to discover (a) how individuals perceived their own good and (b) how they could be educated to do so. This requires, however, that we touch upon Hobbes's views regarding the manner in which individuals learn in general, how human intelligence (and learning) compares with that of animals, how human individuals communicate with one another; then, finally, we may return to the question of the determination of good and evil in human psychology. In the analysis which follows, Hobbes, unlike every important political writer before him, advances the individual – rather than the group (i.e. the family) – as the basic unit of social structure. He dissolves the analysis of the family into an analysis of the physically autonomous individuals of whom familial and other groups are composed.

According to Hobbes, the individual acts and is acted upon. He is a repository of sense impressions, and a source of such impressions: from within, he is subject; from without, object. The individual, as subject, comprehends the world through his senses. These senses essentially operate through the medium of motion, and through the variable pressures which motion generates. 'So that sense, in all cases, is . . . caused . . . by the pressure, that is, by the motion, of external things upon our eyes, ears, and other organs thereunto ordained.'[1]

The individual is capable of varieties of perception originally grounded in his sense impressions. These may stir his imagination, as an explosion generates shock waves. In the way that a knoll may provide a striking view, so the individual's imagination may (albeit imperfectly) keep that view in mind. But the liveliness of these impressions, of the imagination, inevitably decays, and in decay the impressions are stored away as memory. Dreams are nothing more than the operative imagination of a man asleep. Visions occur when a man dreams but thinks himself to be awake. Understanding is the 'imagination that is raised in man . . . by words, or other voluntary signs . . .'[2]

For Hobbes, there is a continuous train of thought set up by sense impressions. None of these thoughts is accidental. But the order in which each comes may either be 'unguided' or 'regulated'. To think in the first manner is to do so at random, as in dreaming or day-dreaming, without any effort to direct or control the succession. To think in the second manner is to do so with deliberate effort, 'as being *regulated* by some desire, and design'.[3]

[1] *Leviathan*, I, I, p. 8.
[2] *Ibid.*, I, 2, p. 13.
[3] *Ibid.*, I, 3, p. 14.

Both men and beasts are capable of directing their thoughts to the realisation of their desires. They do this (a) by recalling the connections between past events and their causes (remembrance); and (b) by imagining the probable outcome of a present or future event (prudence). Hobbes recognises no necessary distinction between the intelligence of human individuals and that of creatures belonging to other animal species, except one grounded in education. 'For besides sense, and thoughts, and the train of thoughts, the mind of men has no other motion; though by the help of speech, and method, the same faculties may be improved to such a height, as to distinguish men from all other living animals.'[1] What distinguishes human intellect from that of other animals is therefore not actual use but capacity for use; not a difference of type but a difference in potential scope and degree of application. For while an animal also remembers, and demonstrates prudence, the human individual can push these abilities to the point, 'when imagining anything whatsoever', of seeking 'all the possible effects, that can by it be produced . . .'[2]

Hobbes's analysis of this question, however, is not altogether clear. For he may have meant that humans are capable of a greater *volume* of reasoning than animals; or that they are capable of more *abstract* reasoning; or that a quantity of reasoning after a certain point *converts into* abstract formulae, embodying a quality of 'mental discourse' which only humans can enjoy. Whatever the case, it is at least certain that, for Hobbes, human intellect was distinctly characterised by a vast capacity for regulated reasoning. This last required speech as a means of communicating and recording its deliberations.

Speech performed two general functions. A word may be used to label an occurrence, or a thing: hence nouns. A word, moreover, may assert a connection between two nouns: hence verbs. Speech, so understood, permits four general activities; research, education, social accommodation and control, and entertainment. We are interested in it in respect of the third of these activities.[3]

Speech is essential to social control and mutual accommodation, since it is only by means of its use that we 'make known to others our wills and purposes, that we may have the mutual help of one another'.[4] Hobbes lays great stress upon the importance of definitions, upon being clear about the meaning of words, in order to ensure, from a social point of view, that 'our wills' are properly communicated. But despite this stress, he comes to the implied conclusion that no matter how great our

[1] *Ibid.*, I, 3, p. 17.
[2] *Ibid.*, I, 3, p. 15.
[3] *Ibid.*, I, 4.
[4] *Ibid.*, I, 4, p. 19.

attentiveness to the meaning of words, there comes a point beyond which such of these words that 'affect us' signify more about the user than about the 'facts' in respect of which they are used. That is to say, Hobbes comes to the conclusion that there is something inherently peculiar to speech which prevents our using it with complete objectivity in so far as we are concerned with human affairs.

Politics and social organisation in general involve decisions, conflicts and developments which 'affect us . . . which please and displease us'. Hobbes insists that 'different constitutions of body, and prejudices of opinion, gives every thing a tincture of our different passions'. Given different natures and dispositions, the effect of sense impressions will not be constant for all human individuals. For the difference in each individual's constitution will enter into (or influence) the very manner in which he conceives these impressions. Thus, words not only refer to data but reflect our (various) reactions to data. It is in this way that Hobbes explains how two individuals may observe the same act, which one might call 'cruel', the other 'just'.[1] What Hobbes here begins to attempt therefore is a demonstration of the ultimate impossibility – even given the utmost desire for objectivity – of humans reaching complete rational agreement in politics. For in matters which affect their interests differently (and this is inevitable) they will prove incapable of common accord.

It becomes essential for Hobbes to set out the relationship, within the individual, between reason and passion. Unlike Plato, Aristotle, Cicero, Bodin (in part) and so many other writers before him, Hobbes does not suppose that reason, as such, is somehow superior to passion. Rather, he supposes that, when properly cultivated, it serves as a hand-maiden to passion, providing 'the light of human minds' by which what is passionately desired may be more effectively acquired. Thus, it is less true that men are governed by reason than that reason is governed by desire. Hobbes is often and aptly quoted to the effect that 'thoughts are to the desires, as scouts, and spies, to range abroad, and find the way to the things desired . . .'[2] The ultimate implication of this conclusion is that philosopher-kings are redundant; that wisdom is subservient to will, that reason, as such, cannot lead; while the clear expression of a single will is essential to order in human societies.

For Hobbes, reason is ultimately incapable of distinguishing between good and evil. Rather, 'whatsoever is the object of any man's appetite or desire, that is it which he for his part calleth *good*: and the object of his hate and aversion, *evil* . . .'[3] What a man finds 'desirable' is good; what

[1] *Leviathan*, I, 4, p. 24.
[2] *Ibid.*, I, 8, p. 46.
[3] *Ibid.*, I, 6, p. 32.

he finds hateful is bad. But by projecting into the future the consequences of present action, his desire may be further provoked or attenuated by the foresight of a probable chain of events, which may promise either good or evil. The implication of this position is that reason can only 'control' passion in the sense that it cautions restraint with a view to the optimum realisation of desire. For Hobbes, therefore, no external event is 'good' or 'evil' in itself, these words being taken to signify nothing more than the favourable or unfavourable attitudes of those who use them towards an event.

One may say (I suggest) of any act or decision that it is right, wrong or indifferent, or that it is good, bad or indifferent. When one thinks exclusively of a moral agent, and of his general disposition (and not merely of a single act) the words used to assess his moral character are most frequently 'good' and 'bad'. Overall judgement (or assessment) of an agent or person tends to become assimilated to the category of aesthetic judgement; one characterises persons as one would paintings or poems. In both cases of judgement, where we are speaking of an act and of the character of an actor, where our assessments relate to 'rightness' and to 'goodness', there is the suggestion that these judgements (although possibly mistaken) are in themselves of an objective nature. But Hobbes uses these terms in a different way.

Hobbes believes that these judgements have some certifiable cause, but not that they are 'objective' in the usual or ordinary sense. For him, 'good' and 'evil' merely register the agent's immediate responses to external stimuli. Judgements of 'right' and 'wrong' are more sophisticated, but they are ultimately intended to perform an identical function. For 'right' and 'wrong' are fluid judgements and have no fixed or 'natural' character; they are *ultimately* derived from common agreement; they are *mediately* derived from an arbitrary convention or command. What men agree upon, according to Hobbes, is the good of security and the evil of war; what a train of reasoning (in fact or impliedly) leads them to is the conclusion that security can only be achieved – in so far as it ever can be – by virtually complete obedience to a single authority, and that this obedience is right while disobedience is wrong. Judgements of good and evil are grounded in the human disposition (without which one is without consciousness or life) to interpret, understand and assimilate experience in terms of its painful and pleasurable effects. Given that all men are like this, Hobbes concludes that there always exists a basis for agreement and harmony between them. Whether at war or at peace, what they share is a common disposition to value peace and to abhor its absence. Thus, not only are judgements of good and evil always present among individuals, but, equally, judgements of right and wrong – derived as they are through reason from the basic and common (even if minimal) desires, abilities, impulses and fears of men.

As we have seen, Hobbes believes 'good' and 'evil' to be inevitable, but idiosyncratic, terms of judgement; unlike 'truth' and 'falsity', they say more about the subject than about the object; which is to say, they attest to individual dispositions, interests and passions. Judgements of 'right' and 'wrong', however, are not immediately (in themselves) subjective. They are ultimately grounded in subjective judgements, but, immediately understood, they are merely deductions from these; in this sense, they do not represent a subjectivity but a spelling out of the implications of this subjectivity (whether the initial judgement of 'good' is confined to a single person or generalised among a group of them). Thus 'right' and 'wrong' can be viewed as objective judgements, in so far as they constitute logical entailments. But they could never be 'objective' in Bodin's sense – merely because the ultimate judgements they represent are arbitrary; the deductive results to which they lead (because of their ground or beginning) can only be conventional. Right and wrong merely record a process of reasoning, initially based upon agreement, and leading back to this at a later point and in a more detailed degree.

For Hobbes, 'good' and 'evil' are not 'objective' simply because, in the end, what is good for one individual may be bad for another; and this means that one and the same object (or event) can be both good and evil. This must be equally so, up to a point, for right and wrong, since these judgements are derived from the former set. Hobbes notes that 'the doctrine of right and wrong, is perpetually disputed, both by the pen and the sword . . .'[1] Disputes over right and wrong, however, are in their nature objective; not because they ignore contrary attitudes embodied in judgements of good and evil, but only because they start from a conventional agreement about the designation of good and evil in some particular respect or sphere. Argument about right and wrong can then be rational – in character, it is rational. It is in fact possible, according to Hobbes, to demonstrate to a man that a judgement or act is 'objectively' right or wrong. One can demonstrate to a man (to 'persuade' is more difficult) that rebellion is 'wrong'; that the act of rebellion is mistaken. This is not because one can persuade him that what he feels immediately to be good is not so, but because one can show – rationally, logically – that his good cannot actually be obtained by the means he proposes. To do this presupposes conventional agreement upon what is good, or what is desired; where that presupposition collapses there can be no discussion of right and wrong, only of good and bad; and this is not to discuss but to declare.

[1] *Leviathan*, I, II, pp. 67–8.

Hobbes assumes that discussion of right and wrong is, in itself, entirely rational. It does not really involve, for that reason, dispute about desires, but about means to the attainment of desire; it involves, in short, the release of argumentative, probing scouts and spies, that 'range abroad and find the way to the things desired'. The discussion of right and wrong can then be assimilated to the sphere of mathematical debate, to 'the doctrine of lines, and figures',[1] and the achievement of this assimilation becomes Hobbes's purpose. He believes that the discussion of right and wrong can be set (in itself) on a scientific basis; and '*Science* is the knowledge of consequences . . .'[2] It depends upon the possibility of speech, wherein assertions may be made, and the implications (or content) of these drawn out. It involves the assertion of premises, and the deduction of conclusions. All that is required is agreement about premises (Hobbes's assertions about human self-containment and egoism are offered as such) and these premises are treated as self-evident.

This discussion is necessarily brief, but it is hoped that it will prove adequate to its purpose. This is nothing more than to set out broadly Hobbes's view of the individual, which is essential to his view of the structure of the state. Too many criticisms have been provided of Hobbes's moral theory, and of the inadequacies of his views of human psychology, to warrant any echo of them in the present discussion. The vital points to be noted are that the individual, for Hobbes, is the basic unit of all social structure; that he is not part of a larger organism but is biologically self-sufficient; that although his ideas may be borrowed, they are inevitably sifted through the prism of a unique locus of understanding; that he is self-contained and largely egotistical; yet that he is rarely alone, impinging upon others (they reciprocating) both in war and peace, both in his most 'natural' and most 'civil' states of being; that only education, science and reason bridge the gulf between one individual and another; that peace among men is not natural, but an aberration, the consequence of effort, of speech, of understanding, of imagination; and that the problem, empirically, is to provide a comprehensive statement of the way in which individuals actually do come to live in peace, order or harmony.

It is important to stress Hobbes's view that hostility is more 'natural' than accord. The primary reason for such hostility, according to Hobbes, springs from the fact of every individual's self-containment – in so far as self-containment expresses both a measure of egotism and an inevitably limited view of, and response to, the world. This narrow view of the world ultimately derives from the simple fact of the individual's

---

[1] *Ibid.*, I, 11, p. 68.
[2] *Ibid.*, I, 5, p. 29.

biological autonomy. The fears of individuals are grounded in their own immediate pains; and a fear for others, which is sympathy and understanding, is indirect, not immediate, is based upon imagination rather than upon biology. Thus the individual feels; but ultimately or initially his feeling can only be for himself. He is merely the centre of his own pain, not everyone's, the centre of his own happiness, and others cannot always join in. Individuals, being 'self-centred', are thus more prone to conflict than accord; for they are almost always related to one another – which Hobbes might have called 'natural' – but they are never 'naturally' related to one another in peace; for this requires an effort, demands an education, is in fact 'artificial'.

Given this picture of Hobbes's individual, and of his conflict-prone nature, the problem is to disengage those elements in his nature or education which permit him to live among others in an ordered or peaceful manner. Hobbes's overall solution to this problem seems not to occasion any difficulty: men are biologically autonomous; they see things differently; they can never be sure of one another; they inevitably distrust one another – hence conflict. But conflict, competition, rivalry are dictated by man's desire for security; as he is equipped with speech, he is also equipped with reason, and reason (which Hobbes himself supplies to supplement the deficiencies of others) shows that the security he seeks may be attained by submission more readily than by war – at least in certain circumstances. These circumstances are: that contiguous individuals recognise the need for, agree upon and abide by an authority that is always vested in a single individual or body, without any restriction whatever upon his or its power, except that individuals who are immediately threatened in life or security (but not individuals who are not so threatened) may take such steps as enable them to avoid the execution of the threat. What this boils down to is the assertion that in any ordered or civil society, each individual accepts the need for a single person or body to wield complete authority, which is to say that he consents to obey one or a set of rulers, up to the point where his own life and security are placed in real and immediate danger. In general, therefore, Hobbes's idea is that peace or order comes only to exist among individuals where one person (or group of persons) commands, and a second (or many) obeys.

However fulsomely we may praise the clarity of Hobbes's analysis, we certainly cannot accept it as adequate. Hobbes tends to believe that political and social organisation are based solely upon *one* type of relationship: that of command and obedience. It is clear that not *all* relationships are of this type. There are relationships of friendship where there is no command and obedience. There are even formal relationships of equality in which command and obedience do not obtain: in a corporate group, like a law firm, where the partners are agreed that no action can be taken on matters of importance except where all the partners are agreed, the simple command and obedience principle is excluded from a central sphere of decision-making. In a state where one agent or body must concur with another before certain steps can be taken, the simple command and obedience principle is again absent.

A part of Hobbes's difficulty lies in his diagnosis of the problem. Not all men seek peace. Nor is it necessarily desirable that they should always do so. Nor will complete obedience to a sovereign necessarily secure it. If we are to obey completely a ruler or government, then he or it may treat us in any manner they like. If we are to render complete obedience, except where our own lives are threatened, we may find that it is too late and our own resources too limited to preserve ourselves. No ruler is completely obeyed. But even if one were, complete obedience to him would clearly provide no guarantee against maltreatment by him. It is clear that rulers commonly employ force – violence – where (at least some) laws are not observed. But even if all laws were observed (a purely hypothetical situation), rulers still could (and through pure sadism often would) employ force or violence in their relations with (not necessarily control over) the ruled. Violence often breaks out where there is disagreement. But equally often there is disagreement and no violence. Violence often breaks out where some do not obey others. But equally often those who unquestioningly obey may and do have violence used against them. Complete obedience to a government therefore does not necessarily, nor (I would argue) even probably, secure peace: it only ensures that the resort to violence will be the exclusive preserve of the government, or (at least) that violent sanctions will never be utilised against it. Since the construction of order does not necessarily exclude the use of violence, the chief question is not whether we enjoy peace but in what degree we are the beneficiaries of justice.

Chapter Fifteen

Mother and Infant

For Hobbes, all social organisation depends upon a command relationship of superior to inferior in which obedience is required. The command relationship does not exclude consent or agreement; in fact, and to the contrary, it presupposes this; it presupposes that obedience is in some degree freely accorded, sufficiently for the will of the orderer to be acceded to by the individual who is ordered. But of course sometimes commands are obeyed and sometimes they are not; the problem is to determine what factors are present when they are obeyed and what factors should be present if they are to be obeyed. What induces obedience to a particular orderer, in Hobbes's view, is a combination of fear and interest. From a more powerful individual there is both more to be feared and more to be gained. He (or she) may kill one, but may also protect one. Since, in Hobbes's view, one must almost always be related to others, it is reasonable to submit to a person – which, in general, is what happens – who may not only take one's life but also spare it (and secure it).

What is necessary for order, according to Hobbes, then, is an orderer; and the criteria of an orderer (a ruler) are two: (a) that he receives the consent of the ruled; and (b) that he wields sufficient force to break any individual, corporate or sectional move to disobey his commands (the instruments of rule). Where he receives 'consent', but is shorn of the power to enforce, he is no ruler and there is no rule (no peace). Equally, where he can only enforce (as with the slave in chains) there is no consent, and therefore no peace (since there is a tendency towards war following the absence of a legitimate duty to obey). Thus consent and force, for Hobbes, are requisite for social order; and neither directly entails the other.

The three different means by which Hobbes supposes order can be established were mentioned in an earlier chapter. These means were the establishment of (i) control over one's offspring; (ii) control over those captured in war; and (iii) control over those who initially and freely agree to render obedience. The second method involves force; the third, consent; the first is a variant form of the second. These are not instances, however, of different types of rule. For Hobbes supposes that all rule, all social organisation, once established, is fundamentally the same. The despot is no different from the legitimate monarch; family control is no different from that which obtains in the state. The types of control mentioned are not – strictly speaking – different *types* of control; they are merely different means by which it may be initiated; or, more precisely, they merely refer to the first element present (in a particular case) where control has been established.

Hobbes's argument suggests that neither consent nor superior power (or force) can, of itself, produce an ordered, civil or peaceful society. Consent and force must be combined. And neither, of itself, automatically entails the other. In the case of motherhood, Hobbes assumes that it is the initial proximity of the mother which is the historical or spatial basis of her control over the child; she is the first to have the child in her power, so her right is a form of conquest (not consent); but her right is nonetheless a *peculiar* form of conquest, resting on the fact that she has actually 'generated' her own subject. Thus, 'generation' or birth refers to the manner in which the child came to be in the mother's power. But, for Hobbes, her control is only complete (if one likes, 'legitimate') where her power over the child, her ability to dispose of it at will, is combined with some notion of the consent of the child, whether tacit or express. Superior power, on this view, therefore, may precede consent; and it may establish the basis for it; but it does not in itself imply consent, and by itself, therefore, it is insufficient for rule (or proper peace). The first question to be considered, for our purposes, then, is whether a mother seems generally able, singly and exclusively, to wield an original power over her offspring. The second question is whether parental control over children actually satisfies the general conditions of political and social control laid down by Hobbes as characteristic of all government.

This chapter is primarily about Hobbes's conception of the establishment of maternal authority over children. It has to do not only with the superiority of the mother's strength over the child (which means that its life is in her hands), but also with the grant of the child's consent to the mother's authority – which consent is required (in Hobbes's view) to make it authoritative. Hobbes not only argues that the mother is the first to have the child in her *power* ('it is manifest that he who is newly born, is in the mother's power before any others');[1] but also that she possesses the initial *right* to wield authority over the child ('dominion over the infant first belongs to him who first hath him in his power').[2] Hobbes advances an argument, then, which relates to the questions

[1] *De Cive*, II, 9, 2, p. 106.
[2] *Ibid.*

(*a*) who has initial *de facto* control over a child, and (*b*) who has the first *right* or legitimate option to assume authority over the child. Hobbes answers that it is the mother in both cases. We are not primarily interested in determining or discussing who it is that Hobbes thinks *ought* to be accorded a right of control over the child. But it is difficult not to be concerned with this matter because Hobbes's argument suggests that the *right* of control can be deduced from the *fact* of control: the mother's original dominion seems to be deduced from the fact that she is the first to have the child in her power (based on the assumption that original *power* of control over X equals an original right to exercise *authority* over X). Thus, if Hobbes is 'mistaken' about the mother's original power over the child, then, within the framework of his own argument, the contention that the mother has the original right or authority to control the child must fail (it will be 'wrong'). In what follows, the purpose will be to show not that Hobbes's argument for the mother's original authority is 'wrong', but that his contention that she possesses an original or initial power is rarely true, and therefore that the contention is false, or 'mistaken'.

Hobbes argues that 'original dominion over children belongs to the mother'.[1] As noted, he intends this both indicatively and normatively. The object of the argument is to demonstrate that anyone else who acquires control over a child must do so indirectly and subsequently, i.e. through the mother. One obtains control over a child by obtaining control over its mother (by marriage or conquest) and also where one assumes a control which the mother has entirely relinquished (as when she abandons her child). The object of Hobbes's contention that the mother has an original power over the child is to show how a social and political structure pyramids, how it is organised, how control over the individual leads into control over others. The difficulty is that the foundation of this organisation is rather shaky; for it hardly requires more proof than the statement itself to convince the reader that mothers, empirically speaking, rarely are the first who either do, or are in a position to, acquire initial power over newly born children. (We are not now discussing authority, or a 'right' of control.) The assertion that mothers are or have ever been (either all the time or most of the time) the first to acquire such control is unconvincing – at least according to the present state of our knowledge.

In Hobbes's day, it was usually the midwife and occasionally the male physician (in difficult births) who attended mothers in labour and were thus the first, prior even to the mother, in a position to wield power over the child following its emergence from the womb. If having power over a child in the first instance means, as Hobbes seems to intend, having the

[1] *De Cive*, II, 9, 3, p. 107.

first opportunity following birth to dispatch it, deprive it of life, then clearly this is usually a power which the mother simply does not wield. Even 'Roman and Arabian medicine [we are told] recognised the need of a physician in difficult deliveries'.[1] But usually obstetrical practice everywhere 'remained in the hands of midwives . . .'[2] There appears to be general agreement that 'Among the Egyptians, Hebrews and Greeks the skilled attendants for women in childbirth were women'; and further: 'After the middle of the 17th century . . . parturient women began to call on men to attend them in natural labours.'[3] What is in question here is not, of course, whether men or women have customarily attended the labours of expectant mothers, but whether the latter were attended by or dependent upon any other humans at all. The answer to this for our own day is obvious. The point of the citations is to show (against the argument that present practice may not have been that of Hobbes's own time) that, in all large-scale societies at least, attendance upon pregnant women by others has been, to the best of our knowledge, universal. Centuries before Hobbes was born, women were customarily attended by fellow women during childbirth, and as *Leviathan* emerged from the press it was becoming customary even for men to assist in difficult deliveries. These facts, of which Hobbes must have been to some extent aware, tends to puncture his belief that 'original dominion over children belongs to the mother'.

But because the facts are so obvious, we must ask why Hobbes took no account of them. To this, no certain answer can be given. One possible line of defence for Hobbes would be to say that, whatever present practice was, or past practice had been, such practice merely represented a convention, not a necessity; and that the generality of mothers (at least a majority) were able to choose whether or not to be attended by others (which again leaves them with an original power). But neither can this *sortie* withstand the weight of counter-argument. In the first place, it will as often be an expert (a prospective grand-mother, a midwife or a physician) who is first aware of pregnancy as the mother herself. Secondly, if there were a question of prematurely terminating or aborting the pregnancy, the mother could not do this without considerable risk to her own life, and so there would be a significant need for assistance. Even in cases of perfectly normal delivery, a mother generally needs some help, without which she may place her own life in danger which, following Hobbes, no one should do (or sanely can do). Thus we find no support for the notion that women in labour generally do not have or do not require assistance.

[1] *Collier's Encyclopedia*, vol. 18, p. 52.
[2] *Ibid.*
[3] *Encyclopaedia Britannica*, vol. 16, p. 680.

Hobbes's suggestion that mothers have an original *power* over children is simply not borne out by the facts. In practice, a mother usually has no such power. In principle, she could not freely place herself in a position to exercise it, at least for the reason that this would endanger her own life (which Hobbes believes no one can sanely do). It is rare for a mother to give birth alone, and it always involves considerable risk. This speaks for the universal need for assistance, and that brings the curtain down on any original and exclusive power of maternal governance of children. As this view is so obviously mistaken, we must now inquire why Hobbes bothered to advance it in the first place.

The point is that Hobbes is primarily *arguing against an original paternal power* of control, *rather than in support of an original maternal power* of control, grounded in the generative, the procreative function of the parent. What Hobbes is really objecting to is the view that the *paterfamilias* wields a natural power and right of control over his children; that he has a power over them, to take or spare their lives, because he has given them life. Hobbes must destroy this argument if he is to establish any real continuity and identity between the nature of rule within the family and its nature within the state. For if the power of the *paterfamilias*, and his authority, stem from his generative capacities, he wields a peculiarly exclusive power which must proscribe that of the sovereign, and thus confirm arguments for the family being autonomous within its sphere. If the family were truly different from other corporations (including the state) then one might argue, perhaps, that it really ought to be treated differently from them by the state. In Bodin, the father's right to his children's lives was deemed to derive from the fact that he gave them life; and in Bodin the family was treated as a unique and largely autonomous body. But Hobbes did not accept that any argument for or assertion of familial autonomy or uniqueness could be left to stand. Thus he sought to show that the father's control, despotic as it might be, was not based on his biological contributions, was not derived from any masterly procreative indulgences.

The quality which renders Hobbes so ridiculous is the same which gives rise to his truly brilliant incisiveness: his logical acumen. Given a premise, he will push it so far beyond its commonplace attachments that it simply evaporates into an absurdity (compare his definition of the slave). But the same disposition prevents him from taking any argument for granted, and so he refutes conventional assumptions with ease, or deepens the range and depth of their implications. Thus Hobbes exasperates while he delights, as with his refutation of the argument for a natural right of paternal rule.

A father does not acquire control over a child because he impregnates its mother. Paternal dominion 'is not so derived from the generation, as if therefore the parent had dominion over the child because he begat him . . .'[1] Hobbes is scornful of such pretensions. If a man impregnates, the women conceives, and each is indispensable to the finished labour. How can it be pretended that the father's right or power is superior to the mother's? A child cannot be equally subject to both (on which point Bodin agrees); but that must prove that the father's power, in whatever it is grounded, cannot be grounded in his biological function, for in this he is merely equal to the mother. Hobbes pushes the argument further. Suppose the father had a power and right biologically grounded: who other than the mother is able to say that he is the father? Given that 'it cannot be known who is the father, but by the testimony of the mother; the child therefore is his whose the mother will have it, and therefore hers'.[2]

Hobbes wants to push his argument much further, however. He not only wished to show that the father had neither power nor right grounded in his procreative ability, but that the power of parents in general was divorced from the mere fact of 'generation', from the fact that they physically produced children. The full force of the argument was directed against pretensions to an original paternal power. It attempted to deflate paternal power by deriving it from a form of control over the mother, she being granted an original power over offspring. Hobbes probably did not see any difficulty in his argument supporting maternal power simply because he recognised that in civil society, i.e. under present practice, mothers had no ultimate or entire power over children anyway. It would have been sufficient, he may have supposed, to deprive the father of a natural and original right over children by referring this to the mother; in which case the person (the mother) who was supposed to possess an original power and a natural right in actual practice had neither power nor right (which redounded to the father); and thus the father's authority could be regarded as being conventionally political. It was as artificial as the monarch's. The father's authority was, therefore, no more impervious to state control and supervision than was the mother's to paternal control and supervision. In short, because the only argument which Hobbes believed it necessary to counter was that supporting the notion of an original paternal power, he overlooked the defects attached to an argument which would transfer this power to a party – the mother – whom no one supposed ever had a proper right or even opportunity to exercise it (given the establishment of a civil society).

If we go back to Hobbes's starting point, which is that 'the dominion over the infant first belongs to him who first hath him in his power', we

[1] *Leviathan*, II, 20, p. 130.
[2] *De Cive*, II, 9, 3, p. 106; *Leviathan*, II, 20, p. 131.

are forced to conclude (contrary to Hobbes) that this is rarely the mother. If Hobbes had been rigorously consistent in holding to the principle that control over a child belongs to whoever first has it in his power, then he would have concluded that it was the physician or mid-wife who usually possesses an original power (and right) of dominion over the infant. For this power must belong to whoever attends the child's emergence from the womb. And such attendance is usually indispensable because of the risk to life (the mother's) in cases of abor-tion and solitary delivery. A mother is usually only free to dispose of a child's life after the umbilical cord has been cut. If she wishes to do so earlier, there is danger to herself; also, others (who are as likely to be aware of her pregnancy as she) can as readily abort her unborn child as she (for example, by harming her). To await the birth of the child affords the advantage that its life is separable from the mother's. But it is in labour that a mother requires to be attended, and it is particularly at this time that she is most exhausted and helpless, leaving not only the infant but also herself at the mercy of those who attend her. Following these facts, Hobbes should have concluded that, if there were anywhere an original power, it must rest usually with someone other than the mother. But had he drawn this conclusion – depriving *both* parents of an original power over children – his argument would have appeared more absurd still.

Hobbes tries to assign to the mother an original power because he wishes to deprive the father of a supposedly original power, and by implication to establish that, even in the most basic of socio-political structures (i.e. the family), authority (given that it in fact rests in the father) is based upon or initiated by superior power, rather than by blood, birth or generation. The attempt to equip the mother with an original power is not inconsistent with Hobbes's ultimate analytical aim: to destroy the argument that 'generation' as such affords a basis for social organisation. His purpose is to show that 'generation' cannot be success-fully established, whether through the claims of the mother or the father, as a basis for rule. Although Hobbes's support of the mother's right is mistaken – according to his own logic – he only really advances it in the form of a *reductio ad absurdum* of the father's right. In his argu-ment for the mother's claims Hobbes does not contradict his principle; he merely provides a mistaken example of it. His principle is that authority can be initiated by conquest. The corollary, in this case, is that 'dominion over the infant first belongs to him who first hath him in his power'. The mistake lies in the contention that the mother, in some general or universal sense, is necessarily the first to acquire this power. It might be anyone, but most generally it is the midwife. Hobbes, nevertheless, can withstand this buffetting. For he has so far said nothing to detract from his principle. His mistake, that is, does not represent an argumentative inconsistency. His whole point is to show that paternal power is arbitrary *au fond*, not 'natural'; and yet that it is legitimate.

We now approach the question whether parental control over infants actually satisfies the conditions laid down by Hobbes as generally characteristic of all political and social control. Hobbes requires that a mother's right of control over a child be based upon her immediately superior power (the child is supposedly accessible to her before anyone else) conjoined with the child's consent to be ruled. Hobbes's argument suggests that not only parental power but filial obligation (based upon consent) is present from birth: 'a son cannot be understood to be at any time in the state of nature, as being under the power and command of them to whom he owes his protection as soon as ever he is born, namely his father's or his mother's, or his that nourished him . . .'[1] Hobbes is explicit about the right of paternal dominion: it is derived 'from the child's consent, either express, or by other sufficient arguments de- clared'.[2] The original power over the child is supposed to be the mother's. But the child is not only supposed to be under her power, but also under her *command*, which implies a political, an ordered, a con- tractual relationship. This relationship, further, is supposed to be based not only on the mother's power but on the child's consent, whether express or tacit.

There is a particular difficulty, however, where this argument relates to an infant. For if one is dealing with a creature without any rational faculty, it is appropriate (and necessary) to ask whether its consent is express or tacit. As it cannot even speak, we must reply that its consent is tacit. As it becomes awkward to assert or imply that an infant can tacitly (and intelligibly) assent to its own governance, it becomes appropriate to ask in what the signs of this tacit assent would consist.

The problem with saying that an infant tacitly consents to be governed is that the assertion cannot be refuted – for no infant is ever in a position to reply to the straight question whether it consents or not. One can, of course, build into the meaning of consent the acceptance of certain favours (such as the milk from the mother's breast); when the child reaches out greedily for food, it may be surmised that it has agreed to be governed; but this is a purely definitional, and thus arbitrary, gambit. For the reach of the child may imply nothing more than want; put more seriously, it may imply nothing more than need. But need and accep- tance of assistance do not in themselves entail any necessary intention, even on the part of an adult, to yield obedience to the benefactor.

---

[1] *De Cive*, I, I, 10(note), p. 28.
[2] *Leviathan*, II, 20, p. 130.

Hobbes has been interpreted in this definitional fashion, however. Professor Oakeshott, for example, tends to interpret him thus. In this interpretation, stress is placed upon a *predominance* of will over reason in Hobbes (which is entirely correct). Thus: 'The human being is first fully an individual, not in respect of self-consciousness, but in the activity of willing.'[1] On this view it is easy to say that 'the person is that which is ... even irrational'.[2] But here we are confronted with an exaggeration. If the person, the individual, is indeed irrational, it would be possible to deduce from this that what makes an infant a person is not his reason but his will. But then all animals, including infant humans, betray will. But we do not suppose ducks and gorillas to be *obligated* to us because of the crumbs and bananas with which we regularly supply them. Infants have desires and aversions, and express these, but the expression of a desire for food and protection can scarcely be read as a sufficient expression of personality. One cannot automatically read into an infant's acceptance of favours his submission to rule. To do so would be an arbitrary exercise, as previously noted.

Hobbes's difficulty is as follows: he suggests that all rule is based on command and obedience; these hierarchical relationships imply a conjunction of consent on the part of the subject, together with a superior power held over him by the ruler; these hierarchies are initiated in three different ways: by birth, conquest and agreement. But how can the control which a mother exercises over an infant be said to involve (meaningfully) the infant's consent?

The question is whether an individual (in this case, an infant) is fit for ordered society merely because it has a will. Hobbes's answer tends to be in the affirmative in so far as he suggests[3] that a child is under command (i.e. is obliged to obey) from birth. The difficulty with this interpretation is that if a child qualified for life in an ordered society merely by virtue of the possession of a will, then (as indicated) so would animals be qualified; and Hobbes explicitly argues that animals have wills without living in ordered (political) societies.[4] In fact, Hobbes's general position simply cannot tolerate this interpretation of the infant's capacity for political obligation, for it makes nonsense of the view that political association can only exist between talking, *rational* animals. Thus (*a*) not only is it generally nonsensical to argue that children at birth are capable of obligation (involving consent) but (*b*) it constitutes at the same time a contradictory thorn in the side of Hobbes's general theory. It is only immediately necessary to demonstrate (*a*).

[1] *Leviathan*, Oakeshott Introduction, p. lv.
[2] *Ibid.*
[3] *De Cive*, I, I, 10(note), p. 28.
[4] *Ibid.*, I, 2, 12; II, 5, 5.

How can an infant meaningfully *consent* to his mother's rule? The straight answer, I believe, is that it cannot, except according to some arbitrary arrangement of definitions. If some acts are voluntary and others involuntary, and some are done 'freely' while others are done automatically (rather in the way of conditioned responses), then it is difficult to see how it can meaningfully be said that an infant consents to maternal rule – in so far as 'consent' presupposes conscious choice.

Any attempt to defend Hobbes by drawing attention to his repeated assertion that liberty is compatible with necessity must fail. Suppose we said, with him, that every effect has a cause; that human acts are the responses to, and effectively execute, human will; that will is the *cause* of action, whether deliberate or spontaneous; and therefore that the acts of every adult must follow from necessity (whether they are a result of much debate and lengthy consideration, or of a pinprick); and thus that the acts of a child must be no less necessary.[1] Even were we to agree on all these points, to concede them without reservation, we would still need to distinguish between voluntary and involuntary acts (though both be 'necessary' as Hobbes insists), between acts or notions 'caused' by the marshalling of reasons (and thus involving decisions) and those physically caused, as distinctly occasioned by the impingement of external forces, etc. If one makes this distinction, then an infant's acts can only be caused by the biological demands of his nature and the physical impingement of external stimuli; and this type of cause is significantly different from that which consists in a weighing of alternative measures and being led into a particular decision. If an infant cannot make the latter type of decision, then it cannot (in the most important of conventional senses) *choose*; and if it cannot choose, it cannot (in what may be called an adult sense) *consent* to maternal governance; and he who cannot consent (in Hobbes's schema) cannot be obligated. Here, it may be noted, we are not discussing the slave, nor even a child who can walk and talk, but an infant; and if this infant cannot give consent, then it cannot be maternally governed by means of consent. And this inadequacy would seem to spoil the façade of Hobbes's socio-political edifice. As an infant which cannot walk or talk or even distinguish between individuals is scarcely in a position to 'consent' to anything at all, it becomes important to determine whether this is a genuine or insuperable difficulty, or whether Hobbes can be rescued from it without harm or false consistency.

Hobbes's problem here again can be construed (I believe correctly) as more one of omission and imprecision than one of inconsistency and

[1] Cf. Hobbes, *Of Liberty and Necessity* (1839 ed.), p. 11, para. 5; *Leviathan*, II, 21, pp. 136–8.

contradiction. To begin, Hobbes believes the personality of the individual demonstrates not only the play of will, but also the exercise of reason. But a child (as an infant) demonstrates only' will. An adult shows both will and reason. It is the possession of reason, as a more sophisticated means to the attainment of desire, which makes civil society possible. By implication, therefore, those who do not possess reason (such as infants and beasts) cannot be a party to, or participate in, it – other than as objects. But Hobbes as we know, wants to say that children do participate in civil society. Yet it is clear, at least, that they cannot all do so – given the importance Hobbes attributes to reason in the elaboration of civil society. *They cannot*, that is to say, *in so far as they are not, or have not become, rational creatures.* What we must now fasten upon is a simple fact which may clear up the problem: it is that children are not all of a piece; they are both rational and (merely) willful, depending on the stage of development they have reached; for some children (infants) could be called mere bundles of impulse, as irresponsible and as incapable of responsibility as they are powerless; while afterwards they grow, and learn, and by a gradual process become capable of responsibility. Such is the general meaning of the following: 'Children therefore are not endued with reason at all, till they have attained the use of speech; but are called reasonable creatures, for the possibility apparent of having use of reason in time to come.'[1] Thus Hobbes's position must be taken most consistently to imply that not all children are obligated to, or can enter into, an ordered or inherently peaceful relationship with their mothers. Hobbes does not expressly say this, however, so the remainder of what follows must be regarded as inventive reconstruction with a view to optimal consistency.

The conclusion we immediately reach is that, in Hobbes's system, it is indispensable, where any individual is to be obligated, that he be capable of speech (which is the condition of reasoning). A system of political organisation is really nothing more than a system of obligations. For Hobbes, the basic obligation involved is obedience to rulers. We must conclude independently that some children are, and others are not, capable of speech, and therefore of reasoning, and therefore of obligation. Those who are incapable of speech, to follow the logic of Hobbes's schema, are no different from beasts, in that they cannot join in a political compact; those who are capable of speech escape this condition and become assimilable to a political, civil, ordered and peaceful society. Persons who are mad, or become so, though they have the use of speech, use it (as internal argument and reasoning) in their own private way, according to Hobbes, and by being thus shut off from communication and the possibility of common agreement, are in the

[1] *Leviathan*, I, 5, p. 29.

condition, and may represent the danger, of beasts (because of their strength, of which of course an infant is deprived).

An ordered society requires that its individual members be capable of reason and obligation. The child may therefore be regarded as fully assimilated to its mother's control not merely when it is subject to her power but when it is in a sufficiently rational state to consent to it (either expressly or implicitly). This must be so even where the control relationship is initiated by the mother's superior power. Hobbes thought it impossible to enter into agreement with, or receive consent from, any person or being who would not, or with whom one could not, speak. It was impossible, therefore, to enter into compacts with God or beasts: 'no man can compact with him who doth not declare his acceptance'. By implication (here arises Hobbes's own failure to draw out the implication) it would be equally impossible to contract with, or receive consent from, infants: 'by reason of their want of speech and understanding'.[1] For this lack is no less characteristic of them than of beasts. Leaving aside the question of a potential for speech, it may be said that God or an animal (Hobbes mentions both explicitly) or a child-*qua*-infant (which Hobbes omits to mention) does not 'declare his acceptance'. Thus, to be able to consent to rule means, for Hobbes, being able to enter into a contractual relationship. Although Hobbes does not argue that being able to contract requires a capacity for choice (he claims that elective and all other acts are 'caused'), he does argue that it requires a capacity for reason (minimally this means speech). Thus, children who 'are not endued with reason at all' could not *consent* to maternal governance until 'they have attained the use of speech'. They are nonetheless different from animals, are 'reasonable creatures' even, but only in the sense that they are assumed to have a *potential* for reason, while not yet being able to exercise it.

If we accept that an infant – quite like an animal or a madman – does not declare his acceptance, it is plain that the mother, though *possibly* the first to see it emerge from her body, cannot directly obligate it for all that; for it cannot speak or reason or declare its acceptance of her authority; so it cannot immediately, nor for some time to come, enter into a politically ordered relationship with her; which is to say that it is not, and cannot immediately become, part of a social union; it cannot accept any obligation or political tie.

The soundest interpretation of Hobbes – at least the most coherent – would appear to be one which concluded that newly born children cannot immediately assume the obligations characteristic of political organisation, because they are not rational (in fact), whatever may be their potential for rationality (in nature). Hobbes does not insist that

[1] *De Cive*, I, 2, 12, p. 37.

every human being is obligated in a civil society, so the case of the infant need not contradict him in a general sense. For if the infant offers no consent, and therefore no obligation, and so is no bearer of rights by its own act *vis-à-vis* its fellows, this is obviously true as well, not only of animals, but also of 'madmen' and 'slaves' ('slave' in the strict sense – of a person in chains – which Hobbes imposes upon the term). If Hobbes argues, as he does, that a slave has no obligation because he has not consented to obey, and that the same is true of animals, then it must obviously be equally true of infants (although – as we remarked – Hobbes does not himself draw this conclusion).

Chapter Sixteen

Parent and Child

The question of parental control over children creates certain difficulties for Hobbes in regard to his apparently general contention that order among human beings is based upon command and obedience, and that obedience requires superior power on the part of the person who commands together with the consent of the person commanded.

An infant is obviously in no position to provide such consent. Either the infant must cease to be regarded as a person or he must constitute an exception to the general rule. To argue that he is not a person is scarcely acceptable.[1] To make him an exception weakens the force of the general rule. Hobbes might well have opted to make him an exception but this he nowhere clearly does. The exclusion of infants from obligatory ties, however, becomes necessary to Hobbes's system since an infant cannot meaningfully consent to authority – whether from fear, prudence or rational conjecture. (If an infant could be obligated without its consent, then we would have a case of rule being based solely upon power – which Hobbes does not, of course, allow.) Infants must then be seen as a category of persons who are controlled but not obligated. (Hobbes views slaves, who are regarded as persons in chains, in precisely this light.)

In so far as Hobbes was concerned with a parental *right* over the infant, this would have to be recognised as entailing not the consent of the infant but that of other individuals (or peers), who alone would be capable of legitimating the parents' authority by their acceptance of it. One consequence of recognising a parental right to stem from the consent of peers (as opposed to that of the infant) is that the infant would have to be regarded essentially, despite its humanity, as an item of property, since it would be an object of control but not a subject affirmatively responding to authority. This, in fact, is the position of the slave in Hobbes's analysis. But Hobbes nowhere clearly faces up to it. What has to be faced up to is that there are jural relationships in which

[1] 'In many ethical systems, children are excluded from obligation, yet it is not very plausible to say that they are not persons.' Cf. H. Warrender, *The Political Philosophy of Hobbes: His Theory of Obligation* (Oxford, 1957), p. 17.

some human beings are controlled by others with the consent (implied or express) of the controllers' peers, but without the consent of the persons controlled.

Thus a parent may have *power* over an infant without obligation on the part of the latter. A parent may also have *authority* over an infant, obtained and exercised by some form of consent from the parents' peers and associates, and still without obligation from the infant. In this case the infant may easily be seen as a person lacking in 'speech and under-standing'[1] and thus as an instance of an individual who – for whatever reason – 'doth not declare his acceptance'. In these respects, the infant may be regarded as sharing the status of a beast or a slave. One's 'right' to the beast or the slave or the infant is not ultimately accorded by them but by the community of one's peers. Thus a *right* of control over an infant cannot be regarded as entailing any ties of obligation either towards or from the infant itself: the reciprocity principle is clearly excluded. But when the infant becomes a child capable of 'speech and understanding', capable of declaring 'his acceptance', whether express or tacit, then one may infer (within the logic of Hobbes's system) that its status has changed: from being (legally) a thing, it rises into individuality and becomes a legal person.

It is not inconsistent with Hobbesian logic to assume that an infant which is not bound – and none can be – becomes an adjunct to, but not a participant in, civil society. Thus, where a 'right' exists over him, it must be seen to derive from the consent of others and not from the infant. But the point of this would not be to suggest that infants are born into 'a state of nature' *vis-à-vis* their parents; no more than that they are born into a state of obligation towards them. They cannot be regarded as obligated, because they have no power of consent; nor are they to be regarded as a threat, because – as infants – they have no power to oppose. It is possible to infer from the above an adequate distinction, for Hobbes's purposes, between an infant and an animal. A 'right' over either must be based upon the consent of fellow individuals, because the beings in question are incapable of consent. Both are physically individual. But an infant is dependent, whereas an animal can operate independently (i.e. of man's will). Since an animal can pose a threat, without being capable of consenting to authority, Hobbes could easily conclude, as he does, that humans should 'reduce those [animals] to servitude which by art may be tamed and fitted for use, and to persecute and destroy the rest by a perpetual war, as dangerous and noxious'.[2] But as for an infant, no implicit 'state of war' need exist, since infants *qua* infants cannot be regarded as 'dangerous and noxious'.

[1] *De Cive*, I, 2, 12, p. 37.
[2] *Ibid.*, II, 8, 10, p. 104.

Thus an infant would have to be regarded as neither friend nor foe; neither in a state of 'nature' nor in 'civil society'; but merely as an appendage, which may indeed be preserved and nourished, but the preservation and nourishment of whom can generate no obligation on its part until it reach some stage of understanding which would warrant that it no longer be deemed an infant.

Hobbes is primarily concerned with a reciprocity principle: not only with superior power over, but also with consent from, the ruled. Exceptions to the rule are damaging to his case, and he is not really prepared to deal with them. If we speak of authority being acquired over persons, not with their consent but with the consent of the peers of the person acquiring this authority, Hobbes is inevitably occasioned some discomfort. In fact, where we approach the conclusion that authority is based upon both power and consent, but where the consent is not necessarily that of the person governed, we begin to move away from Hobbes and towards Spinoza, who was prepared to argue that a jural, ordered relationship *could* exist on the basis of conquest (or superior power) alone, without the consent of all the governed.[1] Hobbes tends to insist that a peaceful order is impossible except where *every* person controlled consents to be governed. There must be exceptions to this rule, in the case, for example, of infants and madmen. But slaves may be neither infants nor madmen and yet Hobbes suggests that control over them is just, even though they may be rational and yet do not consent. These exceptions may be fitted into Hobbes's system, but he is not really concerned with them.

Hobbes understands all individuals to be basically equal. His egalitarianism is not, of course, altogether consistent. When he wishes to deprive women of the right to inherit or to govern, he argues that men are generally better fitted for war and administration. When he wishes to destroy the argument that paternal power is grounded in the biological function of the father, he falls back upon egalitarianism, both in order to show that male and female are equally indispensable in the procreative act, and in order to show that males are not so strong naturally that they can get the better of their women (witness the Amazons). In any event, in the pyramiding of authority Hobbes supposes an initial or (if preferred) a 'natural' equality between men and

---

[1] Spinoza argues that an ordered society is possible even where not everyone – including the sane, rational, adult and unimprisoned individual – grants his consent. 'Vous me demandez, écrit-il [Spinoza] à Janig Jelles, quelle différence il y a entre Hobbes et moi quant à la politique. Cette différence consiste en ceci: je maintiens toujours le droit naturel intact, et dans une cité quelconque, je n'accorde au droit au Souverain sur les sujets que dans la mesure où, par la puissance, il l'emporte sur eux.' Quoted by Raymond Polin, *Politique et philosophie chez Thomas Hobbes* (Paris, 1953), p. 185.

women. Given that equality, there is no means by which men as such can enforce upon women a subordinate position. (When compelled to account for this *de facto* position, he pulls out of his hat the conventional doctrine of superior male fitness.) If a man and woman were conceived in isolation from their fellows, there would be no more reason why he should control her than she him. If, in this egalitarian state, copulation should ensue, this would not of itself imply a 'community', that is to say a relationship within which it was the recognisable duty of one party to obey the other. Thus, prospective progenitors would meet as equals where there was no duty (marital or civil) of one party to obey the other. And the biological product of these encounters, according to Hobbes, on the continued assumption of equality between the individuals engaged in them, is to be assumed the property of the mother.

Where more men than one are available, it is obviously for the mother to declare who the father is. Thus he can have no original or natural *right* over the child, simply because his designation must depend upon the mother's will. We are primarily concerned with power, however, not right. And in this connection, Hobbes supposes that the conqueror is 'by right of nature . . . lord of the conquered'.[1] This means that in a state of war it is proper to do what one likes with an enemy. In this situation the right follows from one's power. Power over an infant, who is not a party to any political tie, yields a right over it in that one does not deprive it of life. It is an obligation that Hobbes makes the *infant* assume in view of the favour it has been shown.[2] The relevant point is that the first person to acquire power over it is assumed to inherit this right of command (and of receiving obedience). The next point, as we have seen, is that the mother is supposed to be the first person in a position to wield this power following birth. Thus the important fact is not that the father has performed procreative marvels, or that the mother has given birth, but that one person has acquired power over another – it being assumed that the one with power is in this case the mother because of her initial proximity to the child.

[1] *De Cive*, II, 9, 2, p. 106.

[2] Hobbes is simply inconsistent. His overall position conflicts with his obvious desire to attribute to the infant obligation. The interpretation which seems fairest to Hobbes is one which suggests that the infant has an implicit obligation towards its parent or protector, but an obligation which only becomes real when the infant is no longer an infant but a child minimally capable of reason. This must clearly imply, however, that the infant *qua* infant cannot in fact be obligated, since it is only as a person (a child) with a minimally developed rational capacity that he becomes so. The difficulty stems from the fact that one cannot dismiss Hobbes's claims that a son is never born into a state of nature (i.e. that he has an obligation from infancy) and that his immediate obligation is towards him in whose power he finds himself (by whom he is protected, succoured and otherwise preserved from death).

The question of importance, then, is not who gives birth but who offers protection; not who is the father or the mother, but who has power over the infant, and with this protects and preserves its life. It is through this protection, preservation, shelter and nourishment that it becomes obligated or tied to a superior. Hobbes's assumption is that generally the person who immediately does this, and shall continue to do this, is the mother. It is initially for her to 'breed him up, or adventure him to fortune'.[1] Such breeding up is a continuing responsibility which she customarily assumes. And if 'she nourish it, it oweth its life to the mother; and is therefore obliged to obey her, rather than any other . . .'[2] Thus, given an initial equality between male and female, and assuming the initial advantage of proximity in the establishment of an original maternal power, and supposing the continuation of this advantage, there must come a point[3] where the child, with the acquisition of speech (and rationality), becomes capable of assuming or recognizing its obligation in consequence of the preservation of its life. The question in dispute earlier was whether a child merely *recognises* an obligation (which was there from birth) or whether, with speech and rationality, it *assumes* an obligation (binding from the point at which he can meaningfully be said to assume it). Hobbes's argument tends to imply both.

To choose either of these courses creates a difficulty. If the child recognises an obligation that was there from birth, then it is contended that an individual or being bereft of reason can be a party to a political tie (while Hobbes insists that speech, and the rationality which it implies, is necessary for both consent and obligation). If the child assumes an obligation that exists from the point that he can consent to it, then we have an instance (in infancy) of political control over a human being without its consent. The second course seems to be most congenial, logically, to Hobbes's overall position. I would think, therefore, that it should be taken that it is only after a certain point that the child becomes capable of assuming an obligation towards its mother – not as mother but as protector.

If Hobbes believed that authority could be established purely by superior power, then the control of infants by parents would create no difficulty. But as Hobbes did not believe that authority can be established in this way, the case of parental authority over infants raises difficulties, because if the infant is to be subject to authority he must be capable of consenting to it.

[1] *De Cive*, II, 9, 2, p. 106.
[2] *Leviathan*, II, 20, p. 131.
[3] This interpretation of Hobbes – from the word 'point' – attempts to apply that gloss most consistent with his general position.

If it is argued that Hobbes does not require the infant's consent, we still do not escape our difficulty. Suppose we say that Hobbes suggests that, in a state of war, right follows from superior power, that the conqueror has just authority over the conquered; that the infant, in so far as we assume him not to be a party to a political tie, is *justly* ruled by whoever acquires *power* over him; and that the first person to acquire this power is the mother. Thus, if she abandons her power it may be assumed by anyone who has sufficient strength to do so. And if the mother comes under the power of another, then so do her offspring. Accordingly, a mother *may* contract to submit to another (marriage); alternatively, she may be conquered, may be *forced* to submit (still marriage). Thus the obligation of the child to obey may simply be derived from parental (or protective) power; obligation is implied, it might be concluded, in the very fact of this power.

The difficulty with this argument is that Hobbes insists that all authority, including the parental, is based upon a combination of power and consent; that neither of these, alone is sufficient; and that the one does not entail the other. Hobbes, of course, does not draw any plain distinction between power and authority; they are intermingled in his discussion. But it is clear that he does not believe that *authority* can be based simply on power (force); further it is equally obvious that he does not believe that *power* can merely be reduced to consent. Authority over a man suggests that he is obligated to do what one commands (and that one has power to 'compel' him to do it). Power over a man suggests that one is able to injure him, imprison him, kill him, or otherwise to dispose of his person. Wherever this advantage is converted into the ability to bring such an individual to yield obedience to one's commands, then in this consists an increase of power. But the specific relationship between the person who commands and the person who obeys becomes a relationship of authority. Power over a person, in Hobbes, tends to suggest then an ability merely to do with the individual what one likes. Authority, in Hobbes, tends to suggest the ability to get the individual, by whatever means, to obey one's commands.

Hobbes does not distinguish clearly between parental control over the child as a matter of power or of authority. Authority requires both power and consent; but authority over the child commences from birth; and yet an infant is incapable of consent; still Hobbes insists that parental authority derives not merely from parental power, but 'from the child's consent, either express, or by other sufficient arguments declared'.[1] Hobbes is clear that parental control involves the child's consent. The problem is whether the consent is intended merely to be implied in the parent's power. If so, then the slave must also consent to

[1] *Leviathan*, II, 20, p. 130.

the master's power (even though in chains) simply because he is subjected to it. But Hobbes says this consent may be 'express'. Express consent would certainly exclude infants (and slaves). Hobbes also remarks that consent may be 'by other sufficient arguments declared'. But what would these be? The single expression of a desire for food, and the parental satisfaction of this desire? This would render Hobbes's conception of 'consent' risible. In fact he is clearer on this point. He is attracted by the idea of a child from birth really *consenting* to parental authority. At the same time, the capacity for this self-interested consent must await the attainment of speech, which permits the child to reason towards consent. Thus we can fit within Hobbes's argument a distinction which he does not himself make – that between the infant (incapable of speech) and the child (who has outgrown this incapacity). In so far as Hobbes requires consent to parental authority, this can only really come from the child, never from the infant. Understood in this way, the child is subject to parental power, and its consent establishes parental authority. It consents to render obedience, given the suspension of any present attempt against its life. Thus, for Hobbes, children are essentially individuals like any others, 'sprung up out of the earth', as it were, 'and suddenly (like mushrooms) come to full maturity'. The child, too, is capable of speech, of reason, of consent, and thus of contractual obligation.

A child, according to this interpretation, can only be thought to assume an obligation towards its parent or protector from the point that it acquires a sufficiently rational capacity to recognise its dependence. It is only from this point that Hobbes's analysis of the child–parent relationship applies. The child's obligation to its parents is grounded, first, in a recognition of their separateness; this implies that the relationship is recognised in some sense to be voluntary; the consequence of the voluntary parental act of protection is the preservation of the child's life; and the consequence of the child's recognition of its dependence, and of its conscious acceptance of this dependence, together with an ability to infer the consequence of the removal of the parental protective power, generates an obligation on the child's part towards the parent.

From the parent's point of view, the child must cease to be an infant from the point that it is capable of speech, of sustaining a train of thought, of wielding power, of dispensing (at least in part) with the need for parental assistance, etc., in order to survive. To be able to do these things implies that it is capable of acting against, as well as in the interest of, its protector. Speech implies a capacity for rationality; growth implies an acquired ability for independent, and possibly harmful, activity. It is the increase in strength and independence which creates an implied parental demand for obligation. It is the development of a child's rational faculty which makes obligation to a parent possible (given, of course, the parent's initial power). A child becomes capable of obligation, however, not only when it is capable of speech but when it is able to understand speech. The consequence of such understanding is a capacity to subjoin its will to the will of another. When a child is able to do this, it is also able to refuse to do it, and it is in this sense that it can act against the commands of a parent. Hobbes's assumption is that everyone, given an individual capacity to act, whether this be rationally or irrationally, 'is an enemy to that other whom he neither obeys nor commands'.[1] This is in a state of nature, where two persons are exposed to one another without being bound by a common source of authority (i.e. a positive system of law). In this case the child, *vis-à-vis* its protector, becomes an outlaw to the extent that it refuses obedience. And the notion that it is the child who becomes the outlaw suggests that the parent's will represents the law and that this is just. The supposition from which this notion of justice flows is that an individual who preserves the life of another can only do so in the belief that one who has spared another cannot be taken to have done so in order to endanger his own life. In any event, for Hobbes, all order is built upon command and obedience. Where the order of command is unclear or is rejected, there can be no peace. A child must either be related to its protector as an obedient object of command within a civil society, or it must be treated as an opponent within a state of nature.

Hobbes is interested in meaningfully showing that the child actually consents to parental government. For he is primarily concerned with a 'reciprocal' relationship, with the notion that a subject's consent is implicitly subjoined to a ruler's command in a civil society. He wants to establish this reciprocity between parents and children. We have seen that he does not distinguish clearly between parental authority (*a*) as derived from mere power over the child, and (*b*) as derived from this power plus the consent of the child. But it seems clear that what interests him, as stated, is the reciprocal relationship wherein the child's consent is attached to the protector's power. Hobbes is also unclear whether this attachment is (*a*) automatic upon birth or (*b*) a subsequent development made possible by the child's advances in rational capacity. I believe, as already noted, the second interpretation to be the more generally consistent with Hobbes's overall position. Thus the child consents (expressly or otherwise) only when able to speak or understand speech, since it is only then that it is even theoretically possible to be one who does, as opposed to one 'who doth not declare his acceptance'.[2]

[1] *De Cive*, II, 9, 3, p. 106.
[2] *Ibid.*, I, 2, 12, p. 37.

In summary, Hobbes believed (like Bodin) that all authority is based on command and obedience. But he also believed that this relationship of command requires not only superior power on the part of the person who commands, but equally the consent of the person or persons commanded. A mother's 'original' authority is based upon her originally superior power combined with 'the child's consent, either express, or by other sufficient arguments declared'.[1] Whoever acquires authority over her acquires authority equally over her dependents and offspring. A husband (by contract), a captor (by conquest) or a sovereign (by either means) could acquire this authority. A sovereign, of course, had an ultimate right of control (and power of control) over all families and all members of families collected within the community which he ruled.

As Hobbes wrote, 'he who hath dominion over the person, hath also dominion over all belonging to the person . . .'[2] Further to this, 'if the mother be a subject under what government soever, he that hath the supreme authority in that government, will also have the dominion over him that is born of her . . .'[3] In short, 'the children belong to him or her that commands'.[4] Hobbes, as might be expected, did not fail to draw out the ultimate consequences of this position; for in pursuing the logic of his premises, he concluded that he 'that hath dominion over the child, hath dominion also over the children of the child; and over their children's children'.[5] The end of all this was not only to show what he regarded as a necessary chain of command, given an initial authority, but also to lay bare the basic characteristics of all authority. Maternal authority could be initiated by the favourable emplacement of the mother's power, but it required ultimately to be conjoined with the child's consent. Any authority might be initiated by force or superior power (which is to say that a condition might thereby be created for it) but always had to be confirmed by the consent of those who came under it.

[1] *Leviathan*, II, 20, p. 130.
[2] *De Cive*, II, 9, 5, p. 107.
[3] *Ibid.*
[4] *Ibid.*, II, 9, 5, p. 108.
[5] *Leviathan*, II, 20, p. 132.

Chapter Seventeen

Corporate Structure

'And as this union into a city or body politic, is instituted with common power over all the particular persons, or members thereof, to the common good of them all; so also may there be amongst a multitude of those members instituted, a subordinate union of certain men, for certain common actions to be done by those men for some common benefit of theirs, or of the whole city; as for subordinate government, for counsel, for trade, and the like. And these subordinate bodies politic are usually called *corporations*; and their power such over the particulars of their own society, as the whole city, whereof they are members, have allowed them.'[1]

In the passage cited, Hobbes makes three basic points. The first is that there are subordinate organisations within the state. The second is that these organisations may pursue some limited common interest restricted to their members, or a broader interest in which the entire society shares. The third is that corporations can only legitimately exist if they are expressly sanctioned or tacitly tolerated by the sovereign power. In this passage, however, Hobbes has nothing to say about the structure of authority within corporations.

In *De Cive*, Hobbes's views on corporate structure are not developed further. We do not learn whether they may be grounded in force or whether they are purely voluntary. In *Leviathan*, we are confronted with Hobbes's famous simile which compares corporations to worms in the entrails of a natural man. But he has more to say about them than that. For, from a formal point of view, corporations constitute the parts of the commonwealth. He refers to them as 'the parts thereof', and suggests that they 'resemble the muscles of a body natural'.[2]

Hobbes refers to corporations as regular systems of people, by which he means 'any numbers of men joined in one interest, or one business . . . where one man, or assembly of men, is constituted representative of the whole number'.[3] Thus he draws a direct parallel between corpora-

---

[1] *De Corpore Politico*, I, 6, 9.
[2] *Leviathan*, II, 22, p. 146.
[3] *Ibid*.

tions and states. A corporation is '*absolute*' and '*independent*' when it is subject only to the command of its representative. Thus a state could be regarded as a particular *type* of corporation; so too could a family. And where a state subsumes corporations, it is impliedly no different from an independent family which has expanded to absorb others: the point of this being that Hobbes sees the principle of control within a corporation as no different from what he understands it to be in any other form of regular union or association among men. His conception of the basis of authority suffers no sea-change.

Hobbes also sees corporations as 'systems subordinate', which is to say, as systems inferior to and governed by sovereign power. One kind of corporation he calls *political*, and these are such that 'are made by authority from the sovereign power of the commonwealth'.[1] He gives as examples of political corporations not only merchant companies, churches, colleges and universities, but also governmental assemblies, such as for the conduct of the business of a town, a province, a colony, or even (as in parliament) of a commonwealth.[2] These are all seen as corporations created on the express demand or assent of the sovereign (as opposed to other corporations which are not).

What is distinctive about 'political' corporations 'is their writ, or letters from the sovereign';[3] and these letters set out the express limits to the authority permitted them by the sovereign. Thus, the sovereign stipulates the purpose of the corporation, its procedure, span of life, area of control and so on. A political corporation, for Hobbes, is not identical with what I designated as a public corporation in the discussion of Bodin. The political subsumes the public corporation, and so, as a category, is more inclusive. But the defining principle is that it is expressly instituted by, as already noted, 'letters from the sovereign'.

The other type of corporation to which Hobbes refers is called 'private'. He gives only one clear example of such corporations, and this is the family.[4] But this absence of examples creates no difficulty, for private corporations are distinguished from the political by virtue of the fact that they are regular and lawful, but do not require the formal recognition of the sovereign. However, though Hobbes may insist upon the distinction between private and political, I think it is easy to show that it has rather little significance. Let us examine the example which he gives of a private corporation: the family.

It is of interest to note, in the first place, that Hobbes – unlike Bodin – regards the family as basically just another type of corporation. The

[1] *Ibid.*
[2] *Ibid.*, pp. 150, 151 and 152.
[3] *Ibid.*, p. 147.
[4] *Ibid.*, pp. 153–4.

difference is that it does not require a writ or licence from the sovereign. Our question is whether, in the case of the family, this writ is (a) in fact altogether absent, and (b) even if absent, whether it is important. Assuming that the church is created by writ (as Hobbes implies) and assuming that its writ confers the right of joining individuals in marriage, then the 'writ' which it may confer upon two persons to live together may be regarded as an express sanction from the state. Clearly, where the state itself performs marital ceremonies, this sanction is present. Thus we may say that, given Hobbes's own criterion for distinguishing between political and private corporations, the family does not altogether succeed in its quest for classification as a private corporation. However, assume that it did succeed as a private corporation, as it might in the case of enduring concubinage, where no formal ceremony of union need ever be performed; or as in the case of controlling servants and children, where no licence for control is granted by the state. Even in these cases, where the sanction of the family unit's existence is tacit, there remains an implicit designation by the state of its area of control. Hobbes, in fact, is clear about this. In the first place, he refers to the family as 'lawful', which means in some sense that it is authorised (but 'without letters'). Secondly, he states that the authority of the family head is permitted by law up to the point where his authority runs contrary to the law. Thirdly, he refers to *unlawful* 'private bodies regular' which are constituted 'without any public authority at all'.[1] I would conclude that Hobbes's distinction between political and private corporations – in so far as they are lawful – is unimportant for our purposes. It merely asserts that the sovereign's recognition of a corporation may be written or unwritten. For Hobbes does not even try to formulate a criterion for distinguishing between the sorts of corporation for which it would and would not be appropriate to issue licences. This fact together with other evidence suggests that he sees all lawful corporations as being governed by a common principle of authority. The evidence for this common principle in Hobbes we shall now investigate.

Given that the corporation forms a subordinate part of a larger state structure, it is always related to the sovereign as a subject. This means that it receives commands, and that in turn it issues them (but only to inferiors). This does not mean that all commands issued by corporations stem directly from sovereign pronouncements, but that the sovereign must be understood to authorise them, and can reverse them whenever the situation seems to demand this. Hobbes states the matter succinctly in the following terms: 'In bodies politic, the power of the representative is always limited: and that which prescribeth the limits

[1] *Leviathan*, II, 22, p. 154.

thereof, is the sovereign.'[1] Here Hobbes is only concerned with what he calls a 'political' corporation; but it is clear that what he says equally covers his description of the family as a 'private' corporation. 'For the father and master . . . lose . . . no more of their authority, than the law of the commonwealth taketh from them.'[2] Or again, 'he [the father] obligeth his children, and servants [his wife must be numbered among these] as far as the law permitteth, though not further, because none of them are [sic] bound to obedience in those actions, which the law hath forbidden to be done'.[3] It is clear from this that Hobbes regards subjects as bound to their immediate superior 'as to their immediate sovereign', but only in matters where the declarations of the ultimate sovereign do not run contrary to those of his subordinate. Thus there begins to emerge a definite conception of a chain of command ordering the entire society (of which the government or sovereign forms the topmost part).

For Hobbes, there can be divided authority but not ultimately parallel authorities. This means that authorities within a single hierarchy can operate independently of one another, but not independently of a common superior. It is the command of this superior, or sovereign, which declares through law the limitations upon the power of subordinates. The declaration of law may constitute either the general regulations governing right conduct throughout the commonwealth, or it may include as well specific declarations governing right conduct within a particular corporate unit. But the principle that all corporations are commanded and limited by the sovereign is constant. For 'the sovereign in every commonwealth, is the absolute representative of all the subjects; and therefore no other can be representative of any part of them, but so far forth, as he shall give leave'.[4]

For Hobbes, there are basically two categories of person who are governed by authority: children and servants. And these two reduce to one: servants. Children serve their parents or lords; wives serve their husbands; servants serve their masters; subjects serve their sovereign. Everyone, therefore, who is commanded and obeys is a servant; so that, in the end, all citizens are servants of the sovereign. Now obviously they cannot all wait upon their sovereign. So there must be intermediate rungs of authority, deriving from that which is sovereign. It will now be appropriate to look at this structure in outline.

To begin with authority over children: 'He that hath dominion over the child, hath dominion also over the children of the child; and over

---

[1] *Ibid.*, p. 146.
[2] *Ibid.*, pp. 153–4.
[3] *Ibid.*
[4] *Ibid.*, pp. 146–7.

their children's children. For he that hath dominion over the person of a man, hath dominion over all that is his; without which, dominion were but a title, without the effect.'[1]

To continue with authority over servants. 'The master of the servant, is master also of all he hath: and may exact the use thereof; that is to say, of his goods, of his labour, of his servants, and of his children, as often as he shall think fit.'[2] 'And if it happen, that the master himself by captivity or voluntary subjection, become servant to another, then is that other master *paramount*; and those servants of him that becometh servant, are no further obliged, than their master paramount shall think good; forasmuch as he disposing of the master subordinate, disposeth of all he hath, and consequently of his servants, so that the restriction of absolute power in masters, proceedeth not from the law of nature, but from the political law of him that is their master supreme or sovereign.'[3]

Thus we build up to the notion that the sovereign is the absolute 'representative' of his people, so that all inferior corporate representatives (that are lawful) must be understood to operate by permission and within the imposed restrictions of the sovereign. Hobbes makes it clear that he does not believe that the scope of any corporation's functions is protected by the law of nature; and this means that none can pretend to be sacrosanct or independent other than by virtue of the sovereign's wish. However important the family might be, a single supreme will was impliedly indispensable to give it effect. However essential economic corporations were, the commonwealth's wealth was the king's, and ultimately there could be no limits placed upon his right to it.

Hobbes, of course, repeatedly compares the structure of the state with the human anatomy: the state 'is but an artificial man'. The will of the sovereign, which infuses the body politic with life, is compared to the soul.[4] Public ministers are variously compared to the 'joints' of the body politic[5] and to its 'parts organical'.[6] Corporations are said to resemble 'the similar parts, or muscles of a body natural'.[7] The commonwealth receives nutrition,[8] blood courses through its veins[9] and so on. In any event, the point is that Hobbes sees the state as built up in an extremely hierarchical fashion, and he indicates, without of course

---

[1] *Leviathan*, II, 20, p. 132.
[2] *Ibid.*, p. 133.
[3] *De Corpore Politico*, II, 3, 6.
[4] *Leviathan*, Introduction, p. 5.
[5] *Ibid.*
[6] *Ibid.*, II, 23, p. 156.
[7] *Ibid.*, II, 22, p. 146.
[8] *Ibid.*, II, 24, pp. 160ff.
[9] *Ibid.*, pp. 164ff.

using Bodin's phrase, that it is built upon 'command and obedience'. It is noteworthy that where Bodin thought of the sovereign as *head* of the state, Hobbes sees him as its *soul*. This difference is perhaps to be accounted for by the fact that Bodin in slightly greater degree than Hobbes still somehow assumed the exercise of command to involve an intellectual function; Hobbes saw it far more exclusively as an exercise of will.

For Hobbes, corporate bodies (which he refers to as regular systems of people, whether political or private, that are subject to sovereign power) are governed in the same way as the state: 'where one man, or assembly of men, is constituted representative of the whole number'.[1] The principle is the same. The only difference is that 'in bodies politic subordinate, and subject to a sovereign power'[2] it will sometimes be lawful and proper to appeal against a corporate decision, either to the sovereign power or to an agent thereof; while such an appeal cannot be made against the decision of the sovereign himself.

The interesting thing about Hobbes is the uniformity of his theory of political structure. It is intended to hold for the state, the family and all intermediate corporate organisations. It is intended to be universally true of any political organisation whatever. Men are biologically separate, he argued, with naturally distinct ideas about 'good' and 'bad', in that these words reflect their separate interests, their separate pains and pleasures. The only means of creating order among them consists not in the destruction of their physical separateness, but ultimately in the express or tacit agreement between them to surrender their judgement of right and wrong to a single arbiter, since they cannot otherwise continue in agreement and so enjoy the benefits and security of a settled order. To surrender their separate rights to judge of right and wrong is, in effect, the means of creating unity, or union. Peace requires the surrender of such separate judgements; it indeed entails that men consent to subjection, to unlimited obedience to another. Union is coterminous with peace and order; what it involves is the transfer of a complete right of command from a multitude to a person, together with a superiority or monopoly of coercive power on the part of that person. Thus unity, for Hobbes, consists in complete obedience to a particular person; and the completest or most comprehensive unity is that which obtains when 'the multitude so united in one person, is called a COMMONWEALTH, in Latin CIVITAS'.[3]

The difficulty with Hobbes's overall analysis is that it tends to run in a direction contrary to that sketched in the preceding paragraph. Hobbes stresses the self-containment of human individuals together with the

[1] *Ibid.*, II, 22, p. 146.
[2] *Ibid.*, p. 149.
[3] *Ibid.*, II, 17, p. 112.

difficulty of overcoming this and establishing the basis for communicability; all of which leads into the unquestioned acceptance of an arbiter whose word is intended to serve as the medium of right and wrong, who declares what behaviour is just and unjust. But at the same time Hobbes says that it is not only an individual (whether father, master or monarch) who may command, but also a group or assembly (whether large or small). This is perfectly acceptable, in that we are aware that groups or assemblies do command. But it is impossible to see how a group can meaningfully be given an untrammelled right to command if groups, as such, can only be united if the wills of all members are reduced to that of a single individual.

Here then lies the basic tension in Hobbes's analysis. On the one hand he suggests that the ruler must be granted a complete right and power of command in order (*a*) to create law and (*b*) to make it binding. On the other, he suggests that supreme power can lie with an assembly, even though the members of the assembly, by virtue of their wills not being reduced to that of a single person, would obviously have to debate issues and come to some form of agreement. But if the reason for the complete transfer of right from an assembly to a single ruler arises from the inability of individuals to agree (in a degree sufficient to preserve the peace), then it becomes absurd to expect that sovereign power can reside meaningfully in a group (since its union or unity must consist in the reduction of several wills to one).

Hobbes intends that the unity of a group must reside in the decision of the majority. One difficulty with this is that, if the seriousness of individual self-containment is such as Hobbes implies, there would never be any reason to suppose that a majority of group members could ever agree, assuming that they ever accepted the majority principle to start with. If there were a sovereign assembly consisting of five hundred members, it would be more reasonable to suppose, following Hobbes's conception of the fundamentally conflict-prone nature of humans, that the assembly would splinter into one hundred (or indeed five hundred) sets of ideas about what to do, rather than split into two. An essential point which Hobbes is getting at, of course, is that human individuals can almost never be expected to completely agree upon anything. The majority rule principle is an admission of this. But the principle of submission to a single will, which Hobbes favoured, involves an exaggerated statement of what is required for peace. If the sovereign will can be that of a group (the majority) as well as that of an individual, then the argument for complete and unquestioned obedience cannot be taken too seriously (as the indispensable condition for peace). For if a wide measure of agreement is to be expected from individuals sitting in an assembly, then as much may generally be expected from individuals in the society at large. And if only a small measure of agreement is to be expected from members of the society at large, then there is no reason to expect more in a small representative assembly supposedly serving as a sovereign.

In summary, we find that rationality, in Hobbes, leads one to accept the need for an all-powerful sovereign. This is because there is too much individualism, self-containment, etc., on the part of individuals. But if individuals are sufficiently rational to be able to establish the sovereign, they should be able to come to a wider degree of agreement among themselves. If they can agree on the sovereign, why not on other matters ? And if the sovereign can be plural (Hobbes preferred monarchy, but did not try to demonstrate that it was best) then this fact must itself imply continual debate within an assembly and agreement emerging from it. If agreement can follow from debate, then order does not exclusively and necessarily depend upon command. If it does not necessarily and exclusively depend upon command, then it cannot be demonstrated (*a*) that where order exists there is always an all-powerful sovereign (to guarantee the absence of conflict); or (*b*) that where it does not exist only an all-powerful sovereign can bring it into being.

Again we note Hobbes's concern with the implications of a strict legal hierarchy. He has relatively little to say about subordinate corporate structures, about their mode of organisation and their degree of independence. The subsequent attacks of pluralists were largely directed towards this omission.

Chapter Eighteen

State Structure

MASTER AND SERVANT

For Hobbes, there is no difference in principle between parental and seigneurial dominion. Parental dominion is not derived from, but is associated with, the accident of birth. Seigneurial dominion is not derived from, but is associated with, the accident of conquest. Conquest does not create authority, but it creates a *basis* for authority, which is implied when the vanquished expresses his willingness to serve the conqueror.

Hobbes is quite explicit on this point: 'the dominion of the master over his servant . . . is then acquired to the victor, when the vanquished, to avoid the present stroke of death, covenanteth either in express words, or by other sufficient signs of the will, that so long as his life, and the liberty of his body is allowed him, the victor shall have the use thereof, at his pleasure'.[1] From this, Hobbes infers that 'it is not therefore the victory, that giveth the right of dominion over the vanquished, but his own covenant. Nor is he obliged because he is conquered; that is to say, beaten, and taken, or put to flight; but because he cometh in, and submitteth to the victor . . .'[2] To create an obligation, the immediate circumstance of being in another's power (as in birth or defeat) is not therefore of exclusive importance; for a contractual understanding, either tacit or express, is required on the part of the persons who are obligated.

Superior power does not directly obligate. It creates a condition necessary to, but not sufficient for, obligation. Obligation follows when the inferior accepts his condition in exchange for the security of his life. It follows for Hobbes that all authority is based either upon the consent of inferiors to the rule of superiors or upon the consent of equals to be ruled by one, of whom (by their effective making over of power) they have created a superior. Consent and force are therefore equally necessary to any political order.

Hobbes intends that neither consent nor superior power alone can

[1] *Leviathan*, II, 20, p. 132.
[2] *Ibid.*

produce an ordered, a peaceful, a civil society. For this, consent and force must be combined. In the case of parenthood (parents are masters) what is initially present is superior power, to which is subsequently added the consent, tacit or express, of the child (who is in the position of the vanquished). But it is not necessary that superior power should precede consent. This process may be reversed as, for example, in what Hobbes designates a political society 'by institution'. In this case, men initially consent to appoint a lord, and from this appointment follows (or to it is added) sufficient power to bind those who have committed themselves in word. The effect is the same. Any social or political structure assumes that both consent and force are indispensable. The indispensability of each is not eclipsed because of the fact that one may precede the other.

Hobbes does not, however, regard power and consent as part and parcel of one another. He does not maintain that where one finds consent, one automatically finds superior power; nor that where one finds superior power, consent automatically follows.

That Hobbes does not believe that agreement of itself entails superior power is amply demonstrated by his repeated insistence that contracts on their own are ineffective and lacking in force. In *De Cive* he states that 'the consent of many . . . yields not that security which they seek for, who meet and agree . . .';[1] and in *Leviathan*, in that most famous of aphorisms, he declares that 'covenants, without the sword, are but words, and of no strength to secure a man at all'.[2]

That Hobbes does not believe superior power of itself generates agreement, acceptance or consent is not, of course, demonstrated by repeated stress. Nevertheless, it is demonstrated. One of his central purposes, in discussing the master–servant relationship, is to distinguish between it and the master–slave relationship. In the first case, there is combined a superior's power with an inferior's consent (to be ruled by that power). In the second case, there is to be found only superior power, which by itself cannot entail or generate agreement, consent or obligation.[3]

In the master–servant relationship, the master permits a continuation of life matched by the servant's obligation to obey him. But the obligation of the servant is not reciprocated by a matching obligation on the part of the master. Dominion is established by virtue of one person acquiring control over another, and this must mean that one person becomes unilaterally obligated to another. Here, because of the promise of submission, 'there is as absolute service and obedience due from the

---

[1] *De Cive*, II, 5, 4, p. 65.
[2] *Leviathan*, II, 17, p. 109.
[3] *De Cive*, II, 8, 2.

vanquished to the vanquisher, as possibly can be, excepting what re-pugns the divine laws; for he who is obliged to obey the commands of any man before he knows what he will command him, is simply and without any restriction tied to the performance of all commands what-soever'.[1] Hobbes calls the person tied a servant and 'he to whom he is tied, a lord'. Even though he assumes that what initiates the obligation of a servant is force or conquest, it is clear that this need not be strictly so, since anyone obligated to another becomes the latter's servant. In this sense, Hobbes understands wives to be servants, as are children, and subjects too. For they are all obligated to serve and obey their husbands, parents and sovereigns.[2] But it is not implied that these are reciprocally obligated to their servants. For Hobbes, it would be impossible for masters to become obligated to servants.

An obligation simply consists in the consent of one to be ruled by another, conjoined with the latter's power to compel where service lapses. If two persons are mutually obligated, however, there is no longer an unequivocal chain of command. The first might command the second, and he the first, and to enforce their commands each would have to wield a power superior to the other's. Such a situation could only result in chaos, not in authority, order or peace. Thus Hobbes is forced into this position: 'The master of the servant, is master also of all he hath: and may exact the use thereof; that is to say, of his goods, of his labour, of his servants, and of his children, as often as he shall think fit. For he holdeth his life of his master, by the covenant of obedience; that is, of owning, and authorising whatsoever the master shall do.'[3]

The master–servant relationship is a perfect reflection of that between parent and child, as also that between sovereign and subject. It features an ordered relationship, which Hobbes calls a civil person. The basic ingredient of this state is that one person commands while the other obeys. It does not matter that this relationship may have been initiated by the fact of birth, or conquest, or contract. The effect is the same. Individuals are tied to one another in a command relationship, where the superiority (in power or force) of the commandant is tied to the consent of the person commanded.

For Hobbes, the master–servant relationship is the prototype of every peaceful society. This is what he has in mind when he writes that 'in all commonwealths whatsoever, the necessity of peace and government re-quireth, that there be existent some power, either in one man, or in one assembly of men, by the name of the power sovereign, which it is

[1] *De Cive*, II, 8, 1, p. 101.
[2] *Ibid.*, II, 9, 9, p. 110.
[3] *Leviathan*, II, 20, p. 133.

not lawful for any member of the same commonwealth to disobey . . .'[1] It is for this reason that in our discussion of Hobbes's conception of political structure we are really discussing the structure of a society which he believes to be certainly at peace. This, of course, is in some sense true of all discussions of political and social structure; for the absence of peace in some degree and at some point is read to mean that the society or state as an organised and functional unit no longer exists.

Hobbes sets at a very high level the measure of accord required to constitute an ordered or peaceful society or polity. Short of this, he posits a state of nature in which human individuals impinge upon one another without constituting an orderly arrangement, without possessing a political structure. In this circumstance, they either reveal a disposition towards, or are actually engaged in, war. Where there is neither war nor a disposition towards it, men must know to whom they owe obedience and render it; for when this is certainly known and done, one is presented in such knowing and doing with the substance of political structure, which is what guards against disorder.

Social structure implies peace; this flows from rule and the obedience of servants. For the structure to be firm and peace secure, obedience must be complete. Once a promise of obedience is given, it cannot (justly) be taken away. But to this must be added the consideration that, for Hobbes, no man can be taken to consent to any measure which unequivocably threatens his life. Thus it would be proper for an individual who seeks peace (which is what everyone does or ought to do) to yield complete obedience to his master except where such obedience entails an immediate and certain threat to his life.

For a subject to be a subject, it is required that he know, acknowledge and consent to the power of his master. Without this knowledge and acknowledgement there can be no subjection; for, on the one hand, one cannot know whom to obey, and, on the other, there is no means of determining what is to be obeyed. No man can have a right to make a law unless he receive the consent and covenant, 'either expressed or supposed',[2] of the person who is to obey. This may be rendered expressly when a person voluntarily yields to another to receive protection; it is rendered by implication when a rational individual, who is permitted liberty of movement within a polity (whether state, household or family) receives protection thereby from its lord and master. Thus, where one is rational, and receives security and protection from a superior, one has implicitly consented to be ruled by him.

Thus consent may be either express or tacit. And it may be initiated either with or without the use of force. Hobbes distinguishes between

[1] De Corpore Politico, II, 6, 1.
[2] De Cive, II, 14, 12, p. 162.

233

doing something under compulsion and without compulsion. But the difference is not that one involves and the other excludes consent. One may do a thing because one is forced to do it, or alternatively, because one is attracted by the prospect of doing it. But Hobbes concludes that, in either case, what one does is *caused*; it has a reason, it can be explained. He insists that when one elects to do a thing, without the play of force, one does it freely; and he also insists that when one is compelled (as under the threat of death) to perform an act, one does so freely. This must mean that either force or desire or a train of reasoning may cause one to choose a particular course of action. But in so far as one ultimately does choose, the course of action chosen must in all cases be regarded as one's own; it must be regarded, in some sense, as being 'free'.

For Hobbes, a master requires control over servants 'either by constraint, or by consent'.[1] The classical pattern of acquiring power by constraint obtains 'when after fight the conqueror makes the conquered serve him either through fear of death, or by laying fetters on him'.[2] The classical pattern of acquiring power by consent is when one or more individuals concede power to a master in order to receive protection from him. Hobbes suggests that, in this circumstance, they 'enter into society to help each other';[3] but this was doubtless a slip of the pen, for his general contention is that each individual enters society in order to help himself. Thus: 'The final cause, end, or design of men, who naturally love liberty, and dominion over others, in the introduction of that restraint upon themselves, in which we see them live in commonwealths, is the foresight of their own preservation . . .'[4] Whether men are constrained to obey or whether they themselves initiate this obedience, they do so in each case because they seek their own good, their own security, the preservation of their lives. Thus Hobbes concludes that where a servant is constrained to obey, this merely means that he chooses to do so under duress, and out of fear for his life from the person to whom he concedes obedience. Where a servant initiates his own obedience, prior to any play of force on the part of the person to whom he submits, he still does so out of an ultimate duress, which is from fear for his life; but it is not necessarily or exclusively from fear of the person to whom he submits, but out of a general fear of all others, near or far, who do or may come to impinge upon him. Thus Hobbes views constraint as one cause of submission to a master; 'deliberation'[5] is another.

---

[1] *De Cive*, I, 1, 14, p. 30.
[2] *Ibid.*
[3] *Ibid.*
[4] *Leviathan*, II, 17, p. 109.
[5] Hobbes, *Of Liberty and Necessity* (1839 ed.), p. 33.

Constraint imposes fear; deliberation leads from fear in an attempt to discover a means of escaping the conditions of insecurity which occasion it. Thus the recognition of constraint, and the involvement in deliberation, follow from an initial fear. Similarly, constraint and deliberation cause submission; they are the causes of consent to a master's authority.

The point of this is that, whether a decision proceeds from force (constraint) or reason (deliberation), force and reason are the means by which it is caused. The decision is caused and at the same time 'free'. The fact that it is free is not to be taken to imply that it is uncaused, but merely that the person deciding, up to the point of choosing, believes that he can choose between one or more acts. The decision taken is caused, but decisions are acts that are generally referred to as 'voluntary' or elective. Thus, whether one decides to submit to authority from foresight or from constraint, the decision must be viewed as voluntary or elective and thus (where there is no sovereign power which declares the contrary to be so) as binding.

Hobbes, in fact, is dramatically clear in his view that decisions which result from the application of force are elective or, in a sense, 'free'. 'For when a man is compelled, for example, to subject himself to an enemy or die, he hath still election left to him, and a deliberation to bethink which of the two he can better endure. And he that is led to prison by force, hath election, and deliberate whether he will be hauled or trailed on the ground, or make use of his own feet.'[1]

Hobbes is concerned to show that consent to authority is possible even where one is forced. Thus it is possible to consent to servitude. He insists upon the need for consent, not in order to overthrow, but to establish, the authority of government. And he insists that consent, for the sake of peace, must be complete and forever binding. Hobbes wants to show that government must be based upon consent (for everyone cannot be kept in chains); but he does not maintain that the consent of a people to be governed entails that they may legitimately withdraw that consent when and as they wish (or ever at all). His position is akin to that advanced by Hugo Grotius: 'From the Jewish, as well as the Roman Law, it appears that anyone might engage himself in private servitude to whom he pleased. Now if an individual may do so, why may not a whole people, for the benefit of better government and more certain protection, completely transfer their sovereign rights to one or more persons, without reserving any portion to themselves?'[2] A master exercises a justly unlimited power over his subjects, in the sense that order requires their complete obedience to him. There is no impossibility attached to rendering such obedience, to consenting to servitude

[1] *Ibid.*, p. 26.
[2] Grotius, *De Iure Belli ac Pacis*, tr. Campbell (London, 1814), I, 3.

(in so far as this is distinguished from enslavement *qua* chains and fetters). Submission to authority, whether occasioned by constraint or foresight, always implies consent, and therefore a contractual right to 'engage himself in private servitude to whom he' wishes.

It is important to be clear that Hobbes is discussing the general character of all social organisation. Where social organisation with certainty exists, he concludes that one finds a single person (or collective agent) empowered to command others, matched by the consent of these to obey these commands. Hobbes assumes that consent to rule is given where an individual, in being commanded to perform an act, performs it. If he is irrational, like an infant or a fool, he cannot understand, and thus cannot obey a command, and thus cannot consent to be governed. If he is rational, and refuses to obey the commands of those who have authority over him, he is a rebel, an outlaw, and may be treated as such. Thus, no man can operate within a civil society unless he in effect consents to do so; where he does not give this consent he operates against the society and may be treated as an enemy.

For Hobbes, it is possible to force a man to consent, but consent is not itself implied in a superiority of force. The master–servant relationship is the prototype of all social and political structure – where one individual commands and the other obeys. Where this relationship does not obtain, one has a multitude but not a people; a mass but not a civil person; distinct individuals but no union. A civil person, a social structure, consists in the concentration of superior power in the hands of an agent, to whom is simultaneously directed the complete obedience of a servant (or servants). It should, of course, be clear that every state or government requires force (to fall back upon) and consent (even to be able to proceed against those who revolt or otherwise defy the law). The question is, how much consent is sufficient to establish authority, or to secure peace? On the strongest reading, Hobbes suggests that all persons in a society consent to be governed by its master or sovereign. On a weaker reading, he suggests that all do so except infants, fools and men enslaved, chained and imprisoned. Here we approach a difficulty. Hobbes wishes to persuade men (who may believe and act otherwise) that they are obligated to obey established masters and sovereigns (which means that they should do so). He also wants to show that all (rational) men do obey their masters and sovereigns. He wishes to persuade *and* to explain. On the explanatory level, however, it is unclear whether any society ever can or ever has attained the degree of obedience which Hobbes supposes to be necessary for peace. If obedience is complete in the social structure which he describes, and if we are aware of no social structure in which the obedience of individuals has been (or is likely to be) complete, then Hobbes does not provide us with a general model of actual political activity, but with an ideal model of obedience to which he supposes we should aspire. In this he advances an ideology of order.

SOVEREIGN AND SUBJECT

Hobbes intends that his analysis of sovereign authority should be consistent with (it is here treated as an extension of) his analysis of paternal and seigneurial authority. Thus, one agent is to command, the other to obey; and he who commands, in addition to the implied consent contained in the subject's obedience, must wield a superior power over him.

Hobbes distinguishes between two types of sovereign authority. One is acquired by force, the other by consent. Where a government is initiated by consent, Hobbes calls it 'government by institution'; where initiated by force, it is government 'by acquisition'. But Hobbes makes it perfectly clear that he understands 'the rights and consequences of sovereignty [to be] the same in both'.[1]

Since the command and obedience relationship between sovereign and subject is 'the same in both', it is not to be understood that sovereignty by institution excludes force, nor that sovereignty by acquisition excludes consent. Hobbes is not, in fact, discussing the content of authority in these two cases. He is not suggesting that there is a *difference* in content between them. Rather, he is referring, as suggested, to two distinct means by which authority may be initiated. In one case, the political condition first present is force; effective authority requires that the consent of subjects be joined to this. In the second case, the political condition first present is consent; and authority requires that the power to enforce be conferred upon a sovereign to make consent effective. Thus, a government that is *acquired* by force is not one that is simply *run* by force; here force is merely the first condition present which makes possible the construction of authority. Similarly, a government that is *instituted* by consent is not one that is simply run by consent; consent is historically the initial condition that makes possible the elaboration of authority. The authority relationship itself is constant between the two cases.

Hobbes is quite explicit, in fact, about the continuity in the principle of sovereign authority, whether such authority is established by 'acquisition' or by 'institution'. He was aware that acquisition (or force) might be taken to imply fear, while institution (or consent might be taken to imply its absence. But Hobbes's basic assumption is that all government is established for the 'protection and defence'[2] of men; and

---

[1] *Leviathan*, II, 20, p. 130.
[2] *Ibid.*, Introduction, p. 5.

that their desire for protection in itself implies a basic fear of one another. Thus, for Hobbes, all government is occasioned by fear. When, therefore, we distinguish between acquisition and institution, we distinguish not only between variant initial conditions, but at the same time between the different *sources* of fear which compel men to accept or to establish governments. One source of fear is an existent and powerful conqueror to whose rule men may assent and so take to be rightfully sovereign. Another source of fear is, as Hobbes puts it, an irregular multitude of men, governed by no fixed authority at all, thus endangering all men equally in their lives. Since this danger is common to all of that multitude, they bind themselves to one another to respect the authority (which is to obey the commands) of a sovereign. In short, sovereignty by acquisition 'differeth from sovereignty by institution, only in this, that men who choose their sovereign, do it for fear of one another, and not of him whom they institute: but in this case, they subject themselves, to him they are afraid of. In both cases they do it for fear . . .'[1]

Hobbes assumes some form of consent to be implied in all authority. By authority, he says, 'is always understood a right of doing any act; and *done by authority*, done by commission, or licence from him whose right it is'.[2] So that when a person acts on or with authority, it is implied that his will (whether paternal, seigneurial or sovereign) *represents* that of those on whose behalf he acts; what he does is 'done by commission, or licence'.

When Hobbes analyses a variant form of sovereignty which is initiated by commission or licence or by consent, he does not then refer to a distinct principle, but to a distinct locus of fear (of which we shall say no more) and to an historically prior condition, which is prior by accident as distinct from being prior of necessity. Thus sovereignty by institution begins with consent and from this proceeds to assemble an apparatus of force. The other sort begins with force and joins to it the apparatus of consent.

It is of course true, particularly in *Leviathan*, that so much stress is laid upon the case of sovereignty by institution that the impatient reader can easily be misled to believe that Hobbes treats all authority as being initiated by consent. It is easy to assume that the initial consent of men to a covenant binding each of them to the rest is what effects the transition from the first part of the book (depicting the natural state 'of man') to the second part ('of commonwealth'). But this in fact is not Hobbes's position, as we have seen. For him, all authority is partly based on consent. None is totally based on consent. Sovereignty by institution is merely one of two basic means by which authority may be established.

[1] *Leviathan*, II, 20, p. 130.
[2] *Ibid.*, I, 16, p. 106.

'One, by natural force; as when a man maketh his children, to submit themselves, and their children to his government, as being able to destroy them if they refuse; or by war subdueth his enemies to his will, giving them their lives on that condition. The other, is when men agree amongst themselves, to submit to some man, or assembly of men, voluntarily, on confidence to be protected by him against all others.'[1]

The reason why Hobbes places such stress on sovereignty by institution is easy to deduce. He was, after all, a supporter of monarchical power. He was at the same time aware of various arguments which attempted to base anti-monarchical power upon the consent of the people. And if he could demonstrate that the principle of consent was inherent in all government, even monarchical government; and if he could demonstrate that absolute power was requisite to all orderly governing, even in democracies; then he would have shown that the source and origin of governments was not so important, since the consequences and attributes of sovereign power were the same in all. This argument could have afforded the analytical basis for justifying monarchy in England, not as an ideal regime but as one as good as, and possibly better than, any other which could be installed in its place. The function that would be served then by placing such stress upon sovereignty by institution would be to show that even where government is initiated, and not concluded, by the consent of subjects, in order to be effective it must issue in the transfer of virtually absolute authority to the sovereign.

Although sovereignty may be obtained in different ways, when obtained, Hobbes believed, it is everywhere in substance the same. It involved for him the existence of a clearly defined agent (the sovereign) who wielded superior power, and exercised that power over one or several other agents (the subjects), who owed and rendered obedience to him. The sovereign's authority always requires the consent of the person who becomes a subject. But this consent never implies a mutual contract. The vanquished may consent to be ruled in order to save his life, but his sovereign is in no way obligated to spare him, simply because he has promised obedience. Parties may consent to be ruled in order to secure protection against one another, so that they are mutually obligated, and obligated to their sovereign; but he owes them no obligation in turn. The sovereign may be obligated to God, and it may be proper that he should not be guilty of 'iniquity'; but the sovereign is not, and cannot be, *obligated* to the subject.

In what immediately follows, we shall not be concerned with the manner in which the sovereign obtains authority. Rather, we shall be concerned with what Hobbes thinks to be characteristic of that authority

[1] *Ibid.*, II, 17, pp. 112–13.

– known as 'sovereignty'. The notion of supreme power involves certain implications. To begin, the command of the sovereign is to be unquestioningly obeyed. Where there is a dispute about the meaning of any command, the person who commanded it must be ultimately responsible for its interpretation also. To commands must be attached enticements and sanctions. The latter may be invoked where there are breaches of command, the former to induce obedience. He who issues commands must ultimately determine what rewards and punishments are required to ensure that they are obeyed. Thus the sovereign is the 'sole legislator' or source of law, the ultimate interpreter of the law, and the determiner of rewards and punishments where the law is upheld or violated. Thus the legislative and judicial spheres must belong entirely to him, which must entail that he is above the law, since he is the maker and judge of it.

For Hobbes, the power of the sovereign is absolute, unlimited, inalienable, indivisible and perpetual. Hobbes, however, does not advance these claims in the abstract. All of them reduce to his initial axioms. These are (a) that all secure political and social organisation reduces to relations of command and obedience; (b) that the fixity of these relationships requires the exercise of a superior power on the part of the person commanding together with the consent to be ruled on the part of the person obeying; and (c) that the commands of the sovereign, in so far as he remains sovereign, must be read as coterminous with the designation of right and wrong. Given these axioms, the power of the sovereign is absolute, in the sense that one can designate no human power within the commonwealth greater than his or which is capable of contravening it. Similarly, his power is unlimited in the sense that there is no agent in the commonwealth who may set himself above the sovereign to say, in any particular case, what he may and what he may not do; nor how much he may or may not do. The power of the sovereign is inalienable in that there is no means by which an all-powerful ruler, receiving the obedience of subjects (whose rule of right and wrong consists in his commands), can be said to have forfeited or alienated his sovereignty by virtue of a supposed violation of justice. Sovereign power is indivisible, since to yield a part is to yield the whole; for a sovereign cannot remain so unless he retain the supreme power over the army (force), the legislature (the source of law), the judiciary (the interpreter of law), the economy (taxation) and doctrine (the church). The sovereign's power is perpetual only in the sense that, *qua* sovereign, he cannot be removed and may determine who is to succeed him.

Chapter Nineteen

Conclusion

It may prove useful to reconsider the discussion of Hobbes in the light of the distinction he establishes between sovereignty by acquisition and sovereignty by institution. (It will be recalled that the first means force and the second consent.) Hobbes argues that, in whatever way sovereignty is acquired, the rights attaching to it are the same. It is as well to quote his own statement regarding the range of those rights: the sovereign's 'power cannot, without his consent, be transferred to another: he cannot forfeit it: he cannot be accused by any of his subjects, of injury: he cannot be punished by them: he is judge of what is necessary for peace; and judge of doctrines; he is sole legislator; and supreme judge of controversies; and of the times, and occasions of war, and peace: to him it belongeth to choose magistrates, counsellors, commanders, and all other officers, and ministers; and to determine of rewards, and punishments, honour, and order'.[1]

It does not really matter that Hobbes says that sovereignty by acquisition (or conquest) and by institution (or consent) produce the same effects; that sovereign rule by a group of individuals and by a single individual are equally absolute; that 'the difference between' monarchy, aristocracy and democracy 'consisteth not in the difference of power'.[2] For although, in one sense, there is no difference, in another there is all the difference in the world. There is no difference between them only in an external sense: a state conquered by an aristocracy or a democracy, as Hobbes says, is 'governed but monarchically'.[3] People who are in no way consulted in the process of rule are, formally speaking, in a uniform state of subjection, no matter how their rulers proceed among themselves in the course of controlling those people. But the situation is altered where the ruled are also the rulers, i.e. where the form of sovereign in some sense contains the subject. In this situation, no ruling element, formally speaking, in so far as it contains some or all of the ruled, can be considered as standing entirely above the law. Hobbes himself is

[1] *Leviathan*, II, 20, p. 130.
[2] *Ibid.*, II, 19.
[3] *Ibid.*

also aware that there is an important difference. But he does not describe it as a difference of power; and in fact it is not so much a difference of power as of the *structure* of power and of the consequences entailed by such differences of structure. Hobbes, it becomes clear, is inclined to assume that collective sovereigns are less likely, empirically speaking, to prove as absolute as the monarchical variety. But, of course, to be proved less absolute, in the Hobbesian context, is essentially to be proved less fit for the exercise of sovereignty.

Let us then see what Hobbes has to say about the three kinds of sovereign in respect to their relative 'convenience, or aptitude to produce the Peace, and Security of the people' – about which is best suited to protect the lives of subjects. What we notice is that monarchy always comes off best or at least as no worse than its rivals. To begin, Hobbes argues that under any government, men will promote their private interest wherever it conflicts with the public interest, but that under a monarchy there is less of such conflict than under the other forms. Under a monarchy, following Hobbes, the sovereign may receive an extremely wide range of counsel, and privately; under the other forms, the membership of the assembly is fixed, and the counsel that is given cannot really be given secretly. Under monarchy, the sovereign (like anyone else) may change his mind; under the other forms, members will not only change their minds, they will also disappear and reappear unpredictably, and these fluctuations in attendance increase the likelihood of political affairs failing to receive consistent direction. An assembly, Hobbes contends, can be reduced to civil war; the decision-making procedure of a monarchy cannot be reduced to such depths of internal disagreement. Just as a monarch may deprive a subject of his goods to enrich flatterers, so may an assembly; but whereas a monarch has few favourites, according to Hobbes, an assembly has many. Just as a monarchy may fall into the power of a child, incapable of dissenting from the counsel of his advisers, so may an assembly find itself incapable of acting against the advice of the majority, however puerile it may be. And just as a ruling child comes under a tutor, a ruling assembly may fall under a dictator.[1] Now one can see that Hobbes's object, through all of these arguments, is to suggest that monarchy is basically a better means towards peace than aristocracy and democracy; at the very least, he argues that it is as good as these others and certainly not worse.

Thus although Hobbes argues that every sovereign is as sovereign as every other, whether initiated by consent or force, whether monarchical, aristocratic or democratic, it becomes plain that he regards monarchy far more favourably than the other forms, and not merely out of whimsy but for reasons which are eminently logical, if not sound. These reasons

[1] *Leviathan*, II, 19.

push him towards the conclusion that monarchy, in practice, is always likely to prove the best form of government, although he declines to draw out that conclusion directly. Yet this conclusion is necessary, or Hobbes's argument for such extensive absolutism as he advocates must collapse.

On the face of it, it seems odd to suggest that a sovereign's rights are in all cases the same, whether he is elected by a people or conquers them. The rights which Hobbes outlines seem to be more nearly those of an occupying power than of a popular assembly. The key right indicated is the impossiblity of a subject ever rightfully complaining about the treatment meted out to him by the sovereign. Even if the sovereign tries to deprive a subject of life, the subject may rebel, but not complain that the sovereign was *wrong* to act as he did; for a subject's own consent in any event makes him the 'author of all his sovereign shall do'. From this it follows that, if the sovereign is never wrong in doing whatever he may do to subjects, the latter have no grounds for attempting to punish him or to deprive him of office. Thus, an essential mark or characteristic of sovereignty in Hobbes's analysis is the unanswerability of the ruler to the ruled. The ruler is above the law. He cannot be held to it by any person or group of persons. The ruler also makes the law, which is why he is above it: since he makes it, he can unmake it. Thus, not only can subjects not bind their rulers to observe the law, but rulers cannot even bind themselves.

The essential mark of sovereignty for Hobbes, then, is an absolute power to command without obstruction. I have said previously that Hobbes confers upon his sovereign *virtually* absolute power – since he suggests the propriety of rebellion where a subject's life is threatened. But we may now remove the qualification: Hobbes simply confers upon his sovereign absolute power. For he suggests that a sovereign may well have to kill subjects; that where he does, they cannot complain of injustice; that their rebellion may thus be understandable and natural; but that their very consent gives the sovereign a right to proceed against them should he so decide; and that what they have themselves authorised can scarcely be regarded as unjust. This argument turns back upon the qualification of sovereign power in such a way as to destroy that qualification. The subject, following Hobbes, establishes the sovereign with a view to protecting his own life. The only certain, or nearly certain, way of achieving that protection is to confer upon the sovereign virtually absolute power. But the reader immediately recognises that sovereign power, in Hobbes's scheme, because it must be entirely unfettered if it is effectively to protect, simultaneously becomes readily capable of destroying the life it is designed to preserve. In this, what one surrendered to preserve one's life becomes, paradoxically, the means by which one's life is again put at risk. We have noted in passing the tendency for Hobbes to be portrayed in some degree as an individualist. But given that such power as he recommends *is* conferred upon the sovereign, it is not *virtually* absolute, as Hobbes depicts it, but totally absolute – in the sense that the sovereign operates according to no fixed principles (since the sovereign may rightly make or unmake law at will), cannot be justly removed and cannot be rightly limited. One can readily understand the Lockeian objection to such an argument: how could Hobbes think men 'so foolish that they take care to avoid what mischiefs may be done them by polecats or foxes, but are content, nay, think it safety, to be devoured by lions' ?[1] In short, how much less a danger to life and property would there be under an absolute government than under a weaker form? Hobbes contends that an absolute government is the only means of achieving security; and yet it must also create great insecurity in respect of the intentions of the sovereign. Hobbes was wrong about the supposed efficacy of absolute government in giving security to subjects.

The most immediately relevant consideration, however, is that Hobbes went much too far in assimilating the absolutism of an assembly to that of an individual. We have seen that Hobbes maintains that sovereign power, however initiated, must be absolute, there being no other way to protect subjects in their lives. Apart from the consideration, already entertained above, that such absolute power would appear as much a threat to life as a means of protecting it, the question arises whether a group of individuals acting as a sovereign legislature can, in the nature of things, be as absolute as a sovereign individual might be.

Hobbes suggests that because of the self-containment, combativeness and irrationality of human beings one cannot depend upon mere agreement to produce peace. In effect, there must be a determinate human superior who declares what is to be done and has sufficient power to enforce such declarations. Thus it is easy to see how an individual might be sovereign, but not a group of individuals. For *within* a collective or plural sovereign no single *individual*, by definition, can be sovereign. So how can a plural sovereign work? Since it is the group, rather than any individual in the group, that is sovereign; since the group is not organic, but – let us say – psychological or legal or social; since its existence presupposes not only separate organic existences but some form of relationship among the latter; then it follows that what creates the group (or assembly) *qua group*, i.e. what distinctly constitutes its *unity*, what defines it and gives it (let us say) life, is in fact that *relationship* that obtains among its members. But the relationship among individuals that makes them into an assembly essentially

[1] *Second Treatise of Civil Government*, VII, 93.

reduces to those rules or laws that guide the manner and end of their operations, as an assembly. A single, absolute, organic individual is not, of course, created by rules, and it is just conceivable that he may escape, in large measure, being governed by them; but an assembly of persons, acting as a sovereign, is not only created by rules but must also be governed by them, since otherwise they cannot function as an assembly and, as such, cease to exist. Where it might possibly make sense to say that an absolute individual may rule unrestricted by law, it can obviously make no sense whatever to say the same of a legislature: for it is only law, or a set of rules, that can bring it into being and maintain its existence. However, we may see in this that it is more fitting to speak of legislative rule as rule by law – or, more accurately, as at least rule of (some) law – than as rule by persons. For these persons only exist *as an assembly or legislature* by virtue of those rules defining the relationships of members to one another. But if men are so contentious as to require absolute rule to be related to one another in peace, it is difficult to see how such absolutism can be exercised by an assembly. Not only may we expect to find within an assembly as much contention as Hobbes argues is to be found in society generally, which must check their corporate absolutism; but we must also accept that their corporate existence is subject to the rules defining it. And if the collective sovereign is not only a source of law but is also subject to the law, then it cannot be sovereign in the sense that Hobbes requires.

Suppose a legislature assembles. Its members decide to become a government. Sovereignty is to be assumed by the assembly itself, and no one is to sit outside it. Society and government in short are to be co-extensive. This assembly, because of the quarrelling within itself, is to give itself absolute power. Because of its inability to agree, it is to set itself up as a final arbiter and decider so as to ensure that there is agreement. It proscribes debate, pitches upon a specific and exclusive form of religious practice, censors political and other literature and so on. But what does all of this mean? It means that what should be an incoherent mass of people, for Hobbes, is actually an effectively governing body – in the sense that it decides what to proscribe and censor, how to worship, how not to, whom to fight and when and so on. How is this possible if people are so self-contained and irrational as Hobbes suggests? What does it mean to suggest that the assembly is only orderly and peaceful in so far as it itself has absolute power? There certainly is no one person who stands outside the assembly and forces it to agree. If there were, that person would be called sovereign. There certainly is no one person inside the assembly who forces members to agree, since it again follows that he, not they, would be sovereign; and if we suppose every member equal to every other, then all, collectively, are more powerful than any minority. There certainly is no *group* of persons inside who force members to agree; for then *this* group would be sovereign – and the question how a collective sovereign can function arises yet again. Where a majority of members decide a particular issue it is to be assumed that the membership as a whole accepts the principle of majority rule. And this brings us back to the conclusion that a collective sovereign can only be so to the extent that it recognises some principle enabling it to judge when and under what conditions final decisions are or have been made. Such a principle (or principles: for example, validating unanimity rule, bare majority rule and so on) is essential to its life as a sovereign assembly. But here we can see that the assembly will only have absolute power to the extent that it actually agrees on a course of action that is binding on the entire membership. As this principle is and has to be internally binding, it becomes apparent that the membership, as a collective organisation, has to bind itself if it is to exist in a corporate fashion at all. But this very capacity and necessity to be self-binding betrays a great potential, contrary to Hobbesian principles, for rational agreement and co-operation among human beings, quite independently of the play of force. It suggests not only that the collective sovereign *can* bind itself, but that it *has to* if it is to exist at all.

If one were speaking of the sovereignty of a king, it might make sense to say that, in his presence, the power and honour of subjects vanisheth. But what sense can it possibly make to say that the power and honour of the members of a sovereign assembly vanish in the presence of the sovereign assembly? No more than it makes sense to say that the power and honour of an all-powerful king vanish in the presence of the crown. The members of an assembly may certainly be distinguished from their office, but only in the way that the person of a king may be distinguished from his office. Hobbes, however, does not show any inclination to make the latter distinction anyway, nor therefore the former, and in both cases for good reason. To distinguish the person of a king from his office implies that the latter expresses or embodies certain rules to which the king *qua* person is subject; and for a king to be effectively subject to rules means that he cannot be – in the Hobbesian sense – sovereign. The same holds for the distinction between the individual membership of the assembly, on the one hand, and their collective office, on the other: it is implied that rules exist which govern the operations of the assembly and which its membership is in some sense bound to observe. Without these rules the assembly has no fixed manner of making decisions and therefore no determinate character. But if it is bound by rules (without which it cannot exist) then Hobbes can no longer call it sovereign. It becomes obvious that Hobbes simply extended his description of royal absolutism to cover parliamentary rule too. But it will not in fact cover parliamentary rule. For although a king, being one person, might conceivably be regarded as absolved from the observation of all rules, this cannot possibly be so with an assembly since, if an assembly is not bound by any rules, most essentially of a procedural kind, it can have no determinate character, and, *qua* 'regular assembly of men', cannot be considered to exist at all.

It might of course be contended that any sovereign authority, whether single or collective, is bound by rules – the rules which create the authority in question. In this one could maintain that an all-powerful individual is no more completely above the law than is an all-powerful collectivity. This contention overlooks, however, an important consideration. An all-powerful individual and an all-powerful group are both limited by the authorisation they receive, however they receive it, from the governed. But a sovereign group is doubly limited by the *procedure of authorisation* which it must impose upon itself if it is to govern at all.

The power wielded by an assembly is significantly different from that wielded by a single individual: where an assembly is sovereign it follows that its membership in certain essential matters cannot be above the law. This means that the membership of the assembly is always to some extent limited by law. And this must mean that the sovereignty of the assembly is expressed by reference to the rules that make it an assembly of a certain sort operating in some particular way. The assembly is not a natural person, like a man, but is a defined set of relationships among persons. The fact that a mass of individuals exist side by side does not mean that these people constitute a regular assembly. It is only when they are mutually related by rules that an assembly of some description can be considered to come into being. The will of a king can be said to exist, come what may: whatever he commands may be said to express his will. But the will of an assembly does not exist so naturally; some of its members will recommend one course of action, others another; there must be rules governing the expression and the acceptance of the recommended courses of action; and these rules will not only relate to when an act is effectively commanded (as by various types of majority vote, ascending to unanimity) but also to how it is expressed (abusively ? temperately ?) and how much argument may precede the authorisation of a command (as with rules relating to points of order, of information and cloture).

We are led to the conclusion that if the power of the sovereign can be wielded by an assembly as well as by an individual, then Hobbes's argument for such an extensive absolutism no longer holds. For if an assembly can rule itself, it cannot simply do so by fiat. It must achieve a large degree of accord which, in the nature of things, an assembly cannot *command itself* to obtain; where such accord is reached it reflects a considerable area of agreement among the membership. Hobbes does of course argue that the sovereign may not only be collective, but collective in two quite different ways. On the one hand the sovereign may be 'an assembly of all that will come together',[1] in which case it is a democracy; or it may be 'an assembly of a part only', in which case it is an aristocracy. But to suggest that, in a complete democracy of the sort Hobbes envisages, men are as absolutely subject as in any other government, is simply nonsensical. In an aristocracy, it is obvious that those who comprise its membership are less *subject* to the law, since they participate in making it, than are those who stand outside the governing élite. But if, in a democracy (as Hobbes defines it: an assembly of all that will come together), citizens are not bound by the law, are above the law, then there can be no law, and democracy, as a form of government, cannot exist at all. It is unnecessary for us here to entertain the question as to whether or not democracy *can* exist – for two reasons. First, Hobbes assumes (naturally in small polities) that it can exist. Secondly, what we are concerned with are the *internal* relations of a sovereign assembly, which does not affect in principle the question whether that assembly merely governs itself alone, or additionally acts as a ruler towards persons outside its membership. In so far as no one of its members effectively *rules* an assembly, the latter can meaningfully be said to be ruled by rules. And this creates insuperable difficulties for Hobbes's assimilation of corporate absolutism to individual absolutism.

A sovereign assembly rules itself, which means that it is ruled by rules. It makes no difference whether the assembly is a democracy (rules no one outside its membership) or an aristocracy (rules itself but also others, who are not members of it). In so far as it rules itself, whether or not it rules persons external to it, its members can make no distinction among themselves between rulers and ruled. Collectively its members are rulers, while individually they are ruled (this approximates to one of the positions which Rousseau takes). But this is only another way of saying that the members of the assembly are subject to the 'constitution' of the assembly and to such other legislation as is drawn up according to that constitution – which means more nearly that certain rules are sovereign rather than certain persons. This is really to say nothing more than that, in either a democratic or an aristocratic system, everyone who is a member of the assembly is in that sense as much a sovereign as anyone else who is so; and this means that there is no sovereign, at least for the membership; and this should mean, according to the Hobbesian model, that the members of that assembly are in a state of nature, or war. We should then expect each 'to master the persons of all men he can', that none would have pleasure, 'but on the contrary a

[1] *Leviathan*, II, 19, p. 121.

great deal of grief, in keeping company, where there is no power able to overawe them all', that every man should be an 'enemy' to every other.[1]

It is no use arguing that this does not follow, that the assembly is *in fact* sovereign and able to overawe its members. The question is, how can an assembly possibly become sovereign, if to become so requires not – as Hobbes's argument suggests – one will to overawe all its members, one will to issue commands and to be obeyed, but instead a general agreement on rules of procedure by the membership. Now Hobbes is quite explicit that we cannot escape the sort of conflict he describes as obtaining in his putative state of nature merely by agreeing to certain rules of conduct. We could never agree upon these rules, but only upon the fundamental fact that we need to confer power upon some discrete authority to declare, without argument, what the rules are to be. But we may see that a sovereign assembly confers no such power upon anyone; and that if it does, it is either no longer sovereign or it reserves a right of review (which means that the rules declared are not in themselves final – or absolute). Thus, any group of men who assembled and formed themselves into a sovereign legislature could not possibly be as absolute as Hobbes suggests, since to exist at all they would have to subject themselves to laws which they would generally be required to observe, and these laws would necessarily come from no persons other than themselves.

It becomes increasingly apparent that Hobbes was really far more concerned with monarchical government than with any other form. His basic argument for absolute government immediately breaks down when we consider the internal structure of a corporate sovereign. For no collective body can be sovereign in the way that Hobbes requires. Further, Hobbes's entire argument for the absoluteness of the sovereign flows from the assumed impossibility of men being governed by *rules*: for him there are too many conflicting interests and rules are always interpreted differently according to the interest of the interpreter. Instead of rules, he argues, there must be *someone*, or some group, some undivided human will, to spell out, interpret and back up the rules – in the course of which that someone is inevitably placed above them (above both the rules and those subjects governed by them). But what becomes clear is that a *group*, internally considered, cannot rule in this way. We saw that Hobbes always distinguishes between persons in a hierarchy of command: father over wife, parent over child, master over servant, sovereign over subject. He assumes that even intermediate corporate groups are governed by the same principle. Someone has to be above others and above the rules governing those others if there is to be peace and order. And obviously the only form of government with

[1] *Ibid.*, I, 13, pp. 81–2.

which this outlook is genuinely consistent is monarchy, not forms involving a collective sovereign. Where a parliamentary assembly is sovereign, it represents the co-operation of a group of people no one of whom alone is able to overawe the rest, wherein no member sovereignly *commands* the rest. Any command issued by the assembly necessarily implies a wide measure of agreement among the members, whether a bare majority or a more considerable majority, or the unanimity of all the members – and this even implies agreement about what is to be taken at any given point to constitute agreement. But this sort of situation must be about as fluid, from a Hobbesian perspective, as that obtaining in the state of nature. Thus it would seem that however often he stated that democracy and aristocracy were potential wielders of sovereignty, he could not have meant it seriously, or he committed a serious mistake in failing to perceive the differences between these forms of government and monarchy (*vis-à-vis* the intrinsic limitations upon the absolutist potential of the former). In fact, he not only committed the oversight but was also far more committed to monarchy than is usually suggested.

Hobbes's whole point is that people are only minimally capable of intercommunication in political affairs; for their passions are involved; they require an exclusive will to bind them together. Such passion, however, as we can see, would as readily destroy accord in an assembly of the whole society, or any smaller part of it, as in a pre-governmental assembly of the whole society. If aristocracies and democracies *can* work, and Hobbes suggests – perhaps tongue in cheek – that they can, then this diagnosis must have been mistaken. Things cannot have been as bad as he suggests. But if human nature is as bad as Hobbes describes it, then surely *only* a monarchy (if any government at all) can work effectively. Only there is the will of the state expressed by a single, organic, non-metaphorical voice. Only there does the unity of the state project a biological coherence. Only there can the person of the sovereign (unlike the persons of congressmen or MPs) be regarded in virtually every sense as being above the law. The power of an assembly may well become 'as great, as possibly men can be imagined to make it',[1] but this must certainly entail that the power of its members, at least *vis-à-vis* one another, be deliberately limited in order to create that power. This power of the group, being built upon the limited power of members, does not therefore imply that the membership of a sovereign assembly is above the law. They may in fact be placed above some laws (*vis-à-vis* non-members), but if they are placed above those laws or rules which alone define the character of the assembly, then naturally that assembly must cease to exist.

[1] *Leviathan*, II, 20, p. 136.

Almost all of Hobbes's arguments supportive of monarchical as against degrees of popular government are for various reasons pretty spurious. We need not criticise them, for the key to the matter is this: Hobbes supported monarchical absolutism. He did so because he believed that human contentiousness demanded it. To the question, why not democracy or aristocracy? Hobbes's reply is, in effect, that where they work, i.e. keep the peace, they are quite as absolute as monarchy. But his suggestion is that they are less likely to work. It is easier for students of Hobbes to see that collective sovereigns can work extremely well. This is certainly a question which we need not argue further. The more important question is whether the principle upon which collective sovereignty is built is significantly different from that of individual or monarchical sovereignty. I think it is now clear that it is and has to be.

Hobbes is right (up to a point) to argue that in every state there should be a final arbiter. But no form of government can be so devised as to ensure absolutely that this exists. Any one person who is made unfettered arbiter over everything may easily alienate popular support and so lose his finality. And a group, assembly or legislature cannot, by definition, be unfettered. Division or separation of powers is possible at least where there is a minimum of overlapping jurisdictions. But for there to be a fairly widespread acceptance of such jurisdictions, there must be a fairly high degree of co-operation in a society. And the potential for this is far greater than Hobbes ever supposed it to be (but it will necessarily vary according to conditions and issues). In the same way that the members of an assembly may recognise and consent to be bound in their proceedings by rules, so to a large degree do the members of a society associate with one another in most matters touching their ordinary lives in a manner sufficiently reasonable to preclude coercion.

The problem with Hobbes is not so much that he makes a mistake as that he commits an oversight. Command relationships are escalated to the point of excluding all others. Hobbes failed to analyse properly the character of legislative sovereignty. The latter presupposes a wide range of shared assumptions, as well as that the persons of the collective sovereign are not and cannot be – in significant ways – above the law; and therefore that they cannot be absolute. In viewing collective sovereignty in that light, Hobbes could have concluded that the essence of sovereignty, or the real basis for peaceful rule, is less absoluteness – which as often invites rebellion – than finality; this, as we saw in the analysis of Bodin, does not require indivisibility or totality or perpetuity or absoluteness of sovereign power; moreover, we must recognise that finality is not absolutely attainable either. There really is no *certain* way of securing law and order. To say that it will exist where all subjects obey their rulers has no higher claim to rationality or truth than the claim that it will exist where all rulers consult the ruled. There is truth in both positions. But how does one persuade the ruled to obey? How does one persuade rulers to become more consultative? Will perhaps rulers become more consultative as the ruled become more obedient or will the ruled become more obedient as their rulers become more consultative?

It is plain, in any event, that Hobbes devoted his attention to only one aspect of the problem. He is only concerned with one means to peace – obedience – and that is simply inadequate. On the one hand, it is not always clear as to what is to be obeyed; on the other, where commands are clear, it is equally unclear whether they ought always to be obeyed. Rulers, even under monarchy, can be extremely indecisive. Even if decisive, they may issue or validate contradictory commands. Even where consistent, their commands may be ambiguous, full of loopholes and inequitable. A sovereign may be decisive, in the manner of a boxer who refuses to be floored, and blunder fatally for knowing only how to persist and not when to give in. Seeing all these difficulties, we may not only agree that at critical moments in history there may be no meaningful commands to obey, but that it is absurd to expect that all commands, however foolish or cruel (Eichmann comes to mind), should be obeyed – even where clear and unambiguous in the first place.

Hobbes has not only a narrow view of human nature but a narrow understanding of the range of institutional possibilities open to men. The civil war, of course, must be accounted as much responsible for Hobbes's views on these matters as anything else. Here we return to the essential importance of distinguishing between solutions really directed to the problems of one's own times and solutions directed to the human condition universally conceived. Here too we pitch upon a distinction between solutions or conclusions which, at one point, appear to be inescapable, but which, at a later point, merely seem to betray a want of creative imagination.

PART FIVE

CONCLUSION

'Law says the judge as he looks down his nose,
Speaking clearly and most severely,
Law is as I've told you before,
. . . .
Law is The Law.'
W. H. Auden, 'Law Like Love'.

'Men naturally aspire to the civil state; nor can it
happen that men should ever utterly dissolve it.'
Spinoza, *Tractatus Politicus*.

'In the first place, it can be said quite definitely that in all
known human communities social order is preserved to some
degree. There is no wholesale violence or unrestrained
aggression. But, on the other hand, there is no passive conformity
to an ideal of the good of the community.'
Raymond Firth, *Human Types* (New York, 1958), p. 109.

Chapter Twenty

The Ideology of Order

THE JUSTIFICATION OF ABSOLUTISM

The political theory of absolutism flows historically and logically from the notion that no human organisation can survive under differentiated leadership (in the same way that it is argued that a servant cannot have two masters). More than one authority can authorise more than one act, and these acts may conflict. Where acts authorised are mutually contradictory, the person (subject or citizen) who is enjoined to obey these contradictories is effectively licensed to choose between them. Where persons may themselves choose which laws they are to obey, and where their choice is not the same, they can hardly be said to live under the same laws. And where men do not live under the same laws, although they may not actually be in conflict because of that fact, their potential for conflict must certainly be deemed far greater than it would be otherwise. Therefore, it is concluded, power should be absolute or as highly concentrated as possible.

In the above it is implied that absolutism is essentially an argument for an 'unlimited' concentration or centralisation of power. But the increased centralisation of power can be promoted without recourse to the specific argument of the previous paragraph. One can argue for a greater concentration of power at a given moment, in a given country, for a specific reason, without ever suggesting that the concentration recommended is good in itself or necessary for all time. One might argue for a greater concentration of power in Russia in order to industrialise; or for a greater concentration of power in the United States in order to promote social welfare services or to diminish racial discrimination; or for a greater concentration of power within and between African or European states in order to create larger and more viable political units. Thus in different cases the arguments for greater concentration may not be the same, and such arguments are not necessarily incompatible with other arguments for greater decentralisation (as they relate to other countries; or to the same, but in relation to other periods or other problems).

A MISLEADING CONCEPTION OF ABSOLUTISM

Although absolutism argues for a greater concentration of power, arguments for greater concentrations of power are not necessarily absolutist. This point often escapes even the best writers, such as Tocqueville, Proudhon and Sorel, and, *a fortiori*, therefore, some of the more superficial, such as Max Beloff.[1] If we take the latter's understanding of absolutism merely as an example, we see that it veers between identifying absolutism with the violation of civil liberties and identifying it with the mere concentration of political power at a given locus, these variations finally reducing to the assumption that centralisation destroys liberties. Beloff argues that the UK and the USA are not absolutist in the way that the USSR is; the reason, he suggests, is that the former enjoy a number of independent power centres, such as corporations, trade unions, churches, universities and organised minority groups which impose 'a limitation upon the absolutism of the state' (pp. 172–3). But it is clear that the absolutism said to be limited is of two distinct types: (*a*) absolutism as centralisation and (*b*) absolutism as an improper violation of certain civil rights. Taking note of the expanded powers of modern governments, Beloff suggests that the 'history of absolutism is only just beginning to be written' (p. 180). From which it is to be guessed that the history of either (*a*) or (*b*), or of (*a*) and (*b*), or of (*b*) because of (*a*), is just beginning to be written. The author's apparent concern seems most fully contained in the last alternative (the notion that the violation of civil liberties increases in direct proportion to the increasing concentration of governmental power). The overall tenor of the book suggests that absolutism is some form of error or evil (with which, on one level, one may agree); and since the substantive content of absolutism is identified as centralisation, then this, too, is identified as some form of error or evil (a conclusion which is obviously silly). For the rest, the historical and argumentative leftovers of an author who advances the sort of position indicated can easily be anticipated, consisting of little more than faint and tattered photocopies of Tocqueville: the seventeenth century will be regarded as perfecting centralised 'governmental techniques'; these will be said to be 'appropriated by the successors of the absolutist regimes that created them'; the pre-revolutionary French monarchy will be said to have 'paved the way' for 'Revolutionary and Napoleonic France' by 'its levelling and destroying tendencies'; whence we advance to the conclusion that the Age of Absolutism 'comes to an end only to give way to the new age of "Democratic Absolutism"'; this being understood to mean, as already indicated, that 'the history of absolutism is only just beginning to be

[1] Max Beloff, *The Age of Absolutism, 1600–1815* (London, 1954).

written' (pp. 18–19 and 180). Thus it is plain that Beloff identifies the history of absolutism with the growth of centralisation, and that absolutism becomes basically synonymous with centralism.

Absolutism, however, is not to be equated with the centralisation of power. The term refers not so much to the fact of centralisation as to a universal justification for limitless movement towards centralisation. If we contrast absolutism, as a form of political organisation, with pluralism, we can grasp this point more clearly. To begin, absolutism cannot be equated with concentrated power; if that were so, then pluralism would prove a form of absolutism. This follows for the reason that absolutism implies a single and self-subsistent centre of power, while pluralism implies a multiplicity of such centres of power; but although absolutism implies one, and pluralism several, concentrations of power, both involve some sort of concentrated power. In so far as pluralism involves concentrated power, and in so far as absolutism is equated with concentrated (or centralised) power, then it must be concluded that pluralism is an absolutism – and this is a highly unsatisfactory conclusion to have to draw. Accordingly, we must avoid identifying absolutism with centralisation. It involves centralisation, in the way that farming involves land, but the two are not identical.

To the above it might be objected that the arguments for one centre of power (absolutism) and several (pluralism) are significantly different (with which one is obliged to agree): and thus that the reduction of the one to the other simply cannot be achieved (with which one must again agree). This position may be further elaborated to suggest that since the relevant distinction between pluralism and absolutism is that they involve different quanta of concentrations of power, it is pointless to conclude that they both involve concentrated power since it is not the concentration but the quanta of concentration that distinguishes them. (Yet again one agrees.) But the upshot of this is that we secure at this juncture what we first sought: the conclusion that absolutism cannot be identified with the mere concentration of power. For the sorts of arrangement promoted by various types of pluralism, which negate absolutism, also involve some form of concentrated power. Although absolutism *involves* concentrated power, the latter cannot be identified with it *per se*. The only problem raised by the notion that absolutism involves some greater concentration of power is that we have no means of determining how much greater such a concentration must be to be styled 'absolute'. If the distinction between the absolute and the non-absolute is a mere matter of degree then the stipulated cut-off point will inevitably prove both variable and arbitrary. In these circumstances, it is possible that any power of which one *disapproves* will be termed 'absolute'.

It might now be objected (starting anew) that absolutism should be opposed to pluralism in the sense that the one involves movement towards the concentration of power and the other movement towards its diffusion. Thus movement in one direction cannot be readily confused with movement in another. (This argument is in some degree perfectly acceptable.) One may well contrast the concentration of power with its diffusion and, accordingly, absolutism with pluralism, so conceived. There is, however, at least one difficulty involved in this operation, and it is a fairly serious one: in so far as absolutism is identified with the concentration of power, and in so far as absolutism so understood is generally construed to be evil, one must regard any move towards concentrating power as evil. This raises the serious moral question as to whether any move towards concentration of power must necessarily be regarded as mistaken or evil or bad. If so, then power as such must be construed as evil or bad. For all power involves some concentration; and in the elaboration of this power what is at least initially involved is always some form of movement towards a concentration. When, for example, any family is created, in so far as the family shows a unity, what is revealed is a movement towards the concentration of power. When any corporation or club or new government department is created, what is again revealed is a move towards the concentration of power. When any federal government is established, such as that of the Americans in 1786 or that of the Swiss in 1848, what is revealed yet again is a move towards the concentration of power – and in these two cases towards a *greater* concentration than existed over the same geo-political area immediately before. Speaking more generally, the diffusion of power from one centre always involves some form of concentration at another. A parent, for example, who delegates authority over the youngest child to the eldest, has at one and the same time spread his own authority and increased that of the eldest child. A government, for example, which delegates authority to a colony, or, if it is a federal government, to a state (relating to taxation or education or whatever) spreads its own power but simultaneously increases and concentrates that of the colony or state. Diffusion and concentration go hand in hand; diffusion of power from one centre involves concentration at another; concentration at one point siphons off power from another; thus no diffusion or concentration of power is really absolute but only relative to certain loci. Although movements towards the concentration or towards the diffusion of power can be distinguished from one another, this is only so in respect of some arbitrarily determined locus.

Since, considering the matter generally, concentration involves diffusion and vice versa, we cannot consistently say that one or the other is in itself evil, except in respect of some specific power centre from which it is diffused or in which it is concentrated. We may say that it is *undesirable* to deprive a family head, or feudal magnate, or tribal chieftain, or captain of industry, or state governor, or federal president or reigning monarch of all (or some degree of) power; we may also say that it is *desirable* to increase the power of any one or all of these figures. To increase the power of the family head may be to decrease that of the spouse or of his (or her) offspring, as well as that of the state; to increase the power of the state or provincial governor may be to decrease that of the counties and of the central or federal government. Similarly, to decrease the power of the president or the prime minister may be to increase that of the Congress or state governor or the monarch or capitalist or segregationist or whatever. Since concentration (at some locus) involves diffusion (from some other); since one can promote neither concentration nor diffusion without in some way promoting both; one cannot, therefore, consistently maintain the desirability of either except in respect of some specific power centre which one wishes either to create or preserve. It is impossible meaningfully to oppose or promote centralisation of power as such. It is accordingly unhelpful to label any and all movement towards centralisation as 'absolutism', since that is only another way of condemning it or giving it a dirty name. Using Beloff as an example, I have suggested that some writers are inclined to equate absolutism with centralism. I have also argued that the equation, for various reasons, is unsatisfactory and useless. There may be many good reasons for moving towards centralisation of one sort or another (just as there may be many good reasons for moving in a contrary direction). But the determination of right and wrong cannot be made abstractly but only in relation to what is actually being centralised or decentralised. Thus when we describe Bodin and Hobbes as absolutists, we do not merely mean that they promoted centralised power, although they did; but that they promoted centralised power in a certain way. Now that we have seen what absolutism is not, as also the most important of its justifications, we may return to a fuller statement about what it is.

ABSOLUTISM AS NORM AND FACT

In this discussion of absolutism it is important to realise that I am not merely defining, or revealing the essential meaning of, a term. I am referring to an experience of a particular kind which, on one level, involves the justification of universal movement towards centralised power and, on another level, merely involves the act of being motivated to achieve some form of universal movement towards centralised power. In themselves, justification and motivation are fundamentally the same. But the same core phenomenon must often be looked at from

CONCLUSION

different perspectives. In the present context, 'justification' is to be seen as a matter of ethical argument; the actual 'motivation' as a matter of historical record (although reliable records of motivations are dauntingly rare). In regard to justification, which covers the normative aspect of the matter, absolutism may be most conveniently regarded as a recommendation of universal application for movement in the direction of more centralised power. In regard to actual motivation, which covers the merely factual or descriptive characterisation of the absolutist norm, absolutism may be regarded as the specific historical impulse as demonstrated by any particular agent or agents to achieve illimitably centralised power. The distinction indicated here, then, is between absolutism as a norm and absolutism as the historical manifestation of that norm in operation. One or a group of agents who *recommend* absolutism may be called absolutist; but merely to *describe* absolutism will not necessarily qualify the describer as recommending it. We should keep it in mind that the historical 'description' of absolutism is only usefully a description of a motivation, not of centralisation *per se*, given that some forms of centralisation, like the poor (and the rich) are always with us.

The distinction between norm and description is necessary. To advance the norm allows us to recommend the movement. Merely to advance the description, by contrast, allows us to condemn the movement, or to remain neutral about it, or (which is very important) to assume an appearance of neutrality while covertly recommending it. A writer who *describes* the character of centralised power is not necessarily to be regarded as an absolutist: he may oppose it. One who recommends centralised power *in some particular context* is not necessarily to be regarded as an absolutist either: he may think the broader claim harmful or unnecessary or impossible. To the extent that Bodin and Hobbes are regarded as describing the movement towards greater centralisation as 'objectively' necessary, inevitable and illimitable, they may be regarded as covert absolutists (i.e. they accept morally what they may be supposed – merely factually – to describe). More obviously, to the extent that Bodin and Hobbes directly recommend greater centralisation, in some universal and illimitable manner, they must be regarded as overt absolutists. Their absolutism cannot be reduced to the mere fact that they recommend that power be more highly concentrated at a given centre. They become absolutists, or approximate to becoming absolutists, where or in the degree that they recommend (overtly or covertly) the concentration of power in an *a priori*, which is to say illimitable, fashion.

Where political organisation persists, political power or authority can no more be made absolute than it can be absolutely destroyed. It is not destroyed (i.e. non-existent) where anyone exercises influence or control over someone else. It is not absolute (i.e. entirely concentrated in one locus) where the controller requires any degree of assent from either co-controllers (actual or potential) or from those controlled. In every social organisation someone influences or controls someone else and no ruler rules without some degree of assent from the ruled or from co-rulers. Political pluralism is impossible in so far as it recommends a 'complete' diffusion of power. Political absolutism is impossible in so far as it recommends a 'complete' concentration of power. To restrict our concern to political absolutism, we can see that it is built around a recommendatory exaggeration. In the strict sense, it is plain that power cannot be made absolute; hence it is foolish to wish it so. But this is so obvious that it is difficult to believe that anyone could ever have recommended it. Bodin and Hobbes, for example, were absorbed by the problems of their own times; a problem for one's own time, of course, is not necessarily a problem for all time; it almost, indeed, seems that it is necessarily not so, given the *radical* differences that exist between any given period and some other (but not necessarily *any* other). One might therefore conclude that Bodin and Hobbes were not writing for all times but for their own time. And there is inevitably some truth in this – enough truth, in fact, to occasion the three brief chapters of historical background that have been provided on Machiavelli, Bodin and Hobbes. There is, nonetheless, an even more obvious case of a contrary kind that has to be made. This is that Bodin and Hobbes were generalising from their own historical condition to the human condition *per se*; their solutions were therefore carried over in an equally universal manner. They were making a recommendation not merely for their own times but also for posterity, and their most serious mistakes were contained in the propositions they vouchsafed to the future.

That one should be most mistaken in the arguments one wills to the future seems almost inevitable. There is a great deal to be said for the view that any social theory tends to be more valid for the writer's own than for some earlier or later period. C. B. Macpherson, for example, argues that recommendations are inescapably geared to existing social facts; and that Hobbes's recommendations were basically appropriate to the facts of his own day – but not universally.[1] Without following Macpherson further and without trying to defend him from a variety of different attacks, I would suggest that the general point is valid. This position may be more fully developed in the following way. A social or political 'scientist' will often write with a view to locating universal truths. Those truths will usually or always escape him; and what he will

[1] C. B. Macpherson, *The Political Theory of Possessive Individualism: Hobbes to Locke* (Oxford, 1962), p. 13.

capture instead are features that are universally recurrent, or nearly so, *in his own experience* (his experience of course may be more or less broad). He can only generalise from what he knows. What he knows may assume the character of a problem or puzzle or abuse or good. This he may wish to solve or end or promote. His theoretical response, by virtue of being a 'response', will always in some fashion be related (indeed, 'bound') to his circumstances or at least to the manner in which he understands those circumstances. In this sense, a writer's 'philosophy' cannot be entirely dissociated from his 'history' – his recommendations are limited by, and are related to, his perception of the existing social facts. It becomes extremely difficult, accordingly, to will these recommendations to the future.

Having indicated that absolutism involves a significant exaggeration, which is difficult to sustain, and yet that the exaggeration is nonetheless built upon a basic appreciation of certain extant social facts, we may proceed to the consideration that an essential concern of the absolutist, whether in his own or any other time, is to eliminate any source of ambiguity or equivocation in the ordering of human affairs. The absolutist, or the man who recommends increasingly centralised power as a matter of principle, or as a sort of political reflex action, is liable to equate ambiguous control with anarchy. He accordingly insists upon the elimination of all overlapping authority; the elimination of all ambiguous sources of control such as divine or natural law; the transformation of 'rule of law' into rule by determinate men; and the recognition of all control, and therefore of all law, as positive, in the sense of flowing from some determinate and specifiable human superior.

Absolutism is easier to analyse in its normative than in its descriptive aspect. The idea of absolutism as a universal *recommendation* for increasingly centralised power is easier to deal with than the idea of absolutism as a *fact* of *a priori* or universally motivated movement towards increasingly centralised power. For where power is made more concentrated, it may be that the motives of those responsible for this concentration are *ad hoc* and not principled, or principled and not *ad hoc*; and since absolutism cannot be equated with just any move towards centralised power, the distinction – as we have said – must lie in the motives of the promoters of such power; and since motives are notoriously difficult to elicit, absolutism as a fact becomes proportionately difficult to tie down. Accordingly, I do not wish to probe absolutism, in the present context, with a view to discovering what historical periods or what governments were or are absolutist (implying that the majority of agents involved were or are committed to the norm of absolutism); I shall only assume instead that absolutism can be invoked as a norm and, further, that it is, has been and will be posited by various agents over time. This is an elementary assumption and no difficulty whatever attaches to proving at least part of it since both Bodin and Hobbes (although Hobbes more than Bodin) may be adduced as ready examples of men who promoted this norm.

COUNTER-ARGUMENTS TO THE ABSOLUTIST NORM

If we regard absolutism for the moment simply as a recommendation or norm promoting increasing and illimitable concentrations of power, we can see that arguments of the sort set out in the opening paragraph of this chapter may be advanced to support it. There are various ways of questioning or – if you like – testing the tenability of a recommendation or norm. One of these ways is by questioning the evidence or arguments advanced in support of it. (By contrast, one might, for example, posit a higher norm and argue that the lower norm is inconsistent with it.) If one questions this evidence, one may conclude that the latter is either true or false or uncertain. Assuming that the recommendation is made or the norm is held because of the evidence, to conclude that the latter is false or uncertain undermines the norm; but even if the evidence is accounted valid, one might yet conclude that it does not support the norm, that it tends to lead to a quite different type of stipulation regarding what ought to be done. I consider that the most important supportive argument for absolutism is that set out in the opening paragraph of the present chapter. Since I regard absolutism as containing or expressing an error or mistake of some kind, it will be necessary to indicate what sort of an error or mistake is involved. Here we shall look into the matter from two aspects: (*a*) whether the basic supportive argument for absolutism is somehow mistaken; or (*b*) whether that argument is basically correct but mistakenly assumed to support the absolutist norm. There is also the question (*c*) whether the error involved somehow or in some degree overlaps both (*a*) and (*b*).

When we review the supportive argument for absolutism, it seems convincing at a number of points. A multiplicity of authorities can authorise a multiplicity of conflicting acts; such authorisations are nothing less than rules or regulations or laws; and where these genuinely conflict the implication is that there really is no law; for an authorisation that is not clearly applied (i.e. with internal consistency) cannot be clearly or consistently followed; and where laws are unclear (which they inevitably are if internally inconsistent) the predictability of behaviour becomes equally unclear, since there are no fixed and generally accepted rules to be followed: and in the degree that there are no such rules, in such degree there is no security.

In objection to the above, it might be suggested that all authority is or should be based upon popular accord. The difficulty, however, is that social order does not just exist, it has to be devised. Devising it always depends, indeed, upon some degree of accord; but this accord is always far from complete; for though men may be agreed upon certain general principles or rules (which, in fact, not *all* men are agreed upon), there are always significant differences between them in regard to the interpretation or application of those principles or rules. These differences of interpretation and application are important. Consequently, social organisation implies and requires not only agreement about rules, but also agreement regarding the designation of some determinate interpreter of the rules. In any social system, where the rules governing it have any fixity, the assignment of responsibility for decision-making must also assume some fixity. For to be able to know clearly what the rules are requires that one be able to determine, equally clearly, who decides what the rules are, and how they are applied. The effect of this is that government, if *complete* agreement between the governed is not to be expected, cannot be entirely based upon consent and, therefore, must in some degree prove arbitrary. Since this is true, it is reasonable to conclude that men *should consent* to *some arbitrariness* in the governing process, given that otherwise there can be no government. This basic point is, I believe, perfectly valid.

The real question that arises, however, relates to the *degree* of arbitrariness that the governing process can be said minimally or necessarily to involve. Disagreement is endemic, so a coherent social system must at crucial points ensure that there is some means of getting round it. Common courses of action must be decided upon even though complete accord on the substantive issues in question can almost never be reached. The need for this cloture principle, the need for some form of finality in the direction of affairs, pinpoints the sort of arbitrariness that the governing process necessarily involves. This need for resolution, fixity, finality – which cannot escape being arbitrary in a degree – means, as indicated, that we must not only be able to say what the rules are, but also who decides upon their content and mode of application. But to say that the governing process must in some degree prove arbitrary, as we have noted, does not tell us *in what degree* it must prove so. Thus, although the basic point, as already conceded, *is* valid, we must recognise that it is also *ambiguous*.

We may as easily remark of an isolated individual, as of an association of individuals, that he or they must not only contemplate proposals but activate them, must not only contemplate decisions but actually decide, must not only *debate* what is to be done but actually *do* something. Indecision within an individual is the parallel to disagreement within an assembly. Indecision and disagreement must at some point be resolved.

But to say that differences *have to be* resolved is not to say *when* they must be resolved: here we have an ambiguity. Further, in the case of a group, to say that differences must be resolved is not to say *how* they should be, or can be, resolved: here we have another ambiguity.

Any existing society must be regarded as a group, some sort of assembly, in the sense that the whole is held together by reference to a cluster of rules or norms which are actually operative – i.e. both issued and obeyed. The society exists in so far as it demonstrates accord and we may assume that that accord is never complete. The accord that actually exists, which indicates a matching of rule-issuance with rule-acceptance, is itself a form of finality: the rule *in operation* is the only real sort of finality that a society or polity can achieve. It may be argued that a society or a state, conceived as some form of committee of the whole, should resolve its differences, i.e. achieve finality (which is accord, the accepted operationalisation of some rule or rules) by empowering a single individual to decide. It may equally be argued that finality should be achieved by empowering a limited number of individuals to decide. Or it may be argued that the group as a whole ought to decide the matter for itself.

What we must note, however, is that whether we say that an individual, or a restricted number of individuals, or the group as a whole, should be asked to decide a matter or take a decision of some sort for the group (as a whole), we are in all cases arguing that the entire group should reach or accept a decision of some kind. Either it must agree to empower one person to make further decisions or it must agree to empower a restricted number of persons to do so, or it must accept to take such decisions for itself. In no case, therefore, is it possible to avoid the problems which attend the achievement of accord – or finality. Agreement will not necessarily be more difficult in the last case than in the first. It might indeed be easier. An assembly, or a society as a whole, might be far more inclined to try to decide all matters for itself rather than surrender – if such were its only alternative – all authority to decide to a single individual among the membership. Since the group as a whole must decide upon some one of the courses of action indicated, it does not, by pitching upon any one of them, avoid, but rather instances, the achievement of finality. It would seem more likely in any event that what would determine a group to assign a decision-making responsibility to one of its sub-units (whether one person or several) is not so much the difficulty of achieving *agreement* within the group as the more obvious limitations of time and space. The conclusion we come to is that the delegation of authority to sub-units of an organisational whole may proceed from a desire for efficiency, but it does not in any case bypass what the act of delegation itself instances – i.e. agreement, finality.

Finality may be desirable, but there is never any way of guaranteeing it, and it assumes no particular form which can be regarded universally as best. If the difficulty is simply that men are inclined to disagree, then there is no simple or single way of overcoming the difficulty. To get them to agree that one person should have a final power of decision in all spheres would be a most extraordinary – politically a virtually impossible – achievement. For them all, in any sizeable polity, actually to exercise in common a final power of decision would only rarely prove possible (if ever) because the attention of many would be absorbed by other matters and such a deliberative body would of course prove unwieldy. The general tendency would presumably be for a final power of decision to be delegated to, or be accepted as the proper preserve of, some intermediate body or bodies. But even within an assembly where every member (at some point) agrees upon a particular course of action, that assembly cannot guarantee that each member will adhere to his original opinion and himself abide by the common course decided upon. All the less likely is it that an intermediate group, which actually excludes the vast majority of those who will be affected by its decisions, can possibly *guarantee* (in whatever fashion its legal prerogatives may be described) that those who are excluded from its counsels will abide by the rules that result from its deliberations. In the end, the only finality, or order, that we achieve in society is when the rules laid down are those actually observed. We may say that co-incidence is more likely where consultation is more extended; but this may also mean that many rules will not be issued where consultation reveals that they would be rejected. *Guarantees* of co-incidence, of the matching of rule-acceptance to rule-issuance, are not possible.

Final decisions, whoever issues them, have to be complied with to prove effective. This means that one does not escape the difficulty of achieving accord merely by setting up an *external* agent to establish it. Separate authorities create difficulties because they may conflict. But the case is the same with separate individuals. Separate individuals may disagree and ask another to judge. Separate groups of individuals may disagree and ask another group to mediate. But if separate individuals have agreed that there must be a judge, they are at least agreed in that particular. Where the judge is an individual, he must somehow make up his mind. Where the mediator is a group, its members must agree among themselves in order to come to any sort of conclusion. In all cases, whatever is decided has to be accepted and thus the process of rule-issuance, whatever the source, cannot in the end be divorced from that of rule-acceptance. They are a conjoint activity and, as such, constitute whatever form of order a society or state may achieve. Legal finality, in short, is after a point a will-o'-the-wisp. The ordering of any society is always ultimately a twofold activity, and no agent or body, when conceived merely as a supplier of rules, can *of itself* establish whatever order is desired.

In so far as complete agreement is not possible, a political system is to be described as arbitrary in the degree that the approximation to such agreement recedes. Our assumption here is that no system operates on the basis of complete agreement and thus that every system is in part arbitrary. This is not to say that every system must be arbitrary in the degree that it actually is. Most could probably operate far less arbitrarily than they do. If a political system existed in which everyone was agreed, the finality of decision involved in this circumstance would exclude arbitrariness. Assuming that no political system exists in which everyone *is* agreed, each system is in such degree arbitrary. Agreements reached, or decisions made, in excluding the full consent of all, are 'final', but arbitrarily so, which means not entirely so, since not everyone accepts them. He who exercises final discretion – since his exercise of it is not entirely accepted by others – wields also, necessarily, some form of arbitrary authority.

Finality, considered for all practical purposes as a form of arbitrariness, is often regarded as involving some kind of 'lawlessness'. We frequently hear of an opposition between a 'government of laws' and a 'government of men'. Strictly speaking, no such opposition is possible, since laws are devised by men and men are regulated by laws. Even where an individual (the despot, the 'absolute' monarch) exercises a final power of decision in all spheres of government, this can be assigned by law. Where such authority is exercised by a body of men, the same will hold. An agent's sovereignty may be 'lawless' by reference to past or projected laws, but not necessarily by reference to his own.

Lawlessness, of course, involves the notion of agents not being bound by various types of procedure. And every sovereign is in some degree so placed; but they are placed so in different degrees. A law which assigns to a single individual a final right of decision in all spheres of government effectively places that individual above the law – apart from that law which itself confers such a sweeping competence. A law, however, which confers such authority upon a collectivity (the typical parliamentary or congressional regime) places the latter above the law in a far more restricted degree. First, in so far as the law actually defines the sovereign's competence, then the latter is lawful. Secondly, where the sovereign is an assembly, it is necessarily bound by rules of procedure without which, as an assembly, it could not exist. Even where a sovereign assembly wishes to alter its procedure, it must follow its procedure. Thirdly, there is a necessary distinction (and potential conflict) between the individual identities of the members and their collective

267

identity as the sovereign. Since an individual member is not equivalent to the entire membership, he cannot automatically make himself unaccountable before the law when he infringes it – even though it is law which he himself may have participated in formulating. In these senses, accordingly, a collective sovereign is necessarily less 'lawless' than an individual who is sovereign. Thus, although the process of finalisation, where there is not absolute unanimity, is necessarily arbitrary, the more inclusive is the composition of the sovereign, the less arbitrary or 'lawless' (in the sense indicated) can the sovereign be regarded as being.

Finality involves arbitrariness, and arbitrariness, in some degree, involves being above the law. Finality, however, exists on two different levels. First, it exists in the sense of actually instancing conformity to rules. Secondly, it exists in the sense of residing in different loci. On the first level, assuming that absolute conformity never exists, finality is always arbitrary and never absolutely achieved. On the second level, finality can be said to exist in some degree, but always in *different* degrees. Thus the membership of any organisation can only rarely if ever achieve complete accord. At the least there can be agreement about some procedure which will permit the organisation, even if arbitrarily, to conduct its business and conclude its affairs. Where an organisation exists it must entertain some procedure by which final decisions are reached, and these procedures may specify that one or more individuals (up to and including the entire membership) should exercise that final power.

On the one hand, we have in effect suggested that any order, if it is to exist, must prove arbitrary. On the other hand, we have suggested that any order, however arbitrary, must be based upon accord. What this means is that where any order exists it is in some degree arbitrary and that this arbitrariness is in some degree accepted. What we started from was the notion that every order must contain some procedural means for securing finality. What we end with is the notion that this finality can only ultimately reside within, not outside, that order – which means that there is no certain means of achieving it as well as that its character is intrinsically ambiguous.

The basic supportive argument for absolutism, understood as some form of factual assertion, is that where an order exists, it involves a resolution of disputes, a finality of decision, and that such resolute finality is in part necessarily arbitrary. Although the argument is sound it is also true that 'order', as well as being ambiguous, is not completely realisable. Since finality is based upon accord between rule-issuance and rule-acceptance, and since complete acceptance of rules is unlikely, complete or absolute order is equally unlikely. Since, again, finality is based upon accord, and since there can and will be different levels of accord, the forms of order established will vary greatly in degree and kind. The degree and type of arbitrariness involved in one form of rule or government or order will not be the same as that involved in another. Since these differences are real, what plainly falls out is that, whatever may be said in support of the supportive argument for absolutism, it certainly does not follow that any degree or type of order is equivalent to that of any other. It does not follow from the fact that *some* arbitrariness is an inescapable component of government, that *any* degree of arbitrariness that does or may come to exist is equally inescapable.

In no society can there be 'genuine' security, outside of some degree of common accord regarding the propriety of different men's aspirations and actions. This common accord is not necessarily secured by formally delegating all decision-making responsibility to one or to a very restricted number of individuals. One may delegate responsibility to a single individual, but this very delegation betrays some common accord. If there ever exists *some* common accord, it is always possible that more may be forthcoming. Where a group is delegated, or takes upon itself, a decision-making power, then for it to continue as a group, taking such decisions, it must again show a large measure of accord.

The notion of 'accord' is not reducible to that of 'security'. Accord involves intrinsically an element of risk, which may undermine security. Since all government is based on some level of accord, or mutual accommodation, every order which a government projects is on some level inherently unstable. The very fact that men can agree means that they can disagree. One can indeed achieve a measure of 'agreement' by resorting to 'force'. But if one attempts to achieve agreement by use of force, and the use of force has in turn to be agreed upon, one is caught up in a circular impasse. Force can generate or impose accord; its use can also destroy accord; therefore it is no universal answer to the problem of social disorder or instability. One man may be allowed to decide in order to settle other men's differences, but he cannot do so if they all oppose his solutions. Many men may decide to compose their own differences, but they cannot do so if unprepared to concede some things which they would prefer not to. Absolute order must be based upon absolute agreement, and since the latter is unlikely so is the former. We cannot escape this conclusion by sanctioning as final either an individual or a collective will.

If we can agree to obey one man, we can agree to obey a majority of men. Both moves involve accord. Both moves involve the establishment of arbitrary ends to argument. There is no way of *guaranteeing* accord. What is certainly false is the assumption that obeying one person necessarily produces greater stability than obeying a majority; or that always creating more rules makes an order more stable than it would be with less; or that penalising all infractions of rules ensures fuller rule-observance in future; or that harsher punishment is an ever-appropriate response to more infractions of existing rules.

BODIN AND HOBBES AS ABSOLUTISTS

To describe either Bodin or Hobbes as an absolutist will meet with predictable objections. These are justifiable to the extent that the expression 'absolutist' is simply used as a means of writing them off – whether intellectually or morally. Such attempts to write them off are fatuous; and yet it seems perfectly clear that both, within the limits of the present understanding of the term, can appropriately be called absolutists. Those who wish to defend Bodin, but object to Hobbes, are likely to complain that the two 'belong to altogether different and incompatible traditions' – but this is to exaggerate. J. U. Lewis, who has written in these terms, is, however, perfectly right to complain of the general tendency *merely* to read Bodin 'as a primer for an understanding of Hobbes'.[1] Although Bodin *is* a proper introduction to Hobbes, the latter can in no way be treated as a mere deduction from the former. To argue so leads us to lose sight of Bodin's insistence upon *just* law, upon its conformity, on one level, to natural and divine law, and, on another, to social utility, all of which suggests that Bodin's argument yields more than a merely monomaniacal defence of sovereign power.

Some of those who defend Hobbes, whatever the position taken on Bodin, are inclined to argue 'that Hobbes is not an absolutist precisely because he is an authoritarian'. I am not entirely clear as to what precise meaning should be attached to this formula, but looking at the matter in the round, I feel bound to conclude that Professor Oakeshott has pushed much too far his defence of Hobbes.[2] It is simply not true that Hobbes's civil society does not exclude 'the freedom of the individual'. On the most elementary level, it is plain that every actual society limits, and that proposed solutions to social problems must presuppose such limits being placed upon, 'the freedom of the individual'. But, beyond this, *Leviathan* goes about as far as it is possible to go in terms of recommended extensions, whether held in reserve or activated, of sovereign power – proposing a rigorous censorship, the complete elimination of open political debate and religious worship, and virtually total opposition to every conceivable check that might be placed on governmental power. It is not even the case that Hobbes recommends these moves on

[1] J. U. Lewis, 'Jean Bodin's "Logic of Sovereignty" ', *Political Studies*, vol. 16, no. 2, (1968), pp. 220, 222.
[2] See Michael Oakeshott's Introduction to *Leviathan* (Oxford, 1955), p. lvii.

an emergency basis; being far more consistent than Bodin, he contends that they are essential to orderly government at all times, no matter what the circumstances. Either Hobbes is an absolutist or no one is. This conclusion does not preclude the concession that Hobbes, viewed personally, appears extraordinarily individualistic; nor that his argument is based upon an individualistic premise. Although we cannot contend that Hobbes is not an absolutist precisely because of his authoritarianism, we can contend that his authoritarianism becomes so extreme, to the point of becoming absolutist, because of his recognition, not of the sinfulness, but of the inevitability, of individualism. In *Fear of Power* I argued that anarchism is the *reductio ad absurdum* of liberalism or individualism conceived in a strictly doctrinaire fashion. It did not occur to me at the time, but seems transparently obvious now, that this same conclusion was implicit in all that Hobbes wrote. It is because Hobbes regarded men as unavoidably individualistic, fated to misunderstand and therefore to contend with one another, that he became such a complete authoritarian absolutist. Hobbes's basic concession to individualism may make him an individualist, but only in the most minimal sense – for he uses that concession only to demonstrate how truly dangerous individualism is.

It is appropriate that Bodin and Hobbes be studied together. Yet it is necessary to point out that Bodin is not a mere exponent of just law nor Hobbes of state supremacy. In different argumentative ways they were both concerned with increasing the degree of peace, order, stability and security in their respective societies. And the forceful initiation of the argument by Bodin, in terms of the necessity of sovereign power being absolute and perpetual, was entirely pertinent to a fuller attempt at the justification of absolutist policies by Hobbes.

A CRITIQUE OF BODINIAN ABSOLUTISM

Although there is a great deal of validity in the supportive argument for absolutism, that argument, if accepted, does not necessarily commit or require one to adopt the absolutist norm. It will be recalled that the latter was stated to consist in a recommendation of universal application for movement in the direction of more highly centralised power. The transition is made from the wholly acceptable notion that social order requires the clear designation of human depositories of authority (no less than of rules governing its exercise), to the unacceptable notion that genuine social order and security require that the nature of the authority conferred must be totally undifferentiated or absolute. To say that genuine social or political order requires the establishment of a total and undifferentiated power on the part of the ruler or ruling group, which is not subject to any law but above it, is just another way of recommending that, in any political time or circumstance, one ought (always or universally) to promote a fully centralised and integrated form of human authority. Universally to recommend as highly centralised a form of authority as is humanly possible is, in turn, just another way of advising those under authority to render to the latter, where centrally defined, a virtually total and absolute obedience, irrespective of the circumstances.

The classical theory of sovereignty both contains the basic supportive argument for absolutism and, of course, makes the transition to normative absolutism, as a projection from that argument. Bodin is the chief exponent of the theory and stakes a claim for normative absolutism in terms of the propriety and necessity of state power – the power of the ruling element in any polity – being absolute and perpetual. This is to be interpreted as a recommendation directed to rulers and ruled, the first in regard to the desirability of a virtually total concentration of power and the second in regard to the desirability of virtually total obedience to such a concentration of power. A full analysis of this position is provided in chapters 10 and 11, so we may here rely upon a summary of the analysis and criticism provided there (especially chapter 11), and from that draw further conclusions.

To begin with, there is the question as to what 'absolute power' really means and whether it can possibly be made to exist anyway. If 'absolute' means 'total', and if a community definitionally consists of more distinct individuals than one, then is it at all possible for one such individual, however much loved or feared, to dispose of or control the entirety of that power exercised by all other individuals ? In so far as the answer to this question is in the negative, then the absolutist goal, interpreted as an aspiration towards 'total' power, becomes absurd because unrealisable. (Ought implies can.)

To continue, there is the question as to what 'perpetual power' really means and whether it, too, could possibly be regarded as a realisable goal. If 'perpetual' referred to a power that somehow continued unending through time, then it would only be necessary to show that no sovereign, whether an individual or a group of individuals, has continued so; and that it appears improbable that they could do so; from which it would seem to follow not only that no sovereign or stable government ever has existed, but that none is ever likely to exist. If literal perpetuity of power is required as a precondition of orderly government, then the latter seems an impossibility, from which we may conclude that to seek after either is absurd.

Finally, there is the question of whether and in what sense any power can be regarded as unlimited. If we look at power as being exercised

THE IDEOLOGY OF ORDER

from any given centre, the latter may show greater or less facility in its operations, and perhaps exercise a broader or narrower sway. But however extensive an authority's power, it would always be possible to say that it could not just do anything, it could not do everything, and that there were always certain specific achievements, even if desired and sought after, which could not be accomplished. The power of a single individual who rules through underlings is limited in what he can do through his dependence upon them. The power of a single individual who rules without underlings is limited by the very fact that he lacks their assistance. A group of individuals who rule as a group are limited in what they do by virtue of the necessity of their recognising, and not infringing, those rules which impart to them the character of some sort of regulated collectivity. No individual or group, though one may have more power than another, can meaningfully be said to have unlimited power. (But even if it were conceded that the power of some particular sovereign were unlimited, this notion could only begin to make sense if applied in the context of domestic, not foreign, politics: for no *one* government has ever – not even formally – held sway over the entire world.) Given the impossibility of unlimited power, a striving after illimitability must also be regarded as absurd.

The argument for illimitably centralised power – in Bodin's terminology, for absolute and perpetual power – is absurd because the goal posited is unrealisable. This suggests that the transition from the notion that 'social order requires some sort of clear chain of command' to the notion that 'the power of the topmost commander must be completely centralised or absolute' is not only unnecessary but impossible. To a large extent, Bodin is aware that illimitably centralised (i.e. absolute and perpetual) power is impossible to realise. But he is not always aware of this; and so he falls into inconsistencies and exaggerates. In his own time and circumstances he wanted to *increase* the power of the sovereign; he wanted to make it far *more* unquestionable than it then was. But to the extent that his argument is of this kind, it is of merely limited application and not absolutist at all. The difficulty is that Bodin's argument is of both kinds: of limited historical application, but largely and inconsistently promoted as a panacea – and therefore promotive of absolutism, in the sense we have given the expression.

A CRITIQUE OF HOBBESIAN ABSOLUTISM

In order to compensate for the endemic conflict that is characteristic of the human condition, Bodin argues (normatively) that state power *ought* to be, and (factually) that, where a polity is stable and orderly, state power *is*, centrally, totally, absolutely and perpetually centred in the hands of the sovereign or ruler. This is the position which Hobbes starts from and develops with extraordinary skill and completeness. For Hobbes, men are self-contained and mutually incomprehensible to an exceedingly dangerous degree; a psychological and epistemological solipsism renders them excessively conflict-prone; rival powers or shared authority do not resolve but exacerbate the problem; men aim to achieve peace and security; these they can only achieve through unity; the only path to unity is authority; authority is merely the agreement of some men to obey some other man or men; where that authority is contested or withdrawn there can be no unity, nor therefore any peace or security; thus either authority is entire and unquestioned, or law and order are undermined. It is because Hobbes constructs this stark choice between untrammelled authority and unbridled anarchy that he inevitably pitches upon the former and, in this, ceases to recommend merely some extension of sovereign authority and recommends instead its illimitable extension: hence his normative absolutism. We have noted previously that there is some value in the analysis of the predicament, i.e. the supportive argument for absolutism. The chief question is whether the absolutism necessarily follows from the supportive argument. The absolutism is essentially a request for the bestowal of unlimited power upon a particular authority: this is intended as the solution to the problem of political insecurity and disorder. The most obvious difficulty that arises from this solution, noted long ago by Locke, is that, if the authority is a single individual, and we confer upon him absolute power to settle our differences, such a conferral is equivalent to our agreeing to do whatever that individual commands or thinks fit; but he may command us to do many things which are entirely unacceptable, and he may arrange that we be treated in a manner that is entirely contemptuous; in which case we may discover, following the establishment of this authority, that our lives are governed by greater insecurity, unpredictability and fear than ever before. Thus, to look only at absolutism, not at the supportive argument advanced, and considering that absolutism is intended as a solution to the problem of fear, insecurity and disorder in human arrangements, we must conclude that it is not a wholly convincing or satisfactory solution. For it is conceivable and perhaps probable that a majority of men might feel far more secure under a looser, more diffuse, even tenuous arrangement, than under a government entirely subject to the whim of a single individual: they might well and reasonably prefer the risks of civil war to those attendant upon such an extraordinary and uncontrollable concentration of power. Now the above counter-absolutist argument is not an argument against any and every uncontrollable concentration of power; it merely indicates that one might often and reasonably forego the risk that absolutism invites one to take. This limited conclusion is quite adequate to our purpose. But it destroys the universality of the absolutist appeal; it defeats the suggestion that extraordinary concentrations of power are appropriate in any and all circumstances if peace, order and security are to be achieved.

This argument, however, was only directed against a particular kind of absolutism: that which universally recommends the unlimited concentration of state power in the hands of *a single individual*. There are other counter-arguments of a similar kind that could be invoked, but I find them less direct and forceful and so shall forego any mention of them here. We must now concern ourselves, however, with a quite different sort of absolutism: that which universally recommends the unlimited concentration of state power in the hands of *a plural sovereign*, or *a group*. Hobbes's absolutism is (formally) of both sorts. He argues that the unity of a group, and thus the peace and security of a society, may spring from its members being represented by the will either of *one*, or of *several*, of their number. We have already considered the case where the will of a single individual is established as sovereign. Now we must consider the situation where a group of individuals serve this purpose. The first point to note is that it is far more difficult to conceive of a group, collectively speaking, having a single will, than it is to conceive of a single individual having such a will. A single individual is a biological unit; a group of individuals is not. There is of course nothing startling about this reflection. Indeed it can be regarded as the elementary beginning of Hobbes's own analysis: single individuals are not at one and the problem of politics is to make them so. The difficulty is, that if this is a problem for society as a whole, it must remain a significant problem for any smaller group within the society, even if such a group is sovereign. Thus, if it is contended that the only means of escaping social disorder and insecurity, made inescapable by the solipsistic and conflict-prone nature of man, lies in obedience to an absolute sovereign, it becomes plain that we have not removed our difficulty if that sovereign is plural; for the same difficulties that obstruct accord in the wider society must be assumed to operate in a similar way within the governing élite (if it is such a group *qua* group that is sovereign).

On the face of it, this argument appears to be open to two possible rejoinders. One: the Hobbesian may argue that although a sub-group is sovereign, it is in turn dominated by a single individual within it – a 'sub-sovereign' – and that it is the exercise of the latter's will which will impart unity to the plural sovereign. Such an argument, however, would reduce to surrendering the notion that a group, as opposed to an individual, can ever govern effectively at all – i.e. be sovereign; and if the argument for a plural sovereign were surrendered, the implied impossibility of the thing would offend common-sense; further, the objection to the sovereignty of a single individual advanced two paragraphs above would again apply.

Two: the Hobbesian may argue that the sub-group is sovereign, not because it is in turn reduced to the will of a single individual, but because the group itself achieves a collective will through the principle of majority rule. This argument is startling, however, in that it seems to suggest that not only a human individual may be sovereign but also an abstract principle – in this case, 'majority rule'. On one level, of course, there is nothing at all surprising about the notion of a group being sovereign and of that sovereign group being governed by the principle of majority rule. What it is important to recognise, however, is that the fact of being governed by majority rule considerably depersonalises rule; majorities may shift and drift, not being determinate beings; so that stipulating that the majority decides is not essentially a matter of determining *who* decides, but of agreeing upon *how* a group may be said to decide. A majority is not a determinate being, but a variable procedure adopted by a group for determining which directives will and which will not be regarded as legitimately emanating from the group. If a 'group' can be sovereign, then what has been demonstrated is that Hobbesian absolutism, as applied to groups, is quite impossible, for the minimal prerequisite of group rule is that some *principle* of decision-making be adopted; and as such a principle constitutes the group it must also be said to bind it, for otherwise it cannot persist as a group. If there are no basic, fixed procedures, then the sovereign group cannot operate as a sovereign group; there is no way of tying it together, of saying that it has decided a matter one way or another, and therefore of meaningfully saying that it even exists. Where Hobbes contends that the sovereign cannot be bound, either by himself or another, it is clear, in fact, that if a sovereign group is not somehow bound to at least minimal rules of procedure, it cannot function at all. Although we may say, as a matter of common-sense, that groups can indeed be sovereign, we are also bound to say that they cannot be sovereign in the manner Hobbes requires: illimitably and absolutely. Yet again the absolutist norm appears untenable.

It would be unwise to delay too long in our discussion of this matter. It is plain that no contemporary writers of note argue for the type of political absolutism espoused by Bodin and Hobbes. They are all too aware of the feasibility of effective government being secured by plural sovereigns; they are also aware, if less clearly, that plural sovereigns cannot be regarded as absolute in the manner prescribed by Hobbes, not merely as a matter of accident, but also of necessity. A plural sovereign can be significantly absolutist *vis-à-vis* those who have no say, directly or indirectly, in its deliberations, but it generally cannot be so over those who do. This is the essential reason why those who oppose the injustice of plural sovereigns (towards particular sections of a community) generally express their opposition by arguing for extensions of the franchise to those sections which have been unjustly affected or treated. (It goes without saying that this approach does not always work.) Where a group is genuinely sovereign, it is necessarily rule-bound; and although neither this nor any other stipulable condition can guarantee the justice of its operations, it does imply and require that the degree of whimsicality attaching to its operations, at least *vis-à-vis* those who exercise any influence over it, is to that extent restricted.

IS ORDER DESIRED?

First, it is clear that some disobedience does not mean complete disobedience and thus that *some* disorder does not mean *no* order. Secondly, even where there is a clearly established authority in a community, so organised that it puts out few conflicting directives, and where most members of the community feel they should (and where most do) obey the authority's directives, it would still be fair to say that the existing order was not, and therefore that *no order can be, absolutely stable and certain*. Thirdly, since rulers often themselves create disorder by being too severe or callous or feckless, etc., towards their citizenry; since they may frequently ensure against disorder by percipience, sympathy, accommodation of popular demands, etc.; it clearly follows that the complete obedience of subjects to rulers *is not the only way* to attain peace or achieve greater stability. Fourthly, it becomes clear for the same reason that obedience by subjects to rulers *is only one among other ways* to attain peace. Having reviewed these possibilities, I would suggest that the absolutist argument, that there can be no order without a proper sovereign, typically means that an existing order (*a*) is uncertain unless, and (*b*) can *only* be made sure where, subjects render complete obedience to their sovereigns. We can see of course that any order *is* uncertain where subjects do not render *complete* obedience, but we can also see that this means we can speak of *no* order as being *certain* or absolutely stable. Nor is it desirable that any order should be – since none is absolutely just. Further, although an order would come *closest* to being absolutely stable where all subjects yielded unconditional obedience, we can also see that such a form of obedience would be completely irrational and could not fairly be demanded: for rulers, being like other men, commit their share of errors and excesses too, and these often require to be disobeyed and opposed. (The onus lies upon both rulers and ruled to behave sensibly and with restraint and neither obstinately to command nor blindly to obey.)

The *factual* proposition, 'without a proper sovereign there can be no order', is used to support the recommendation that sovereigns *ought* to be completely obeyed and as such presupposes that the presence of order is better than its absence. It assumes that order is better than disorder, and thus that whatever is necessary must be done to establish the one and avoid the other. The establishment of a proper sovereign, which is the rendering of complete obedience to an authority, is relevant in so far as it furthers this purpose. Since the heart of the matter does not lie in the factual position but, rather, in the preference or normative inclination it indicates (that order is *better* than the lack of it) we must directly consider that preference.

A basic absolutist preference, underlying all the factual arguments, is for order over its absence. Hobbes suggests that this preference does or should hold for every individual in all circumstances except where the latter's support for 'order' would itself directly endanger his life. Whether or not this preference *should* hold, it is clear in fact that it does not by any means always do so. *All* men do not prefer 'order' to 'disorder' and not even *most* men do so all the time. It happens with surprising frequency that people will risk their lives, where otherwise their lives would not be at risk, because in doing so they believe that what they do is right (not to speak of those cases where courting danger is positively enjoyed). And it is because people do not always prefer order to its alternatives that it is impossible to conclude (from the assumption that they ultimately and always *do* prefer order) that they ought always to obey their rulers.

The proposition that an order is uncertain (unstable) unless subjects render complete obedience to authority only demonstrates – where it is taken to be valid – that no political system or order can be completely certain or stable. This uncertainty is an inescapable feature of the human condition. There can be no ironclad guarantees of obedience no matter how a government is structured. Since 'order' can in fact represent *any* sort of order, the presence of peace, accord, agreement, acquiescence or whatever is not always to be regarded as more desirable than its absence. The absence of order, like its presence, is in any event always partial. The question cannot meaningfully be whether or not we want order *per se*, but what type and degree of order we want, and how far we are prepared to go to defend some particular arrangement, some particular set of relations, which we desire (and accordingly label as 'order'). It is clear that few people, *pace* Hobbes, actually desire order above all else. If they did, we should be hard put to explain all the wars, civil and national, all the strikes, peaceful and bloody, all the strife, protest and conflict with which we are everywhere and continually confronted. Since order cannot be achieved *per se*, it is pointless to demand it as such. Since order cannot be established in any total sense it is important to recognise that the demand for it is always impliedly a demand for some specific kind of social arrangement, for some limited species of order. Probably very few people really desire order quite simply in itself for the elementary reason that (very) few are likely to divorce the demand for it from some more or less explicit conception of the *type* of order under which they would wish to live. 'Order' is in some sense both desired and desirable, but the real question is whether the particular form it will assume at any given point will or should be regarded as just.

ABSOLUTISM, TOTALITARIANISM AND LIBERAL-DEMOCRACY

The issue is not whether a group sovereign may not wield more power than an individual sovereign; nor whether a group sovereign may not commit the same injustices as an individual sovereign, and even exceed them; the issue, rather, is whether a group sovereign is or is not bound by certain principles or procedures which, in binding it, limit what it can do, and in principle subject its membership to certain laws (but not to all laws) which they cannot rise above.

The important differences between group sovereigns derive essentially from the range of their inclusiveness (membership) and from the differences of principle or procedure that structure their operations. It is from the latter differences that flow in turn, for example, a spirit of staidness, intolerance and doctrinal rigidity; or one of frivolity, tolerance and compromise. A group that is limited, in the way that an individual sovereign is not, as regards its internal mode of operation or its constitution, may nonetheless project liberal or racialist or class or religiously doctrinaire or other principles by which it commits itself to be guided. For a group sovereign to be limited by its principles is not necessarily a virtue since its principles may be effectively evil. But it is nonetheless limited by them. Principles are not alien to law; law enshrines them. A bill of rights is nothing less than a set of principles subjected to legal definition. An apartheid act directed against Blacks or an extermination order against Jews has precisely the same character. What a group sovereign does, how far it goes, may be largely determined by what it initially commits itself to; the logic of the commitment will impose its own not entirely predictable limitations upon practice; for a group does not change its 'mind' without persuasion or argument or some form or other of communication within itself and such communication will, to a greater or lesser degree, be enclosed within the framework of its original constitution – i.e. that declarative act (or series of acts) that determined either the mode or the end or both mode and end of its functioning.

The absolutism of an individual is significantly different from that of a group. Similarly, the essentially secular and personal absolutism promoted by Bodin and Hobbes differs significantly from the secular and collective absolutism promoted by modern parties. 'Totalitarianism', in so far as it is a descendant of absolutism, is not an exclusive descendant. In so far as it promotes the concentration of political power, it is not alone in this. The power of liberal-democratic regimes in times of crisis (the perception of 'crisis' always contains a subjective element) – as during the Second World War and during the McCarthy period in the United States – may become extremely concentrated, involving considerable concomitant restrictions upon civil liberties. Totalitarian states will evince similar alternating contractions and expansions of powers and of civil liberties, depending on a variety of circumstances. In any event, of course, given that no power or authority can be 'total', no state can, strictly, be totalitarian. Given that no state can secure the entire agreement of its citizenry, none can, strictly, be 'democratic'. Given that every state depends in some degree upon force, every one of them must in some degree prove 'illiberal'. Thus the difference between totalitarian and liberal-democratic regimes is to be seen as a matter of degree, not kind, a difference vitally affected by the range of inclusiveness (or representativeness) of the ruling group and by the order of ends which it projects and promotes. Totalitarian regimes generally betray far greater concentrations of group power than do liberal democracies, together with far more irreverence for civil liberties. But, like the liberal democracies, they do not necessarily (with the exception, *perhaps*, of fascist regimes) promote extremes of centralisation universally or on a temporally unlimited basis. Marxism–Leninism, for example, as in the Russian context, has not insisted upon the universal indispensability of government (the state, after all, is intended to wither away) nor upon the prior importance of personal security (it is assumed that security for certain classes of citizens is inimical to the welfare of the people as a whole); it has insisted instead upon the transitional importance of concentrated power in order to move a society forward in a particular direction (as by achieving rapid industrialisation). Similarly apartheid, in the South African context, has not insisted upon the universal necessity of concentrated governmental power; given the racialist goal, and the possibility of its accomplishment, it is assumed that such concentrated power (as expressed in the detention laws, press laws, etc.) may cease to prove necessary when the goal stipulated is achieved; in the meantime, the exponents of apartheid do not regard themselves as totalitarian 'idéologues', a label which it is extraordinarily difficult to deny them, but as hard-headed 'pragmatists', who are only doing what is necessary to achieve a valid end. Modern collective sovereigns, whether totalitarian or liberal-democratic, do not generally promote unlimited concentrations of power universally and for all time. In this respect, too, modern collective sovereigns must be distinguished from their predecessors.

The successor governments to the absolutist type have been group sovereigns. Between individual absolutism and collective sovereignty there are significant structural differences, as we have seen. We have also seen that between collective or group sovereigns there are significant differences too, which it would be impossible to list exhaustively. Here we only draw attention to the current distinction between those group sovereigns that are 'totalitarian' and those which are 'liberal-democratic'. Both forms of collective sovereign tend to be pragmatic. In this respect they project an image significantly different from that which attaches to their antecedents. Most modern states evince a commitment to great power concentrations only in order to achieve specific aims. The poorer totalitarian states tend to commit themselves singlemindedly to the pursuit of industrialisation. The richer liberal democracies commit themselves to economic growth, but the need is less pressing, and their more obvious commitment comes to centre on proceduralism, civil liberties, compromise, indeed, on *pragmatism*.

A truly vital consideration in relation to group sovereigns centres around three related questions: what chief end each serves, how effectively that end is being served, and how desirable or acceptable is this end within the context of a variety of competing ends. We can never assume that a government, given the complexity of the society it administers, can be governed by a sole end. But it is obvious that every government must assign some priority among the competing ends by which it is guided. Thus the fundamental question becomes not so much that of determining what end, but what *priority* of ends, a power concentration is intended to serve; and thus not what end, but what priority of ends, is desirable. The question concerning the degree of power concentrated at any particular locus relates more to the problem of means than to that of ends. It is pointless to try to determine whether a particular power concentration is desirable or not until we know what it is for. It is in this sense that we must move away from power for power's sake, as well as away from pure proceduralism, and so bring into sharper focus the ends which both powers and procedures are intended to serve and are capable of serving.

THE DEFENCE OF ORDER

Any order has more to it than meets the eye: it is characterised by a great number of rules and goals, and it is very difficult to say that the removal of any one of these rules endangers the retention of the rest. Systems of norms are constantly undergoing change, some norms being dropped and others inserted, not only specific norms but the priority of norms being altered. To accept self-defence of the system as a fundamental and overriding goal, therefore, is not so simple as it seems. For no system as a whole can be defended, nor is such defence desirable; and no specific norm can easily be argued to be so fundamental that the elimination of it somehow implies or entails the elimination or overturning of all or most of the rest. To spell out a danger to an order is merely to spell out a danger which threatens a part or parts of this order. To defend the order, therefore, is not to defend the order as such but some parts of it. This selection of parts to stand in some form of supportive relationship to one another establishes a system of priorities. But this system of priorities merely affords one way of seeing and manipulating the system as a whole. The system, the order *per se*, cannot in the end be identified with or reduced to the particular priority imposed by a particular moral or political perspective.

The ideology of order is essentially the justification of order *per se*. An order is some form of stable relationship among individuals. The relationship, or at least the stability of the relationship, involves the conformity of a plurality of individuals to some discrete norm or norms. Where an order exists it can be said that there is some congruence between norm-issuance and norm-acceptance. This congruence may obtain in relation to the sharing of very few or very many social norms. In whatever degree that an order exists, its existence can be revered.

The demand for order is always a demand for the elimination of some form of conflict. One way to eliminate conflict is to urge obedience to a common law. One way to make that obedience coherent is by referring it, or submitting it, to the will of a single man or body of men. The dead letter of the law only comes alive when interpreted. The pronouncements of legislators only have meaning when coherent. The coherence of law exists as a pattern of expectations. If we take the law as merely patterning expectations, then wherever expectations are disappointed, order – the projected order which each pattern contains – is disrupted. In this sense there can never be any absolute order. Expectations are always being disappointed, for the codified wishes of a group never match exactly the specific wishes – or interpretations – of each member of the group. Thus any general call for order can only reduce to a

THE IDEOLOGY OF ORDER

demand that some particular interpretation of the group's codified expectations be accepted and imposed as the proper one.

ORDER AS CONSERVATISM

To the extent that absolutism survives, it tends to do so, not as a distinctive form of government, but as an ideological residue that unpredictably surfaces here and there, sovereignly oblivious of national frontiers, generally with a view to justifying the irately repressive or tidily conservative whim of the moment. It will be recalled that the basic justification for absolutism flows from an insistence upon the need for order. This need is indeed genuine and cannot be flippantly ignored. But we have also seen (apart from the fact that some form and degree of order always exists) that in the absolutist's view, nothing is more important than order, that virtually anything should be done to secure it, that, in fact, there is virtually nothing which we may not be forced to sacrifice – to authority, to government – to obtain it. Hence the belief that the power of government must be absolute, perpetual, unlimited, above the law – if it is to do its job properly. What is reflected in all this is the clear assumption that any species of order is better than none. The absurdity of the position, however, is that the projected choice between some order and no order is false. If one were ever restricted to a choice between some order over none one would of course choose the former. But since the choice is false, this dichotomous argument merely reduces to a covert defence of some particular conception of the *status quo*.

A call for order need not *logically* imply fuller obedience (or some variation on this theme) to present rules; it could imply obedience to an entirely new set of rules (and therefore disobedience to the old). Nonetheless, the call for order has generally come to be associated with a call for the protection of the whole or a part of some existing order. By contrast, a call for a new or altered order has come to be associated, at the extreme, with a call for revolution (often reduced simplistically to disorder). If, however, a call for order is ultimately intended to mean little more than 'protect and preserve what is', it proves a somewhat less compulsive call than when formulated in the more general way indicated.

ORDER AS JUSTICE AND ORDER *v.* JUSTICE

In so far as there is social organisation, order exists. In so far as social organisation can (in some degree) break down, a greater degree or different kind of order may be needed. A call for order is essentially a call for the observation of rules. Since there is an almost infinite variety of rules that can be observed and, therefore, promulgated, it is plain that a specific call for order always presupposes that certain rules in particular, not just any rules at all, will be observed. To ask people to obey just any rules at all is to ask them to do what they like – or to continue so doing. To call people to order is to ask them to become related to one another in some particular fashion, which is only possible in so far as they are somehow bound to observe the same rules. Thus, although the observation of any rules whatever may be constitutive of an order, where an order exists it is based upon a specific system of rules. Thus a call to order, implying the defence or alteration of specific rules, always contains or projects a concept of justice.

Order is not abstractly necessary: one cannot claim an abstract need for something of which one is already and necessarily possessed. A society is definitionally characterised by some species and degree of order; a member of a society, therefore, in so far as he is that, makes a request which is redundant in so far as he makes an abstract appeal for order, as distinct from an appeal for some specific amendment to present arrangements. Ultimately one cannot posit an abstract need for order for the reason that one is never ultimately able to maintain that there is *no* order.

When one says that order is necessary one may mean that it is inevitable or that some particular form which the inevitable has assumed is bad. Every form of order which manifests itself is necessarily concrete. Every concrete order projects a hierarchy of norms. These hierarchies do not exist *prior* to what they control, but as *a part* of what they control. A political order, a political system, taken as a rank order of norms, does not precede justice; rather, it is an expression of a reasonably, but never a totally, coherent conception of justice. Order does not precede civilisation: 'civilisation' merely labels a favoured order. Order does not precede justice: it only labels what many will often regard as a 'higher' form of justice. Order does not exist prior to 'art', 'culture' and the rest. But any concrete order will be of a kind which will favour or attack or prove indifferent to them.

A system of order which effectively precludes depiction of the human form will not produce Michelangelo. A system of order which effectively outlaws the dance (as sinful and erotic) will not produce Nijinski. A system of order which will not give free rein to the individual imagination cannot possibly tolerate types like Rabelais and Joyce. An order which is committed to the exclusion of certain categories of citizen (or subject) from the arts and sciences and destroys their hopes of fulfilment within these spheres necessarily cannot serve as a way-station to the sort of cultural flowering that may be desired. An order that contains an unjust rule or system of rules automatically is not to be regarded as an indispensable means of achieving what the system, in this particular, rejects. Justice is not built upon an order, but is contained within it; and where an order contains an injustice, one does not build justice upon it, but merely changes the particular that is regarded as unjust; and if the injustice is monumental, change of a proportionate dimension may be required, and the existing order disordered in order to achieve a better one.

Thus we approach the conclusion, not so much that order is prior to so many other projected goods – the chief of these being justice – but that every order of itself contains, embodies, supports different types and degrees of justice and injustice. Where, therefore, we confront a proposition of the kind 'order is prior to justice', we are confronting more nearly a recommendation than a fact. The recommendation is essentially that existing injustices should be accepted before they are rejected; or that the existing order should be accepted as a whole, together with its injustices, for fear that otherwise there will be no order at all.

But of course there is always an order, and a socio-political order of the size of a nation always contains countless rules. Further, it is difficult to imagine that the elimination of one or some of these rules will equate with the elimination of rule, of order, *per se*. When one thinks indeed of a system, of an order, being overturned, one rarely imagines the event to be identical with all (or even most) of the rules in the system being undermined. Where it is proclaimed that there is a serious threat to any system, there is virtually always a divergence of views as to whether this is true, simply because members of the system will hold different ideas about which rules are crucial to the survival of that system. Since a system or order in its totality can never be overturned – i.e. since the members cannot possibly unlearn or ignore all of the norms which have been inculcated within the system – it follows that only parts of the system can be overturned. Where members feverishly defend particular parts, they are often likely to do so by conflating those parts with the whole. Similarly, where members attack certain parts, they are equally likely to do so by conflating these parts with the whole. What we must recognise is that everything turns round those parts, those norms, which members believe it important to defend or attack. Seen in this light, spuriously factual statements about order preceding justice may be converted into plain ethical arguments about the relative merits or demerits of certain norms contained within a system of control.

The doctrine of the priority of order – that is, the ideology of order – wherever it raises its head, whether in the United States of America or Czechoslovakia, Hungary or Northern Ireland, South Africa or Sudan, is essentially a recommendation for the perpetuation of the *status quo*, to be effected through the medium of unquestioned obedience to established authority or continued acceptance of existing rules. It is at this stage that we can detect the continuity between this doctrine and absolutism. Where absolutism demanded an illimitable concentration of power in the sovereign, what it was simultaneously demanding was the subject's complete obedience to the sovereign: the one ultimately implied the other. The ideology of order begins at the other end. It demands obedience to the government, unyielding defence of (certain) established rules or practices with which the government is identified; and in whatever system such obedient defence is conceded without question, we are merely led back to the point whence absolutism began.

A call to order always contains an ethical element. It assumes the propriety, rightness or justice of the agents or rules which, either explicitly or implicitly, we are enjoined to accept. Thus an argument for order can never be regarded as being ethically superior to the demand for justice. It is merely another way of saying often covertly, that some particular order ('all told', 'on balance', etc.) *is* just. This covert promotion of 'order', that is, of order *per se*, is characteristic of absolutism, but carries over into any form of government where the latter is more exclusively concerned with defending some conception of the *status quo* than with setting wrongs to right.

APPENDIXES

Appendix 1

Bodin on Female Rule

In the text I may have underemphasised Bodin's conception of the *intellectual* inferiority of women *vis-à-vis* men. It may prove useful to indicate more fully the precise lengths to which Bodin goes to make this point. First, he justifies the command of husband over wife as an expression (in Knolles's translation, *Republique*, McRae ed.) of 'reason' over 'affection' (p. 15). In the French, 'affection' is not rendered so quaintly, but rather as 'bestial appetite' (*l'appetit bestial*); there is also occasional reference to 'reason' over 'cupidity'. Such remarks, however, are of a subsidiary character (bk. 1, ch. 3), and attend but do not dominate the central point: that in any order, in any system, the will or command of some one person must dominate that of the rest. Bodin does maintain, as indicated, that woman's supposed 'cupidity' must be subjected to man's 'reason'. But what is to be noted is how uneven is his emphasis upon this point. For his fundamental contentions are two: the law of *God* commands the subservience of women to men; and in all nations such is the practice (*de facto*). The superior wisdom of men is by no means consistently held to in Bodin, as it is in Aristotle. The supposition is indeed equivocal: the glory of the wife *should* depend upon that of her husband; men '*ought* [my italics] to excell their wives in wisdome and virtue' (McRae ed., p. 19). But to suggest that men *ought* to excel their women in wisdom is not the same as contending that they in fact do so. Nevertheless, Bodin returns to the idea that women may be less rational than men: they ought, where they have broken the law, to be more lightly punished *either* because they (women) are more passionate, *or* because they are less rational, *or* because (being gentler) they are more susceptible to pain than are men (McRae ed., p. 776). There is too great a disposition, however, for translators to convert Bodin's *prudence* into 'wisdome' (as, e.g., McRae ed., p. 746). Bodin's major stress appears to be upon God's command rather than upon man's superior wisdom. In the text, we have already indicated how appalled Bodin was at the thought of female rule – 'how wise soever she be' (McRae ed., p. 747). Similarly, Bodin says that Isabel of Castille 'was one of the wisest princesses that ever were', but merely objects that it was difficult for the dignity of her subjects to put up with the government of a woman (McRae ed., p. 748). This theme arises again and again: female rule offends male dignity; not that it necessarily replaces the rule of the wise by that of the ignorant. Indeed, Bodin is sportingly inclined to conclude that in the end it does not much matter whether a woman is sovereign or if the sovereign is obedient to women, as long as there is unity ('c'est tout un que les femmes commandent en souveraineté, ou bien que les Princes souverains obeïssent aux femmes': *Republique*, 1608 ed., bk. VI, ch. 5). Bodin certainly supposes that no man, and more especially no sovereign, should be subject to any woman's will. But it is difficult to suppose, in the end, that this most deep-seated of Bodinian prejudices had much to do with the Aristotelian justification which Bodin occasionally trots out for our edification. The bulk of Bodin's arguments are really utilitarian and biblical: female rule is vastly *inconvenient*, on the one hand; on the other, women are basically *lustful* (not stupid) creatures.

Bodin probably had more in mind the Old Testament picture of Eve proffering her apple to Adam than the Aristotelian picture of woman simply being intellectually inferior to man. This point is worth stressing if only to underline the continuity in principle between Bodin's views on female rule and his views on rule in general. In the same way that Bodin sometimes suggests that the many (a collective as opposed to a monarchical sovereign) are somehow inferior, 'mediocre', etc., so he sometimes makes similar statements about women *vis-à-vis* men. But in the same way as his primary concern is that there be finality of decision in the state, so is he concerned with finality of decision in the family. Obviously it is no misfortune for a state to be governed by a wise prince, no more than it is so for a woman to be ruled by a wise husband. But it is difficult to suppose that in either case Bodin is genuinely concerned to justify the need for such finality in terms of the wisdom of the sovereign or controlling agent. Bodin certainly supposes that a prince will generally be wiser than his subjects, and a husband wiser than his wife. But if wisdom were the criterion upon which the conferment of authority turned in either case, Bodin would *have to conclude* that a stupid prince should be overturned, that a wise queen should be revered, and that an intelligent wife should control an unintelligent husband. But although perfectly prepared to admit that male authority, private and public, might be stupid, Bodin was never prepared to admit that this was a reason for overturning such authority, and never a reason for accepting wise female rule or authority in its place. Thus, although most writers, like Fournol (1896, p. 36), draw attention to Bodin's insistence upon the intellectual superiority of men over women, I argue, on the contrary, that within the overall context of Bodin's argument, such statements cannot be regarded as vital and cannot accordingly be conceded a fraction of the significance that similar remarks carry in earlier writers, most notably in Aristotle.

Appendix 2

The Justice/Order Problem in the Bodinian Concept of Law

A key assumption in any analysis of Bodin's concept of law is the notion that virtually all acts conform to some divinely and naturally ordered scheme of things such that he who looks for that order is likely to discover it. Reference to such an assumption can lend us some assistance in resolving the tension between Bodin's disposition to invest absolute (or humanly unrestrained) power in the sovereign and yet assume that the latter will not behave in a merely tyrannical and willful manner. I am inclined to stress, however – quite apart from this aspect of the 'great chain of being' assumption so evident in Bodin – a somewhat different element. This is the residual assumption that natural law is not perfect, or that it cannot be perfectly known by all, thus requiring that we accept that an ultimate and exclusive will, a decider, in his ultimacy, must somehow become, or be regarded as, unrestrained.

No discussion of this problem is to be found in Franklin (1963) although it would have been appropriate in his book. In the case of Moreau-Reibel (1933), however, we encounter a much more detailed appreciation of the distinction between a natural law (*droit naturel*), and a universal law (*droit universel*) or a human law (*droit humain*) (p. 31). Moreau-Reibel discovers in all this a significant distinction between simple utility on the one hand, and pure justice on the other ('Sans doute nous retrouvons cette idée du droit d'utilité, opposé au juste pur . . .': p. 32). One need not stress the importance of such a distinction in determining the degree of arbitrary power to be conferred upon the sovereign. If what is naturally right is perfectly evident to and acceptable by all, then there is no need to confer such extensive power upon the monarch. It is necessary for the monarch to have such power only if either there is no natural right (or law), or if it is not universally recognised (which is almost the same thing), or if it is recognised but flouted.

The question that arises in this last case, however, is why should we suppose the monarch or the sovereign to be any better able to recognise natural law, *in its true nature*, than anyone else. To such a question a number of answers arise, but most importantly this: that if someone does not humanly decree and consequentially uphold some notion of what is right, no such notion will be upheld at all. This is the chink, as I see it, in Bodin's armoury of natural law. And it is this which begins to take us towards legal positivism. (My own position, as stated, is that human organisation is inevitably full of chinks and that this is a situation which we must consciously accept, rather than build up dikes against lateral shifts of opinion and inclination which will inevitably sweep such opposition away: finality, legal and otherwise, is unattainable, although in some degree and circumstances it is appropriate to seek after it.)

Moreau-Reibel (pp. 151–2), however, continues to see Bodin as per-fectly consistent in his concept of law: the power to command is both public and private but both must conform to natural law (*droit naturel*). In this, Moreau-Reibel sees Bodin as continuing a tradition perfectly consistent with that of his (medieval) predecessors. Nonetheless, Moreau-Reibel (pp. 167ff.) is brought back to the central difficulty: Bodin admits simultaneously of the superiority of both *roi* and *loi*, of the sovereign and of law. It is no use saying that Bodin subjects the king to the law, for as we have made abundantly clear, he also places him above it (as interpreter, but also as its conscious modifier). Obviously, the king is not enjoined to dispose of the law lightly, but the power to dispose of it is nonetheless conferred upon him. One cannot simply return, as Moreau-Reibel does (p. 169), to the notion of the prince as sovereign legislator, otherwise being bound by what he decrees, since according to Bodin's own reasoning a sovereign cannot tie his own hands in such a manner. Thus one is brought back to the distinction between such law as *does* bind the sovereign and that which does not. Bodin, we have made clear, presupposes some such distinction. The problem derives from the fact that it is not a distinction which can ever be made perfectly clear, because all that Bodin is really saying is that the sovereign should be able to do exactly as he pleases when he is right (when what he does is *just*), but not otherwise. And this raises the obvious question, not strictly a legal question, as to whether we have at hand or can otherwise produce a reliable criterion of justice.

Garosci (1934), like Moreau-Reibel, also appreciates the distinction in Bodin between *roi* and *loi*. But just as Moreau-Reibel is disposed to reduce Bodin's *roi* to *loi*, Garosci is similarly disposed to reduce Bodin's *loi* to *roi*. He is led to this conclusion primarily because he insists upon reading Bodin as perfectly continuous with Machiavelli. Distinguishing between Bodin's law of *ragione* and that of *utilità*, Garosci assimilates Bodin's concept of law more to the latter than to the former notion. He explains Bodin's utilitarian concept of the law in terms of 'una lesione di un diritto, con cui l'opera del vivere civile è cominciata' (p. 193). Garosci thus falls back upon some concept of a prehistorical state in Bodin, characterised by a lack of law, out of which some authoritative *princeps* must arise, in order to impose an order – an order which must, in the nature of things, prove (at least partly) arbitrary. Garosci sees Bodin as developing from Machiavelli some concept of a distinction between ethics and politics (*politico e morale*: p. 199) which of course can only reinforce the autonomy of the sovereign. He does not actually suggest that *diritto* is in Bodin subjected to *utilità*, but that it occupies a position of enormous importance, if for no other reason than that the contemplation of the *good* (to employ the classical formula) requires a commodious and *utilitarian* setting – i.e. a peaceful political order – in which such contemplation can take place (p. 202).

We have no need to push too far this distinction between natural law and human law. But, as I have maintained, it provides the link between Bodin's natural law theory and his state absolutism. As Bodin argues explicitly in the *Tableau du droit universel* (1580), if the law, in whatever degree it may derive from nature, did not also flow from the needs of man, one would be able to say (with the Stoics) 'justice is natural, not conventional', and less a matter of prudence and judgement than of science (pp. 83–4). For Bodin, justice is less a matter of distinguishing the true from the false than of distinguishing between the useful and the useless, between the good and the bad. Bodin, of course, nowhere argues that such distinctions are simply arbitrary; the important point is that they are not scientific; they are not of a mathematical character; and dependence upon human authority in such matters is by implication greater than in science. Even conceding this distinction between justice and science, Bodin is, as we have seen, further concerned to distinguish between natural law and civil law. He held to no absolutely fixed views regarding the differential content of natural and civil law. But he thought of natural law as being expressed in such views as supported, for example, obedience to God, respect for the family, gratitude towards benefactors, the protection of private property and punishment for the wicked. Civil law, by contrast, is highly variable, depending upon time and circumstance, etc., but always requiring some manner of conformity with utility. (Bodin's own distinction is between *jus naturale* and *jus humanum*, the latter being further divided between a *jus gentium* and a *jus civile*.) The fact that a law is *universal* does not necessarily mean that it is *natural*. It is in this sense that all civil law (I am using this expression as an equivalent for *jus humanum* or *droit humain*) is conventional. As such, such law is the preserve of the sovereign. It may be fitting for a consultative or parliamentary body to be consulted about, and even to decide upon, the law; but it is solely for the sovereign to command it and resolve to carry it out.

In effect, Bodin accepts that there can be no pure government of laws. Such a conclusion is reasonable enough. There are, even given laws, differences of interpretation, and somewhere it becomes appropriate to suggest that even arbitrary decision may be better than none at all. If there were a wholly encompassing natural law, and assuming that all men could recognise and agree upon it, the whole case for legal finality (or positivism) would fall to the ground. Bodin perceives that justice is a chief category, but he also appears to be aware that there is some sort of gap between the ideal it enshrines and the necessary modicum of coherence, of order, he supposes that we require. It is in this important sense that he begins to move in the direction of Hobbes and of legal positivism. (What we may be in danger of forgetting along the way, however, is that there is no such thing or state of being as order *per se*. There is no fully attainable fixity, finality, coherence or order in human affairs, however much we insist upon conferring unrestrained powers upon one or some individuals, or however insistent we are upon upholding the letter of the law whatever form at a given moment such law happens to assume.)

Perhaps I should note, finally, that J. U. Lewis (1968) has recently suggested that 'the view that Bodin belongs at the beginning of the Hobbesian–Austinian tradition of political and legal theory needs reassessment' (p. 212). This, as it happens, is a view which I have both reassessed and reaffirmed. Lewis regards such reaffirmation as mistaken. He writes: 'to lift Bodin's definition [of sovereignty] from its context and set it alongside Austin's is anachronistic' (p. 215). The basic thrust of Lewis's article must be regarded as an attempt to dissociate Bodin from the Austinian tradition. But I believe that the thrust peters out, that the attempt fails.

Lewis would have done better to recognise that, from our own contemporary perspective, Bodin necessarily participates in and contributes to two traditions: the one is the natural law tradition (to which in fact Bodin has nothing new to add, except a heightened awareness of its problems); the other is the tradition of legal positivism. This joint participation flows from Bodin's dual conception of law as being both natural and human (or civil). It is no use trying to wish away the difficulty which this dualism creates for Bodin. The problem must be placed within the context of the demarcation to be established between natural and human law. To the extent that Bodin requires this line of demarcation to be established by men – and this must ultimately mean by the sovereign – to this extent he serves as a vital tributary to the tradition of legal positivism. Bodin of course had his own (shifting) views about what natural and/or divine law consisted in. Plainly, to the extent that he held firm views about its content, to that extent he believed the sovereign ought *to agree to be bound* by that content. But to the extent that Bodin believed the sovereign had an appropriately arbitrary (i.e. unquestionable and unrestrained) right of command, to that extent he was enjoining total obedience upon subjects.

I remarked above that Lewis attempts to dissociate Bodin from the Hobbesian–Austinian tradition; I also remarked that he failed in this. I should now point out that this failure is ultimately reflected in Lewis's own concluding remarks: 'social and political order rather than justice is given a priority all through the *Six Books*; and there is nothing [according to Bodin] that can secure these so much as a strong will' (p. 218). Although Lewis's attempt to divorce Bodin from the tradition of legal positivism collapses, he is of course correct to suggest, as we have done, that there remain significant differences between the work of Bodin on the one hand, and that of men like Hobbes, Bentham and Austin on the other.

Appendix 3

The Sovereign as Legislator in Bodin

I have not treated this issue with sufficient fullness in the text and there-fore return to it in an appendix. A variety of views have been advanced regarding the prior role which Bodin attaches to *legislation* as a mark of sovereignty. Most commentators stress the view that Bodin's concept of legislation is central to his concept of sovereignty. I, by contrast, think it better to perform a work of de-emphasis. I wish to stress that the chief mark of sovereignty for Bodin is simply an ultimate power to *command*. Bodin conceived of legislative bodies as essentially advisory in character. This opinion was largely valid for his time. In arguing for ultimacy of command as the chief mark of sovereignty, Bodin was not arguing that legislatures in monarchical or other states had no role to play. Nor, obviously, was he arguing that ultimate power was to be regarded as lying with legislatures or perhaps with those (the people) whom such legislatures represented (as perhaps in Locke). Bodin, in regarding sovereignty as undivided, looked upon it as an ultimate or final power of control *in all spheres* of government – whether legislative, executive or judicial. And since Bodin did not regard the sovereign as being empowered to make just any law he wished, he clearly did not intend the legislative sphere to be more completely subject to his con-trol than any other – nor, conversely, that other spheres were less com-pletely subject to his control than the legislative.

Let us take the case of Zygmunt Izdebski (1965) as representative of the view that the sovereign is especially a *legislator*: he is supreme, unique, solitary and from his legislative powers flow all others. There is some validity in Izdebski's position, as in the similar position taken by many others. Let us employ Izdebski's own phrasing: 'Le souverain est surtout un législateur. Il est le législateur suprême et unique. La marque essentielle de la souveraineté consiste en la législation, de laquelle dependent toutes les autres marques de la souveraineté', etc. From this point the author goes on to quote Bodin (*Republique*, 1, 1, ch. 9) to the effect that 'there is, properly speaking, only this sole mark of sovereignty'. What Izdebski failed to note, however, was that Bodin's reference (in the matter of this mark of sovereignty) was expressly to the notion of *commanding law*, not *legislating*, the latter being something rather different, and indeed something rather less.

Before we return to the substantive argument, it is as well to note that Moreau-Reibel (1933) at least is one of those few writers who do not insist upon a distinctly legislative superiority as the chief mark of sovereignty in Bodin. Moreau-Reibel argues succinctly: 'The sovereign remains the supreme judge and officer of state, whether he be people or king. He disposes of all powers of adjudication and administration' (p. 163). He goes on to remark that the sovereign must of course delegate these powers ('elle [i.e. delegation] dérive de la nature des choses') but he clearly understands Bodin to regard the sovereign as performing an ultimate and generally encompassing function, summarily referred to in the *Republique* as *commanding law*.

It is certainly true that Bodin wished to extend the role of the sovereign, particularly in the *Republique*, so as to make it more dynamic, less static. This means that there was in Bodin a significant shift from the idea of the prince as a judge to the idea of the prince as a 'legislator'. To this extent I agree with most commentators on Bodin. But there is a problem in this way of stating the case. To say that Bodin argued that 'legislation' was the distinguishing characteristic of sovereignty tends to presuppose ways of thinking, political categories, which are more appropriate to the eighteenth than to the sixteenth century: namely, the now conventional distinction between legislative, executive and judicial functions. Even John Locke, who is generally assumed to have contributed significantly to the separation of powers theory, only distinguished between an executive and a legislative power (subsuming the judicial function together with foreign relations – i.e. the 'federative' power – under the executive). Even Montesquieu, despite the differences between himself and Locke, was disposed to regard the judiciary as a branch of the executive. If this threefold distinction was not well-established in the minds even of such men as Locke and Montesquieu, it will be difficult to argue that it could have been so in the mind of Bodin.

We may readily see that the stress upon the supremacy of a 'legislative' power in Bodin is likely to mean something rather different from what it would mean, for example, to Locke, and certainly to us. When Locke stresses the supremacy of the legislative power what he really means is the supremacy of the legislature, i.e. of the English parliament, over the (English) monarch. Such an intention as this was completely foreign, of course, to Bodin's intentions.

It seems most reasonable to suppose that Bodin was thinking not in terms of the dominance of one branch of government over another (or others), but in terms of the chief characteristic of a sovereign power in the state. The primary characteristic of a sovereign would be his (or its) ultimate power to command in every sphere of government. To command is to order another (or others) to perform an act (or acts) and to receive obedience in the course of so doing. The law, for Bodin, is a written command; as pronounced by an officer or magistrate of the state it becomes a spoken command. It would not therefore be the 'legislative' act, as some form of specialised function, which Bodin conceived as the chief mark of sovereignty, but 'ceste meme puissance de donner & casser la Loy' – the *power*, in effect *to give and break the law*. For Bodin, the sovereign is he who 'lays down the law'; but such a being is not quite the one we have in mind when we speak of the 'legislator'. A legislator we are generally inclined to think of as one who formulates laws and nothing more. The Bodinian sovereign is one who gives law and takes it away, who commands what is and what is not to be done, and who, in this sense, makes war or peace, promotes, demotes or dismisses officers and magistrates, imposes taxes or removes them, and so on (*Republique*, I, I, ch. 9). Contrary, for example, to Izdebski, I maintain that the essential mark of sovereignty for Bodin does not 'consist in *legislation*' but in the power to give and break the law – which is a much grander, a far more encompassing role.

As I have indicated, Bodin primarily saw parliamentary bodies as serving in an advisory capacity. There was never any question for him of such bodies serving as sovereigns; nor therefore did he think either of legislators or of the specialised legislative function as being sovereign. He did of course think of sovereigns as possibly being monarchs, aristocracies or democracies. He also thought that each of such sovereigns might employ parliamentary bodies to serve in some form of intermediate capacity – but not ever of a parliamentary body *per se* being sovereign. This position is held to both in the *Methodus ad facilem historiarum cognitionem* of 1566 (the *Méthode de l'histoire*) and in the *Republique* of 1576.

It is a quite different problem, of course, to determine in what sense more persons than one, i.e. a group (as distinct from a solitary individual), can serve as a sovereign in the sense that Bodin requires. We shall see that the same problem arises even more acutely for Hobbes. Bodin at least consciously recognises that there is a problem. For although he reduces all true sovereigns to three types (the one, few and the many), he plainly concludes that the one (monarchy) is best in the sense of being more sovereign – i.e. less divided, more united and decisive – than the rest. But then Bodin's problem is only to persuade all parties that the monarch should be placed well above the fray. Hobbes's problem is the more difficult one of persuading parliamentarians that if their power *is* sovereign – and either theirs or the monarch's must be – then it must be no less absolute than that of the king.

Hancke (1894) grasps, in a way that most commentators seem not to do, this notion of the first mark of sovereignty in Bodin really consisting, not so much in the control of a legislative power, as in the control of a *highest* power – *die höchste Gewalt*. Hancke at least draws out what Bodin himself – if not most commentators – seems to make clear. I was struck by the attention which Hancke addresses initially and most importantly to the notion of a *highest* power – possibly because I read Hancke *after* I read Bodin – and found his analysis, at least on this point, to coincide with my own. ('Souverain ist, wer die höchste Gewalt im Staate besitzt, das heisst, allen Anderen befiehlt und Niemanden über sich anerkennt, als Gott', p. 10.) Most commentators begin with the notion that the chief mark of sovereignty in Bodin consists in control of the legislative power. Hancke begins more generally, and more correctly, with the notion of it consisting quite simply in the highest power (one – perhaps the – chief element in which is of course the power to 'command law').

Appendix 4

Bodinian Absolutism from the *Methodus* to the *Republique*

One of the reasons for avoiding (in the text) analytical treatment of the entire corpus of Bodin's work is that it reveals as a whole far greater internal incoherence than does the work of Hobbes. The *Republique* appears in the middle of the French religious wars and can relevantly be read against that background in a fairly distinct way. The *Methodus* (1566) is in a marginally different position in terms both of its content and the time of its appearance. (Hobbes, by contrast, was telling roughly the same story in the *De Corpore*, *De Cive* and in *Leviathan*, even though they date from the late 1630s to the early 1650s, so that no particular analytical problem arises from considering them all together.) Despite differences between the *Methodus* and the *Republique* significant enough to warrant my dealing with the latter more or less on its own, I shall maintain that the development of Bodin's doctrine of absolutism, or of sovereignty, is more markedly continuous than discontinuous. More than a few reputable scholars, as is well known, take a contrary view of the matter, and it will accordingly be appropriate to pay at least some passing attention to such views. It should be understood, however, that my views regarding the fundamental continuity between the *Methodus* and the *Republique*, even though I regard the fact of such continuity to be clearly marked, are not in any way to be taken as affecting one way or the other my central argument: that a highly significant theory of absolutism (one of the most basic historical theories about the nature of political order) is advanced in the *Republique* and that this theory merits distinct consideration in its own right.

Beatrice Reynolds (1945), in the Introduction to her translation of the *Methodus*, argues that 'too much stress has been placed upon Bodin as the author of the *Republic*; too little notice has been paid to his earlier and more liberal work [the *Methodus*]' (p. x). Reynolds does not here follow through this argument. On a number of small points she proves surprisingly unreliable. Her major work on Bodin, which we shall come to, was completed over a decade before, and so we discover her in a mood to argue not merely that the *Methodus* is more 'liberal' than the *Republique*, but – more interestingly – that the *Republique* itself is more 'liberal' than we are normally disposed to think. Thus she writes, for example, that Bodin 'disclaimed any support of absolutism', that 'he objected to the increase of royal power' – but all of this occurs in the Preface to a *1608* edition of the *Republique*. (Bodin, it will be recalled, died in 1596.)

Reynolds's earlier work (1931) is, however, far better than the Introduction referred to (1945) would lead one to expect. She has more to say than this about the discontinuity between the *Methodus* and the *Republique* and it is worth paying attention to, even if I cannot regard it as altogether convincing. Reynolds originally sought (1931) to portray Francis Hotman as an apologist for self-government and Bodin as an apologist for state absolutism (p. 106). She quickly discovered that such differences did not correspond to the facts. Reynolds is correct in arguing that Bodin (in the *Methodus*) regarded the sovereign as being bound by law (p. 117), that he believed high officials should be appointed for life so as to be insulated against royal whimsy (p. 119). But these views are not alien to the *Republique*. She maintains (p. 124) that there are 'companion passages in the two books which are absolutely contradictory'; although this is true, she fails to cite these passages, and personally I remain unaware of (what I would regard) as significant contradictions. Reynolds later (p. 143) maintains that Bodin 'eliminated from *La Republique* his most forceful statements in favor of constitutional limitations upon the king'. But she is unable in fact to substantiate this assertion textually. Even had that been possible it remains clear, nonetheless, that in the *Republique* Bodin goes quite far in arguing for various types of limitation upon sovereign power.

The formal difficulty for the student must remain: *not* whether Bodin believed that the monarch should labour under the laws of God, etc., but whether and in what degree Bodin envisaged some species of division of powers or of countervailing powers to check the monarch's unlimited sway. Bodin's insistence upon unity and finality as the hallmark of sovereignty – in both the *Methodus* and the *Republique* – runs consistently counter to the tenability of such a position. It may sound a small distinction, but I believe it more accurate to say that the *Republique* argues more forcefully than the *Methodus* for unrestrained public power – not that it contains fewer arguments for greater restraint upon public power. And this is a very good reason for considering the major arguments of the *Republique* quite separately from those of the *Methodus*. Bodin does say that the prince can do nothing contrary to the law (*Methodus*), but his later position (*Republique*) is not a repudiation but a qualification: the prince cannot alter *natural* law; but *customary* law (civil law, etc.) is different. (Cf. the contrary implications in Reynolds, p. 179.) Bodin's basic view of the prince in relation to the law remains reasonably constant; what changes are Bodin's views regarding what is and what is not basic or natural law. He always assumed that 'the prince-ship should be kept within the power of the law'. But he *never* maintained that he should be 'checked by the power of the people' (cf. Reynolds, pp. 181–2).

John L. Brown (1939), following in the steps of Reynolds, argues that 'Bodin's attitude of hostility towards the idea of the *princeps legibus solutus* which he expresses in the *Methodus* . . . undermines the conventional conception (based on a superficial reading of the *Republique*) of Bodin as the advocate of an absolute and completely unrestrained monarchy' (pp. 132–3). Here the writer suggests there is at least superficially a great gap between Bodin's treatment of absolutism in the two works; Brown further suggests that in neither case is Bodin properly to be seen as an 'advocate of an absolute and completely unrestrained monarchy'. In the text I have cited and partly supported the views of Shepard and Conde who advance similar views. Thus we are already aware of something of the intricacy of Bodin's position. Suffice it to say here, in regard to Bodinian absolutism, that Bodin does, by his own admission and in his own words, advocate 'absolute' monarchy. It would be inappropriate to raise yet again, in this appendix, the question as to how absolute Bodin's absolutism is to be taken to be. Our more relevant task must be to consider the extent of the gap asserted by Brown to exist between the *Methodus* and the *Republique*.

For the moment, we shall simply restrict ourselves to reconstructing Brown's position. Brown argues (p. 153) that 'in the *Methodus* . . . Bodin's idea of the monarch was that of a king bound by law, by custom, by the will of the three estates'. The question for us is to what extent Bodin diverges from such a position in the *Republique*. The only point that I would wish to make is that in the *Republique* Bodin still insists upon the king, the sovereign, being bound by law – which could be expressed in customary procedures or through the will of the three estates, so long as it was in conformity with *natural law*. Brown continues: 'Bodin's ideal of monarchy expressed in the *Methodus* is clearly the medieval ideal of the king living under law, the servant of his people as well as their ruler, receiving his power from the people, and responsible to them for his use of it.' Such a view as this is clearly exaggerated. Certainly in the *Republic* Bodin regards the source of law as being the sovereign, not the people – except in such circumstances where the people were sovereign (i.e. in a democracy). But such a position is not fundamentally different from that argued in the *Methodus*, where Bodin expresses utter contempt for the people, regarding them as capable of wielding sovereign power but as being completely unfit for it. (See the argument against democracy in the Mesnard edition (1951) of the

Methodus, pp. 412ff.) Brown is largely right to say that the *Methodus* conceives of the monarchy in the medieval fashion: the king, created by and responsible to the people, is bound by natural and divine law, by custom, by legal contracts, by the *leges imperii*, by the *loi Salique*. The point, however, is that the *Republique*, too, makes all of these points – except that both it and the *Methodus* regard a king who is created by the people not to be sovereign but subject, subject indeed to the sovereign people. But I need not repeat Bodin's contempt for such a form of sovereignty. To say that Bodin (in the *Methodus*) rejects Aristotle, where the latter argues that a king is not a king if he is bound by the law, proves nothing. In numerous passages in the *Republique* Bodin also says that the king *is* bound by law. Bodin, of course, makes both this point and its contrary. So we witness the usual confusion attendant upon any analysis of Bodin's work. What Brown must establish, however, is that the notion of some form of indisputably unrestrained absolutism is far more marked in the *Republique* than in the *Methodus*. There is surely room for argument, enough indeed to lead me to conclude that the point cannot be made.

In fact, the more traditional analyses lead in the opposite direction. Both Baudrillart (1853) and Chauviré (1914), for example, argue for continuity rather than discontinuity as between the *Methodus* and the *Republique*. Baudrillart is more disposed to assume rather than to argue for such continuity, although he does state that Bodin 'put all of his ideas' into the *Methodus*, 'ten years in advance of the *Republique*' (p. 145). Chauviré speaks more expressly of 'an essentially profound continuity between the *Methodus* and the *Republique*' (p. 271). He is disposed to explain what he regards as certain minor differences ('variations légères') by reference to changed historical circumstances. In general, he concludes that 'the differences between the *Methodus* and the *Republique* are actually more apparent than real: they involve different *nuances*, accounted for by changing contemporary circumstances, as expressed by a single doctrine which remains essentially true to itself' (p. 273).

Mesnard (1941) develops the argument for continuity more forcefully still. In the introduction to his French translation of the *Methodus* he states expressly that 'Bodin here categorically affirms the superiority of royal government'. He rejects the view that in the *Methodus* Bodin somehow decisively opposes monarchical absolutism. 'The concept of an hereditary monarchy in conformity with the Salic Law leads him [Bodin] directly to this clear and distinct idea – that sovereignty is indivisible – and it is this idea which will serve as the pivotal concept of the *Republique* . . .' (p. xvi).

Enough has been said by now to demonstrate significant differences of opinion regarding the relative stress of the *Methodus* as against the

Republique in the matter of the propriety of royal absolutism. It will be clear that differences of stress are difficult to assess and it is for this reason that I do not wish to assign to such a problem any considerable methodological significance. It will suffice, perhaps, having drawn attention to the existing differences of opinion, to reconstruct the basic continuity (as I see it) in the development of the theory of royal absolutism from the *Methodus* to the *Republique*.

In Bodin's work one confronts an important question regarding the relationship between the apparently rival notions of the prince being abcve the law and (at the same time) subject to the law. This problem must certainly be seen as internal to Bodin's *Republique*. There it is clearly argued that the prince or the sovereign wields an absolute and perpetual power, but that he wields this power (or authority) subject to the law of nature or of God and (in some cases) of man. The problem, as we have seen, arises in regard to the determination of the will of nature or of God and thus also which laws of man (e.g. contracts) are to be regarded as binding upon the prince. If the determination of such matters is left to the prince, then clearly it does not mean much to say that the prince is above human law but subject to natural and divine law – for the simple reason that the prince, himself would always be able to say what this natural or divine law was. The problem of whether and in what way Bodin's prince is subject to divine law is not so easily resolved, however, for the reason that Bodin does accept that other human beings – e.g. judges – in effect have some right to interpret natural and divine law, such that where princely decrees conflict with such law, judges are not obligated to implement those decrees. All the same, this represents a very modest check upon sovereign power. Bodin indeed rejected the whole concept of a mixed state, a *stato misto*, and in so far as this rejection is central to his whole analysis, so too must be any notion of countervailing powers. In brief, Bodin's position in the *Republique* was not far removed from the notion that the sovereign must be regarded as having been placed above his fellows by God, exercising a rightful authority of virtually unlimited sway over them, an authority basically obstructed only by a proper (princely) consideration of God's will rather than by the express wishes of subjects.

In the text I have restricted my concern to the *Republique*. But we have seen that it is of some interest to inquire in what degree the position advanced there is consistent with that which Bodin adopts in the *Methodus*. We shall now briefly review the chief ideas expressed in the *Methodus* in order to discover to what extent they accord with those expressed in the *Republique*. (Latin and French citations below from the *Methodus* refer to the Mesnard edition of the collected works, the *Œuvres philosophiques de Jean Bodin*, 1951.)

To begin, Bodin draws a clear distinction between debating a measure, on the one hand, and implementing a law, on the other. Debate may be appropriate to a parliamentary body, but the actual proclamation and implementation of the law remains the preserve of the sovereign (p. 289). The sovereign may assume only one of three forms – monarchy, aristocracy or democracy – and no other. The sovereign, whatever form he assumes, is humanly superior within the system concerned; he is not subject to other human elements within it ('n'est déjà plus un magistrat, mais le prince', p. 330; 'non jam magistratus, sed princeps erit', p. 168). Bodin accuses Aristotle of having had no proper appreciation of the nature of sovereign power. For Bodin, the sovereign is one who in effect exercises the supreme power – not one (or some) who merely gives counsel (*consilio*) or appoints officials or enforces law. Even private citizens may give counsel, but this does not make them sovereign. Even the humblest of men, too, may assist in the enforcement of law, without for that reason becoming sovereign. For Bodin, the appointment of officials comes closest, among the Aristotelian categories, to being a sovereign function. What we must see, however, is that Bodin is here thinking of high officials as representing that power which is most approximate to the variety we label as sovereign. This in no way – as in the *Republique* – distracts him from proclaiming: 'but it is even more directly the province of sovereign power to promulgate laws or to rescind them, to declare war or end it, to act as a final court of appeal' and so on (p. 351).

In delineating the character of sovereignty, Bodin is clearly not concerned merely with issuing or not issuing law, with judging or not judging cases, or even with implementing or not implementing law, considered as distinguishing characteristics of sovereignty. It is rather the level on which any or all of these activities takes place – as argued both in the *Methodus* and the *Republique* – that counts. It is only the highest instances of issuing law or of judging cases or of implementing commands, and only the highest agents performing these functions, which and who are to be accounted sovereign. Bodin is particularly concerned with the unity of any association denominated a state. His query is: in what may we hold the unity of a state to consist? Whatever the case, however awkward the facts, he always attempts to argue that a state can only be regarded as united, as a genuine state, where certain final powers of command internally attach to some specifiable, distinct, determinate body within that state. He inquires, for example, whether the Swiss cantons of his day form a united state ('une seule Republique') and his answer is negative, in effect because the Swiss cantons at that time retained independent powers of final decision, and thus were *associated* with one another, but not *united* with one another as a single state (cf.

pp. 355–6). This analysis brings Bodin very close to our contemporary distinction between confederal and federal states, i.e. between state associations of a loose kind which ultimately either do or do not allow of secession to member units. In so far as this is true, one could conclude that Bodin would have recognised federal states to be 'genuine' states, even though his characterisation (in the *Republique*) of the nature of that unity (as absolute, perpetual, indivisible, etc.) would have to be regarded as extremely faulty.

In the *Methodus*, just as in the *Republique*, Bodin argued vehemently against any form of mixed state (*imperium temperatum*). Differentiating between governments in terms of the *number* of rulers characterising each (one, few or many), rejecting the utility of further distinctions based on the goodness or badness or upon the morality or immorality of such governments, Bodin went on to suggest that no sovereign state was simultaneously monarchical, aristocratic and democratic (wherein a single leader, an élite, and the vast mass of people have an equal say). For Bodin, the real problem was to determine who exercised a final right of decision, or command: one, a few or the many? He both assumed and argued that such power could only be exercised from one locus. Accordingly, writers like Polybius, Cicero and Machiavelli were simply wrong to suggest that the Roman or any other state was of a mixed or 'temperate' kind. Bodin seems desperately anxious in the *Methodus* to assign the principle of authority in any given state to a fixed and distinct locus. It is possible that, in this context, many writers have been misled by Bodin's attribution of sovereignty to the people in the Roman Republic. If one assumed that in the sixteenth century 'liberals' argued for popular rule and 'conservatives' for monarchical rule, then Bodin's insistence, particularly in the *Methodus*, that Roman rule was of a popular type might lead one to suppose that he was 'liberal' in this work, turning 'conservative' in the *Republique*. But all that Bodin was doing was insisting that the Roman constitution was not of a *mixed* type, that it had a distinct sovereign focus, one which, in the event, was democratic. But of course Bodin, unlike Machiavelli, despised 'republicanism', or 'democracy' in our contemporary sense of the term. He expanded at tiresome length in the *Methodus* on the Roman constitution: yes, in it authority *was* conferred upon the senate, *and* upon dictators, but it was not withdrawn from the tribunes of the people, and he concluded in myriad ways that final authority rested with the people – as in Athens and in Venice. But Bodin insists that the best and only really stable state is a monarchy, and a hereditary monarchy at that.

One can easily appreciate Bodin's inclination to think that state cohesion ultimately requires the final command of some discrete orderer. It is almost certain that he would have conceded the United States Federal

Government the status of a 'state'. But it is difficult to see how he could do this in terms of the more specific attributes by which he characterises a state. Certainly it represents a system in which reasonably final decisions of a reasonably coherent sort can be taken. But if Bodin were to regard sovereignty as reposing in a 'democracy', in 'the people', then the same sort of circularity would appear as in his discussion of the Roman constitution. The immediate problem would arise, within the context of his own discussion, of how a 'people' – diffuse and disunited in themselves – can be 'sovereign' anyway. If it is argued, as it reasonably may be on one level, that the 'ultimate' coherence of the federal system derives from the fact that one body – in this case a body of jurists – is ultimately empowered to declare what the law is, it will be noted that the United States Supreme Court commands neither votes nor battalions. Thus it is the highest organ within the federal system as regards the interpretation of the law. But it remains true that its interpretations must be accepted. Beyond this, it is plain that the states may amend the constitution, as may the Congress; and the President, in concert with the Congress, may pack the court. Thus we discover a cycle of control, not a straightforward 'command and obedience' syndrome. Because of this cycle, the wheel of control may and does turn; and it is difficult to say, for anything other than a specific act or moment, that X, in such a federal system, = a final orderer. Thus Bodin's argument against the possibility of a 'mixed' state is less cogent than it at first appears. Every state seeks finality, but finality, considered over time, is not genuinely attainable. Finality may be interpreted as a form of predictability. It may also be interpreted as a form of coherence. But no system of laws can ever be entirely coherent, or even nearly so. Nor can the form in which such laws will be applied be entirely predictable. It is also inappropriate to think of sacrificing justice for predictability and coherence. The latter have to be regarded as subsidiary functions of the former.

Bodin could not make it clearer than he does in the *Methodus* that he was a monarchist, an absolutist, an 'order first' theorist of a rather extreme kind. Let us consider now his general preference for monarchy. Bodin at no point supports Machiavelli in his plea for popular government as an ideal type. On the contrary, he mentions Machiavelli's defence but then adds that he (Bodin) 'does not believe it necessary to agree with his [Machiavelli's] views in the matter' (p. 412). Bodin proceeds to cite conventional attacks on democracy in terms of such regimes being 'sworn enemies of all public virtue', etc. In this connection he even attacks Plato as being too liberal. Modern commentators usually cite Aristotle's attack upon Plato's *Republic* where Plato is criticised for making his state too much of a unity. These citations have

APPENDIX 4

as their point a liberal thrust: to wit, Plato urges too great a degree of corporate unity. Bodin, by contrast, is so far from bearing a republican or popular orientation, in the modern sense, that he cites Aristotle's attack upon Plato in order to demonstrate that Plato's insistence on unity was merely a ludicrously extreme argument for egalitarianism. Karl Popper regards Plato as such an unbridled anti-egalitarian that it is difficult to imagine there would be any room left in his conceptual framework to accommodate a theorist like Bodin. It is certainly plain that a writer like Brown (1939) is quite mistaken to suggest that Bodin betrays in the *Methodus* some significantly more liberal disposition than in the *Republique*.

According to Bodin (*Methodus*, 1951, p. 412), nothing is more un-natural and detestable than extreme equality (of the kind Plato is sup-posed to have favoured). In a democracy, the fundamental principle projected is that of an equal right to command. But command requires prudence at least (if not *sagesse*). And this, of course, not all men possess. Therefore, concludes Bodin, nothing could be more absurd than a democratic 'order'. He advances similar arguments against aristocracy (p. 414). The latter consists of a body of persons, however limited in number. Since the majority must carry the day, and since the mediocre are more numerous than the prudent, then the mediocre will govern. Bodin argues here – as well as, and still more elaborately in, the *Théatre de la nature universelle* (1596) – that nature, by contrast, ex-cludes such anarchy: in nature, every species in the animal kingdom is characterised by the domination of each group by one leader. As this is true in nature, he implies that the appropriate lesson for man cannot be less clear. For Bodin, divided power is dangerous, God himself decrees unity, and unity should always be as great as possible. This sort of argument leads Bodin into a defence of monarchy. As we have indicated, Bodin, in order to avoid all disorder, and this includes any form of interregnum, pitches naturally upon an hereditary rather than upon an elective monarchy as best. It is clear that much of what Bodin says in the *Methodus*, particularly about the 'mediocrity' of the people, whether in a democracy or an aristocracy, is similar to and possibly influenced by Plato's views. But as I have argued in the text, the concept of intelli-gence, of wisdom, of sagacity, is in no way really central to Bodin's concept of the appropriate qualifications for rule. Bodin is distinguished by placing equal and indeed greater stress upon will, prudence, judge-ment. If he were more concerned with wisdom as the chief quality of the ruler, then it would be better, as in Plato, to make the ruler elective rather than hereditary. But since Bodin is more concerned with estab-lishing a final locus of power, he is far less concerned with the personal virtues of the prince who represents such a locus. It is in this sense that a writer like Lewis (1968) is mistaken in attributing to Bodin an 'insistence that the sovereign must be a wise and just ruler'. This position would thus be consequently mistaken, too, in assigning Bodin and Hobbes to 'incompatible' traditions (p. 220).

Having come now to the discussion of monarchy as a distinct form of sovereignty, it may be said that a great deal has sometimes been made of the difference in treatment of this subject in the *Methodus* as against the *Republique*. The suggested difference is, in my view, much exaggerated. The key to the issue is that Bodin discusses different types of monarchy and this discussion is likely to be confused with his *recommendation* of one type over another. Bodin, in discussing the first species of monarchy, clearly indicates (*Methodus*, 1951, p. 377) that 'very few princes . . . are disposed to subject themselves to the slightest laws and, in their own words, never bind themselves'. Bodin proceeds to discuss a second type of monarch, which he partly characterises as Christian, and under which the prince swears to govern the state for the good of all. Such a monarch is obviously bound by law. (But we have already seen that the type of monarch recommended by Bodin in the *Republique* is also understood in important senses to be bound by 'law'.) Now given that monarchs can be bound by such engagements (as also argued in the *Republique*), it follows (for Bodin) that Aristotle was mistaken in arguing that kings who are bound by laws are not kings. (In the *Republique* Bodin argues that if a prince who has 'absolute power is one not subject to any law, then there can be found no sovereign prince on earth . . .') Bodin argues in the *Methodus*, as in the *Republique*, that a king may be bound by a variety of laws: the Salic law, those natural and divine, some that are civil and contractual (such as obligations the king undertakes in his dealings with others). The interesting point about the *Methodus* is that there Bodin concludes that 'there is thus this difference between legitimate kings, in that some are bound by some laws of the kingdom and others are entirely unfettered' (p. 378). It is plain that such a conclusion could easily make Bodin appear *less* liberal in the *Methodus* than in the *Republique*, since in the latter he states, as we have noted, that there is *no* king on earth who is not bound by natural and divine laws.

With regard to the character of sovereignty, or royal absolutism, I conclude that Bodin makes his position clearer in the *Republique* than in the *Methodus*, but I do regard this as *clarification*, and thus as the continuous rather than the discontinuous development of an argument. In the *Methodus* Bodin defines the essential attributes of sovereignty as (*a*) appointing the highest state officials and setting out their duties, (*b*) laying down laws or annulling them, (*c*) making war or peace, (*d*) acting as a final court of appeal, and (*e*) granting pardon or otherwise in cases of life and death. He sets out these attributes in the order given and indeed qualifies the first – the appointment of high officials – as the most important (in the French text, 'le plus important', p. 359, col. 2, ll. 36–46; in the Latin text, 'una est ac praecipua' pp. 174–5, ll. 55–60 and 1–4). In the *Republique*, by contrast, Bodin advances the *commanding* of law (not 'legislating') as the first and chief mark of sovereignty – that which (logically) subsumes all the rest. This change from the appointment of high officials to the commanding of law (as the chief mark of sovereignty) doubtless came to seem more logical to Bodin – as indeed it is. If officials are appointed to perform a job, then the logically prior consideration is the stipulation of the job – the setting out of the law including the duties of officials under such law. Bodin obviously came to regard the commanding of what was to be done (in the *Republique*) as *logically* anterior to the designation of those who were to do it (the reverse of the position taken in the *Methodus*).

Appendix 5

Comments on the Source of Political Obligation in Hobbes

A. E. Taylor (see Brown, 1965) distinguishes between Hobbes's psychology and his ethics. Psychology has to do with the *facts* of human motivation, ethics with what men *ought* to do. Following Taylor, Hobbes's psychology is built upon *egoism*, his ethics upon the making of implicit or explicit *promises*. Thus the reason why a man should obey his sovereign is not that by doing so he preserves himself, but because, given the contract, he is bound by his own promise to do so. The principle that one is bound to observe one's promises is, in Hobbes, an element of natural law, and so must be understood to be commanded by God. I accept the importance of the distinction between Hobbes's psychology and his morality. But I do not accept that Hobbesian morality binds the sovereign as well as the subject. The subject may be obligated because he promises. But of course the Hobbesian sovereign does not himself make any promises. The subject is obligated to his fellow subjects and therefore to the sovereign upon whose institution they have agreed. But there is no further human agent to whom the sovereign is in turn obligated. Of course it is true, just as in Bodin, that the Hobbesian sovereign is obligated to uphold the laws of nature and of God. But, again as in Bodin, the problem arises as to whose word one takes to be the word of God. It does not matter whether Hobbes was or was not an atheist. The position is simply this: if what God declares must be humanly 'divined', and if the ultimate interpreter of the divine word is the sovereign, then obviously the latter is not bound to obey God in the sense in which Hobbes demands that this sovereign should be obeyed by subjects. Hobbes's subject, after all, is left little room in which to interpret as he chooses his sovereign's commands. But the sovereign himself, for Hobbes, is the only human agent who may ultimately interpret the will of God. Theirs are obviously two quite different types of 'subjection'.

As indicated, I accept the distinction between Hobbes's psychology and his morality. But I argue that Hobbesian obligation rests less upon promise in general, than upon the implied principle that men ought always to try to preserve themselves. It is because they *should* try to preserve themselves that suicide, were it genuinely possible, would be wrong; the same reason dictates that men should try to escape from the state of nature; and it dictates further that men must make these *promises* of mutual forbearance, and accordingly establish so powerful a sovereign, in order to protect their lives. I argue, in short, that self-preservation in Hobbes is the basic implied *duty* of mankind. For Hobbes, men *do* try to preserve themselves, but his laws of nature indicate that they *ought* to try to preserve themselves: this is the linchpin, in my view, of Hobbesian political theory, of Hobbesian ethics, and of Hobbesian political obligation. The chief law of nature is that one should do nothing 'which is destructive of his life', nor anything which 'taketh away the means of preserving the same . . .' (*Leviathan*, ch. 14). If indeed one should promise obedience in order to preserve one's life; if, further, one may freely disobey where one's life is placed in danger; then, clearly, the prior area of concern has to do with a duty of self-preservation, rather than with the subsidiary duty of observing promises.

Stuart M. Brown (in K. C. Brown, 1965) in effect insists that Hobbes derives his norms from his facts. To a certain extent I agree. I have myself no doubt that Hobbes seriously thought that he could demonstrate how men *should* behave on the basis of some understanding of how they *do* behave. But it seems to me equally clear that Hobbes not only grounded 'the civil rights of sovereigns, and both the duty and liberty of subjects, upon the *known natural inclinations* of mankind' (my italics), but also 'upon the articles of the law of nature'. The law of nature was not, of course, a physical fact, but – if one likes – a moral 'fact'. Hobbes suggests not only that it is 'the natural inclination' of man to preserve himself, but also that this inclination is right, i.e. that we are *obligated* to follow it. He suggests at times that one *ought* to seek to preserve oneself because one *does* seek to do so; and he also suggests that one ought to because one ought to: it is a law of nature or a command of God or an expression of reason or simply an imperative which we all, for whatever reasons, do accept. If we follow the first trail, we can accuse Hobbes of falling into the naturalistic fallacy (Moore). But we can instead follow the second trail, which would seem preferable since it leads Hobbes into more defensible territory: we strengthen Hobbes's argument, and therefore make it a more interesting object of attack. Neither path, of course, is invulnerable to attack.

In regard to the first, and as Macpherson (1962) rightly argues, to insist that Hobbes derives his theory of obligation (exclusively) from his concept of human nature is to reduce that theory to ruins. There is no way in which one can logically derive the notion that men *ought* to preserve themselves from the assumption that this is something that they always in fact *do*; the notion of an act being done in no way logically contains the notion that it ought to be done; thus there is no way in which one can even pretend to *deduce* from a fact of nature any form of duty to government. Hobbes cannot escape this objection. (At this point, therefore, I disagree with Macpherson, who thinks Hobbes can.) But although such an objection as this is perfectly *appropriate*, it cannot be taken as an *exclusive* answer to Hobbes. To do so merely makes his argument appear trivial, which it is not, for Hobbes is also involved in the business of deducing – or of attempting to deduce – express norms from covert norms: the express duty to obey the sovereign from the covert (although sometimes overt) duty to preserve oneself.

As regards Hobbes's second line of argument – where he 'derives' a norm to obey from the principle of self-preservation – this, too, can be attacked. But it is certainly a more difficult position to overrun. It invites inconsequential attacks, such as the question as to how one can speak of a *duty* to obey a principle in a state of nature where the conditions for Hobbesian obedience do not obtain. This sort of attack, in my opinion, merely leads towards infinite regress or circularity. Clearly what one ought to do (in many respects) when there is no government will differ from what one ought to do when there is; in the first case one is inevitably one's own ultimate arbiter on a wider range of issues, while in the second case one more frequently defers to the decisions of others, and rightly so. Under a government we might say that we ought to do something *because* we have promised. If asked why we have promised, we might say that this was in order to preserve ourselves. If asked why we ought to preserve ourselves, we might reply that to do so conforms to natural law. If asked why we ought to conform to natural law, we might answer that it is the supreme embodiment of Reason. If asked why we should conform to Reason we might say it is because through this God's commands are made known. If asked why we should obey God's commands, we may concoct similarly regressive replies *ad infinitum*. Alternatively, we might return a circular answer: to obey God's will is the indispensable condition of self-preservation. And then the question again arises: why should we preserve ourselves? Such questions, then, about the source or origin of the duty to preserve ourselves, when applied to Hobbes, will lead into infinite regress or circularity. Consequently I am not disposed to regard as interesting the question: Whence does Hobbes derive the duty to preserve oneself? It is only important, basically, to realise that he does regard it as a *duty*, whether one lives under a government or not, in times of civil war or other, in a 'state of nature' or of 'civil society'. And since Hobbes regards self-preservation not only as a fact but also as a duty, the more interesting questions become those of assessing (*a*) the validity of this supposed duty *per se*, and (*b*) the validity of the deductive relationship he insists upon as obtaining between his Basic Norm (self-preservation) and his 'derived' norm (virtually total obedience to an established sovereign).

It may, of course, be argued, as is explicitly stated by Hobbes and emphasised by Warrender (1957), that the *first* or most *fundamental* of the laws of nature is to seek peace. But I would argue that what is here advanced as a first duty is really intended as a derived duty: peace is regarded less as a good in itself, an initially binding principle, than as a means towards the end of self-preservation. Thus, within Hobbes's system the first principle is really this: preserve thyself. It is indeed due to a certain formal ambiguity as to which of the two duties is prior, to preserve oneself or to seek peace, that Hobbes's system becomes open to another line of attack. In order to preserve oneself, it might at times be best to wage war. To seek peace (by erecting an all-powerful sovereign in the way that Hobbes suggested) might lead with the greatest speed to self-destruction (as Locke rightly observed). Of course, Hobbes made it clear that he thought it inappropriate – in a state of nature – for one to seek peace where to do so would put one's life at risk. But he seemed not to appreciate that the sort of concentrated power that he sought to confer upon a sovereign might create as much insecurity and risk to human life as civil war itself. In any event, what is important is that Hobbes's clear conclusion – that to seek peace is not morally enjoined where it creates significant risks to life – of itself suggests that the first duty in his system was that of self-preservation.

Although Hobbes's concept of political obligation can be traced back *both* to his psychology and to the command of God, I argue that neither, strictly speaking, is *necessary* to his argument for obedience to the state, on the assumption that obedience affords a means of self-preservation and on the further assumption that self-preservation (for Hobbes) is what men *ought* to desire. The basic point here is that Hobbes's argument is not *merely* conditional: he is not just saying that if men desire self-preservation they may find it through peace, and peace only through total submission to a sovereign. This suggests a detachment on Hobbes's part which does not correspond to the reality. As Hobbes himself said of *Leviathan*: 'That book now fights for all kings . . .' He assumed that men should, like himself, desire self-preservation, which would in his view require them to accept that means which he regarded as indispensable to its achievement. Thus Hobbes's argument was of the form: *as* men *do* desire to preserve themselves, etc. There is, of course, a certain ambiguity about saying that one *does* desire to preserve oneself. It may suggest that one is merely describing a psychological state. But it may also suggest that the item desired is in itself 'desirable'. Hobbes is not merely describing what others desire, but what he – and what he thinks others – accept as desirable.

Warrender (ch. 9) argues that self-preservation in Hobbes is a right and not a duty – that it is an option which we may take or leave, claim or yield, but not an obligation which we must follow unwaveringly. On this analysis it would be right to preserve one's life, but not wrong to surrender it. Here I believe Warrender to be mistaken. Like any commentator, he provides an *interpretation* of what Hobbes intended. In saying that he is 'mistaken' on a particular point, I am suggesting that some alternative interpretation is better.

Warrender suggests that the Basic Norm of Hobbes's state is not (*a*) 'preserve thyself' (as I argue) but (these are not Warrender's words) (*b*) '*preserve all men* to the extent that doing so is not inconsistent with preserving thyself'. (Warrender's *own* words are: 'act so that all men can be preserved, except where this is inconsistent with your own preservation'. I cannot locate this formula in Warrender, 1957, but only in his essay in Brown, 1965.) Even if we could accept formula (*b*) rather than formula (*a*), it would seem clear that the fundamental condition which it contains – that preserving others is enjoined '*except* where this is inconsistent with your own preservation' – shows that one's prior concern must be to preserve *oneself*. My argument is that the prior duty asserted by Hobbes is self-preservation, and that the seeking of peace is to be regarded as a function of this. If peace, however, is promoted from a means to an end, it becomes much more difficult to justify. Why should one seek peace, after all, unless it is to preserve oneself? To 'endeavour peace' is, for Hobbes, a law of nature. But to think that he really regards it as the *first* consideration is in part to ignore what he himself says: 'all laws of nature . . . tend to nature's preservation' (*Leviathan*, Oakeshott ed., p. 103). If to seek peace is a law, and if this law is a law of nature, then it must, like all such laws, have the effect of preserving nature – i.e. life, and most especially one's own. Hobbes suggests that anyone who does not observe the laws of nature 'seeketh not peace, but war'. What is interesting is the reason he gives for seeking peace and avoiding war: 'he that . . . observes them [the laws of nature] not himself, seeketh . . . consequently the destruction of his nature by violence'. By implication, the duty to 'endeavour peace' is a function of the duty to preserve oneself. One might object to Hobbes that the seeking of peace could lead to self-destruction. Hobbes's answer would be that the mere seeking, the endeavour *per se*, could not achieve this effect. I would not care to argue the point: but it would seem clear that any attempt to conclude a peace (as with Hitler, for example) could carry as great a risk to life as the resolve in certain circumstances to go to war. So it would be useful to ask Hobbes whether war, as opposed to peace, could ever preserve life. His answer is revealing: 'it can never be that war will preserve life, and peace destroy it'

(*Leviathan*, p. 104). Clearly, however, one may *peacefully* submit to the hangman; but it is difficult to maintain that doing so preserves life. It seems plain that Hobbes thought peace was good and war evil because the latter destroyed life and the former preserved it. Obviously, matters do not always fall out in this manner. When Hobbes characterises the seeking of peace as a law of nature, he does not merely mean of course that *he* regards it as a duty. He thinks that everyone, explicitly or by implication, does so. It is in this sort of circumstance that his psychology and his morality merge. Hobbes confidently asserts that 'all men agree on this, that peace is good' (p. 104). The assertion is doubtful on two counts: that *all* men (psychologically speaking) *do* agree that peace is good, and that all forms of peace are *morally* right.

In arguing that Hobbes lays down the seeking of peace *as a function* of self-preservation, I am of course completely opposing Warrender's view (1957, p. 218) that in Hobbes, 'the fundamental principle which the individual is obliged to follow is one which enjoins peace *rather than* self-preservation as such' (my italics). For Hobbes, a 'right' confers upon one a liberty to act or forbear; a 'law' imposes upon one a *duty* to act or forbear. Thus, as we noted earlier, Warrender attributes to Hobbes the view that self-preservation is a matter of right rather than of law; it supposedly describes a manner in which we are at liberty to act but not under an actual obligation so to do. But this characterisation of Hobbesian self-preservation simply turns it inside out.

For Hobbes, 'the Right of Nature . . . is the liberty each man hath, to use his own power, *as he will himself*, for the preservation of his own . . . life' (my italics). The important thing for Hobbes about this right of nature, which gives us a *liberty* to act, is that it leads into *war*, which is evil: for it authorises a man to do anything, *as he will himself*, anything, which '*he shall conceive to be the aptest*', *anything at all* which an individual should decide provides him with a means of preserving his life. This right of nature, therefore, does exist, but Hobbes conceives of it as containing highly anarchical and destructive implications. Hobbes's whole object is to replace that right by law, the liberty by a duty, with the effect of binding men in such a way that war between them is eliminated. Thus the chief right of nature is understandable, but anarchical, and thus has to be replaced by a law. But this law, if ever it is to be accepted and applied, must meet the condition of self-preservation while eliminating the condition of individuals deciding upon such means of self-preservation as *they* 'shall conceive to be the aptest', etc.

So we must ask: What sort of *law* will or can replace this sort of *right*? Well, of course, the law of nature must simultaneously build upon and displace the right of nature. The first question, contrary to the

Warrender assumption, is not: What is the *first* or *fundamental* law of nature? It is, rather: What is the law of nature *per se*? Hobbes's answer to this question, as below, is absolutely fatal to Warrender, even though Warrender quotes the same text: 'A law of nature', says Hobbes (meaning any law of nature at all, fundamental or otherwise) 'is a precept or general rule, found out by reason, by which a man is *forbidden* [my italics] to do that, which is destructive of his life, or taketh away the means of preserving the same; and to omit that, by which he thinketh it may best be preserved' (*Leviathan*, p. 84). A right confers a liberty, but the law imposes an obligation. The whole point of Hobbes's argument here is to suggest that the exercise of the *right* of nature conflicts with the duty of a man under the *law* of nature. And the law of nature imposes upon man the *obligation* to do whatever is truly rather than falsely *required* to preserve his life. The difference between the right of nature and the law of nature is essentially this: the *right* confers upon an individual a liberty to perform *as he will himself, as he himself shall conceive* to be the aptest; whereas the *law* imposes upon an individual the duty to act to preserve himself *in a manner conformable* to such precepts or general *rules which are 'found out by reason'*.

The right of nature gives an individual a liberty to preserve himself *in any way he chooses*. The law of nature (every law of nature) imposes upon an individual the obligation to preserve himself, not by adopting just any means he chooses, but *by adopting means which are rational*. The right of nature, therefore, *presumes* that a man will act somehow to preserve himself; the law of nature *enjoins* that he do so in a rational manner. It is clear, from this, that Hobbes regards self-preservation not merely as a motive but as a proper motive, i.e. as a duty. The difficulty is of course that every man, in exercising the right of nature, will doubtless assume that the way in which *he* chooses to preserve himself is indeed rational, or conformable to reason. But Hobbes necessarily assumes a distinction between rational and irrational, or between reasonable and unreasonable, means. His object, assuming that we are all agreed on the end (which is a moral consideration), is to demonstrate the appropriate, and indeed for him the only possible, means of achieving it. If his argument is sound, then the *law* of nature – as he describes it – will oblige us to accept the consequences (i.e. the institutional notions which fall out from his argument). (If one must ultimately find out for oneself, even with Hobbes's help, what is 'found out by reason', then a 'civil society' is always in some degree a 'state of nature'. But this is a problem for Hobbes's analysis, not for us.)

The right of nature confers upon man a liberty to preserve himself (in *any* fashion); the law of nature imposes upon him an obligation to preserve himself, a duty to avoid that 'which is destructive of his life' (in a *rational* fashion). It is appropriate for Warrender to underline the Hobbesian distinction between right and law, but mistaken to suggest that for Hobbes self-preservation is merely a right and not a law (or duty). For Hobbes there are several laws of nature, but they all derive from the duty of self-preservation. The first law of nature is not so much a 'good' (i.e. 'the object of any man's appetite or desire', *Leviathan*, ch. 6, p. 32) as a 'general rule of reason' (ch. 14, p. 85). The function of reason, for Hobbes, is to lead us safely to that which we desire. In the state of nature we are at liberty, but are not *obligated*, to adopt any means at all of preserving ourselves, because the 'reasoning' upon which we fasten may only lead us to an '*apparent, or seeming good*' (ch. 6, p. 39). But in this same state of nature we are also obligated to follow, and are not at liberty to ignore, those rules of reason which advance us beyond the perception of a merely '*apparent* good', and which truly lead us to the attainment of what we desire. Hobbes says that we all desire peace and that we all desire self-preservation. But the latter is the good (what is both desired and desirable) and the former is the chief rational means we are obligated to follow to achieve it. If indeed to preserve himself is man's fundamental motive (as Warrender concedes), it is also, following Hobbes's argument, man's fundamental good (again: what is both desired and desirable). Reason, Hobbesian reason, will lead us to the attainment of this good. The laws of nature which Hobbes sets out, since they will lead us to this end, obligate us.

The first obligation (to seek peace) is merely the chief means of attaining the underlying good (self-preservation). The second obligation ('to defend ourselves') is *not* the second law of nature. In Hobbes's words, it is merely the second 'branch' of the first or fundamental law of nature. Thus the first or fundamental law of nature expresses two duties: (*a*) to seek peace and (*b*) to defend ourselves. On this point Warrender is guilty of a significant omission. For he asserts that, in Hobbes, 'the fundamental law of nature is not "preserve thyself", but "seek peace", and the further laws of nature are derived from the latter precept' (1957, p. 216). I should remark parenthetically that I regard Goldsmith's analysis (1966) of this problem as more accurate than Warrender's. He clearly states, for example, that 'self-preservation is the end to which the laws of nature are the means' (p. 116). Nonetheless, the analysis is overtaken by a certain hesitancy, and eventually trips up over the same difficulty instanced by Warrender. For Goldsmith concludes: 'still, the first and fundamental law of nature is not *preserve yourself*, but *seek peace*, and this seems to support the contention that self-preservation is not a duty' (p. 122). Warrender (and Goldsmith) *should have said*, as does Hobbes, that the first and fundamental law of nature is to 'seek peace' *and* to 'defend ourselves'. Because Warrender omits the second part of the fundamental law of nature, he commits a second error: the suggestion that the remaining laws are merely derived from the principle of seeking peace. This is obviously false. They are derived from the *conjoint* principles of peace-seeking and self-defence. Since Hobbes views these conjoint principles as one, it can impose no distortion upon his system to try to see them as such by disengaging the underlying notion which binds them together. Both to seek peace and to defend oneself simply means that one should try to attain peace in order to preserve oneself and on condition that the attempt does not undermine one's security. This fundamental precept stems from the assumption that peace-seeking provides a means which is most apt to achieve the end, *the good*, of self-preservation.

Warrender appears to assume that 'self-preservation' and 'self-defence' are used by Hobbes in an identical way. Accordingly, he states that *if* Hobbes thought 'self-preservation were meant to be taken as the principal duty of each individual, one would expect Hobbes to have regarded the precept that we should defend ourselves as a law and not a right . . .' But the first thing to note is that Hobbes does not use these expressions ('self-preservation' and 'self-defence') interchangeably. The primary good is self-preservation. According to Hobbes, men in a state of nature seek to achieve self-preservation through aggrandisement, through an endless pursuit of power, and this may obviously involve the deliberate initiation of war. One might also seek to achieve self-preservation through concessions, mutual limitations, the seeking of peace – which Hobbes infinitely prefers; but not, of course, on condition that one surrender the minimal right of self-defence should one's efforts fail. Thus one might seek to preserve oneself through acquiring mastery over all those about one; or one might seek to do so by giving and obtaining fair and equitable mutual concessions, but not in such a manner that one was deprived of the right to self-defence. Hence self-preservation was the end, in regard to which self-defence could never be ruled out as a potentially necessary means. Although the aim of self-preservation (for Hobbes) most rationally involved the seeking of peace, this seeking of peace – because of the governing end initially posited – could never be divorced from the equal obligation, should occasion demand, for self-defence (which is thus regarded as a *minimal* means of self-preservation).

Another and connected mistake arises out of Warrender's analysis. It is simply false to suggest, as Warrender does, that Hobbes did *not* regard 'the precept that we should defend ourselves as a law and not a right'. A law of nature, any law of nature, imposes an obligation to take such steps as will best conduce to the preservation of ourselves. The first of these laws dictates both (*a*) that we seek peace and (*b*) that we defend ourselves. Thus, if the precept 'seek peace' is a law and not a right, then so too is the precept enjoining self-defence. 'Defence' is a means towards self-preservation, which is reconcilable with seeking peace, in a way that 'attack', for example, is not. But it is clear that Hobbes makes it a duty at least to defend, but not to attack. It is then attack which in natural circumstances is a right; but defence is always a duty. Self-preservation *per se* is accordingly never a right, but always a duty. How could it be otherwise? If a law of nature, which means any law of nature, which means *all* laws of nature, obligate us to act in a manner best calculated to preserve ourselves, then the preservation of self must in itself be regarded as imposing an obligation. How can it not be a general duty to preserve ourselves if all the specific laws of nature obligate us to take proper steps to avoid self-destruction? Self-preservation for Hobbes is a *duty*; the point is merely that any irrational means thereto is at best only to be regarded as a *right*.

I think, as does Warrender, that the question of suicide is a key issue in deciding whether or not 'preserve thyself' is the underlying norm of Hobbes's system. If Hobbes regarded self-preservation as a duty, then suicide must constitute an offence against natural law. Warrender is inclined to conclude that Hobbes regarded suicide as neither illegal in civil law nor 'as a breach of natural law' (pp. 217–18). I think Warrender is right but for reasons which stare him in the face and are yet significantly contrary to his own. In so far as suicide (for Hobbes) is *not* an offence against civil or natural law, it is simply because 'naturally and necessarily the intention of every man aimeth at somewhat which is good to himself, and tendeth to his preservation' (from *A Dialogue of the Common Laws* but quoted by Warrender himself at p. 217). Hobbes cannot admit that anyone could ever 'hurt himself voluntarily': he cannot *conceive* how any man can bear 'so much malice to himself'. Hobbes is forced therefore to conclude that suicide, self-murder, is simply an impossibility. Where a man *does* kill himself, accidents apart, 'it is to be presumed that he is not *compos mentis*', is somehow 'distracted'. If suicide, as a species of act, simply cannot be committed, then clearly it cannot be regarded as constituting any form of violation or breach of any species of law. But this in no way suggests, as Warrender implies, that Hobbes regards suicide as a *right*. If Hobbes regarded suicide as being possible then he would be bound to regard its occurrence as a breach of duty, a violation of natural law. For if one had no *intrinsic duty* to preserve oneself, one could inherit no *consequential duty* to seek rational *means* of preserving oneself. Apart from this inference, it seems virtually impossible that Hobbes could regard suicide as a right, for the simple reason that, in his system, a right confers a liberty and Hobbes cannot, as he says, *conceive* 'how any man can . . . kill himself'; he cannot conceive of any man being at liberty, of any man deliberately and voluntarily willing, that very greatest *malum in se*, his own death.

Of course the difficulty is that if one cannot intentionally kill oneself (if one can only kill oneself accidentally or when the balance of one's mind is disturbed – in either case suggesting that one does not really know what one is doing), then it would equally follow that one cannot intentionally preserve oneself either. That is to say, if I am *caused* or *determined* or *made* always to seek to preserve myself, then the notion of my being so caused is incompatible with the notion of my being able to choose, or to elect, *not* to preserve myself. I may be able to choose different *means* of preserving myself, some more rational and effective than others, but I cannot *choose* to preserve myself *per se*. It is necessary that I *be able* to do what I have a *duty* to do. If then I have a general duty to preserve myself, this must imply that I can intentionally choose not to preserve myself. Hobbes suggests that we cannot *but* choose to preserve ourselves. But if that is so, we really have no choice in the matter at all, and Hobbesian self-preservation would consequently have to be regarded as a psychological fact rather than as a duty. Such indeed is the conclusion to which Warrender was brought. But we must accept that the difficulty reflected in this is intrinsic to Hobbes's system, and we must hew our own way out of it.

What we must first discard is Hobbes's suggestion that we are inevitably disposed to preserve ourselves and that any apparently contrary acts only indicate some form of mental aberration. In fact, we may choose either to preserve or to destroy ourselves. To suggest that all suicides are mad, whatever we may agree 'madness' to mean, is contrary to fact (although we might incorporate into the notion of suicide 'madness', as Hobbes does, but this would prove a merely circular procedure). Since we can intentionally destroy ourselves, and since many people do not merely kill themselves, but do so intentionally (thus suicide), then we cannot accept, as a mere matter of motivation, as a matter of universal psychological fact, that *all* men do seek to preserve themselves. In suggesting that self-preservation is a universal motive, Hobbes is clearly mistaken. But whatever the cause of the mistake, we must consider its consequences. As I argue in the text, to say that all men seek to preserve themselves is also to say that the speaker, as a man, seeks to preserve himself, along with everyone else. To *describe* a man's motive is not necessarily to *approve* of it, but this is only on the assumption that one does not share it. Since Hobbes by implication shares the end of self-preservation, he must also by implication approve of it, in himself and in others. It is hard to believe that he only approved of it in his own case and not in all others.

Hobbes's approval of self-preservation, his inclination to regard it as a duty, is both overt and covert. This derives from the fact that Hobbes regards self-preserving motives with approval and yet takes them to be inescapable. He seeks to derive his laws of nature both from the supposed universality of self-preserving motives and also from assumptions regarding their propriety. If everyone accepts self-preservation as a good, then the specific laws of nature will only detail rational means of attaining it. But since Hobbes considers the laws which detail the means as obligatory, he must also regard the end as obligatory. It is one thing to say 'if you accept the end, you must accept the means'; it is another thing to say, as Hobbes does, that *since* we (you included) accept the end, we (you included) are obligated to concede the means. For Hobbes, all laws of nature in general set out rules 'by which a man is forbidden to do that, which is destructive of his life, or taketh away the means of preserving the same'; even more clearly, by such laws is a man 'forbidden . . . to omit that, by which he thinketh it [his life] may be best preserved'. The *duty* stipulated here is *overt*. But it is found out by reason. Reason, for Hobbes, is a scout or spy which ranges abroad to find 'the way to the things desired'. What we desire, the good we seek, is of course the preservation of ourselves. But we can only derive a duty from a duty. So natural law, which obligates us to adopt a series of rational means, must derive from the good we all desire. And here the *duty* stipulated becomes *covert*, because Hobbes is less inclined to *argue* that it is a good than to *assume* it to be so. This is plainly shown by his inclination to state that the good, the desire for self-preservation, is shared by us all. And this way of putting the matter, as we have seen, merely presents as a fact what is inevitably a recommendation: that we *ought* to preserve ourselves.

I would not care to try to undermine Hobbes's argument by simply saying that he mistakenly attempts to derive a duty from what he supposes to be a fact. I have no doubt that he does do this but I also have no doubt that he simultaneously conceals a higher norm within what he supposes to be a universal psychological fact. The difficulty that this dualism creates for Hobbes is rather different from that involved in the naturalistic fallacy (deriving 'ought' from 'is'). As regards suicide, for example, Hobbes is hamstrung by the suggestions (*a*) that it is *impossible* and (*b*) that natural law *forbids* a man to attempt to do that which is destructive of his life. More generally, he is hamstrung by the notions (*a*) that we inevitably *do* try to preserve ourselves and (*b*) that we have a *duty* to adopt those precepts most conducive to this end. We could have no duty to adopt the means, of course, unless we were somehow obligated to accept the end. Hobbes wants to say that the end is somehow *imposed* upon us. But it is clearly not imposed upon us – unless in some moral sense. He never fully makes out a case in this sense; but he does in part and the rest is implied. Accordingly, Hobbes's ethic of self-preservation is both overt and covert. When the ethic of self-preservation is stated as a universal motive it automatically takes on the character of a political recommendation – upon which Hobbes erected an absolutist ideology of order.

Watkins (1965) also objects on several grounds to what he describes as 'the Taylor–Warrender thesis'. I agree with Watkins in his contention that 'Hobbes's account of political authority starts out from individual wants' (p. 86); but at the same time I urge the need to accept that the 'wants' which Hobbes initially asserts are ambiguous: they refer to both the 'desired' and the 'desirable', to a psychology as well as an ethic, to motives and to duties. To insist that Hobbes merely derives *obligation* (the laws of nature) from the *fact* of a supposedly universal psychological motive (as Watkins seems to be disposed to do) renders Hobbes's doctrine 'coherent', but it also, immediately, reveals its procedure to be illogical. To insist that Hobbes *merely* derives his laws of nature from a higher norm (such as Reason or God's command) does not necessarily render his doctrine incoherent, but it does raise problems (as Watkins suggests) which Hobbes himself anticipated and objected to: it would be, in Watkins's phrase, 'a merely moralistic "law"', or one, as Hobbes wrote, 'built in the air'. Clearly there is a form of 'dualism' in Hobbes, but of a largely deliberate kind, in which he advanced a *duty* of self-preservation, but simultaneously advanced the performance of that duty as a *fact* of human nature. It was vital that Hobbes should discover an area of universal agreement among men, where the desired and the desirable were identical, in order for his system to work at all. And it is basically because such universal agreement (upon self-preservation) cannot be established as a fact, and cannot be looked upon as an exclusive good, that his system fails. Thus, although I agree with Watkins that 'Hobbes's ideas hang together', my agreement is entirely literal: because the two parts (the desired and the desirable) are so inextricably intertwined, the result for the system proves unavoidably fatal.

I agree with Watkins that Hobbes's 'Laws of nature persist through the state of nature into civil society' (p. 87). I further agree with him in so far as he contends that they are not necessarily morally obligatory '*because commanded by God*'. (If self-preservation is a good *per se*, and if the laws of nature only show us how we may best achieve it, then although we may be additionally enjoined to obey these laws because God commands it, clearly the initial good, if it is really a good, is sufficient to obligate us to adopt such means.) But I disagree where Watkins argues that Hobbes's laws of nature are not '*moral* laws'. One way of arguing that Hobbes's laws of nature are moral laws is that followed by Warrender: covenants without the sword are but words; obligation in a civil society is built upon obedience to a civil superior who has power to overawe one; obligation in a state of nature is built upon obedience to a supernatural superior who equally has power to overawe one. (This position creates obvious difficulties of the kind which Watkins notes, p. 86.) I am content to say, by contrast, that in so far as the laws of nature are means, and yet obligate us, they are means to an end which we are impliedly bound to attempt to achieve, and thus that the Hobbesian end is not merely a psychological motive but also an ethical ideal.

We might say that self-preservation is a 'prudential' rather than a 'moral' end. But I must confess to being unimpressed by the distinction as here applied. My doctor may say to me: 'Take this potion.' I may ask: 'Why?' He may reply: 'It will make you better.' Here the assumption would appear to be that *if* I want to get better, I *ought* to take the draught. And the doctor could leave the matter at that. He would be offering me advice, with the proviso that I am perfectly entitled to accept or reject it without in either case incurring any moral blame. But suppose I ask the doctor: 'Why *ought* I to try to get better?' Here the above assumption could be made perfectly explicit. My doctor may say: 'In itself there is no reason why you *ought* or *ought not* to want to get better; and if you do *not* want to get better, then I advise you to refuse the potion.' The doctor's position here would clearly be prudential; he is merely prescribing means to *possible* ends; he only regards the means as obligating me if *I* regard the end as doing so; further, it does not matter to him whether I accept the end or not.

But such is not Hobbes's position, certainly not in any exclusive sense. He may well be offering prudential advice, but his commitment to the end to be achieved by such advice goes far beyond that instanced by my doctor. If I were to ask another doctor, in similar circumstances, why I ought to try to get better, he might well prove committed to the notion that I should try to do so *in order to preserve myself*, irrespective of whether I agreed or not. There are various ways in which he might reveal such a commitment. One of his most obvious moves, for example, would be to suggest that, whatever I may think now, I would later think otherwise; that deep down I do not *really* want what I now say I want, etc. Or he might say that it is simply *impossible* for me not to want to get better, since it is a law of nature that all men seek to preserve themselves. Or he might say that it is *irrational* of me to want to get better, since all living things are disposed to promote their own good, identified at the extreme with self-preservation. Or he might say that I am flouting the will of *God* in acting in such a way as to lead to my self-destruction (I might for example be regarded as the property of God and thus as having no *right* to destroy myself). Hobbes is certainly in the position of such a doctor as this. He is not just prescribing means to a possible end, but – as Watkins sees (p. 83) – to an 'actual end'. The arguments of the second doctor do not treat the end of self-preservation as hypothetical, but as 'actual'. And to treat the end as *actual* does not merely mean that he thinks I accept such an end, but that it is *morally right*, proper, fitting, etc., for me to do so. It further means that the doctor, too, regards such an end as in effect morally obligatory.

Hobbes's argument is not merely 'prudential' but 'moral'. His problem initially derives from the implication that he is playing the role of both doctors at once. But since Watkins, in effect, still regards the arguments of the second doctor as 'prudential', we must show how impossible it is, at this stage, to eliminate the 'moral' element from the second doctor's argument. The end which this doctor accepts is, as Watkins would suggest, 'an egocentric end', but the fact that an end is egocentric does not necessarily deprive it, contrary to Watkins's contention, of 'a distinctively moral character'. One may say that a person is acting 'morally' in at least two different senses. In the first, we may mean that he is rightly complying with some sort of social duty. In the second, we may mean that he is complying with what he *conceives* to be his duty, but wrongly. One may make mistakes both about facts and about acts. One may do what is wrong even while thinking it is right. So even if we do not like egocentrism, it only follows that we can categorise it as *immoral*, not non-moral. The only way in which we can speak of 'an egocentric end' as being deprived of a 'moral character' is on the assumption that self-oriented or egocentric action cannot be posited as a *duty*. Hobbes, indeed, spoke of rational self-preserving means, i.e. of the laws of nature, as 'not only *natural*, but also *moral* laws'. In his system that is indeed the case (and a major source of his difficulty). In so far as men are *not* necessarily disposed to attempt to preserve themselves, rationally or otherwise, then to that extent are they *free* (able) to posit self-preservation as a duty. Hobbes's problem is to disguise the duty such that it no longer appears a duty at all. But irrespective of the disguise, irrespective of the *blending* of the natural with the moral, the distinctively moral element remains. We may well say that he who wills the end wills the means. But it is much more accurate to say that he who wills the means wills the end. Hobbes characterises all rational *means* of self-preservation as laws, as duties, as moral. And in doing so he automatically implies also that the *end* of self-preservation is to be regarded as morally obligatory. He does argue that we cannot escape this obligation because it is *natural*. But because we know that we *can* intentionally (not just accidentally or irrationally) destroy ourselves, we can see that this 'inescapable obligation' is fitted out, is disguised –

partly consciously and partly unconsciously – as 'natural' in order to *persuade* us to accept it.

Watkins says that 'Hobbes did derive his prescriptions from factual premises, but without committing a logical fallacy: for his prescriptions are not moral prescriptions . . .' (p. 76). I am saying, with Watkins, that Hobbes (partly) derived 'his prescriptions from factual premises'. But I am also saying, contrary to Watkins, that he did commit 'a logical fallacy' in doing so. Finally, quite apart from Watkins, I am saying that the fallacy committed does not necessarily trivialise Hobbes for the reason that Hobbes was at the same time 'deriving' means from ends (norms from norms) – or, to put it more accurately, *relating* means to ends.

Hobbes posited a good, an end, which was simultaneously understood to be factual and moral, whatever the difficulties this understanding created for him. The Hobbesian doctor, in Watkins's analogy, does not merely assume that the patient may or may not accept the end of self-preservation, but that he *must*. The logic of the position which stipulates that any and every patient *must* accept the principle, the end, of self-preservation is only another way of saying, as already indicated, that the prescriber accepts it too, along with everyone else. But to say this is not merely to 'describe' social behaviour but to accept self-preservation as a (or the) moral ground for such behaviour: what else can be implied if self-preservation is accepted as a good for everyone, including oneself?

Hobbes's prescriptions are undoubtedly 'moral'. I am suggesting that this is most clearly so for the reason that anyone who projects a 'motive' as universal, where in fact it is not (i.e. is not a mere 'instinct'), is in effect projecting an end, a good, which – not being inevitably chosen – becomes an object or end which is right (or wrong), which it is morally necessary to choose (or to reject). If the Hobbesian doctor is his own patient, then the 'morality' of his prescription, contrary to Watkins's assumption, becomes still clearer. After all, 'an ill doctor' (in Watkins's words) 'whose *overriding aim* [my italics] is to get well again' cannot be seen merely as an isolated individual whose acts have neither social content nor moral consequences. If his desire to become or to remain well assumes the form of an *overriding aim*, then that desire (for him) becomes desirable, the aim (for him) becomes a good, and his motive in this case *is* his morality. Otherwise one would have to identify 'morality' with a specific morality of selflessness. A doctor who regarded his duty to himself as prior to his duty to others, we might perhaps characterise as *im*moral, but certainly not as *a*moral. He might project the end of self-preservation as fundamental for himself as well as for others, such that it consistently and fairly predictably dictated the character of his social relationships in general.

Apart from the consideration that the projection of any supposed motive as universal involves simultaneously the projection of a morality, I have in effect suggested that we consider a further, equally important, argument. This has to do with the fact that Hobbes regards all rational means to self-preservation as morally and unconditionally obligatory. Warrender of course contests such an argument. But assuming it to be correct (as I argued earlier), then it seems difficult not to conclude, given that the means are unconditionally obligatory, that the end is not similarly obligatory. And if the end is obligatory, is right, then it is obviously 'moral'. Hobbes certainly wished his argument to be received, in Watkins's phrase, as an 'eye-opener'; but whatever he might have *wished*, our eyes must remain open to the fact that his argument only operates as a 'hidden persuader'.

We might say that self-preservation is a bad ethic, an unworthy end, but it may nonetheless serve as the focus, the ground, of a morality. There is in any event no end whatever, even though promoted as morally just, which when exclusively promoted will prove just, or which (less disputably) will be universally accepted as just however it is promoted – whether it be the golden mean, liberty, equality or any other projected ideal. In this connection, Macpherson's analysis, whatever its particular faults, is helpful. For it urges us to accept Hobbes's system *as* a moral system, as consecrating a certain form of individualism, egocentrism and acquisitiveness. More broadly, the same sort of point may be made for Warrender's analysis. For even if God is not a necessary source of obligation for Hobbes's system, the system does set out a very significant ethic, with clearly prescribed duties, with continuing contemporary consequences. Moralists, since Hobbes, have increasingly tended to urge upon us obligations in the form of an explanation of facts. Hobbes has the distinction of being the first modern moralist to do this effectively. He attempts to convince us (in the most powerful manner conceivable) that we should obey established authorities not simply because to do so is in our interest but because between self-interest, rational duty and divine command no possible distinction can be made.

Gauthier (1969) in effect follows Watkins in trying to deny 'the charge that Hobbes commits a logical fallacy in deriving normative conclusions from factual premises' (p. 22). In this particular, Gauthier's position can only be described as confused. Hobbes either is or is not – whatever else he may be doing at the same time 'deriving normative conclusions from factual premises'. If we say that he is, as Gauthier does, it is for us to show how the procedure avoids being in error. Let us say that men are *caused* to want to preserve themselves in such a way that the motive of self-preservation is ultimate and inevitable; in such circumstances, it seems plainly illogical to assert that men *ought* to take rational steps to preserve themselves. It only follows if what we initially assert is true and (as Spinoza would argue) that being *compelled* to want to preserve oneself, one *will necessarily* take such steps as lead – by one's own (defective) lights – towards this end. If the end is regarded as merely inevitable, it is a nonsense to suggest that one *ought* to adopt rational means to achieve it: for one will inevitably adopt such means as seem to one best suited to the realisation of the end. It is no use suggesting that the Hobbesian duty to obey follows from the fact that we do not always judge the best means to our ends, for one cannot *knowingly* believe what is *false*; one cannot pursue a genuinely accepted end by *intentionally* adopting *irrational* means. Thus if it can be said that I am strictly and unarguably motivated to achieve some end in such a way as to preclude my having any choice in the matter, it can only be inferred that I shall necessarily adopt such means as appear to me best suited to achieving that end – it cannot be inferred that I *ought*, or that I am obligated, to choose such (rational) means. I do not, of course, accept that anyone is in this sense ever compelled to achieve any end – but this is not a consideration to be taken up here. The point is merely that, since one cannot legitimately – neither Hobbes nor anyone else – derive 'normative conclusions from factual premises', it is important for anyone who thinks we can either to specify in what way he thinks such a procedure can be legitimately followed or to concede that the procedure (to the extent that it is attempted and no matter who attempts it) is faulty. Gauthier only concludes that this derivation 'seems', but never really demonstrates how it *could* be, 'a quite legitimate procedure' (p. 23).

Writers often become tiresome in their endless exegetical attempts to manufacture consistency where none exists, and this is particularly true in analyses of Hobbes. McNeilly (1968) wants to remodel Hobbes, so that the latter's arguments for self-preservation reduce to 'the formal concept of frustration of all one's desires', replacing 'the material concept of death' (p. 181). What this suggests is that Hobbes should be understood to mean that what men chiefly seek is not self-preservation but the realisation of desire (which might be a desire to achieve some higher end at the cost of self-destruction). Fortunately, McNeilly realises that to apply such an interpretation would be 'to take a liberty with the text', but he is not convincing when reassuring us that it would be only 'a very *small* liberty'. Reconstructions of this sort, I repeat, simply become tiresome. If people wish to elaborate their own theories of human motivation or whatever they should certainly feel free to do so. But it is my own, no doubt eccentric, view that we have reached a point in 'Hobbes studies' where we might profitably concede that Hobbes's analysis is irredeemably confused. Thus one may accept that McNeilly's 'reconstruction', for example, reflects a more accurate view of the facts of life, but we must also recognise that it significantly distorts or reconstructs in a highly selective way) what Hobbes actually said.

We today can see (if with logical hindsight) and should accept (with however much regret) that Hobbes's predicament, self-imposed, quite precludes all hope of release. Hobbes (at the very start of his analysis) is caught in a cleft stick of his own fashioning and with every attempt at release he is borne down upon by an ever-increasing weight.

Gauthier argues (in, to my mind, an excessively elaborate and often mistaken fashion) that Hobbes both does (formally) and does not (materially) have a 'moral' theory. This may sound rather like the 'cleft stick' position which I advance. In substance it may well be. But Gauthier's argument seems so unsound at so many points that I honestly cannot be sure. In order to make plain my own position I shall try (with Gauthier in mind) to cut clear to the heart of the problem of obligation in Hobbes as I see it.

Hobbes does indeed intend, as Gauthier states, that 'not to defend oneself is neither rational nor psychologically possible' (p. 34). But as this is the case, I infer Hobbes to mean (a) that we always *do* and (b) that we always *ought* to try to preserve ourselves. This is his difficulty. For if we always *do* try to preserve ourselves it is pointless to argue that we should. And if it is meaningfully suggested that we *should*, then it cannot be the case that we inevitably do try to preserve ourselves. (Of course, what Hobbes actually says is that we ought to try *rationally* to preserve ourselves. But it is difficult to see how this can mean much more than that we ought *really* to try to preserve ourselves. If we knowingly adopted inefficient means it could scarcely be contended that we were really committed to the end.)

Since (a) and (b) are mutually contradictory in such an obvious way, Hobbes's defenders are disposed to argue either that he is advancing (a) or that he is advancing (b), but certainly not both. They may say against (a) that 'Hobbes admits that death is not always the greatest evil to a man who is *compos mentis*' (Gauthier, p. 24). They may say against (b) that since 'men are necessarily bent on their own preservation' we are prevented 'from classifying Hobbes's system as moral' (Gauthier, p. 98). They do in fact say more, but so much for the present. The point is this. If anyone contends that Hobbes argues that men *do* always try to preserve themselves, someone else may cite the odd contrary passage, or develop the odd contrary implication, that this is *not* something which Hobbes thinks men *always* do; similarly, if anyone contends that Hobbes argues that men are morally *obligated* by the laws of nature, then someone else may cite the less odd contrary passage, or develop the pervasive contrary implication, that this is not something which Hobbes can seriously mean since his men are *bound* to act with a view to preserving themselves (whence the inference is drawn that men's acts are at best 'prudential', not 'moral'). These arguments and counter-arguments, however, seem to me merely to confirm how hopelessly entangled Hobbes is within the mesh of his own system.

First, let us lay out fully the logic of (*a*), the first prong of the fork, under which Hobbes commits himself to the position that men always *do* act (wisely or foolishly) with a view to preserving themselves. Under Hobbes's *right of nature*, each man has a liberty 'to use his own power, as he will himself, for the preservation of his own nature'. This suggests, not that one is free to choose either to preserve or to destroy oneself, but merely that *one will oneself decide how to preserve oneself*. Under the *law of nature*, a man is 'by reason . . . forbidden to do that, which is destructive of his life' or 'to omit that, by which he thinketh it may best be preserved'. This suggests, not that one is forbidden to destroy oneself, but that one should always attempt to *act rationally* rather than irrationally *while attempting* to preserve oneself. The suggestion which this contains is that the difference between Hobbes's right of nature and his law of nature is *not* that one gives us a liberty to preserve ourselves while the other imposes an obligation to do so. The suggestion, instead, is that we are always disposed *in fact* to do whatever *we think* we have to do to preserve ourselves (the 'right' = some form of capacity, possibility, what we *may* do) and that it is rational for us to adopt those means which are most likely to preserve us (the 'duty' = the most rational means of achieving an actual end). Hobbes seems to assume then that we all do try to preserve ourselves, but often in foolish ways; he suggests that we may choose, or are at liberty, or have a right, or enjoy a capacity to choose, between a variety of what we *conceive to be* possible means. But he also implies (not merely that we 'ought' to, but) that our nature will *compel* us, *oblige* us, *obligate* us, *make* us, adopt those means which are *seen* or which *reveal themselves* to be most rational. Finally, Hobbes does not merely assume that we shall try to preserve ourselves, he actually says so: 'every man is desirous of what is good for him, and shuns what is evil, but chiefly the chiefest of natural evils, which is death; and this he doth by a certain impulsion of nature'.

In so far as it is true that everyone inevitably seeks to preserve himself, it becomes pointless to say (*a*) in a *general* way that we ought to do what we are already and inevitably doing, and equally pointless to say (*b*) that we ought to seek *sound* (i.e. rational) means of achieving our end. For it must follow that our nature necessarily prohibits us from *intentionally* seeking unsound (i.e. irrational) means of achieving our end. It is plain, of course, that such means as I *think* efficient may not in fact be so. But this ineliminable gap between appearance and reality still leaves no room for me or anyone else to say what I *ought* to do, considered more minimally as an item of 'prudence'. For if I necessarily seek to preserve myself, then I necessarily seek to do so by those means which appear to me most rational.

We may consider the situation both from the perspective of one who takes advice and from that of those who give it. One who takes advice, being necessarily compelled to do what strikes him as most rationally consistent with his chief end, can never say to himself that he *ought* to follow any given course of action. For he will inevitably take that course of action which he deems most apt to achieve his end. As for those who give advice, they must be seen initially as occupying exactly the same position as the recipient: they can never say to themselves individually that they *ought* to follow any given course of action. And if an 'adviser' can never even say to himself 'I ought', it is difficult to conceive how he can consistently or meaningfully say to anyone else 'you ought'. The adviser is, in another respect, in the same position as the advised: since he *will* do only what he *thinks* is best, he cannot assume for the advised, any more than he can for himself, that what he advises *is* best. The 'adviser' then is never telling me what I 'ought' to do. Such a formula, for him, would have to be meaningless. He is merely in the position of a mathematician who is given a problem to solve. When he has solved it, or when he *thinks* he has solved it, he merely details the nature of the conclusion that he has come to. He is not able to tell me in any sense that I 'ought' to accept his conclusion; he cannot himself even be *certain* that it is correct. All that he does, then, when 'advising', is to lay bare his own reasoning upon the particular matter in hand. He is not telling me in any sense to do this or that; he is only saying, given a particular problem, that a particular train of reasoning (his own) may provide the correct solution. The adviser knows that if I *see* his possibility as *the* solution I shall *necessarily* accept it. So he is only reporting on his state of mind. If I agree, I agree. But there is no independent basis on which he can say I *ought* to agree. Merely to report what one thinks to be true is not necessarily to *recommend* it. Or to turn it around, to 'recommend' a train of reasoning is merely to say that one thinks it is true.

Of course it may be that some persons are so placed or endowed that they know more about some matters than other persons. A mathematician might construct a valid proof which most of the population could not recognise to be sound. Equally an adviser might detail a sound economic or political policy which even his immediate superiors – forgetting about the rest of the population – might be incapable of recognising as such. But the policy could no more be 'recommended' than the proof. They represent possible solutions which will simply be accepted or rejected. But if one accepts a proof or a policy without really understanding it, we may say, in an important sense, that one does not really 'accept' it at all. There is an important difference between 'accepting' in the sense of 'understanding' something, and 'accepting' in the sense of 'taking the word of some authority' on the matter in question. Hobbes provides us with no reason why we should accept anyone's word on matters of truth or correct reasoning. He certainly does not ask his readers to 'take his word' for it that absolute rule ought to be accepted. He has tried to *demonstrate* its necessity by a flow of argument. He assumes that we do accept his (self-preserving) premises, and further that, if we follow his reasoning aright, we will simply *recognise* the truth of his conclusions (as to the inescapability of absolutist rule).

This reconstruction of Hobbes, as disengaging a series of deductions from the assumption that we always do try to preserve ourselves, naturally has its drawbacks. Given that, in fact, we *can* intentionally destroy ourselves, to insist that we cannot do so merely betrays obtuseness, or *a priori* dogmatism, or hidden normative assumptions (that we ought not) and probably a bit of all these things. If Hobbes saw himself as merely describing how men *necessarily* behave, then he would have to concede that his *description* of that behaviour, assuming the description to be correct, could have no possible effect upon it. If men necessarily seek to preserve themselves, they necessarily seek to do so rationally. If in practice rationality always manifests itself as what is *recognised* to be rational, then there is no way in which men can be *enjoined* to perform in one way as distinct from another, whether we describe such injunctions as 'moral' or 'prudential'. Agents will simply be confronted with a variety of possible options, as these are conceptualised by a variety of men (including the agent himself), and the choice made has to be read as that dictated by the chooser's nature. No one therefore can tell him that he ought to act or to have acted in any manner other than that instanced by his actual choice. On this model advisers never tell the advised how to act. They merely throw up possible courses of action. At the very best, therefore, the adviser is never saying anything more than 'if X, then possibly Y': if you want to achieve X, I think Y may be a means of doing so.

'If X, then possibly Y' might be described (following Kant, and Watkins) as a 'problematic hypothetical imperative'. But Watkins and Gauthier, for example, are clear that Hobbes is advancing a *genuine* imperative, the lugubrious 'assertoric hypothetical', etc.; thus, '*given X*, then Y': i.e. 'since we want to achieve X, then Y is the only certain means of doing so'. It is clear that a proposition of the form 'if X, then possibly Y' commits neither the propounder nor the hearer to any course of action, whether we label it moral, prudential or otherwise. One might say: 'if you wish to torture an opponent, then you may (= can or might) apply electrodes to', etc. But such a statement does not entail that one *recommends* either the end or the means. Even when the propounder says *'given* that *you* want to torture X, you may (= can or might) apply Y', it does not necessarily follow that he is *recommending* the means. (Since he does not imply that he accepts the end, he might well insist that the means was efficient but immoral.) Hobbes, however, is not merely saying *'if X'*, nor even *'given X'* (for you). He is saying: *'we* accept X, and therefore *we* must or ought to accept Y'. He is not merely holding up a possibility for himself; he is insisting upon a moral certainty for everyone. If we accept that Hobbes *was* concerned to *persuade* men to submit to established rulers, then it is at such a point that his psychological positivism (i.e. the notion that men necessarily do try always to preserve themselves) collapses. Finally, it seems to me to be perfectly possible to defend (which is not to say that one accepts) a 'prudential' morality; to characterise a 'prudential' morality as *non-moral* is really only another way of objecting to it as *immoral*. It is one thing to say that Hobbes's ethics are immoral; it is indefensible to suggest that he has no 'genuinely' ethical system at all.

Now let us develop as fully as we need the logic of (*b*), the second prong of the fork, under which Hobbes commits himself to the position that men always *ought* to act (wisely, not foolishly) with a view to preserving themselves. What we have already said about Hobbes's 'right of nature' and his 'law of nature' we shall (almost) repeat – albeit more briefly – here. Hobbes's right of nature does not stipulate a mere liberty to preserve oneself. Nor does his law of nature directly stipulate a simple *duty* to preserve oneself. The *right* of nature only indicates that one may (will or must) *oneself* decide how to preserve oneself. And the *law* of nature stipulates that one ought, in the pursuit of self-preservation, to adopt *rational* means. For Hobbes, it will be recalled, a right confers a liberty (when 'liberty' = 'permission'); an obligation or duty takes it away. The right that we have (it is ambiguous, implying 'permission' and/or 'capacity') is to preserve ourselves *as we think best*. The duty that we have is *to think rationally* in devising means of preserving ourselves. Hobbes assumes a difference between what we do (or may do) and what we ought to do. What we *may* do (now regarded as mere 'capacity') by natural right, given that what we do is sometimes foolish, is frequently at variance with what we ought to do by natural law (which is always reasonable and rational). The formulation of the right of nature presupposes that we both are and ought to be trying to preserve ourselves, and also that we may be mistaken about the proper means of doing so. The stipulation of the law of nature, in directly stating that we ought to seek self-preservation *rationally*, presupposes indirectly that we ought

333

to seek self-preservation *per se*. It is difficult to imagine how we can *deliberately* adopt irrational means to achieve our ends. And if we could, it would be difficult to see how we could truly seek to preserve ourselves if we pursued this end in an *intentionally* irrational manner. And assuming that we can commit suicide and remain *compos mentis*, are we not in fact able to *choose* to preserve ourselves ? Just as it would be foolish to say that we ought to try rationally *to preserve ourselves* if we were not somehow *at liberty* to preserve ourselves; so it would be foolish to say that we ought to try to preserve ourselves *rationally* if it were not assumed, more minimally, that we ought quite simply to try to preserve ourselves. Self-preservation *per se*, as Hobbes implies (in his discussion of the difference between a right and a law), cannot of course be both 'obligation, and liberty', a right and a duty. To suggest that one is free to preserve oneself rationally is to presuppose that one is able to destroy oneself 'irrationally'. The 'right' of nature is relevant, but because it refers to a 'liberty', it is ambiguous; for 'liberty', as we saw, may suggest both moral *permission* and physical *capacity*. We shall say that the right of nature refers (among other things) to a physical capacity to destroy oneself, but does not confer any form of moral permission to do so. Thus the right of nature and the law of nature are consistent. For the right indicates an actual capacity for action (self-destruction) which the law indirectly proscribes (preservation to be achieved by rational means). (They would only be inconsistent in so far as the right granted a permission which the law took away.) The duty of self-preservation does not suspend a supposed *right* of self-preservation. Rather, the liberty (capacity) to behave irrationally is confronted with (not replaced by) the duty to behave rationally. Thus the law of nature does not suspend the right of nature; on the contrary, it presupposes it. For one can have no *duty* to perform unless one enjoys a *capacity* to perform. One can have no *duty* to preserve oneself unless one is *able* to destroy oneself.

To say that one has a *right* to do something does not mean that one ought to do it. To say that one *may* do something does not mean that it is a rational thing to do. The Hobbesian right, conceived as a mere possibility, is not negated by the law, conceived as a duty. For without the possibility, there could be no duty. The right, where conceived as instancing an irrational act, is not necessarily negated by the law, its contrary – but impliedly it *ought* to be.

Of course Hobbes supposes that no one can ever *really* intend to destroy himself. But this is only another way of concealing his basic ethical premise – by taking it for granted that the end of self-preservation is shared by his readers. The basic norm is self-preservation; this requires the application of rational means; these norms (both ends and means) presuppose the possibility of self-destruction (even if merely foolishly); all of the laws of nature, including contracts or covenants, are to be regarded as applications of the basic norm; and the breaking of covenants is evil principally because it is subversive of the end of self-preservation.

Having laid out the logic of Hobbes's forked argument that (a) we always do try to preserve ourselves and (b) we always ought to, we have seen how plainly and viciously the two parts, brought together, destroy the overall tenability of the Hobbesian position. We can see further how each fork, deliberately extended within the limits of its own logic, collapses upon itself. If we *do* necessarily always try to preserve ourselves, then it follows that we necessarily *try* to do so rationally; we must impliedly have no choice in the matter, since we do what (we think) we have to do, both as relates to the end and its attendant means; thus no room is left for any form of moralising, whether prudential or otherwise; and this would appear to be an absurd conclusion to draw. On the other hand, if we always *ought* to try to preserve ourselves, then we must value our individual lives above all else; but when the matter is put in this way, it is probable that most readers, while accepting that one is rarely called upon to sacrifice one's life, would reject the notion that survival is preferable to all other goods or that it is to be preferred in itself no matter what form or style it assumed. To say that self-preservation is the highest good in itself may, also, be regarded as absurd.

Gauthier concedes that 'Hobbes's concepts are . . . moral in so far as "moral" means "practical", "concerning what to do", but not in so far as "moral" means "opposed or superior to prudential" ' (p. 28). Basically he is right. But we should take note of one of the difficulties which this position creates. In so far as Hobbes's morality dictates a commitment to self-preservation, and given that at some point we might rationally and sanely prefer and choose to die, the moral commitment would dictate the omission of an act (self-destruction) which (from our perspective) the agent might regard as positively advantageous. If we care to, we may follow Gauthier in characterising Hobbes's system as one 'of rational prudence' (p. 97). But what we must recall is that Hobbes does not characterise this system as one 'in which all reasons for acting must reduce to considerations of what, in each situation, is most *advantageous* for the agent' (my italics). Hobbes's position is more minimal: no action should subvert the end of *self-preservation*. He assumes naturally that self-preservation constitutes an advantage. But we have already seen that adherence to self-preservation may reasonably contradict self-advantage. If, therefore, we regard 'moral obligation' as a function of selflessness, as acting against what one projects as being to one's own advantage (or in one's best interest), it is clear that a clinging to life may be indulged merely because one regards it as a *duty*, and despite the fact (possibly *because* of the fact) that it serves the needs or meets the interests of others, rather than of oneself. Although I disagree with Gauthier where he argues that 'in no system of rational prudence . . . can moral obligation be introduced', it seems clear to me that the position which he describes cannot accurately be attributed to Hobbes anyway. Hobbes's concept of 'self-preservation' is much narrower than Gauthier's concept of what is 'advantageous for the agent'.

Gauthier thinks it a serious mistake to suppose that 'Hobbes's concept of obligation must be defined in terms of his concept of the law of nature' (p. 29). I have of course stated that Hobbes advances a concept of obligation or duty in his formulation of the law of nature and that this law, conceived as a duty, does not negate the right of nature (or 'liberty') conceived as a possibility, but merely stipulates that the right should not be exercised irresponsibly – i.e. that irrational possibilities (or means) should be excluded. Gauthier states that 'the laws of nature do not create obligations'; rather, 'men create obligations for themselves by acting on the second law of nature' (pp. 66–7). (Hobbes's second law of nature, in brief, enjoins us to observe contractual obligations.) Here Gauthier is not directly concerned with the cleft stick problem, with whether Hobbes is arguing either (*a*) that men do act so as to preserve themselves or (*b*) that they should do so – or both. He is concerned, rather, with reconciling what appear to be two distinct types of 'obligation' in Hobbes, where Hobbes argues (i) that laws 'without the sword' are not laws properly speaking and (ii) that there are laws of nature, in the state of nature, which are *binding* despite the fact that there exist no legal means of enforcing them. He tries to effect this reconciliation by upholding (i) and eliminating (ii). Thus he concludes that, for Hobbes, no obligations exist in the putative state of nature, but only in civil society. Accordingly, the laws of nature are not binding (cannot lay down obligations).

Gauthier's attempt to eliminate obligation from the law of nature is primarily based on the strategy of collapsing the *law* of nature into the *right* of nature. The right of nature, for Gauthier, may basically be formulated as '*A* may do *X*' (p. 31). (Gauthier does not appear to recognise the ambiguity of the word *may*; as we have seen, it can suggest 'capacity' *or* 'permission'; Gauthier states only that it 'conveys permission', p. 30.) Gauthier then equates '*A* may do *X*' with '*A* doing *X* is in accordance with (right) reason'. But since in this context 'acting rightly' means 'acting rationally' (i.e. in accordance with right reason) and vice versa, the law of nature for Gauthier is only really the right of nature. Let us reiterate that Hobbes's 'right' or 'liberty' (of nature) implies both capacity *for* action and permission *to* act. His law of nature (where it stresses duty) resists being reduced to his right of nature (where it stresses capacity) for this reason. A *duty* to do X obviously presupposes a *capacity* to do X, *as well as* the contradictory of X, but certainly not a rightful or *legitimate* permission to perform the contradictory of X.

I would regard it as a mistake to pay *too* much attention to the Hobbesian distinction between obligation in the state of nature and in civil society. Hobbes clearly assumes that there is obligation, for whatever reason, in both cases. He would like to make these forms of obligation more consistent than they appear. It is for this reason of course that he refers to the commands of God in the state of nature as paralleling those of the sovereign in civil society. What we must ask is in what way these forms of obligation differ. They differ, as Hobbes suggests, in the sense that the set of civil obligations is backed up by sovereign force, while the set of natural obligations is not immediately – i.e. in this life – backed up by any (legal) force at all. Hobbes then thinks that natural laws do obligate us, but (quite literally) without the *force* of civil obligations. We ought to observe these laws, he thinks, because we ought to preserve ourselves, and the laws are mere means to this end. Hobbes does not assume that any one man can by sheer force subject an entire community to his control. What he does assume is that for a community to be created, one agent (a single or a plural agent) must be sufficiently, completely and willingly *obeyed* in order further to strengthen the likelihood of obedience from dissident elements. Hobbes is less concerned to encourage kings to display force than to encourage subjects to submit unquestioningly. He is not so much saying that subjects *ought* to fear all-powerful sovereigns, as that they ought to agree to establish such power in order to remove (or come as close as possible to removing) a more fundamental, immediate and destructive fear – that which they understandably entertain of one another.

Gauthier wishes, as shown, to argue that Hobbesian obligation is only assumed when men voluntarily lay down their rights: thus obligation does not exist for Gauthier in Hobbes's state of nature, and is not created by divine command nor imposed by natural law. One way to test whether this interpretation is valid is by asking under what conditions Hobbes would think it proper for men to violate contracts. If obligation is created simply by virtue of the fact that men make promises, the only question is whether in any circumstances such promises could be voided. If there are cases in which Hobbes will allow promises to be voided, such cases will presumably give evidence of obligation to some higher norm, by reference to which the norm of contractual obligation would have to be regarded as inferior and subordinate.

For Hobbes, the 'way by which a man either simply renounceth, or transferreth his right, is a declaration or signification . . . that he doth so renounce, or transfer' (*Leviathan*, p. 86). To yield one's right, Hobbes argues, 'is a voluntary act'. And he adds that the object of any voluntary act by any man 'is some *good to himself*'. But it is clear that one can make promises, thereby creating obligations, which later turn out not to be *good to oneself*. Hobbes argues that in such circumstances a man cannot be understood to have made a valid promise in the first place. But this is just another way of saying that no promise *per se* creates obligations: certain further conditions, at the least negative, must be met. If for example a man promises not to resist attack, imprisonment or attempts upon his life, he is not, following Hobbes, bound by such promises – they are void. All this means is that where one voluntarily promises to do or not to do *X*, and where this promised action or inaction contradicts one's prospects of self-preservation, one's prior obligation relates to self-preservation rather than to the keeping of promises. This means that any promise is voided where keeping it undermines self-preservation. This must mean that Hobbes's higher norm is self-preservation and not the keeping of promises. Such indeed is the logic (according to Hobbes) of *all* the laws of nature. In effect he states that a (i.e. any) law of nature dictates sound or rational means by which we are always obligated to act in conformity with the preservation of ourselves (*Leviathan*, I, 14, para. 3).

It seems to me difficult to suppose (this is contrary to Gauthier) that one could possibly define 'Hobbes's concept of obligation' other than 'in terms of his concept of the law of nature'. For the law of nature stipulates that we are obligated to adopt self-preserving means of a rational kind. The norm 'preserve yourself *rationally*' necessarily presupposes the more basic norm '*preserve* yourself'. So we return to the position where we recognise Hobbes to be indirectly enjoining self-preservation *per se* as a duty and simultaneously to be regarding it as a necessary and inescapable motive in all human conduct. Finally, on the assumption that one might really prefer, under various circumstances, to die rather than live, the injunction to preserve oneself can easily be regarded as constituting a form of 'selfless' duty. Although the laws of nature necessarily have no legal force where there is no legal structure, they are for Hobbes nonetheless compelling – and not simply because God supposedly commands them: they are compelling, as Hobbes sees it, because they are (more especially when they are *recognised* to be) conducive to our self-preservation. If we have extra reason to obey a sovereign because of our fear of him, according to Hobbes we have even *greater* reason to fear (one another) where no such sovereign exists at all. It is certainly true that the duty to preserve oneself is usually disguised in Hobbes. But it is there. And it is ultimate. It is no use asking Hobbes the further question: *why* ought we to preserve ourselves? He never really thought the question could arise. And he could only offer to reply to the effect that we *do*, or that God commands it, or that it is irrational not to, or with some combination of these views.

BIBLIOGRAPHY

This bibliography does not and cannot aim to be comprehensive. A large number of important and relevant works are not listed at all. My purpose is simply to ensure that most of the materials referred to in the text and appendixes are set out according to a summary and orderly plan. Naturally some additional sources are listed apart from those actually cited in the book.

I GENERAL

AUSTIN, JOHN, *Lectures on Jurisprudence* (London, 1832).
CASTLES, F. G., in D. J. Murray and D. C. Potter (eds), *Decisions, Organizations and Society* (Penguin and Open University, 1971).
DUGUIT, LÉON, *Jean-Jacques Rousseau, Kant et Hegel* (Paris, 1918).
GOUGH, J. W., *John Locke's Political Philosophy* (Oxford, 1950).
HART, H. L. A., *The Concept of Law* (Oxford, 1962).
KANT, IMMANUEL, *Foundations of the Metaphysics of Morals* (1785).
　The Metaphysical Elements of Justice (pt I of *The Metaphysics of Morals*) (1797).
KELSEN, HANS, *General Theory of Law and the State* (Cambridge, Mass., 1949).
KENDALL, WILLMOORE, *John Locke and the Doctrine of Majority Rule* (Urbana, Ill., 1941).
KING, PRESTON, *Fear of Power* (London, 1967).
　'An ideological fallacy', in P. King and B. Parekh (eds), *Politics and Experience* (Cambridge, 1968).
　'Against federalism', in R. Benewick, R. Berki, and B. Parekh, *Knowledge and Belief in Politics* London 1973.
LOCKE, JOHN, *Two Treatises of Government* (1690).
MACHIAVELLI, NICCOLÒ, *The Prince* (1513).
　Discourses on Livy (1532).
ROUSSEAU, JEAN-JACQUES, *The Social Contract* (1762).
SPINOZA, BENEDICT DE, *Tractatus Theologico-Politicus* (1670).
　Tractatus Politicus (1677).

II ABSOLUTIST PERSPECTIVES

ARMSTRONG, E., *The French Wars of Religion* (London, 1904).
ASHLEY, MAURICE, *England in the Seventeenth Century* (Penguin, 1961).

343

BELOFF, MAX, *The Age of Absolutism, 1600–1815* (London, 1954).

BURCKHARDT, JACOB, *The Civilisation of the Renaissance in Italy* (London, 1937).

COUZINET, L., *'Le Prince' de Machiavel et la théorie de l'absolutisme* (Paris, 1910).

CRANSTON, MAURICE, *John Locke, A Biography* (London, 1957).

GARDINER, S. R., *History of the Great Civil War, 1642–49*, 4 vols (London, 1894).

HANOTAUX, GABRIEL, *Études historiques sur le XVIe et le XVIIe siècle en* (Paris, 1886). *France*

HAUSER, H., *La prépondérance espagnole (1559–1660)* (Paris, 1933).

HEXTER, JACK, *The Reign of King Pym* (Cambridge, Mass., 1941).

HILL, CHRISTOPHER, *Puritanism and Revolution* (London, 1962).

JONES, I. DEANE, *The English Revolution, 1603–1714* (London, 1931).

JUDSON, MARGARET ATWOOD, *The Crisis of the Constitution: An Essay in Constitutional and Political Thought in England, 1603–1645* (New Brunswick, N.J., 1949).

LASLETT, PETER, *The World We Have Lost* (London, 1965).

NEALE, J. E., *The Age of Catherine de Medici* (London, 1963).

PLUCKNETT, T. F. T., *Taswell-Langmead's English Constitutional History* (11th ed., London, 1960).

ROMIER, LUCIEN, *Les origines des guerres de religion*, 2 vols (Paris, 1913–14).

SABINE, G. H., *A History of Political Theory* (3rd ed., London, 1951).

SIMONDE DE SISMONDI, J. C. L., *A History of the Italian Republics* (Anchor Books, 1966), abridged.
Histoire des républiques italiennes, 12 vols (Paris, 1807–18).

THOMPSON, J. W., *The Wars of Religion in France, 1559–1576* (Chicago, 1909).

VIÉNOT, JOHN, *Histoire de la Réforme française de l'Édit de Nantes à sa révocation*, 2 vols (Paris, 1926–34).

VILLARI, PASQUALE, *Niccolò Machiavelli and his Times*, tr. L. Villari, 2 vols (London, 1878).

WEDGWOOD, C. V., *The King's Peace, 1637–1641* (Fontana, 1966).
The King's War, 1641–1647 (Fontana, 1966).
The Trial of Charles I (Fontana, 1967).

III JEAN BODIN

BODIN, JEAN, *Les six livres de la Republique* (Paris, 1576).
Les six livres de la Republique (Lyons, 1579).
De Republica libri sex, latine ab autore redditi (Paris, 1586).
The Six Bookes of a Commonweale, out of the french and latine copies done into English by Richard Knolles (London, 1606).
Six Books of the Commonwealth, abridged and translated by M. J. Tooley (Oxford, 1955).
The Six Bookes of a Commonweale, a facsimile reprint of the Knolles

translation of 1606, edited with an introduction by Kenneth D. McRae (Cambridge, Mass., 1962).

Das Heptaplomeres. Edition of *Colloquium heptaplomeres* in German and Latin, ed. G. E. Guhrauer (Berlin, 1841). *Colloque de Jean Bodin*, etc. Slightly abridged French edition of *Colloquium heptaplomeres*, ed. Roger Chauviré (Paris, 1914). (The *Colloquium heptaplomeres* was only discovered after Bodin's death and although it was circulated privately it was first published in the Guhrauer edition of 1841.)

La vie chère au XVIᵉ siècle: la response de Jean Bodin à M. de Malestroit, 1568, ed. H. Hauser (Paris, 1932).

The Response of Jean Bodin to the Paradoxes of Malestroit, and the Paradoxes, translated from the second French edition of 1578 by George Albert Moore (Washington, 1946).

Methodus ad facilem historiarum cognitionem (Paris, 1566).

La méthode de l'histoire, traduite [from the 1572 edition] pour la première fois et présenté par Pierre Mesnard (Paris, Algiers, 1941).

Method for the Easy Comprehension of History, tr. Beatrice Reynolds (Columbia, 1945).

Demonomania (Paris, 1578).

De la demonomanie des sorciers (Paris, 1580).

Universae naturae theatrum. In quo rerum omnium effectrices causae, & fines comtemplantur, & continuae series quinque libris discutiuntur (Lyons, 1596).

Le théatre de la nature universelle, traduit du latin par M. François de Fougerolles (Lyons, 1597).

Œuvres philosophiques de Jean Bodin, texte établi, traduit, et publié par Pierre Mesnard (Paris, 1951). This is vol. 5, no. 3 in the Corpus général des philosophes français, and it includes *Le discours au sénat et au peuple de Toulouse* (1559), *Tableau du droit universel* (1580), and *La méthode de l'histoire* (1st ed., 1566; but, as above, this translation is based on the 1572 edition).

BAUDRILLART, H. J. L., *J. Bodin et son temps* (Paris, 1853).

BROWN, JOHN LACKEY, *The Methodus ad facilem historiarum cognitionem of Jean Bodin: A Critical Study* (Catholic University of America dissertation, Washington, 1939).

CHAUVIRÉ, ROGER, *Jean Bodin, auteur de la 'République'* (Paris, 1914).

CHURCH, WILLIAM FARR, *Constitutional Thought in Sixteenth-century France* (Cambridge, Mass., 1941).

CONDE, FRANCISCO J., *El pensamiento político de Bodino* (Madrid, 1935).

FEIST, ELIZABETH, *Weltbild und Staatsidee bei Jean Bodin* (Halle, 1930).

FOURNOL, E., *Bodin, prédécesseur de Montesquieu* (Paris, 1896).

FRANKLIN, JULIAN H., *Jean Bodin and the Sixteenth-century Revolution in the Methodology of Law and History* (Columbia, 1963).

GAROSCI, A., *Jean Bodin: politica e diritto nel rinascimento francese* (Milan, 1934).

HANCKE, E., *Bodin. Eine Studie über den Begriff der Souverainetät* (Breslau, 1894).

IZDEBSKI, ZYGMUNT, *Quelques observations sur les idées politiques de Jean Bodin*, Lodzkie Towarzystwo Naukowe, no. 59 (Lodz, 1965).

LEWIS, J. U., 'Jean Bodin's "Logic of Sovereignty" ', *Political Studies*, vol. 16, no. 2 (1968).

MOREAU-REIBEL, J., *Jean Bodin et le droit public comparé dans ses rapports avec la philosophie de l'histoire* (Paris, 1933).

OLIVIER-MARTIN, FRANÇOIS, *L'organisation corporative de la France d'ancien régime* (Paris, Liége, 1938).

REYNOLDS, BEATRICE, *Proponents of Limited Monarchy in Sixteenth-century France: Francis Hotman and Jean Bodin* (Columbia dissertation, New York, 1931).

RIESENBERG, PETER NORMAN, *Inalienability of Sovereignty in Medieval Political Thought* (Columbia, 1956).

SHEPARD, MAX ADAMS, 'Sovereignty at the crossroads: a study of Bodin', *Political Science Quarterly*, vol. 45, no. 4 (1930).

IV THOMAS HOBBES

HOBBES, THOMAS, *The English Works of Thomas Hobbes*, collected and edited by William Molesworth, 11 vols (London, 1839–45).

Thomas Hobbes Malmesburiensis – opera philosophica quae Latine scripsit, omnia in unum corpus nunc primum collecta studie et labore Gulielmi Molesworth, 5 vols (London, 1839–45).

Behemoth: or The Long Parliament, edited for the first time from the original manuscript by Ferdinand Tönnies (London, 1889).

The Elements of Law, Natural and Politic, edited with preface and critical notes by F. Tönnies (Cambridge, 1928).

De Cive or the Citizen, ed. S. P. Lamprecht (New York, 1949).

Leviathan, edited with an introduction by M. Oakeshott (Oxford, 1955).

BOWLE, JOHN, *Hobbes and his Critics: A Study in Seventeenth-century Constitutionalism* (London, 1951).

BRANDT, FRITHIOF, *Thomas Hobbes' Mechanical Conception of Nature* (Copenhagen, 1928).

BROWN, K. C. (ed.), *Hobbes Studies* (Oxford, 1965).

CATTANEO, MARIO A., *Il positivismo giuridico inglese, Hobbes, Bentham, Austin* (Milan, 1962).

DAVY, GEORGES, *Thomas Hobbes et J.-J. Rousseau* (Oxford, 1953).

ELIOT, T. S., *Selected Essays* (New York, 1950).

GAUTHIER, DAVID P., *The Logic of Leviathan, the Moral and Political Theory of Thomas Hobbes* (Oxford, 1969).

GOLDSMITH, M. M., *Hobbes's Science of Politics* (Columbia, 1966).

GOUGH, J. W., *The Social Contract* (Oxford, 1936).

HOOD, F. C., *The Divine Politics of Thomas Hobbes: An Interpretation of Leviathan* (Oxford, 1964).

KOSELLECK, R. and SCHNUR, R. (eds), *Hobbes-Forschungen* (Berlin, 1969).

KROOK, DOROTHEA, *Three Traditions of Moral Thought* (Cambridge, 1959).

LAIRD, JOHN, *Hobbes* (London, 1934).

LYON, G., *La philosophie de Hobbes* (Paris, 1893).

LUBIENSKI, Z., *Die Grundlagen des Ethisch-politischen Systems von Hobbes* (Munich, 1932).

MACDONALD, HUGH and HARGREAVES, MARY, *Thomas Hobbes: A Bibliography* (London, 1952).

MCNEILLY, F. S., *The Anatomy of Leviathan* (London, 1968).

MACPHERSON, C. B., *The Political Theory of Possessive Individualism: Hobbes to Locke* (Oxford, 1962).

MINTZ, SAMUEL I., *The Hunting of Leviathan* (Cambridge, 1962).

PETERS, RICHARD, *Hobbes* (Penguin, 1956).

POCOCK, J. G. A., *The Ancient Constitution and the Feudal Law: A Study of English Historical Thought in the Seventeenth Century* (Cambridge, 1957).

POLIN, RAYMOND, *Politique et philosophie chez Thomas Hobbes* (Paris, 1953).

ROBERTSON, G. C., *Hobbes* (Edinburgh and London, 1886).

SALMOND, J. H. M., *The French Religious Wars in English Political Thought* (Oxford, 1959).

SMYRNIADIS, BION, *Les doctrines de Hobbes, Locke & Kant sur le droit d'insurrection* (Paris, 1921).

STEPHEN, LESLIE, *Hobbes* (London, 1904).

STRAUSS, LEO, *The Political Philosophy of Hobbes* (Oxford, 1936).

TAYLOR, A. E., *Thomas Hobbes* (London, 1908).

TÖNNIES, F., *Thomas Hobbes, der Mann und der Denker* (Leipzig, 1912).

WARRENDER, HOWARD, *The Political Philosophy of Hobbes: His Theory of Obligation* (Oxford, 1957).

WATKINS, J. W. N., *Hobbes's System of Ideas* (London, 1965).

Index